LOCKHEED

TRISTAR

THE MOST TECHNOLOGICALLY ADVANCED COMMERCIAL JET OF ITS TIME

GRAHAM M. SIMONS

AIR WORLD

AIR WORLD

Lockheed TriStar
The Most Technologically Advanced Commercial Jet Of Its Time.

First published in Great Britain in 2021 by Air World Books,
an imprint of Pen & Sword Books Ltd,
Yorkshire - Philadelphia

ISBN: 9781526758828

Typeset in 10pt Times by GMS Enterprises
Printed and bound in India by Replika Press Pvt. Ltd.

Pen & Sword Books Ltd incorporates the imprints of Air World Books, Pen & Sword Archaeology, Atlas, Aviation, Battleground, Discovery, Family History, History, Maritime, Military, Naval, Politics, Social History, Transport, True Crime, Claymore Press, Frontline Books, Praetorian Press, Seaforth Publishing and White Owl.

For a complete list of Pen & Sword titles please contact:

PEN & SWORD BOOKS LTD
47 Church Street, Barnsley, South Yorkshire, S70 2AS, UK.
E-mail: enquiries@pen-and-sword.co.uk
Website: www.pen-and-sword.co.uk

Or

PEN AND SWORD BOOKS,
1950 Lawrence Road, Havertown, PA 19083, USA
E-mail: Uspen-and-sword@casematepublishers.com
Website: www.penandswordbooks.com

Contents

Acknowledgements

A book of this nature would not have been possible without the help of many people and organisations too numerous to individually mention. I am indebted to many for providing photographs and information - first-hand and anecdotal - for this story, but in some cases it has not been possible to identify the original photographer or information source and so credits are given in the appropriate places to the immediate supplier. If any of the pictures have not been correctly credited, please accept my apologies.

I would however, like to offer my special thanks the Fellows, Members and Associates of the Worldwide Society of Civil Aviation Enthusiasts (WSCAE) - many of whom work in the global aviation industry as flight or ground crew or indeed 'on the spanners' - for letting me have free access to their collections of images and information, including Dee Diddley (Ireland/Eire), Ameen Yasheed (Middle East), Wan Hunglo and Tsai Ing-Wen, (China and Far East), John Hamlin, Bob Lehat, Kirk Smeeton, Ian Frimston, Hugh Jampton, Peter Clegg, Matt Black, Alan 'Al' Conberry, David Lee, (all UK and Europe), Carrie Åberg (Scandanavia), Temil Sokhet (Asia), Simon Peters, Robin Banks, Rick O'Shea, Adam Brookes, Emma Dayle, Dr Harry Friedman, (USA, Caribbean and Canada) Trymore Simango, Kim Bolton and Phil McCrackin (Africa and Europe) Bill Armstrong, Autair, and Edward 'Ed' Posey, Court Line Aviation and Richard Vandervord.

Introduction

The advent of the generation of wide-bodied transport aircraft provided the Lockheed Aircraft Corporation with an opportunity to re-enter the commercial aircraft market and Rolls-Royce with access to the US market. However, this became a period of extraordinary turmoil for both the airframe manufacturer and the engine company, with only the former coming out alive, albeit weakened. Fortunately, ten years after the maiden flight of the RB211-powered TriStar, Rolls-Royce (1971) Ltd and Lockheed were finally able to look with pride on what was still the most advanced jetliner then in service.

When in 1966 Lockheed started work on what was to become the most technologically advanced jet airliner in the world, the company was able to draw upon its experience of developing the triple-sonic high altitude SR-71 Blackbird along with the development of the mammoth C-5 Galaxy, the C-141 Starlifter and the Jetstar.

The avionics suite on the TriStar was five to ten years ahead of the competition. Lockheed Autoland was the only system the Federal Aviation Administration would allow to land in zero-zero weather for many years. The L-1011 pioneered commercial flight and transport flight management. The Lockheed Flight Management System worked in conjunction with the autopilot systems to provide fuel savings while significantly reducing crew workload.

Partnering the technologically-advanced airframe was the Rolls-Royce RB211 high bypass turbofan engine - the largest, quietest, and most fuel-efficient turbofan of the time.

From a safety standpoint, the L-1011 was designed with redundancy on all systems. It had four separate and independent hydraulic systems, four electrical systems, three environmental control systems, and two separate automatic landing systems, each with dual computers.

Despite all the advanced technology, success in airline service could not overcome the effects of a worldwide industry recession, and on 7 December 1981, Lockheed announced its intention to terminate L-1011 production in 1984.

I first saw the L-1011 at the 1971 Paris Air Show - a few days later, I was at what everyone used to call 'Castle D' - more correctly East Midlands Airport - sneaking into the Rolls Royce viewing. The next year it was the Farnborough SBAC Show and a trip to Luton to see the Court viewing. By 1973 I actually flew on one - my only Court Line trip - an Ian Allan away-day to the Paris Air Show aboard Golf Bravo Alpha Alpha Alpha. 1974 was a spectacular display at Farnborough with a PSA 'Smiling Bird' brightening up a very wet event - mind, you, the thought of the PSA Flight Attendants helped!

Over the years, I flew in many TriStars. Often it was British Airways to and from the Mediterranian - usually Athens, and numerous Delta DL037/DL036 flights into and out of Cinci. An early BA TriStar flight was aboard G-BBAE operating as BE562 on 12 April 1978 into Athens. Nineteen years later, I caught the same aircraft, on almost the same route - but from Gatwick not Heathrow - by now flying as Caledonian Airways operating as CKT980 on 15 August 1997. That was the only disappointing TriStar flight I ever had. The aircon packs were on the fritz, and for the entire three and a half hour flight, my feet were either boiling hot or freezing cold!

Writing this book has proved to be challenging - reading it may be the same. As usual with much of my work, the use of American quotes brought forth difficulties that spring from treating quotes as sacrosanct. I am English, so I write in that language; however, as a sign of respect to the nation that built the L-1011, if I am quoting an American, I use their spelling and phrasing. This directly clashes with the differences of the so-called 'common language' British and Americans share. Color becomes colour, program becomes programme, and of course, American phrasing is often different from English.

Then there is the dreaded use of plane instead of aircraft; I don't care what anyone says, a plane is a cutting tool used to smooth wood!

This brings me to the conundrum of whether to use Imperial or metric units of measurement. Invariably there are times when I must use both, but by and large my writing rules are simple: if the aircraft was designed using Imperial units, so I use Imperial measurements.

I was lucky enough to access many copies of *The Lockheed Star,* the company in-house newspaper. This provided tremendous insight into the day-to-day goings-on by the many thousands of staff directly involved.

Use of this valuable resource also provided insights into the overall corporate structure, revealing that there was a whole series of acronyms - sometimes appearing as all capital letters, sometimes not - that were used internally that have, by necessity, been included in any quotes used. Logically, this means these need decoding for the uninitiated:

CALAC Lockheed California Company, with headquarters in Burbank with plant facilities in Burbank, Palmdale, Rye Canyon and Watts-Willowbrook. Operating semi-independently is the Advanced Development Projects group. Principal activities included the L-1011 and P-3/CP-140 programmes, aerospace research and the classified work of the Skunk Works.

CORAC The Lockheed Corporation.

GELAC Lockheed-Georgia Company based in Marietta, Georgia with additional facilities at Charleston in South Carolina, Clarksburg in West Virginia, and Meridian in Mississippi.

LMSC Lockheed Missiles & Space Company Inc in Sunnyvale, California, and other Alabama, California, Florida, South Carolina, and Washington facilities is primarily responsible for the company's submarine-launched ballistic missiles and its military and NASA space activities. LMSC is also engaged in ocean mining, deep submergence rescue and research submarines, and alternative energy development.

LAS Lockheed Aircraft Service Company, headquartered in Ontario, California, has facilities in Europe, the Middle East and Africa. Its activities include aircraft maintenance and modification, air traffic and air defence systems management and operations.

LEC Lockheed Electronics Company Inc in Plainfield and Denville, New Jersey, provided a variety of electronic products, systems, and services to military (radar and gunfire control systems), industrial, and commercial (air traffic control) customers.

LSCC Lockheed Shipbuilding and Construction Company had three shipways in two yards fronting on the deepwater port in Seattle, Washington. Among the ships built by LSCC have been ferries, light cruisers, drill vessels, barges, destroyer escorts, hydrofoils, bulk carriers, assault transports, icebreakers, and submarine tenders

LEMSCO Lockheed Engineering and Management Services Company Inc with headquarters in Houston, Texas, and offices in Missouri, Nevada and New Mexico, provides key technical support to NASA and other federal agencies.

LAT Lockheed Air Terminal Inc provided operational services at the Burbank-Glendale-Pasadena Airport (owned by Lockheed until 1978), and fuelling and other services at 25 airports in the United States, Panama and Guam. LAT also offers airport consulting services.

LFC Lockheed Finance Corporation in Burbank finances or arranges financing for buyers of Lockheed products, services and related projects, as well as general equipment for airlines and the aerospace industry.

I do not think there can be any doubt that the TriStar was the most technologically developed of all the wide-bodied airliners of its era and deserved better sales than it eventually received. This then is the story.

Graham M Simons
Peterborough UK
June 2021

Chapter One

What came before

The history of Lockheed Aircraft can be traced back to Allan Loughead and his brother Malcolm, who had operated an earlier aircraft company, Loughead Aircraft Manufacturing Company, which was operational from 1912 to 1920. The company built and operated aircraft for paying passengers on sightseeing tours in California and had developed a prototype for the civil market, but folded in 1920 due to the flood of surplus aircraft deflating the market after World War One.

The early venture failed to find a market, and the Loughead Aircraft Manufacturing Company suspended its operations. It was 1920. For six years, the Santa Barbara factory lay dormant following the failure to find an S-1 Sport Plane market.

There was much confusion as to how the brothers' last name was spelt. Allan once explained the apparent confusion over the spelling of the name. 'The true pronunciation of our name is Lock-heed, but so many people pronounced it Logheed, we decided to legalise the phonetic spelling.'

The brothers separated. Malcolm Lockheed left the company to develop an invention of his own for the automobile world, an idea for a superior brake. He worked out a method for putting brakes on all four wheels of an automobile. The system worked by hydraulic pressure from a small pump mounted on the brake pedal, pushing the fluid to work the brakes in each wheel. Its use - with minor variations - can be found on virtually every vehicle today. The company he founded, Lockheed Hydraulics, became a world-wide subsidiary of the Bendix Corporation.

Meanwhile, Allan Lockheed entered the real estate business but stayed with his dream of building a better aircraft. But he had no money and no aircraft to make. More discouraging was the fact that nobody wanted any new machines. He still had faith that the right design would catch the public's attention. At least, he believed from talking with flying men that there could be a market developed if a designer could come up with the right kind of product.

Fred S Keeler, a Burbank businessman, who had also invested in Malcolm Lockheed's brake venture, was one of those who expressed a great deal of

Allan (left) and Malcolm Lockheed at the controls of the Lockheed F-1 flying boat. *(Lockheed)*

interest. He offered to put up all but $2500 of a stock subscription for $25,000. Allan Lockheed himself put up the other $2500, and they formed a new company known as the Lockheed Aircraft Company in December 1926. Operations began in a small building at Sycamore and Romaine Streets in Hollywood.

Keeler became President, Allan Lockheed the vice-president and General Manager. They immediately hired back Jack Northrop, who had previously worked for the Lockheed brothers, and left to join Douglas Aircraft Company as Chief Engineer. Allan Lockheed - the name had been officially changed - and Northrop worked tirelessly on a new concept which they felt would create its own demand.

In the factory on Romaine and Sycamore in Hollywood, construction was started on the new Lockheed-Northrop design, a high-wing, ultra-streamlined monoplane built around a moulded plywood monocoque fuselage, similar to the construction used in the S-l sports machine.

Construction of the company's first aircraft, the beautifully streamlined Vega cantilever monoplane began. While the Vega was under construction, the Lockheed Aircraft Company succeeded in selling it to George Hearst Jr, the wealthy publisher of the *San Francisco Examiner*, who wished to enter it in the August 1927 Oakland-to-Honolulu Dole Derby. Following flight trials and modifications to its vertical surfaces, the aircraft, flown by John Frost and Gordon Scott, took off from Oakland on 16 August 1927, bound for Oahu. Although the first Vega disappeared on its way to Hawaii, its advanced design had already attracted other customers and the Lockheed Aircraft Company was forced to move to larger quarters in the partly occupied building of the Mission Glass Works on Empire Avenue in Burbank in March 1928. The company completed four more Vegas and began the construction of the Air Express and Explorer. Off Empire Avenue behind the factory, a narrow piece of land some 1,500 foot long was graded to serve as its airstrip.

The single-spar wooden wing of the new aircraft was a radical design departure. There were no struts to support it. By the year's end, reported sales exceeding one million dollars.

Three months after the move to Burbank, Jack Northrop and Ken Jay left the company and were replaced by Gerald F 'Jerry' Vultee, chief engineer, and Whitley C Collins, as secretary/treasurer. Going on from success to success while being flown by many of the most famous pilots of the time, the hand-built Vegas were produced at a remarkably high rate - two in 1927, twenty-nine in 1928 forty during the first six months of 1929 with many more under construction. Besides, the company completed two Air Expresses in 1928 and five of this type during the first six months of 1929. The first Explorer, which had been started in 1927, was also completed during the first half of 1929. From 1926 to 1928, the company produced over eighty aircraft and employed more than 300 workers who, by April 1929, were building five aircraft per week.

The company was making money as long as Allan Lockheed retained control. But the money interests completely disregarded internal recommendations. Mercilessly, stockholders began to milk the thriving company of dividends. The treasury ran dry. No money was provided for research. Its engineers and designers, who had built the reputation with continued improvements and new designs, were not allowed to maintain the pace. And in aviation, there is an axiom that has never failed to prove true - 'keep five years ahead of the times, or you lose your shirt'. Lockheed had its five years ahead with its 'Vega' series and the other stars that followed the line, for all came from the same basic moulds. But for five years, it stood still. Engineers had stretched to the limit the basic wooden fuselage common to the Vega, Sirius, Air Express, Altair and the Orion.

With business booming and a healthy cash flow fuelled by a steady stream of orders, Fred Keeler saw an opportunity of realising a large profit by selling the Lockheed Aircraft Company while the going was good. Over the protest of Allan Lockheed, Keeler began in April 1929 to negotiate the company's sale with Edward S Evans, the president of Detroit Aircraft Corporation. The sale agreement, which became final in July 1929, said much for Keeler's business acumen as three months later, the 1929 stock market crash plunged the USA into the Great Depression, and the bottom fell out of the aircraft market.

Upon acquiring eighty-seven per cent of the assets of Lockheed in July, the Detroit Aircraft Corporation - a Michigan holding corporation with controlling interest in various aviation ventures including aircraft manufacturers Ryan and Eastman, Grosse Isle Airport in Detroit, the Park Air College in East St Louis, and other entities - reorganised the company as a division. To head the new Lockheed Aircraft Corporation, the Detroit group sent Carl B Squier, the founder of one of its other subsidiaries, Eastman Aircraft, as general manager and retained Jerry Vultee as chief engineer. It appeared that the change of owners was not going to affect the business, and the operationally independent Burbank team went on producing their own designs.

Besides producing these well-established types, the sale provided much-needed cash to the Detroit Aircraft Corporation after the stock market crash. Lockheed introduced the Sirius, the Altair and the superb Orion. Most of these aircraft were built with the company's traditional plywood monocoque fuselages. But, beginning in February 1932, when the first DL-1 Vega was completed in Michigan, Detroit Aircraft Corporation made nine Vegas and one Sirius with a metal fuselage of Detroit construction and Lockheed-built wooden wings. Detroit, using the same combination, also built the XP-900 two-seat fighter prototype in 1931. Initial design work for an Army observation biplane and an exceptionally clean flying-boat was also undertaken, but lack of funds prevented the realisation of these projects.

Despite this flurry of activity amid the Depression, the future looked bleak for Lockheed as rising losses from its parent company's other operations drained it of its profit. Finally, having lost $733,000 in 1929 and seeing its stock, with a par value of fifteen dollars plummet to twelve cents, the Detroit Aircraft Corporation could no longer survive. On 27 October 1931, it went into receivership with its Lockheed Aircraft Corporation subsidiary being placed under the aegis of the Title Insurance and Trust Company of Los Angeles. With Carl Squier remaining as general manager, a skeleton workforce built two more Orions and one Altair but, on 16 June 1932, the doors were finally locked.

Only five days after the Title Insurance and Trust Company had shut the company's doors, acting as receivers, a new Lockheed Aircraft Corporation was born. Led by Robert Ellsworth Gross, a thirty-five-year-old San Francisco investment broker, a group of investors submitted to the US District Court in Los Angeles a $40,000 bid for the defunct company's assets. There being no other bids, District Judge Harry Holzer accepted Gross' offer on its presentation, on 21 June 1932. Four investors now

Lockheed used concrete moulds to form the early single-engined aircraft designs from the Vegas to the Orions. It was a similar process to what English company De Havillands used later to produce aircraft such as the Mosquito and Hornet. *(Lockheed)*

Above: the company headquarters at Burbank in 1928. The site was to evolve into the Lockheed Air Terminal, and later into that of the Lockheed-California Company.

Right: the narrow fuselage and cantilever wing of the Lockheed Vega is very noticable in this photograph of one machine under construction.

owned Lockheed: Walter T Varney, the owner of Varney Speed Lines, who provided $20,000; Mr and Mrs Cyril Chappellet contributed $10,000; and R C Walker and Thomas Fortune Ryan III, who each provided $5,000. The investors acquired physical assets worth $129,961 as valued by the receivers, including work in progress, raw material, machine tools, office and engineering equipment, and furniture. At thirty cents in the dollar, it was not a bad investment if you had confidence in the aviation business at a time when the country was at the bottom of the Great Depression.

A native of Boston, Massachusetts, Bob Gross had stepped out of college into the investment business, putting to use his Harvard degree. In 1928, at the height of aviation's Lindbergh' boom,' he had invested in the Stearman Airplane Company and later formed the Viking Flying Boat Company with his brother Courtland. In 1932 he was associated with Walter T Varney in operating the Varney Speed Lines, which was flying West coast passengers in the fast Lockheed' Orions'. When they heard of the

Lockheed situation, Gross, Varney, and Stearman decided to raise capital and buy the Lockheed Company. So it was that day in July of 1932 that Gross appeared in a Los Angeles Federal Courtroom and heard the judge confirm purchase of Lockheed for $40,000! Ironically, Allan Lockheed himself had planned to bid for his own company but had raised only $50,000, which he felt was too small a sum for a serious bid.

The investors elected Lloyd C Stearman, already a well-known aircraft designer, as president and general manager for their management team. Stearman was initially assisted by Carl Squier as vice-president and sales manager; Robert Gross as treasurer; Cyril Chappellet as secretary; Richard Von Hake as chief engineer; and Hall L Hibbard as assistant chief engineer. Their initial tasks were to complete four Vegas, one Altair and seventeen Orions, with all twenty-two aircraft to be delivered by 1934, and to initiate a new product line.

The entire group - all aviation-minded business people - was well aware of Lockheed's reputation as a high-performance aircraft builder. They believed sincerely in past products, but more importantly, they believed in the future of aviation. The same old story and the same old problem had faced Allan Lockheed and Jack Northrop when the Loughead Aircraft Manufacturing Company had suffered its first failure and had to close its doors back in the early twenties. There was nothing wrong except Lockheed needed a new type of design to present to money people and the public. The big question was: 'What kind of a new design to build and still maintain the company's already established reputation?'

Shortly after taking the helm, Bob Gross brought in a young Massachusetts Institute of Technology aeronautical engineer named Hall Hibbard, who had been a consultant for Gross for some time. Hibbard was full of ideas. So was Lloyd Stearman, Gross' other partner. A brainchild both Hibbard and Stearman had been working on was a new twin-engined all-metal transport aircraft design. They also had sketched out a large single-engined transport machine. Together they had tried to convince Gross that one or both of these designs would be marketable to the expanding airline industry.

They needed a facility to build their designs. When Gross bought Lockheed, part of their problem was solved. Maybe the new company would manufacture one or the other of their designs.

The new Lockheed Aircraft Corporation directors spent their time getting the house in order and then started looking for a new aircraft design. The Vegas and the Star series could no longer support the company - there were too many newer designs flying.

The decision as to what to do was up to Gross. He remembered seeing a design similar to the Boeing 247 in Hall Hibbard's office, a sketch which Hibbard and Stearman had shown him a while back. This new design could be the answer to Lockheed's problem.

Lockheed was going to build a small twin-engined airliner. Work was started in a little farmhouse. Engineers Gerschler and George Prudden were charged with the job of turning the Hibbard-Stearman aeroplane into a reality. This was the Model 10, or as they called it the Electra' after the lost Pleiad in the cluster of stars in the constellation Taurus; so another star was born.

There were plenty of birth pains, but finally the engineers had worked up a model to send to the University of Michigan at Ann Arbor for wind tunnel tests. They thought they really had something. But bad news came back from the university. 'Your design needs some more work', a gifted young

Lockheed Model 9 Orion NC984Y of New York and Western Airlines Inc, a subsidiary of Pittsburgh Airways Inc. *(Lockheed)*.

aeronautical engineer working in the university's wind tunnel wrote to Lockheed. 'That single rudder doesn't provide sufficient control with one engine out, and the wing-to-fuselage fillets are likely to cause problems.'

The engineer's name was Clarence Leonard Johnson, known to all as 'Kelly', who was then an assistant to Professor Edward Stalker, the University of Michigan aerodynamicist. Shortly afterwards, Johnson joined Lockheed as a tool designer on a salary of $83 a month. At Lockheed, he designed a twin-tail for the Model 10, loaded a scale model in his car's trunk, drove back to Ann Arbor and did some further testing. This one worked. Lockheed accepted Johnson's suggestions and the Model 10 went on to be a success. It had built-in safety. It was possible to lose an engine on take-off, and it still had good control.

In the light of the unpromising financial results of the company's first six months of operations, the bold decision to proceed with the development of the Model 10 Electra twin-engined transport created an urgent need for more capital. Thus, with the guidance of the Los Angeles investment firm of G Brashears and Company, Lockheed restructured its capital. At the time of its inception, Lockheed Aircraft Corporation had an authorised capital of 50,000 shares of non-par stock; 4,800 of these shares, with a stated unit price of $10, were distributed as follows among the original investors and Robert Gross: 2,000 shares to Varney, 1,000 to the Chapellets, and 500 each to Ryan and Walker in return for their $40,000 investment, with 800 shares going to Gross for goodwill and the rights to the planned single-engined transport. Soon after, Thomas Fortune Ryan III purchased an additional 500 shares for $5,000 and William L Graves acquired 700 shares at $10 per share. The 6,000 shares then outstanding were transferred to a holding company organised as Lockheed Aircraft Corporation of Delaware (the State of Delaware having particularly favourable corporate laws) but known later as the Southern California Aviation Corporation.

When in early 1933, the need for additional capital was recognised, the company's directors authorised an issue of 500,000 shares at a par value of $1. Ninety thousand of these shares were given to the Southern California Aviation Corporation in exchange for the 6,000 shares of the original Lockheed stock, thus providing the original investors

A reunion of founders. Left to right: Carl B Squier, Robert E Gross, Cyril Chappellet, Lloyd Stearman and Walter T Varney, all who put things together for the Lockheed Aircraft Company in 1932. This reunion took place in 1956. *(Lockheed)*.

The prototype Lockheed Model 10 Electra, NC233Y, after delivery to Northwest Airways of St. Paul, Minnesota. Note the original reverse-slope cockpit windshield changed on later models. *(Lockheed)*

with a fifty per cent return in less than one year - quite an achievement amid the Great Depression!

Southern California Aviation also received 34,000 of the new shares to cancel loans for operating funds made by its stockholders to Lockheed. Additional shares were sold on the open market, so by April 1934, 289,471 shares - almost fifty-eight per cent of the authorised capital - were outstanding. The successful underwriting of the new stock and the $25,962 profit realised during 1933 ensured the company's soundness. Moreover, before its maiden flight in February 1934, the Model 10 Electra was ordered by Northwest Airways. Lockheed's future looked bright.

The Model 10 was flown for the first time on 23 February 1934. The performance was excellent. It cruised at an honest 190 miles per hour, had a top speed of 200 mph - the first multi-engined aircraft to boast such speed. The airliner went through a rugged series of tests with Marshall Headle, test pilot, at its

NC17374, a Lockheed Model 12 Electra Junior in flight. *(Lockheed)*

Lockheed 12A Electra Junior taxiing at Houston Hobby Airport, 1940. This aircraft belonged to the Continental Oil Company. In the foreground is a Braniff Lockheed Model 10 Electra.

controls, to pass Civil Aeronautics Authority certification tests as a passenger airliner.

This brought Johnson to the attention of company management, and he was promoted to aeronautical engineer. After assignments as a flight test engineer, stress analyst, aerodynamicist, and weight engineer, he became chief research engineer in 1938.

Lockheed had a respectable order book for the Electra, it was able to obtain in September 1934 a $200,000 revolving credit line from the government's Reconstruction Finance Corporation and thus could finance quantity production. While this was taking place, changes were being made at the top of the company. Walter T Varney disposed of his Lockheed stock in May 1933 to concentrate on his airline ventures, and Lloyd Stearman was also planning to depart. Thus Hall Hibbard took over as chief engineer in 1933, and Gross succeeded Stearman as president on 15 December 1934.

In addition to deliveries to US-based airlines, several European operators added Electras to their prewar fleets. In Latin America, the first airline to use Electras was Cubana de Aviación, starting in 1935, for its domestic routes.

Besides airline orders, a number of non-

Thirty-three years separate these two pictures.

Above: Clarence Leonard 'Kelly' Johnson as a test engineer with Lockheed Aircraft in 1940.

Right: Johnson press conference at the Gazebo Hotel, King's Cross London on 20 September 1973, promoting the TriStar.

Amelia Earhart with her Lockheed Model 10E Electra Special NR16020 at Oakland, California on 20 March 1937. The aircraft and pilot Earhart and navigator Frederick Noonan left Lae in New Guinea bound for Howland Island in the Pacific Ocean. This trip was estimated to take twenty hours flight time, and it seems the aircraft was lost in the sea some thirty minutes before it was due to arrive at Howland Island on 2 July 1937. Search and rescue operations never found any trace of the aircraft or crew. *(Lockheed)*

commercial civil operators also purchased the new Model 10. In May 1937, Henry Tyndall, 'Dick' Merrill and J S Lambie accomplished a round-trip crossing of the Atlantic Ocean. The feat was declared the first round-trip commercial crossing of that ocean by any aircraft. It won them the Harmon Trophy. On the eastbound trip, they carried newsreels of the Hindenburg crash, and on the return trip from the United Kingdom they brought photographs of the coronation of King George VI. Bata Shoes operated the Model 10 to ferry its executives between their European factories.

The most famous use of the Electra was the highly modified Model 10E flown by aviatrix Amelia Earhart. In July 1937, she disappeared in her Electra during an attempted round-the-world flight.

After Lockheed introduced its ten-seat Model 10 Electra, the company decided to develop a smaller version as a 'feeder airliner' or a corporate executive transport. Simultaneously, the US Bureau of Air Commerce also sensed the need for a small feeder airliner and announced a design competition for one. For a candidate to qualify for the competition, a prototype had to fly by 30 June 1936.

Lockheed based its candidate, which it named the Model 12 Electra Junior, around a scaled-down Electra. It would carry only six passengers and two pilots but would use the same 450 hp Pratt & Whitney R-985 Wasp Junior SB radial engines as the main Electra version, the 10A. This made it faster than the Electra, with a top speed of 225 mph at 5,000 feet. Like the Electra, the Model 12 had an all-metal structure, trailing-edge wing flaps, low-drag NACA engine cowlings, and two-bladed controllable-pitch propellers. It also had Electra's twin tail fins and rudders, which were becoming a Lockheed trademark. The landing gear was a conventional tail-dragger arrangement. The main wheels retracted back into the engine nacelles; as was often the case with the period's retractable gear, the wheel bottoms were left exposed in case a wheels-up emergency landing was necessary.

Several Model 12s were purchased for military use as liaison aircraft and given L designations. Australian inventor Sidney Cotton modified two Model 12s that British Airways had purchased to track potential enemy aircraft immediately before the outbreak of war.

Shortly before the War, Cotton was recruited by Fred Winterbotham - then of MI6 - to take covert aerial photographs of the German military buildup. Using his status as a wealthy and prominent private aviator currently promoting his film business and using a series of other subterfuges, including taking on an archaeologist's guise or a film producer looking for locations, a series of flights provided valuable information about German naval activity and troop buildups. He equipped the civilian Lockheed 12A G-AFTL with three F24 cameras concealed behind panels which could be slid aside and operated by pressing a button under the pilot's seat, and a Leica behind a similar panel in the wings. Warm cabin air was diverted to prevent condensation on optical surfaces. Cotton took his secretary, Patricia Martin,

The XP-38 at March Field in January 1939. *(Lockheed)*

along, and she too took photographs in flight. Although the German government dictated his flight plans, he consistently managed to get away with flying off-track over military installations. It seems that Cotton had a very persuasive manner and exploited any advantage he could.

In 1939, Cotton took aerial photos during a flight over parts of the Middle East and North Africa. On the eve of war, he even managed to engineer a joy-ride over German military airfields on one occasion, accompanied by senior Luftwaffe officer Albert Kesselring. With the German at the controls, Cotton reached under his seat, operated the cameras, and captured the airfield on film. Cotton later offered to fly Hermann Göring to London for talks a week before the outbreak of hostilities and claimed that his was the last civilian aircraft to leave Berlin before the outbreak of hostilities.

The Model 14 Super Electra design, developed by a team led by Don Palmer, was a scaled-up version of the original Model 10 Electra, with passenger seating increased from ten to fourteen. It was intended to compete commercially with the contemporary Douglas DC-2 and the Boeing 247. The first Model 14 flew on 29 July 1937, piloted by Marshall Headle. Early 14s used the Pratt & Whitney R-1690 Hornet engine; later, the Wright R-1820 Cyclone 9 was offered.

The Model 14 entered commercial service with Northwest Airlines in the US in October 1937. Aircraft were exported for use by Aer Lingus of Ireland, British Airways and KLM of the Netherlands. Howard Hughes purchased a Super Electra and took it on a four-day flight around the

The first production model 18 Lodestar NX25064 with the tailplane in its original position. From the name 'Sky Chief' on the fuselage side, the aircraft is apparently promoting Texaco's high octane gasoline. *(Lockheed)*

globe in July 1938. Ironically, more Super Electras were built under license in Japan than were constructed by Lockheed. The Model 14 was the basis for developing the Lockheed Hudson maritime reconnaissance and light bomber aircraft operated by the Royal Air Force, USAAF and United States Navy.

In 1938, British prime minister Neville Chamberlain, after signing the Munich Agreement, returned to Heston Airport on board a British Airways Lockheed 14, and was famously photographed beside G-AFGN showing to the crowd the signed document, which he would famously describe as bringing peace for our time.

Five weeks before the first flight of the Model 14 on 24 July 1937, Lockheed was awarded War Department Contract AC9974 for a prototype of its Model 22 twin-engined interceptor. Designed by Johnson and Hibbard, after the Lockheed Model 11 - Air Corps designation XPB-3, later XFM-2 - had lost an earlier competition to the Bell XFM-1, the Model 22 was submitted to meet the requirements of the Air Corps' specification X-608 of February 1937.

First in the Lightning series, the XP-38 brought the Lockheed Aircraft Corporation into the major league of aircraft manufacturers. However, the Model 22 design's progressive nature resulted in a reasonably protracted gestation, with the construction of the XP-38 beginning in July 1938 and its first flight not taking place until 27 January 1939.

Lockheed continued to produce Model 10, 12 and 14 types of transport in the light of intense competition from the Douglas Aircraft Company. Thus by the spring of 1938, Lockheed's order book was down to only a few aircraft when the aggressive promotion of the Model B-14 by Kenneth Smith won for the company its first large scale contract, an order for 200 to 250 Hudson general-reconnaissance aircraft, signed by the British Air Ministry on 23 June 1938. To

Above: parallel production lines of Hudsons and Lodestars, 'sometime in 1940'.

Right: By the end of the war the production lines were full of P-38s and P-80s in the assembly hall at Plant B-1. *(both Lockheed)*

Two views of Plant A-1 at the Union Air Terminal Burbank during the final stages of i's construction. *(Lockheed)*

No, this is not a typical Southern Californian residential area, but the Lockheed factory under camouflage. *(Lockheed)*

fulfil this initial order and follow-on contracts for Hudsons and P-38s, the Lockheed workforce exploded and from 332 people in 1934 to 7,000 employees on 31 March 1940, and to a massive 16,898 one year later.

Even though it had by then obtained a foothold on the military market, Lockheed, spurred by rising profits, wanted to increase its commercial business and, to that end, undertook a two-pronged effort. On the one hand, it incorporated on 17 August 1937, a wholly-owned subsidiary, the AiRover Company, while on the other, its engineering staff studied several new transport designs, which eventually culminated in the Model 49, the famous Constellation.

The Model 14 suffered from several design deficiencies, which led to a further improvement that became the Lockheed 18 Lodestar. The first Lodestars were modified Super Electras sent back to the factory by Northwest Airlines after a series of crashes plagued the Model 14. The fuselage was lengthened to accommodate more passengers while more powerful 1,020 horsepower Pratt & Whitney Hornet engines replaced the 760 hp Wright engines of the Super Electra, increasing cruise speed by 15 mph to 265 mph. The change in power plants constituted a new model, so Lockheed designated them as Model 18s.

Although primarily civilian designs, Lockheed designs were modified into military use; the PV-1 Ventura for the Navy, the Model 18 Lodestar into the C-60... Then came World War Two.

When it was founded in August 1937, the AiRover Company moved into an old red-brick building at 923 East San Fernando Road, Burbank, next door to Lockheed. Its initial tasks were to build from available spares a modified Altair for use as a flying testbed and to design a five-seat feeder transport, the Starliner. Completed in December 1937, the modified Altair, named Flying Test Stand, proved its Menasco powerplant to be reliable. After the AiRover Company had been renamed the Vega Airplane Company during 1938, it was followed into the air on 22 April 1939, by the Starliner.

The war in Europe dictated a better use for the limited plant capacity of Lockheed and its subsidiary. The Vega Airplane Company went on to build five Model 40 target drones of its own design and four NA-35 primary trainers designed by North American, with the trainers being the first aircraft manufactured in the new 750,000 square foot plant built on a 30-acre lot adjacent to the Union Air Terminal, and a mile from the parent Lockheed plant. At about the same time, Courtlandt Gross, Robert Gross' younger brother, took over the Vega Airplane Company's presidency. Earlier, Lockheed, which with its officers controlled Vega's stock, distributed over fifty per cent of Vega shares, with a par value of $1.50 each, as a dividend to Lockheed stockholders.

In its new plant, the Lockheed subsidiary built Ventura bombers under both British and Lend-Lease contracts and, as a member of the Boeing-Vega-Douglas organisation, played a major role in building B-17F and G Flying Fortresses for the USAAF. Vega's design work included the PV-2 Harpoon and XP2V-1 Neptune for the US Navy and the XB-38 and XB-40 derivatives of the Flying Fortress. Its corporate identity was changed on 31 December 1941, when it merged with Lockheed (its stockholders receiving one share of Lockheed for

The ever-expanding Lockheed Air Terminal at Burbank with new hangars being erected in the foreground and a number of Constellations - at least four for American Airlines - being serviced towards the rear. *(Lockheed)*

three of Vega), and its assets transferred to the Vega Aircraft Corporation. Finally, on 30 November 1943, the Vega Aircraft Corporation was absorbed into the Lockheed Aircraft Corporation, and its facilities became Lockheed's plant A-1.

The airport, which Lockheed operated from in the northwest corner of Burbank, was built in 1930. By 1934 it had become Los Angeles' primary airport and was later known as Union Air Terminal. Lockheed increased its commercial activities during 1940 when it purchased the Burbank facility from United Air Lines for $1.5 million. Organised as a subsidiary under the presidency of Cyril Chappellet, and renamed the Lockheed Air Terminal, it continued to be used by airlines and for general aviation operations. It enabled Lockheed to expedite test and delivery flights for the aircraft coming off its assembly lines. Thirty-eight years after acquiring this airport, Lockheed sold it to the Hollywood-Burbank Airport Authority for $51 million, of which $35-5 million came from federal grants by the Department of Transportation to the cities of Burbank, Glendale and Pasadena.

During the 1930s Lockheed Aircraft Company, adjacent to the field, evolved into one the nation's largest aircraft manufacturers, and in 1940 Lockheed purchased the airport. During the war, Lockheed built P-38 fighters, Hudsons and B-17 bombers. The Royal Air Force's Air Technical Services Command and US Army Air Forces Western Technical Training Command had operations at the field. The airport and the Lockheed plant were extensively camouflaged. The main Lockheed plant and runways were made to appear as grain fields and houses, and the parking lot was covered over with netting to appear as alfalfa fields. Also, an extensive smoke screen system was installed to hide the plant under layers of chemical smoke.

Lockheed expanded greatly during the Second World War with aircraft such as the P-38 Lightning - of which they built literally thousands - and in the post-war years continued aircraft production, making the phenomenally successful and startingly elegant Constellation series of airliners (see *Lockheed Constellation*, Air World 2021 by the same author).

Between 1 July 1940 and 31 August 1945, Lockheed produced 19,077 aircraft. Almost seventy per cent of them came from the assembly lines at plant B-1, the remainder being produced at plant A-1. To produce this large number of aircraft, the company was forced to augment its facilities, with floor area increasing from 550,000 square feet in the summer of 1939 to 1,600,000 square feet at the end of 1940 and a wartime peak of 7,700,000 square feet in mid-1943. Most of this expansion took place at plants A-1 and B-1. Still, Lockheed also operated a system of ten feeder plants in California - two each in Bakersfield, Fresno, East Los Angeles and Santa Barbara, and one in both Taft and Pomona and, beginning in March 1942, a modification and service centre in Dallas, Texas. Another service centre was opened

Nathan Price (on the left), and Hall Hibbard examining an XJ-37 turbojet engine. The J37 was one of the first turbojet engines designed in the United States. It was not considered very important when it was first introduced in the 1930s, and development was allowed to languish. By the time it was developed enough for production use, other engines, often British-derived, had surpassed it in performance. The design was later converted to a turboprop, as the T35 and was subsequently sold to Wright Aeronautical. It saw some interest for use on what would become the B-52 Stratofortress before that design moved to jet power. Some testbed examples of the J37 and T35 were built but never entered production. *(Lockheed)*

Civil and military Constellations undergo work at Burbank. Much of this work was done outside, taking advantage of Calfornia's climate. *(Lockheed)*

in early 1944 at Van Nuys Airport, California, to handle modifications of Navy aircraft.

Overseas, Lockheed had set up during 1938 a parts depot in Amsterdam and the British Reassembly Division, LAC Ltd, at Speke, the Liverpool airport. Together with similar units at Renfrew and Abbotsinch near Glasgow, the Liverpool facility handled the task of receiving and assembling the British-ordered Hudsons. Reassembly facilities were also set up in Australia to handle the Hudsons of the RAAF. This experience proved useful when on 3 December 1941, Air Service Command asked the company to establish a maintenance and overhaul base in the British Isles, with repair shops and accessories for thirty-three types of aircraft. Its proposal was accepted, and Lockheed was awarded a contract in February 1942.

Three months later, Lockheed Overseas Corporation set up operations at Langford Lodge, twenty miles west of Belfast in Northern Ireland. Before it closed in July 1944, the facility reassembled and modified 3,250 aircraft, serviced 11,000 more, and overhauled 450,000 components; late in 1943, its employment peaked at about 6,000.

Work on jet propulsion projects had begun at Lockheed during 1939-40 when the Hibbard-Johnson team, including Phil Colman, Willis Hawkins and Gene Frost, undertook preliminary studies for a series of novel twinjet aircraft of highly unconventional design, including the L-133 all-steel aircraft with canard surfaces, which Lockheed had planned to use for its proposed Model 27 transport. In addition, Nathan Price designed for Lockheed the L-1000 turbojet, with military designation of XJ-37, that incorporated several then extremely advanced features such as axial-flow, two-spool turbine stages, high compression ratio and afterburner. Neither the L-133 aircraft nor the L-1000 turbojet projects went into production, and Lockheed sold some of its turbojet patents to Curtiss-Wright. Fortunately for the company, the XP-80 contracted for by the USAAF on 24 June 1943 led to the production of 8,507 related aircraft (F-80, T-33, F-94 and T2V-1) between 1943 and 1958.

Together with the Constellation family (856 Constellations/Super Constellations/Starliners) and 1,051 Neptunes, they assured the well-being

Lockheed's enormous Constitution was one of the world's largest aircraft at the time of its late 1940s debut. *(Lockheed)*

of the Lockheed Aircraft Corporation well into the late fifties.

In the immediate post-war years, Lockheeds fortunes rose and fell. The first full year of peace was a difficult one for Lockheed; the July-August grounding of its Constellation and the Shooting Star was experiencing a high rate of accidents. Furthermore, although initial attempts at operating commercial servicing bases at Linden in New Jersey and Shannon in Eire ran into trouble, the company stuck to the concept and at the end of 1946 organised Lockheed Aircraft Service (LAS) as a wholly-owned subsidiary to handle servicing and modifications of Lockheed's aircraft as well as those of other manufacturers. Other favourable developments during 1946 included the first flight of both the Saturn and the Constitution and the introduction of the first postwar version of the Constellation, the L-649.

At the end of 1946, the financial picture looked bleak. Lockheed's operating loss for the year was \$21.9 million, almost three-quarters of its wartime profit of \$30.4 million realised from 1940 through 1944 before income tax. A federal income-tax credit reduced this loss to \$10.7 million, and a transfer of \$13.8 million from a reserve fund set up during the war to finance transition to peacetime operations enabled the company to post a \$3.1 million net income. Moreover, Lockheed was forced to borrow up to £40 million to finance continued operations.

1947 ended with a \$2.5 million loss, which could no longer be offset by the transfer of funds from reserves. It was intense competition between Lockheed and Douglas, with the DC-6 starting to overtake the Constellation's lead which brought the realisation that sales of the Saturn feeder liner would not materialise in the face of the availability of large

Right: The nearly square cross-section of the C-130's cargo compartment was 41 feet 5 inches long. Here an Army ton-and-a-half truck tests clearances during 1951, using the full-scale mock-up built at Burbank.

Below: the full-scale wood and metal mock-up of the C-130 was built at Burbank during 1951, and was later shipped To Marietta, Georgia. The two prototype YC-130s stayed basically true to the features defined in this mock-up. *(both Lockheed)*

VH-RMA was a Lockheed 188 Electra of Australia's Ansett-ANA airline. *(Lockheed)*

numbers of cheap surplus aircraft, mainly Beech C-45s and Douglas C-47s. At the same time, the Constitution proved too large to attract airline orders.

Increases in world tension following the start of the Berlin blockade saw C-121s, military versions of the Model 749 Constellation, making transatlantic cargo/passenger flights in support of the Berlin Airlift, and LAS obtaining a three-year Air Force contract to operate facilities at Keflavik Airport in Iceland, which all had a positive impact on Lockheed.

Late in 1950, the USAF asked the company to reopen a government plant at Marietta, Georgia. Built by the Defense Plant Corporation, a subsidiary of the Reconstruction Finance Corporation, this 4.5 million square foot facility was operated during the war by the Bell Aircraft Corporation to produce Boeing B-29-BAs but was shut down in 1945. Reopened in January 1951, it was initially used by Lockheed to de-cocoon and prepare for operations 120 B-29s which had been stored for several years at Pyote, Texas, and went on to be used for the assembly of eight Boeing-designed B-47B-LM Stratojets and the production of 386 B-47E-LMs. Later, the Marietta plant was assigned responsibility for the production of the Hercules and JetStar, two prototypes of each type being built in Burbank before the transfer of production to Marietta.

In addition to opening Marietta and modernising Burbank's main installations, Lockheed opened a new facility at Palmdale Airport, California in early 1951 to supplement the Van Nuys Airport's production flight test centre for jet aircraft.

In 1953, following the crash of a T-33A at Van Nuys, in which a housewife was killed, Lockheed transferred all jet production flight activities to Palmdale. Moreover, Lockheed Aircraft Service relocated its main base from the crowded Lockheed Air Terminal in Burbank to Ontario, California, in October 1952.

By the end of 1950, the company's backlog had skyrocketed to $447 million. During the Korean War, Lockheed posted steadily rising sales figures: $173.3 million in 1950, $237.2 million in 1951, $438.1 million in 1952 and $820.5 million in 1953, with net income during these four years totalling $37.5 million, or two and three-quarter per cent of sales. Despite continued Super Constellation production for the airlines, the bulk of sales was from defence contracts; military sales accounted for eighty-five to eighty-nine per cent of total sales from 1950 to 1954.

In the commercial field, the heated competition between Lockheed and Douglas was not turning in favour of the Burbank company as between 1945 and 1958, the year in which the last of the piston-powered transports were produced. It delivered 510

Lockheed C-130E Hercules 61-2358 was the first E-model to be built, making it's first operational flight on 24 September 1957 and the last to be retired on 1 May 2012. *(Lockheed)*

commercial Constellations, Super Constellations, and Starliners than Douglas' 878 DC-4s/DC-6s/DC-7s. Even when including deliveries of military versions of these aircraft, Lockheed was outsold 856 to 1,045 - or 2,210 if wartime C-54s are included in the Douglas total. It was not that Lockheed was lax in its efforts to improve the Constellation series, as in fact, it outpaced Douglas in introducing or attempting to introduce significant improvements. Thus, it pioneered in 1953 the commercial use of Turbo-Compound engines, when on 17 February the L-1049C was first flown, and In 1954 the use of propeller-turbines on a US transport aircraft, when on 1 September the R7V-2 began flight trials. However, the Douglas DC-6 and DC-7s benefited from using a circular fuselage of constant cross-section, which made stretching more manageable and less expensive. Pratt & Whitney R-2800 engines were more reliable than the Wright R-3350s used in the Constellation and thus proved more economical and longer-lived.

Before gaining propeller-turbine experience as powerplants for transport aircraft with the Pratt & Whitney T34-powered Model 1249A Super Constellation - the R7V-2 for the US Navy and YC-121F for the USAF - Lockheed had begun ground testing the Allison XT40-powered XFV-1' tail sitter' in late 1953. This aircraft became inadvertently airborne on 23 December 1953, but officially flew for the first time on 16 June 1954. By then, however, the construction of YC-130 prototypes was well underway, and the turbine-powered Hercules was first flown on 23 August 1954. For a while, Lockheed had been considering offering turbine-powered Super Constellations to the airlines but concentrated its commercial efforts on its last piston-engined aircraft, the L-1649 Starliner.

In the military jet field Lockheed continued during the mid-fifties with the large scale production of T-33As and with the manufacture of T2V-1s, a naval development of the T-33A. Above all, however, this period was marked by the debut of the XF-104, which was first flown on 4 March 1954, and of two highly classified programmes: research into nuclear-powered aircraft and the U-2. The first of these programmes had been started in great secrecy in 1949, and its existence was not revealed until October 1953, and even then only in a guarded statement.

Just about as heavily classified was the work of a special engineering team led by Kelly Johnson in an off-limit area of Burbank, which housed the Advanced Development Projects section, better known as the 'Skunk Works'. The nickname was coined at the onset of the XP-80 programme when Kelly Johnson and his staff were housed in temporary quarters next to a plastics factory. One of the team engineers began referring to the buildings by the same name as the foul-smelling factory in Al Capp's 'Li'l Abner' comic strip. Despite Kelly Johnson's initial dislike for the nickname, it stuck.

This organisation became famous and spawned many successful Lockheed designs, including the U-2, A-12 and SR-71 Blackbird. The Skunk Works often created high-quality designs in a short time, often with limited resources.

Johnson, whose technical genius was greatly

respected in industry and Department of Defense circles, had long been critical of pure research aircraft, even though his own F-104 owed much to the work of Frank Fleming's X-3 Stiletto team at Douglas, which, he claimed, were a wasteful way of spending limited funds. Instead, he advocated designing high-performance aircraft that would serve to advance the state-of-the-art and have specific operational use. Johnson got a chance to practice what he preached when he was secretly apprised of the need of the Air Force and the Central Intelligence Agency for a long-range reconnaissance aircraft with such performance that interception by potential adversaries would be virtually impossible. How well Johnson succeeded with his U-2 - which was first flown on 6 August 1955 - can be judged by the fact that for several years it repeatedly made 3,800-mile flights across the USSR without being intercepted. Finally, on 1 May 1960, Lieut Francis Gary Powers was brought down near Sverdlovsk, and it was ordered back into production as the TR-1.

In a fantastic demonstration of the benefits of free enterprise Kelly Johnson and his team, freed from most governmental red tape and company bureaucracy due to the highly secret nature of the U-2 programme, made the first aircraft ready to fly within eight months of the project go-ahead. Later, the first twenty U-2s and spares for the USAF were completed within the $21 million budget. When the inventory of spares was determined to exceed requirements, Lockheed used these spares to build six additional aircraft for only the cost of labour. Thus, the USAF obtained twenty-six U-2s ahead of schedule and at a remarkably low unit cost of less than $900,000. Furthermore, working with a project and manufacturing staff running a mere seven to twenty-five per cent of that of similar, non-classified, programmes at Lockheed, the Advanced Development Projects group has reportedly obtained since that time profit margins reaching twelve per cent, or more than double the average on most other military contracts. Quite an achievement indeed for a contractor often accused by the press and some members of Congress of being careless with its cost and schedule controls on military contracts!

In 1955 Lockheed again activated design study efforts for a turbine-powered airliner to meet American Airlines' requirements, despite facing stiff competition from Boeing, Convair, Douglas and North American. It was feared that Douglas would have the edge as American Airlines, since acquiring its first DC-2s in 1934, had been a staunch Douglas client and had become the launch customer for the DC-3, DC-6 and DC-7. However, displeased by a dispute over DC-7 pricing, American Airlines was ready to consider alternative suppliers. Thus, after working with Lockheed and Eastern Air Lines in refining the requirements for the four-engined propeller-turbine transport, American, therefore,

The full-scale XF-104 mock-up built at Burbank was not only an accurate rendition of the finished aircraft, but was also a masterpiece of the woodworkers art. *(Lockheed)*

Serial number 61-2775 was the very first of 284 Lockheed C-141A Starlifters and had its maiden flight on 17 December 1963, the 60th Anniversary of the Wright Brothers first flight.This C-141A Starlifter spent its entire career as a test aircraft in numerous programs. It is one of only two remaining 'A' models and is the only known four engine jet used to tow a glider. *(Lockheed)*

became, on 8 June 1955, the Electra's launch customer with an order for thirty-five aircraft. By the end of the year, Lockheed had received sixty-one more aircraft orders and had a $211 million Electra backlog. The future appeared bright for the new type, which made its first flight on 6 December 1957.

Unfortunately, following two accidents, the Federal Aviation Agency imposed on 25 March 1960 a speed restriction on the aircraft. Following the completion of a modification programme funded by Lockheed, this restriction was lifted on 5 January 1961. The cost of this modification programme, together with loss of revenues when production had to be ended with the delivery of the 170th Electra, drained Lockheed of an estimated $25 million. By then, however, the Electra had spawned the P-3 Orion long-range patrol aircraft, which remained in continuous production for many years. When viewed jointly, the Electra and Orion programmes have been solid money-makers for their manufacturer.

Even though its design had been started only in early 1957, almost two years after Lockheed had received an initial order for its Electra, the JetStar business jet and light military transport prototype was first flown on 4 September 1957, three months before that of the Electra. Anticipated largescale military orders for these twin-engined prototypes and four-engined production model jet transports did not materialise. Even though the sixteen C-140A/Bs and VC-140Bs for the USAF were supplemented by 146 commercial JetStars and 40 JetStars IIs, with the two prototypes being built in Burbank and all production aircraft being built in Marietta, the programme did not prove financially satisfactory.

While the JetStar and Electra were undergoing flight trials, Lockheed was also engaged in a ruthless competitive battle with other US aircraft manufacturers and British and French companies to supply the West German Luftwaffe with its first supersonic fighters and to provide similar weapons systems to other allied air forces. Helped in part by the world's records - absolute speed, absolute ceiling and seven time-to-height records it set, and in part by the company's aggressive marketing, the F-104 was a strong contender. Its first and decisive victory in this competition was won on 6 November 1958, when the German Federal Republic's defence committee announced its selection of the F-104G, a specially developed all-weather multi-mission version of the Starfighter, as that nation's standard interceptor, fighter-bomber and reconnaissance aircraft. Only limited production was to be undertaken by Lockheed, with larger-scale manufacturing in Germany. During the following year, the Starfighter was also selected by Canada (CF-104A/D) and Japan (F-104.1/DJ), whilst in 1960 the multi-national programme was expanded to include Belgium, Italy and the Netherlands. This largescale undertaking eventually added 1,789 Starfighters to Lockheed's production of the F-104 and contributed $1.39 billion to the US balance of payment. For Lockheed, it was a major coup which significantly contributed to the company's financial success in the late fifties and early sixties and funded in great part its diversification programme.

Having acquired the Lockheed Air Terminal in 1940, organised the Lockheed Aircraft Service in 1946, and activated its Missile Systems Division in 1953, the Lockheed Aircraft Corporation was better prepared than most other aircraft manufacturers when a 1957 announcement of drastic cutbacks in military aircraft expenditures made it advisable for these companies to diversify their business into helicopters, electronics and even shipbuilding and repair!

In its more traditional aircraft business, Lockheed proceeded during the first half of the sixties with its existing Starfighter, Hercules, JetStar, Orion and U-2 programmes and concluded production of the Neptune and Electra. New aircraft types committed to production during this period included the C-141 StarLifter, first flown on 17 December 1963, and the YF-12/SR-71, the Skunk Works' superb product that began flight trials on 26 April 1962.

Furthermore, after participating in a preliminary design competition for a very large military logistics transport, termed the CX-HLS (Cargo Experimental,

The P-3 Orion was a straightforward development of the L-188 Electra and was built for a number of navies around the world. Closest to the camera is NZ4202 of the Royal New Zealand Air Force *(Lockheed)*

The first C-5A Galaxy, serial number 66-8303, was rolled out of the manufacturing plant in Marietta, Georgia, on 2 March 1968. On 30 June 1968, flight testing of the C-5A began with the first flight, flown by Leo Sullivan, with the call sign 'eight-three-oh-three heavy'.

Heavy Logistic Support) project in December 1964, Lockheed became one of the three contractors invited to participate in the C-5 competition. Thus, at the end of 1964, Lockheed, which then had a backlog of just over $2 billion, a working capital of $161 million, a capital of $75 million and retained earnings of $164 million, appeared to be in a comfortable position. However, serious troubles were soon to beset its new management: Robert Gross died on 1 September 1961, to be succeeded as Chairman of the Board by his brother Courtlandt, and Daniel J 'Dan' Haughton became President in 1961 when Courtlandt Gross had taken his new position.

October 1965 saw Lockheed win the hotly contested C-5 competition when its Marietta division was awarded the contract for the first type of aircraft powered by the new generation of high-bypass-ratio turbofans in the 40,000 pounds thrust class. This award was one of the first under what was called the total package procurement system and was something of a poisoned chalice.

This system came about in 1960 when successful development contracts were generally followed by production contracts with little or no likelihood that the contracts would have to face competition. To ensure this, contracts based on the initial competitions started to include the development effort and requirements for substantial production quantities. Observing this trend, Robert H Charles, ASD (Installations and Logistics), conceived the total package procurement (TPP) concept.

TPP was a major systems acquisition policy introduced in the United States Department of Defense by Secretary of Defense Robert Strange McNamara.

The objectives of this concept were as follows:

- Limit or eliminate 'buy-in' considerations
- Motivate contractors to design for economical production, and minimise any tendency for production redesign
- Encourage subcontracts with, and obtain components from, the most efficient supply sources
- Encourage contractor efficiency through competition, and thereby reduce costs.

According to Charles, TPP would allow the government, like any buyer in the commercial world, '…to make a choice between competing products on the basis, not of estimates, but of binding commitments concerning performance and price of operational equipment.'

It soon became obvious that this any application of this novel type of contracting to a high technology programme was unworkable. This, combined with a sharp increase in inflationary pressures in the USA and with increased difficulties in both obtaining and retaining skilled workers at a time when sharply rising production of military aircraft and jetliners due to the intensifying of the Vietnam hostilities and a boom in the air transport industry forced the manufacturers into a sharp competition for staff. This, in turn, resulted in substantial cost overruns on the company's programmes, especially with the C-5.

Chapter Two

Genesis of a Giant

To a whole generation, the phrase 'beautiful downtown Burbank' especially if you did not have to look it up in your Funk & Wagnalls, meant that northern neighbour of Los Angeles so beloved – and often mentioned - by Dan Rowan and Dick Martin in their *Rowan and Martin's Laugh-in* TV comedy show of the late 1960s. To others, it meant the home of one of the great American airliner manufacturers, Lockheed-California, known internally as CALAC, the Burbank-based manufacturing unit of the parent Lockheed company.

It is safe to say that more often than not, the sun shines on Burbank, California. It was most probably shining on 29 March 1968 - for that date was hailed as a sunny one in the history of the Lockheed company with happy times ahead. Beyond the horizon lay storms of unimagined severity. Still, no-one in Burbank on that now-historic day saw anything but sunshine for Lockheed due to the decision then announced by TWA and Eastern Air Lines to adopt their L-1011 design as future equipment for their domestic US operations. Combined with a deal between Lockheed and the United Kingdom's Air Holdings company, the TWA and Eastern contracts represented a commitment - including options, or 'second buys' as Lockheed termed them - for 144 aircraft - which was more than enough to allow Lockheed to go ahead with production of the L-1011.

Before the new airliner flew its first revenue passengers on 26 April 1972, it was a factor in bringing Lockheed to the brink of bankruptcy and pushing Rolls-Royce over the same edge. By now, the TriStar, as the design was christened – and yes, that is the correct spelling of capital and lower-case letters – following the Lockheed tradition of naming their machines after celestial bodies.

Both in the USA and the UK, the TriStar tribulations, and its RB211 engines were to result in unprecedented public scrutiny of two great companies' financial plight and lead both Capitol Hill and Whitehall to accept a new order of State involvement in the affairs of the aerospace industry. The fact that the TriStar with its RB211 engines survived and entered airline service and in production against a healthy backlog of orders was the testimony to the resilience of the two companies and the fundamental soundness of the engineering design of the airframe and engine if nothing else. But none of this was foreseen in 1968.

The Lockheed TriStar's initial version, the L-1011-1, was a subsonic commercial jet transport designed to operate over short/medium-haul and transcontinental airline routes with larger passenger payloads than any other airliners of the day. Improved passenger comfort, the convenience of schedule frequency, and operation from close-in satellite airports were advantages of this second-generation jet transport. The L-1011 was also designed to comply with the increasing demands for reduced noise, reduced smoke emission, improved all-weather capability, improved safety, and greater passenger and cargo capacity. These demands had primarily developed from the explosive growth of the air transportation market.

This new aircraft had been sized to perform economically within an environment defined by passenger demands for quiet, convenient, and dependable air travel at distances from 300 to more than 3000 nautical miles, and by air-traffic growth anticipated for the next twenty years.

To understand the importance of the initial L-1011 orders to Lockheed, it is necessary to recall that the company at that time had no commercial transport in production and was in danger of losing beyond recall the relationships and reputation it had built up throughout the world's airlines with the Constellation, Starliner and Electra. Throughout the nineteen-fifties Lockheed-California was one of the 'big three' companies on the US West Coast to which the airlines turned for more than ninety per cent of their new aircraft. While Douglas offered the DC-6 and DC-7 family and Boeing produced the Stratocruiser, Lockheed more than held its own with the Constellation and Starliner. Still, when air transport stepped up to the next level, marked by the introduction of gas turbine engines, the Burbank company made what turned to be a fundamentally wrong decision by placing its faith in the turboprop, leaving Boeing and Douglas to press ahead with the pure-jet types for extended range operation. Lockheed argued - as did Vickers-Armstrongs in Britain - that the turboprop was the more economically attractive prime mover for medium- and short-range operations. There was a substantial body of opinion within the airlines that supported this view, and only the most far-sighted of visionaries correctly anticipated, in the mid-fifties, that it was the turbojet that held the key to future success in the airline business.

Inspired directly by an outline specification drawn up by American Airlines, Lockheed committed its resources to the design and production of the Electra, a four-turboprop airliner to carry about 100 passengers over non-stop ranges of up to 2,300 miles. Orders from Eastern Air Lines, Braniff Airways and Northwest Airlines soon followed. However, the Electra suffered a troubled start. Passengers of early aircraft complained of noise in the cabin forward of the wings caused by propeller resonance. Lockheed redesigned the engine nacelles, tilting the engines upwards three degrees. The changes were incorporated on the production line by mid-1959 or as modification kits for the aircraft already built and improved performance and a better ride for passengers.

Unfortunately, three aircraft were lost in fatal accidents between February 1959 and March 1960. After the third crash, the FAA limited Electra's speed until the cause could be determined. After an extensive investigation, it became clear that two of the crashes - in September 1959 and March 1960 - were caused by an engine mount problem. The mounts were not strong enough to damp a phenomenon called whirl mode flutter, analogous to the precession of a child's top as it slows down, that affected the outboard engine nacelles. When the oscillation was transmitted to the wings, the flutter frequency decreased to a point where it resonated at the same frequency or harmonically related ones with the outer wing panels. This caused violent up-and-down oscillation that increased until the wings would tear off.

The company implemented an expensive modification programme (the Lockheed Electra Achievement Program or LEAP) in which the engine mounts and the wing structures supporting the mounts were strengthened, and some of the wing skins were replaced with thicker material. All Electras were modified at Lockheed's expense at the factory, the modifications taking twenty days for each aircraft. The changes were incorporated in later aircraft as they were built. However, the damage had been done, and the public lost confidence in the type - this and the smaller jets that were being introduced eventually relegated Electras to the smallest airlines. Losses to Lockheed were estimated as high as $57 million, not counting an additional $55 million in lawsuits.

The greater misfortune for the company was its failure to launch a turbojet transport as well as, or in place of, the Electra, for production of the latter ended in 1962 with only 170 built far short of the projected break-even quantity of about 400. The Electra provided the structural basis for the P-3 Orion, sold in quantity to the US Navy and other nations, but this was only small compensation for the fact that Burbank had no airliner in production for the first time since the end of the Second World War.

In the early 1960s, two major civil airliner programmes were studied at Burbank. The first of these, starting in 1963, was the design in competition with Boeing of a proposed US supersonic transport (SST), funded by the US Government. Lockheed proposed a fixed-wing delta design, but on 31 December 1966, this was rejected in favour of the variable geometry Boeing project. On subsequent analysis, the Boeing design failed to meet the airline payload/range requirements, and Boeing had to change to a fixed delta layout similar to the Lockheed proposal. In any event, the US SST was cancelled as being far too costly. The second programme, an 'outcrop study' of work done by the Lockheed-Georgia design team concentrating on the CX-4/CX-HLS/C-5 evolutionary programme in an attempt to come up with a civilian derivative.

During the early studies for the P-3C Orion long-range patrol aircraft for the US Navy based on the prop-jet Electra, the first seeds of a possible future commercial jet airliner were sown. During the preliminary design work, two-, three- and four-jet engine layouts were studied, all with the typical Navy-type long, thin fuselage and big wings giving long endurance. One of the twin-engined designs showed a great deal of promise but was rejected by the US Navy due to its lack of enthusiasm for long missions over water on only two engines. Despite the rejection, the aircraft still looked reasonable, and Lockheed's thoughts began to turn towards a commercial derivative. With the capacity of the fuselage increased to carry a large number of passengers, it was studied by the Navy P-3C team in

Opposite page: Although Lockheed did win the CX-4/CX-HLS/C-5 contract for the US Air Force, studies were made to come up with a civil derivative - although without the RO-RO facility! *(Lockheed)*

their spare time, despite the heavy workload. The result was a high-wing, big twin-fan engined aircraft, with the engines hung on underwing pods. The fuselage was oval-shaped, wider than it was high, giving a passenger cabin capacity of 250 persons with a twin-aisle layout. Weight and performance were briefly checked on a wind tunnel model, but the pressure of work on the Orion took over, and the schemes for the airliner were shelved.

William M 'Bill' Hannan, who became Chief Engineer on the L-l0ll TriStar project in its early phases, and later Deputy Director of L-1011 Engineering described the development: 'We had done a lot of study work and a lot of preliminary design work on proposals for the new Navy patrol bomber. We had studied two engine airplanes and three engine airplanes and four engine airplanes. all of which were typical Navy-type with long skinny

An 'artists impression' of one of the early TriStar designs. Note the scalloped out rear fuselage around the aft engine and the apparent downward-sloping tailplane. This picture, along with a number of others were used by Lockheed as part of presentations to airlines during negotiations. *(Lockheed)*

fuselages and big wings and lots of range.'

As a result of market analyses and many discussions with airline technical management, preliminary design studies of short/medium-range transports with large passenger capacities began.

In the Spring of 1966 Lockheed's Chief Engineer Rudy Thoren recieved a call from Frank W Kolk, his counterpart with American Airlines. Kolk wanted to talk to Lockheed about building an airliner which American could operate as a kind of 'shuttle bus' over its heavy-traffic New York to Chicago segment.

Over a long lunch, Kolk and Thoren sounded each other out. 'Bill' Hannan, who was present at the meeting, remembers: 'Frank had a little five-page typed document with him that he called a requirement. It was a very brief description of what he had in mind. a little bit on the performance and so forth. He wanted a 'box' that could carry a maximum number of people at a minimum cost per seat mile. To him, this meant two engines, not three or four. He didn't want the plane to be too big nor like the 747 project which Boeing had talked to American about. He had heard about the big new fan engines too, and he thought they might do the trick.'

'There was one thing though that he insisted on. American had a decided advantage over other carriers because of their close-in LaGuardia Airport, the downtown airport for New York City, where the airline had millions invested in facilities. But LaGuardia had certain geometric constraints. The terminal was already fixed. The finger satellites were fixed, restricting aircraft length to a maximum of 185 feet. The turning areas were fixed. And there was a pier under one of its runways that extended out into Flushing Bay, which at that time was only approved to carry 270,000 pounds gross weight either taxiing or take-off. Frank was determined that the airliner he wanted had to be designed right up to those limits and no more. Even the overall length of the machine was a firm constraint.'

This, combined with the experience gained by the Georgia team, with the use of high-bypass turbofans, had well prepared Lockheed for what was on the horizon. In the autumn of 1966, a few months before the rejection of the Lockheed SST, American Airlines produced an outline specification for a large capacity, short to medium haul transport powered by the new technology large turbo-fan engines then becoming available. Lockheed decided to use this requirement as their basis for re-entering the commercial jet airliner field, although there was a direct competitor in the form of the McDonnell Douglas DC-10. Lockheed worked closely with American to define the design of its airbus. The requirement was for a 250-300 passenger aircraft with a similar performance to the Boeing 727, but a much better economy. American Airlines required a one-stop transcontinental range of 2,130 miles, while some of the other potential customers regarded non-stop transcontinental range as essential. A Mach 0.8 cruise and operations from a 9,000 foot runway on a hot day were also specified. The capability to conduct practical operations from existing and planned satellite airports with short fields was established as a primary design requirement.

Moreover, American Airlines specified the use of two high-bypass turbofans in the 40,000 pounds thrust class such as the General Electric CTF39, the Pratt & Whitney JT9D, or Rolls-Royce RB178-51.

The aircraft was to be a wide-bodied aircraft between the size of the huge Boeing 747 and the smaller Boeing 707 or Douglas DC-8 first generation jetliners. With the loss of the SST programme by Lockheed in late December 1966, there were suddenly about 1,200 surplus engineers available. While some were temporarily laid off, many others were transferred on to the airbus project, allowing it to go ahead with top priority.

Wingspan, overall length, landing-gear geometry, loadability, self- sufficiency and engine exhaust characteristics were some of the many considerations that influenced the design in terms of compatibility with the smaller airports. A requirement for lower loading stresses on runway pavement than those imposed by the current series of stretched DC-8s was also established for the L-1011 landing gear.

Thus, in meeting the listed initial design objectives, 1966 designs had two engines in the 41,000-pound static-thrust class and a passenger capacity of 250 in the all-coach configuration. Typically, a payload of 55,000 pounds could be carried over the required design range of 1850 nautical miles, and the maximum gross takeoff weight was about 265,000 pounds.

Subsequent liaison with a number of potential US operators confirmed these design objectives but also resulted in general agreement on the more specific requirements shown.

The CL-1011-28 configuration of April 1967 met these new requirements with a 250-passenger coach interior (227 passengers with a 20/ 80 per cent mixed

Above: Lockheed-California Company President Robert A. Fuhrman (*b*. 23 February 1925, *d*. 21 November 2009).

Right: William M 'Bill' Hannan holds a model of the proposed Lockheed twin-engined TriStar and points to the stretched version of the advanced technology trimotor. *(both Lockheed)*

interior). Prospective powerplants were either the Rolls-Royce RB207 with 50,300-pounds thrust (projected at the time for the European A-300 Airbus) or the uprated 48,100-pound-thrust Pratt & Whitney JT9D.

The maximum gross weight was 300,000 pounds. The cruise Mach number was 0.84 for services up to 1400 nautical miles, and the aircraft had the capability for 1850-nautical-mile flights such as Chicago-San Francisco.

Meanwhile, early in 1967, studies were also initiated on three-engine configurations with engines of about 35,000 pounds thrust. These were designed to meet the same mission requirements as the CL-1011-28, but had, in addition, a transcontinental range capability.

While establishing a design that met these requirements and achieved the necessary performance, the Lockheed design office evaluated sixty-six different configurations on a computer, leading to a basic layout in the early months of 1967. This was defined as the CL-1011-28, a wide-bodied, low- to mid-wing airframe with two engines located in underwing pods. With a gross design weight of 300,000 pounds, it would carry 250 passengers up to 1,600 miles. Its wingspan was 155 feet and overall length 162 feet. Alternative three-engined layouts were also studied under the designations CL-1011-30, -31, -32, and -33, but the economics of the twin-engined version appeared more promising.

As contacts grew with the major US domestic airlines towards the end of 1966, some important objectives and requirements had been defined. Several of the airlines, notably TWA, were interested with reservations, as although it was just taking delivery of 747s, the aircraft appeared to be too large and uneconomic for its domestic routes, especially Chicago to Los Angeles, and Kansas City or St Louis to West Coast destinations. A 250-300 seat wide-bodied jet would be ideal, but TWA did not like the twinjet idea, in case of an engine failure over the Rockies. A single-engined diversion would require an engine of around 55,000 pounds thrust, and none of that power existed at that time. Eastern Airlines were also interested, but was not happy with a twin-jet because its longest nonstop route was the 1,800 miles from New York to San Juan, much over water. Therefore, like their competitors at Douglas working on the DC-10 design, the Lockheed engineers switched to a three-engined design, with the third engine installed in the aft fuselage and fed through an S-duct with the intake at the base of the fin. Weights, capacity and installed thrust grew progressively, as they did with the DC-10 design, but

Lockheed Corp. Chairman Daniel J. Haughton (*b*. 7 September 1911, *d*. 5 July 1987)

Lockheed was confident of winning American Airlines' launching order for the wide-bodied trijet.

Bill Hannan: 'Frank Kolk's original idea to have a little short-range 'shuttle bus' started to stretch. The other airlines had quite a tug of war going, and the upshot was we decided that to satisfy a market big enough for a multi-million dollar investment, we would have to change our thinking somewhat. We weren't sure the engines available, or soon to be available, would be powerful enough to meet some of the common requirements of the major carriers. There were a lot of ghost stories and claims from the engine people. But even they admitted they weren't positive they had the answers. The obvious thing was to lean more toward a trijet.'

Meanwhile. by the end of June 1967 the 'Air Bus' had a more formal designation: L-1011-365. There were further evaluations. The 'Dash 365' became the 'Dash-385' which meant increased gross weight to 385,000 pounds. 'We arrived at this figure...' Bill Hannan explained '...because if you flew the airplane at that weight, it could satisfy the Chicago-West Coast leg for TWA and United or the Eastern New York-to-San Juan requirement. Or, with a partial payload, it could be used as a 747 back-up on non-stop transcontinental runs. At the same time. if the plane flew at the proper fuel load for American' Airlines requisite on the short-range New York-to-Chicago trip it would still not exceed the LaGuardia pier restriction'.

Passenger appeal and comfort needed to be

improved over the existing narrow-bodied jet airliners, while carrying double the payload on short to medium routes. Higher cruising speeds were required while using existing airport facilities. Higher utilisation had to be achieved through faster turnarounds, and reliability needed to be improved, allied to design for ease of maintenance. Lower operating costs, lower noise levels and an automatic landing capability were all required to provide more reliable operation and a better return on the initial capital investment in the aircraft. All this was needed by the early 1970s, to be followed by a family of models extending the investment over longer business spans by broadening the scope of operations while retaining commonality in spares, maintenance, ground handling and training.

This represented a basic change in thinking because, until that time, the airlines most involved with the project had felt that requiring the new aircraft to have transcontinental-range capability would overly burden the aircraft in its short-range role. The major fact that emerged from the two/three-engine studies was that a three-engined airliner could be built that met all the design requirements set for the 2000-mile range twin-engined aircraft, while also having the desired extra range and consequently improved flexibility.

Thus, although the price of this extra capability represented five to seven per cent of the direct operating cost and a slightly higher initial cost, there were many mitigating factors which collectively were sufficient to tip the scale in favour of the three-engine design.

The initial contacts between Lockheed and the major US domestic airlines led, by the end of 1966, to a list of objectives and design requirements for the new project, including the following:

- Improved passenger comfort and appeal.
- Double the payload of existing jetliners on short-to-medium routes.
- Higher cruising speeds than then available.
- Lower operating costs.
- Ability to use existing runways, taxiways and handling facilities.
- Lower noise levels.
- Higher utilisation through faster turn-round and improved reliability.
- Automatic landing capability.
- Increased flight safety through improved structural and system design.

In the days before desktop computer presentations, the company also made use of scale models to fit 'TriStar' into conventional patterns for ground equipment and loading techniques at existing airports. *(Lockheed)*

In at least one of the presentations to the airlines Lockheed included this sumptuous 'lounge' in an L-1011 underfloor space. *(Lockheed)*

- Design for ease of maintenance.
- Availability in the early 'seventies.
- Provide an aircraft to yield a high rate of return on the initial investment and a planned family of models capable of extending the new investment over longer business spans.

Another consideration was that the operating flexibility of the three-engine design made it a much more saleable aircraft - an attractive proposition to many more airlines. It should be noted that while this consideration entailed obvious benefits to the manufacturers, it was recognised early in this design-study process by the participating airlines that all would benefit by introducing a high level of versatility in the basic design so that it would fit the requirements of more than just one or two originating airlines. Not only would this effectively generate a wider market over which to spread the development costs, but it would also ensure a long-lasting, successful transport programme with all the associated support services well entrenched in a healthy environment.

Specific Design Requirements

It was around this time that a desire for improved operational performance and flight safety led to the inclusion of three advanced technology features in the flight control system: full power controls, backed up by four fully independent hydraulic systems; a flying stabilizer to eliminate the dangers of miss-trim during takeoff; and direct lift control to provide a rapid vertical response in maintaining a required approach descent path.

One of the overall goals in the design of the airframe structure was to provide an essentially unlimited fatigue life and an assurance that the aircraft would not run into a major structural problem during its projected lifetime. Of the various actions taken by Lockheed to satisfy this goal, the commitment to employ extensive metal-to-metal bonding in the fuselage was probably the most important, providing significant advantages for long fatigue life, improved fail-safe capability, and corrosion resistance.

The avionics flight control system, the autopilot, the flight controls, and the cockpit displays were developed with safe and precise all-weather automatic landing as a prime consideration. For the first time, automatic landing was certificated in an initial aircraft certification programme for all-weather landing conditions down to, and including International Civil Aviation Organization (ICAO) category Illa, which allowed landing with zero ceiling conditions and 700 feet of horizontal runway visibility. However, automatic landing was only part of the total avionics flight control system that provided manual or automatic modes of control throughout the total flight envelope, from takeoff to landing rollout.

Through the turn of the year from 1967 to 1968, both Lockheed and McDonnell Douglas were busy refining their designs to be ready for the anticipated orders from the major US airlines. The Lockheed submission was redefined as the L-1011-385 with a fuselage length increased to 175 feet, to allow the

Aircraft Characteristics

Fuselage	
Overall Length (Feet)	177.67
External Diameter (Feet)	19.58
Overall Height (Feet)	26.54
Floor Height (Feet)	5.08
Wing	
Area (Square Feet)	3456
Span (Feet)	155.33
Aspect Ratio	6.95
Sweep, 25% Chord Line (Degrees)	35
Horizontal Tail	
Area (Square Feet)	1282
Span (Feet)	71.58
Vertical Tail	
Area (Square Feet)	550
Span (Feet)	29.67
Overall Height (Feet)	55.33

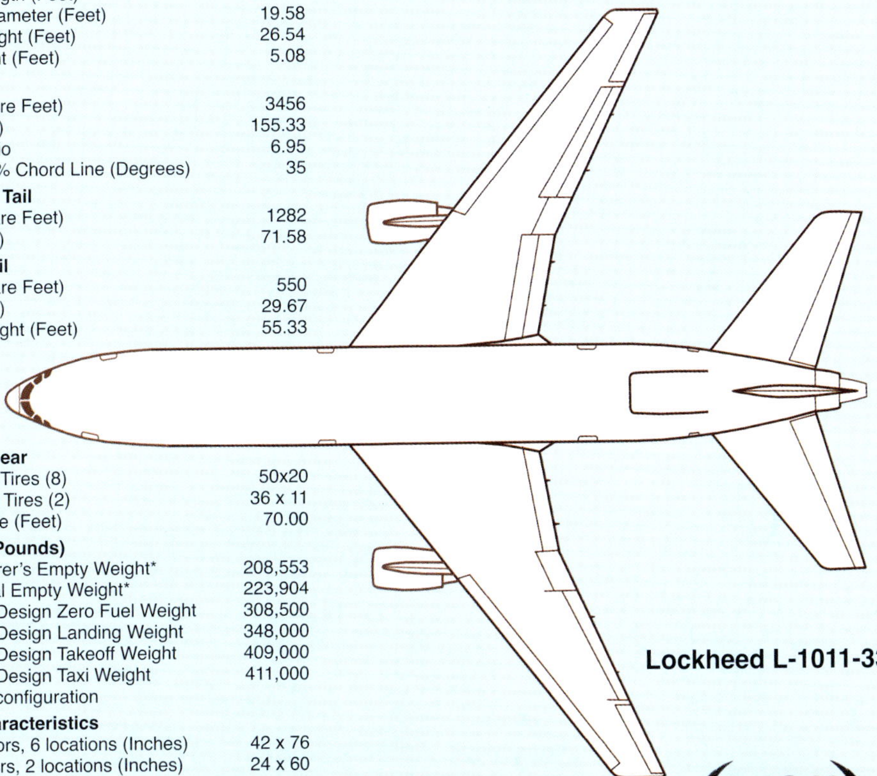

Landing Gear	
Main Gear Tires (8)	50x20
Nose Gear Tires (2)	36 x 11
Wheel Base (Feet)	70.00
Weights (Pounds)	
Manufacturer's Empty Weight*	208,553
Operational Empty Weight*	223,904
Maximum Design Zero Fuel Weight	308,500
Maximum Design Landing Weight	348,000
Maximum Design Takeoff Weight	409,000
Maximum Design Taxi Weight	411,000
*256-seat configuration	
Cabin Characteristics	
Type A Doors, 6 locations (Inches)	42 x 76
Type I Doors, 2 locations (Inches)	24 x 60
Window Size (Inches)	9.5 x 13.5
Window Spacing (Inches)	20
Sidewall Storage, 120 Units (Cubic Feet)	396
Miscellaneous Storage (Cubic Feet)	64.6
Aisle Width, First Class (Inches)	27.5
Aisle Width, Coach Class (Inches)	20
Cross Aisle Width, Aft (Inches)	32
Cross Aisle Width, Centre (Inches)	44
Ceiling Height (Inches)	95

Lockheed L-1011-335-1

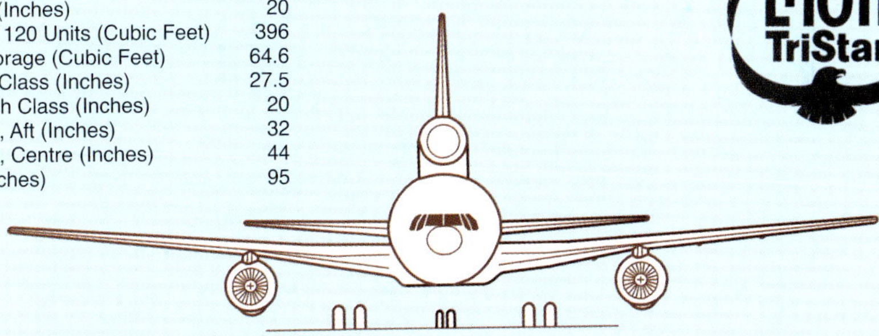

Accomodations

Passengers

	Basic 20/80 mix	Alt 15/85 mix	All coach	All economy	
First Class	52	40			
Coach or Economy	204	228	279	330	345
Total	256	268	279	330	345
Seats Abreast/Seat Pitch - inches					
First Class	6/38	6/38			
Coach or Economy	8/36	8/34	8/36	9/34	9/32

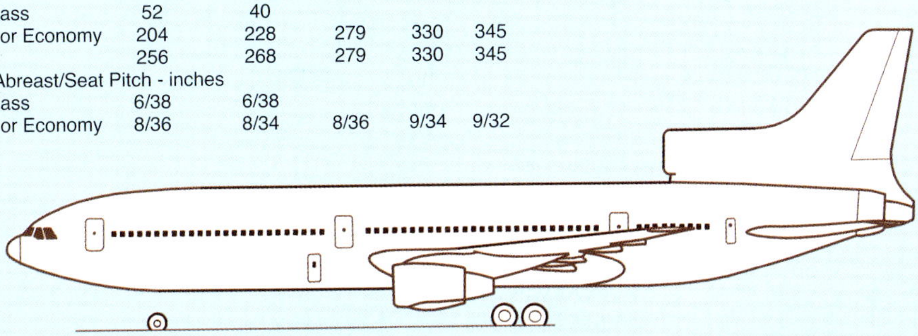

carriage of 250 passengers from the 7,000 foot runway at New York's LaGuardia to Chicago. With power from three 37,000 pound thrust engines, it met American Airlines' needs but was not entirely satisfactory when studied against the transcontinental requirements of TWA and Eastern Air Lines.

The airlines established a policy of compromise in differing individual requirements to achieve commonality of design and a high degree of inter-airline standardisation. While the immediate result was a reduction in the aircraft's initial cost, it was also appreciated that such a policy would prove to be extremely beneficial from the service and spares viewpoints when the airliner began operations.

About the same time that Lockheed presented its formal proposal to the airlines, Douglas was doing the same thing. Douglas and Lockheed sales associates bumped into each other worldwide as they visited potential airline customers' home offices. There was a rumour that Boeing had plans for shrinking its 747 Superjet and coming out with a shorter-range aircraft in the same weight and performance category as the DC-10 and the TriStar.

Airline executives, pilots and flight crews, technical and salespeople and maintenance personnel were also on the move, visiting Lockheed and Douglas to participate in detailed conferences and discussions and view mock-ups of the respective designs. In April 1967, for instance, Lockheed had engaged the firm of Sundberg-Ferar to make preliminary studies of the interior cabin arrangement for 'Dash-385' concentrating on an eight-abreast seating configuration with a unique aisle treatment. A quarter-scale mock-up was shipped to Burbank.

The 'dash 365' offer included both the Rolls-Royce RB211 (a new design derived from the RB207) and the General Electric CF6 (derived from the engine powering the C-5), and it was proposed that the airlines should evaluate the engines, as well as the basic design, and aid in making the final engine selection.

Many changes were made, and it was not until September 1967 that the Lockheed Board of Directors reviewed the full-scale mock-up.

There were also cockpit mock-ups and system mock-ups which all summer long were shown to various airline representatives. The first airline specification standardisation meeting was held over 16-20 October 1967, and, as a result, some 250 change requests were processed.

Resulting from these evaluations, the 'dash 365' grew in seating capacity, engine thrust, and gross weight for additional range. The cruise speed was established at Mach 0.85 to meet a requirement that

Lockheed President Archibald Carlisle Kotchian (*b*. 17 July 1914, *d*. 14 December 2008).

the airliner be competitive with the Boeing 747 on US transcontinental routes. A trade-off study, with the cruise speed variable and certain performance assumptions - 55,600-pound payload, 2500-nautical-mile range, minimum initial cruise altitude of 31,000 feet, 129-knot approach speed - showed excessive weight penalties for speeds approaching that of the 747's Mach 0.88. For example, a Mach 0.88 cruise speed for the L-1011 would have added 30,000 pounds to the take-off weight and required sixteen-per cent larger engines, resulting in a seven and a half percent increase in the direct operating costs. It was decided that a transcontinental flight-time within 15 minutes of that of the 747 (Mach 0.85 cruise) would be competitive without accepting undue penalties in other performance areas.

A second specification standardisation meeting conference was held in mid-December and dealt with points which rose from the first meeting of five major airlines. The air transport community was rife with rumours about who was going to get the big plum, Douglas or Lockheed? A billion dollar rainbow hung over the magic numbers game!

Despite Lockheed's excellent relations with American Airlines, it was something of a shock for the company when on 19 February 1968, the airline selected the DC-10 making it even more important for Lockheed to gain sufficient launch orders.

As the aviation press glowingly reported: 'First

details of the McDonnell Douglas DC-10 252-seat triiet 'airbus' were released on 19 February when American Airlines placed a firm order for twenty-five, at a cost of over $400 million, and placed options on another twenty-five. The order calls for delivery of the first twenty-five DC-l0s beginning in late 1971 and the additional twenty-five during 1973. Unlike options usually associated with aircraft orders, American have committed money they will lose if the options are not exercised.

The DC-10 will be 179 feet 8 inches long, with a span of 155 feet 4 inches and a height of 57 feet 3 inches. The cabin will be 18 feet 8 inches wide and 128 feet 4 inches long, and maximum take-off weight will be 386, 500 pounds. Powered by three Rolls-Royce RB211s or General Electric CF6s (choice still to be decided), the DC-10 will cruise at about 600 mph and have a range of 3,000 miles.'

Bill Hannan recalled that it was a real traumatic experience for Lockheed. 'I can remember our Board Chairman, Dan Haughton, coming in that Sunday after we got the news on Friday night, and Dan first thought he had been hoodwinked. But when all the facts began to leak out as to what really had happened, he realised that we had just been honestly skunked in the commercial set'.

Dan Haughton called a meeting and told staff: 'We're really going to get in this commercial business or we're going to get out, and I guess, if we're going to get in, the way to do it is to get in all the way. The first thing is, I've got the price too high and we're going to cut the price since we haven't sold any yet.' He cut the price down to where Lockheed was substantially lower than Douglas had just signed up for American.

Bill Hannan: 'Then, we went to TWA and Eastern and told them Look, now you got American out of the way, we'll change the design of our airplane to fit your needs right where you want it, and all of Frank Kolk's constraints don't count, anymore.'

'The L-1011-385-1 became the L-1011-410. We didn't call it that we still called it the 'Dash- 385'. We raised the gross weight because TWA wanted the range and raised the thrust requirement to 40,600 pounds. Eastern didn't object, particularly because they had some Mexico City requirements and they needed the thrust. Moreover, they had a seasonal interchange agreement brewing with TWA so they would like to have an identical airplane, anyway. Consequently, these two airlines began working very closely with us. It paid off handsomely.'

By March 1968, the aircraft specifications had grown further to an all-up weight of 409,000 pounds, with a payload capability of 56,200 pounds, equivalent to a maximum of 345 passengers. Three 40,000 pound thrust engines would give a cruising speed of Mach 0.8 at 35,000 feet and a typical range of 3,305 miles. This was an altogether more cost-effective proposal, primarily as the competition was still wide open, as although the DC-10 had achieved

The layout of the L-1011's flightdeck.

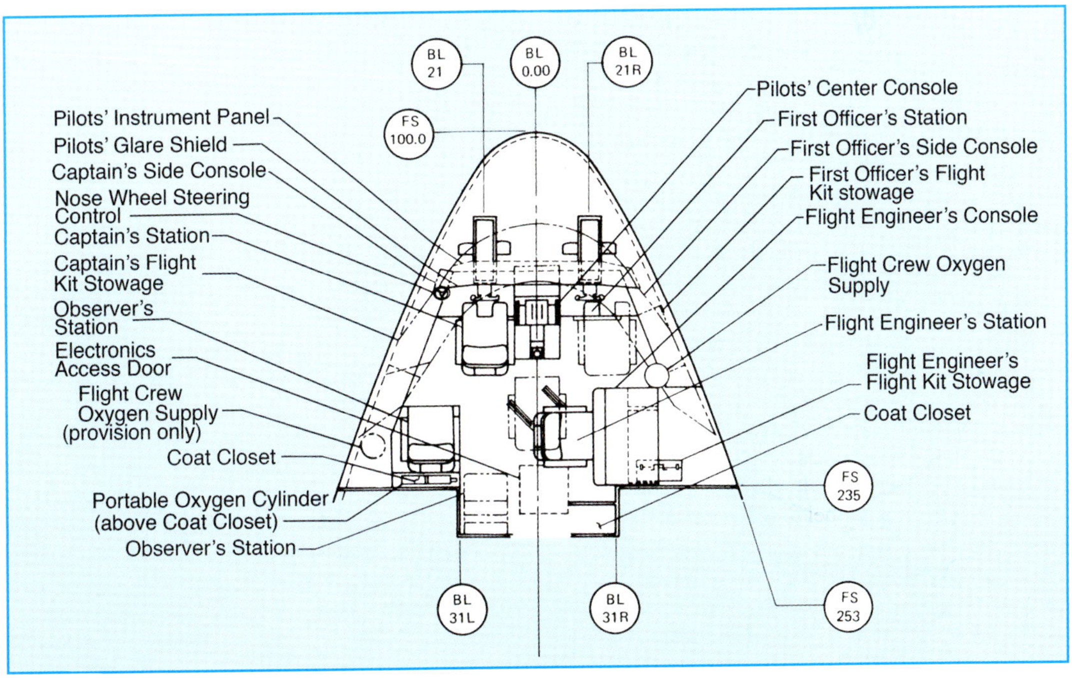

A comparasion of fuselage cross-sections between the Boeing 747 and the Lockheed L-1011.

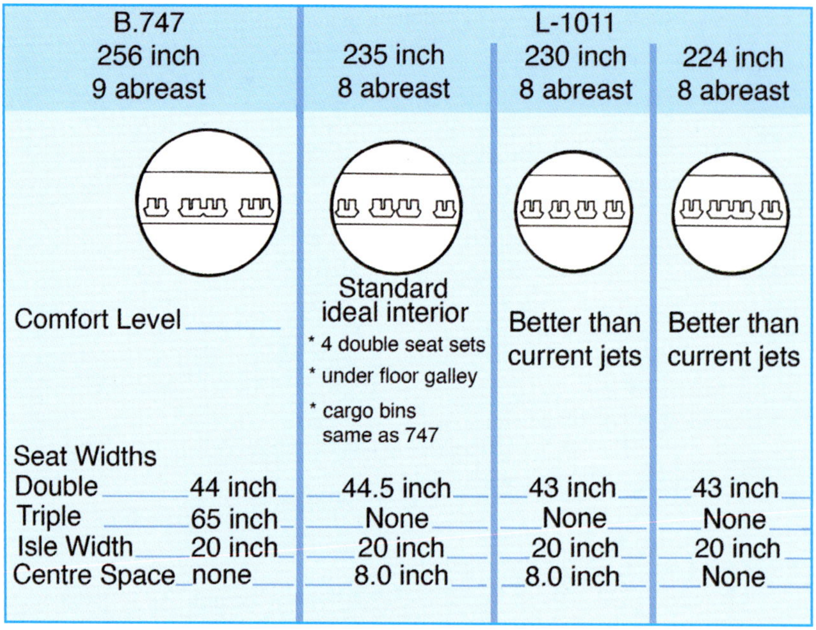

the initial order, it was still not sufficient to launch the programme, intensifying the sales battle between Lockheed and McDonnell Douglas.

Both airlines were well aware of the importance of their choice to the manufacturers, and quite naturally took full advantage of the keenly competitive situation. They both decided in principle to order the Lockheed L-1011 at board meetings on 26 March 1968 but kept their decisions secret. Final discussions were held with the top management teams of McDonnell Douglas and Lockheed, beginning at the Waldorf-Astoria Hotel in New York the next day. A press conference was scheduled for 11.00am on 29 March in the hotel to announce the winner, but it was not until the previous evening that TWA came to a final agreement with Lockheed, and then informed McDonnell Douglas and Eastern Airlines of the decision. Eastern confirmed its plans later the same evening and Letters of Intent were signed over breakfast the next morning in time for the press announcement, launching the Lockheed L-1011 TriStar into production and development.

The definitive L-1011 which won a record value of $2,160 million orders for an airliner still on the drawing board could seat 227 passengers in a mixed-class layout or 300 all economy-class. With 227 seats, the aircraft had a US coast to coast payload-range capability with a cabin capacity load. It could also carry a maximum payload out of LaGuardia on a hot day with enough fuel to reach Chicago.

Development of the Configuration

Over two million working hours were expended during the two years of L-1011 TriStar configuration development, and over 13,000 hours of testing was completed in seven different wind tunnels to establish the most eflicient aerodynamic configuration. Necessarily, much of this work was undertaken simultaneously while establishing the basic airline requirements, as previously outlined.

The fuselage cross-section was established early in the development stages. Many full-scale cross-section mock-ups were built complete with seats, and studies of many more cross-sections were made. The basic wing configuration, including high-lift devices, and the engine layout and installations varied considerably as the design requirements changed.

The major considerations for determining the proper section and diameter for the constant cross-section fuselage included:

- Creation of new norms for passenger comfort.
- Capability for optimal seating provisions.
- Flexibility of seating arrangements.
- Compatibility of aircraft weight and length with satellite air terminals
- Compatibility with convertible passenger cargo and freighter versions.
- Compatibility with future growth in range and capacity.

The fuselage cross-section was influenced by passenger capacity and the overall size-limitations of the aircraft; the latter being based on operational requirements from limited ramp space on existing key airports, such as New York/La Guardia.

Effectively, about 250 to 300 passengers - depending upon the interior layout - had to be accommodated within a fuselage length of about 180 feet, a figure which also allowed for future growth. Two basic approaches - a single or a double-deck arrangement - determined that a wide-bodied cylindrical fuselage accommodated all passengers on one deck with eight-abreast or more seating resulting in a lower deck which met requirements for cargo and other uses. Thus, there was no justification for deviating from this simple concept.

The final design approach for optimizing coach passenger seating was to provide eight-abreast seating in a two-aisle arrangement, with double seats and thirty-six-inch seat pitch. A 224-inch diameter cross-section was regarded as the minimum diameter fuselage to meet the above requirements. However, a design objective had been established to not only avoid triple seating but to eliminate any arrangement in which a passenger would feel trapped or sandwiched between other passengers. This situation could exist in the two centre doubles, but it was shown in a mock-up that it was alleviated when they were separated by eight inches. With this in mind, and using forty-four and a half-inch double seats and twenty-inch aisles, a fuselage diameter of 235 inches was selected to provide the best comfort level.

The 235-inch diameter fuselage selection resulted in new and improved passenger comfort and flexibility of seating arrangement. It gave suflicient space below the passenger floor for a completely new galley concept to prepare and store food away from the passenger cabin compartments. Large capacity compartments for baggage/cargo containers could also be made available. Two of these were sized for containers that were interchangeable with those used on the 747 and DC-10.

A major portion of the aerodynamic development effort was directed toward deriving the most efficient transonic wing design, commensurate with retaining excellent low-speed handling qualities and high maximum-lift characteristics. The wing design was optimised to provide minimum-cost cruise-speed at Mach 0.85 to achieve block-times competitive with the Boeing 747 over transcontinental ranges without undue weight penalties.

This looks like the interior of an actual aircraft - in fact it is the very cleverly designed 2-2 2-2 layout of the partial interior mockup at Burbank. This L-1011 'space' is much smaller than it appears due to the designer's use of full-width mirrors to the rear of the first two darker ceiling panels. *(Lockheed)*

Extensive trade-off studies and wind-tunnel tests were conducted to establish the compromises between aerodynamic efliciency and structural weight for such items as wing area, planform - with both leading edge and trailing edge extensions - sweepback angle, aspect-ratio, wing-thickness distribution, twist distribution, taper ratio, and high-lift devices.

Full-span leading-edge devices and double-slotted trailing-edge flaps, coupled with nominal wing area increases over that required for cruise conditions, result in a configuration providing short-field capability, low approach and landing speeds, and excellent cruise efficiency.

The spanwise location of the wing-engines allowed the use of large inboard flaps, thereby utilising the most efiicient portion of the wing for providing lift, where the wing chord was greatest and the flap pitching-moment contributions were smallest. Further, the engine pylons were far enough outboard to act as efficient fences in reducing the spanwise flow, thereby eliminating any pitch-up tendency. A combination of ailerons and spoilers obtained lateral control.

Aerodynamic data used for performance and stability calculations were based on low and high-speed wind-tunnel test results. Low-speed wind-tunnel models were used to develop the high-lift system, and various high-speed models were used to develop the cruise configuration. In addition to force measurements, various visual means for examining flow characteristics were employed during high-speed wind-tunnel tests. Oil-flow, tuft, and paint-streak methods were used to examine flow patterns on the wing, wing fillet, landing-gear fairing, and aft-body region in the area aft-engine inlet.

The test programme examined forty-five wing

Literally thousands of wind tunnel tests were conducted to prove the aerodynamic qualities of the Lockheed L-1011.

designs, six high-lift systems, twenty-five wing and aft-nacelle coinfigurations, eleven forebody and windshield shapes, twelve aft-body configurations, and six empennage arrangements. These tests also included a detailed examination of wing incidence, wing-body fillets, landing-gear fairings, pylon shapes, flap-track fairings, and engine exhaust.

The wing area selection was based on the results of an analysis which considered the following operational and design criteria:

- A cruise speed of Mach 0.85.
- Federal Aviation Regulations takeoff field length less than 10,000 feet on a 90 degrees F day.
- Initial cruise altitude of 33,000 feet.
- Approach speed of less than 130 knots at normal landing weight.
- Transcontinental-range capability at Mach 0.85 against winter winds (2650 nautical miles equivalent still-air range).
- Payload at the design range of approximately 56,000 pounds.
- Growth in range to 3500 nautical miles.

These design features, coupled with a nominal wing area which was larger than that required for cruise conditions resulted in a configuration that provide short field capability, low approach and landing speeds, and excellent cruise efficiency.

Wind tunnel tests were conducted to examine various means for arranging the wing-mounted nacelles and establish the proper pylon geometry.

Six nacelle configurations were studied in detail to develop the best engine/nacelle configuration. Considerations included the method of mounting, the length of the fan-exhaust duct, and the accessory gearbox location. A quantitative analysis was conducted to evaluate the effect of these configuration changes on the aircraft performance capabilities.

Lockheed thought that the range differences for the pylon configurations were not believed to be

Different engine configurations and wing locations were also studied. *(Lockheed)*

Configuration	Nacelle Mounting	Fan Duct Length	Exhaust / Gearbox
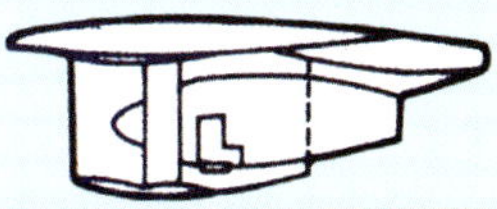 1	Mid Chord	3/4	Bare engine / Core-mounted gearbox
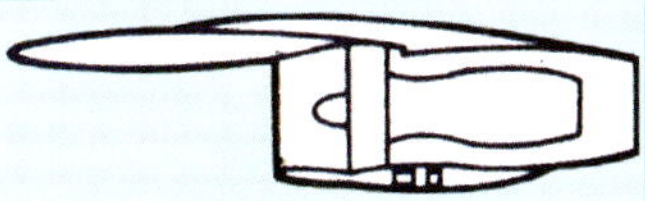 2	Aft Wing	Long (mixed flow)	Integral fan duct / fan-mounted gearbox
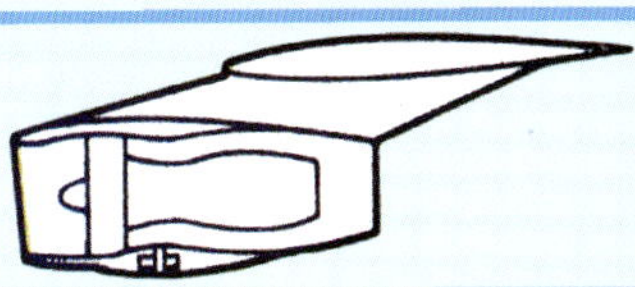 3	Pylon	Long (mixed flow)	Integral fan duct / fan-mounted gearbox
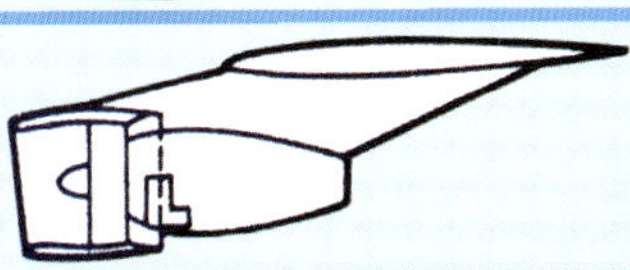 4	Pylon	Short	Bare engine / fan-mounted gearbox
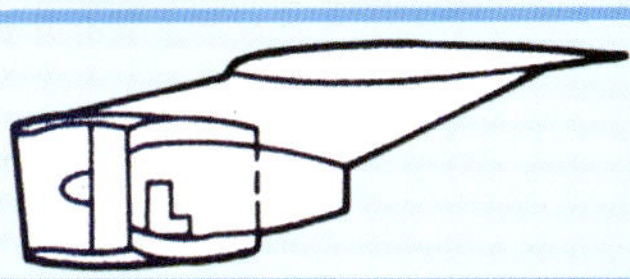 5	Pylon	3/4	Bare engine / fan-mounted gearbox
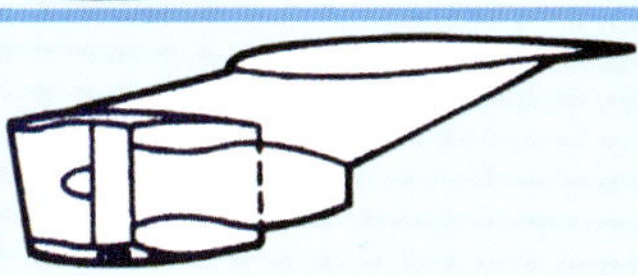 6	Pylon	3/4	Integral fan duct / fan-mounted gearbox

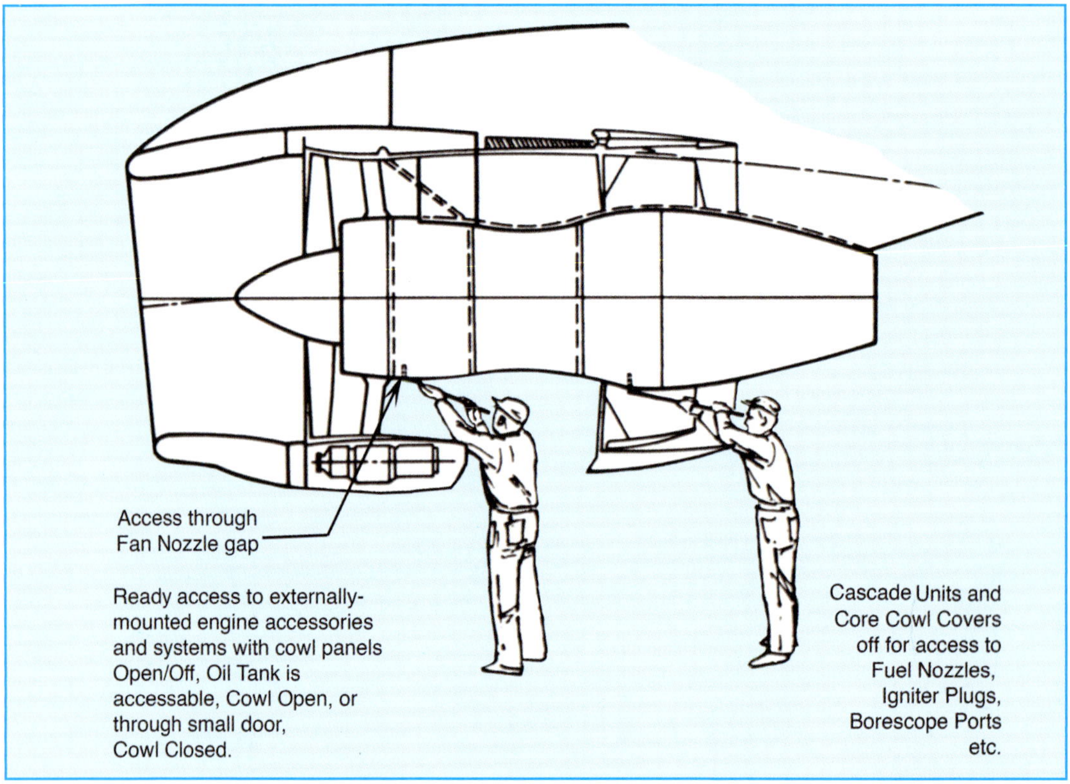

Lockheed took great care to explain the advantages of wing mounted engines. *(Lockheed)*

decisive in themselves, and a qualitative assessment was undertaken to assist in making the final selection. The major factors considered in this assessment were:

- Powerplant installation design.
- Effect on aircraft configuration.
- Noise.
- Maintenance.
- Development risk.

It was concluded based on this study that the three-quarter length fan-duct configuration, with accessories mounted externally to the fan exhaust duct was superior.

Comprehensive studies were conducted to determine the best overall position of the pylon-mounted engines. The spanwise location was selected by determining the most outboard location for weight-relief consistent with the minimum control-speed objectives. Attention focussed on determining a position that allowed for a large inboard flap area and served to concentrate wing lift inboard, thus avoiding the pitch-up problems inherent with large outboard-flap configurations.

From these studies, two positions were further investigated in the wind tunnel to determine the position with the best pitch characteristics at cruise and at low-speed with the flaps up and flaps down.

The summarised cruise data indicated that the outboard position was most favorable from pitch-up considerations.

The longitudinal/vertical nacelle location was determined from wind-tunnel tests. Data obtained showed that by placing the engine approximately 0.95 of a diameter below the wing chord, and the engine primary inlet 1.85 diameters forward of the wing leading edge, the lowest nacelle interference drag was obtained. The selected location was later verified in a test in which air at the correct pressure-ratio was exhausted underneath the wing. The vertical position also met the ground-clearance and maintenance objectives.

The vertical and horizontal inclination angles were also determined from wind-tunnel tests. The data showed that a nacelle vertical inclination angle of four degrees maximised the wing positive-pressure field acting on the nacelle aft-body. The horizontal inclination, or toe-in, provided the lowest nacelle interference drag at approximately two degrees.

The effect of engine location and pylon flexibility on basic wing-flutter characteristics was determined

Above and below: two wind-tunnel models of the No.2 engine intake and S-Duct. *(Lockheed)*

early in the design. It was found that these effects were minor, and no additional stiffness was necessary for flutter considerations to position the engines on pylons ahead of the wing.

One of the most critical and involved trade-off studies conducted during the L-1011 development programme was centred on the selection of the inlet-duct configuration for the aft-engine installation. Four designs were considered and tested in the subsonic and transonic wind tunnels. Cross-wind compatibility was also investigated, as well as the effects of low and T-tail arrangements.

Two designs incorporated an S-shaped duct with the inlet located on the aircraft centreline ahead of the tail fin and the outlet at the cone in the fuselage aft-body. The other designs incorporated a straight-through duct arrangement. More than 550 hours of wind-tunnel testing were expended at both low and high speeds to examine the effects of the aft engine's location on aft-body closure geometry, drag, stability, and control effectiveness. These tests were conducted on two types of model support systems. Gross aft-body closure effects were investigated on the sting support, and the blade support was used to isolate details and tailor the aft-body geometry.

The initial step in isolating the S-duct's aerodynamic characteristics and the fin-mounted nacelle installation was to determine the lowest drag level that might be realised from an optimum aft-body closure, irrespective of nacelle-installation requirements. In combined propulsion, design, and aerodynamic studies, additional aft-body geometries were determined which would realistically represent aft-body closure for the fin-mounted nacelle and the S-duct installation.

The results of these blade support system tests showed that the drag level of the aft-body

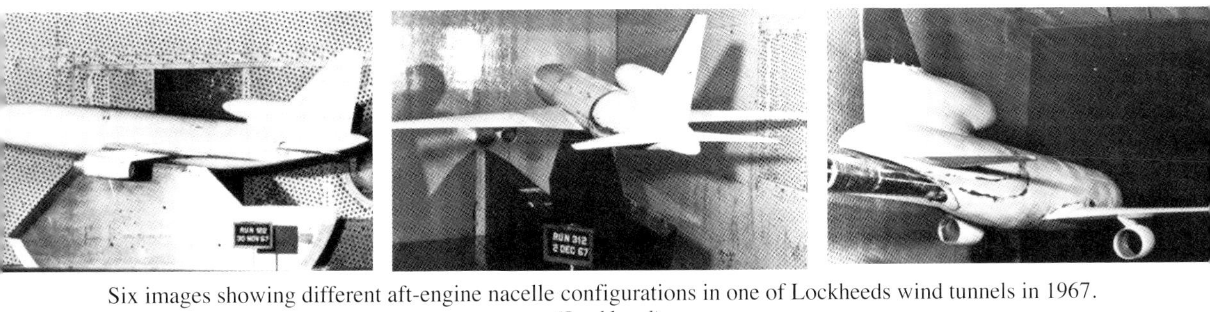

Six images showing different aft-engine nacelle configurations in one of Lockheeds wind tunnels in 1967. *(Lockheed)*

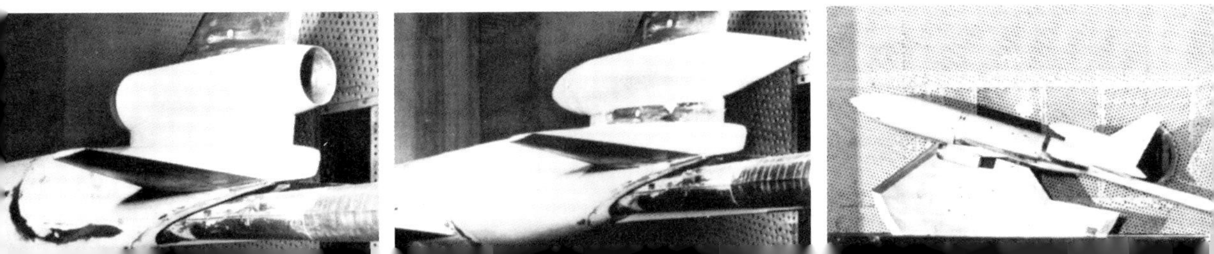

No.2 engine S-Duct was built for Lockheed by Bristol Aerospace of Winnipeg as a test-fixture for Rolls-Royce RB211 testing.

It was used at R-R Hucknall in the UK in an outdoor test stand where cross-flows were simulated and noise measurements could be made. *(both Lockheed)*

representation of the S-duct installation closure was within the data-band expected for the idealised aft-body closure; the location of the engine increasing the effective fuselage fineness-ratio. Further, the aft-body closure configured for the fin-mounted nacelle showed two to four per cent higher aircraft drag than the S-duct throughout the test Mach-number range.

Examination of the wind-tunnel drag polars - that is, the relationship between the lift on an aircraft and its drag - of the complete models representative of the S-duct and fin-mounted nacelle installation showed that the aft-body associated with the S-duct retained the drag level advantage at cruise Mach number and lift coefficient, as indicated by body-alone tests. Increments in drag measured from model build-up tests showed that estimated increments in drag due to the addition of horizontal, vertical, and nacelle components agreed with the normal friction-drag allowance; therefore, there was complete flow attachment.

The effect of both aft-nacelle configurations on the zero-lift pitching moment was a favourable positive shift. Neither the fin-mounted nor S-duct installation affected longitudinal stability. Directional-stability levels of both nacelle installations were also essentially the same.

The wind-tunnel test results of low-speed stability and control characteristics for the S-duct configuration showed that this inlet arrangement had excellent directional stability and control down to the stall, and had the required cross-wind capability.

Other test results showed that the L-1011 had no aft-engine distortion problem up to a cross-wind of fifty knots - well beyond normal operating conditions.

Rudder effectiveness for the lower portion of the rudder was measured in wind tunnel tests. Comparing the lower rudder moment-effectiveness to that of the total rudder area showed that the lower portion, located aft of the inlet, was fully effective.

Flow visualization-studies conducted at cruise Mach number using an 'oil dot' technique demonstrated the high-energy air on the aft-body displacing oil along the local flow lines and that there was no flow separation. Aft-body pressure data further substantiated the excellent flow-recovery in the region of the duct-closure and lower-rudder area. In the same wind tunnel test, rudder trailing-edge pressures were measured and again substantiated the flow quality in the aft-fuselage region.

The L-1011 S-duct configuration resulted from a concentrated model test programme involving low and high-speed wind tunnels and a cross-wind test rig. Scale models of seven S-ducts, and associated variants were tested in an open-throat wind tunnel having a speed capability of fifty knots and a wind vector capability from zero to 180 degrees.

The estimated and measured values of L-1011 S-duct total pressure- recovery at high speed were compared against the performance of an idealised straight-duct configuration. The high-speed model test data, corrected for skin-friction differences between model and full scale, compared extremely well with estimated values.

Tests demonstrated that at a median cruise corrected airflow of 1450 pounds per second, the L-1011 aft-engine inlet was expected to operate at a total pressure-recovery of 0.992. An idealised straight inlet, having a constant diameter equal to engine-face diameter and a length 3.88 times this diameter, had a total pressure-recovery of 0.994. The difference in specific fuel consumption resulting from these values was less than one-tenth of one per cent for the aircraft. Further, if this idealised, straight aft-engine inlet was made practical by utilising a realistic throat diameter followed by a near-optimum diffuser, total pressure-recovery was estimated to be equal for the two concepts.

It was known that the performance and operational characteristics of some existing aft-engine, S-duct installations were not ideal. However, each aircraft had its peculiar installation problems, affecting the duct's efficiency, and it did not follow that all S-duct installations had the same characteristics. Lockheed compared the L-1011 duct

Lockheed's L-1011 Engineering/Manufacturing Mock-up Area. The RB211 in the left foreground is fitted with the Hot Stream Spoiler strangs to translate the spoiler doors to the rear. *(Lockheed)*

to that of the Boeing 727. Both ducts were scaled to a common engine-face diameter. It should be noted that the L-1011 duct had less severe lines; the bend offset was considerably less, and so was the overall length; there was a four-and-a-half degree up-tilt of the engine axis and a straight section immediately ahead of the engine attachment. Also, the cross-section of the L-1011 S-duct was circular whereas the 727 duct had a vertically elongated cross-section throughout most of the duct.

A summary of the study results leading to the selection of the S-duct for the aft engine installation revealed that:

- S-Duct inlet recoveries were equal to recoveries for practical and realistic straight ducts.
- Acceptable total pressure distortions up to a 50-know crosswind.
- Aerodynamic performance and stability characteristics confirmed by extensive low and high-speed wind tunnel tests.
- L-I011 aft-body closure - S-Duct tail configuration - offered drag levels five to ten counts lower than a straight-duct tail configuration.
- S-Duct configuration provided a fully effective rudder installation with excellent directional stability and control characteristics at low and high speeds.
- S-Duct configuration was estimated to be 800 pounds lighter than a straight-duct configuration.
- Aft engine in S-Duct configuration was readily accessible from working platforms positioned directly under the aft fuselage.
- S-Duct installation offered a direct operational cost improvement of 1.2 per cent for a typical transcontinental flight.

Rhio Weir, a research mechanic in Department 76-46 installs a portion of the L-1011 landing gear on the VSS. *(Lockheed)*

The Big Iron Bird

In advance of the TriStar taking to the skies, there was a demand for what Lockheed staff called 'the iron bird' - the L-1011 TriStar Vehicle Systems Simulator at Rye Canyon. Although the VSS would never fly, it was designed to operate and respond exactly how the L-1011 production models would during flight. Steel jigs supported the testing systems, with prototype parts and assemblies installed on the jigs until the production parts become available.

The VSS enabled pilots to 'fly' the TriStar long

Left: Bill Sechrist, a research mechanic, adjusts the instrumentation fitting that contreols the temperatures and pressures of the hystraulic fluid within the VSS. Right: John Enlow, a research electrican in Department 76-55 wires an instrument panel. *(both Lockheed)*

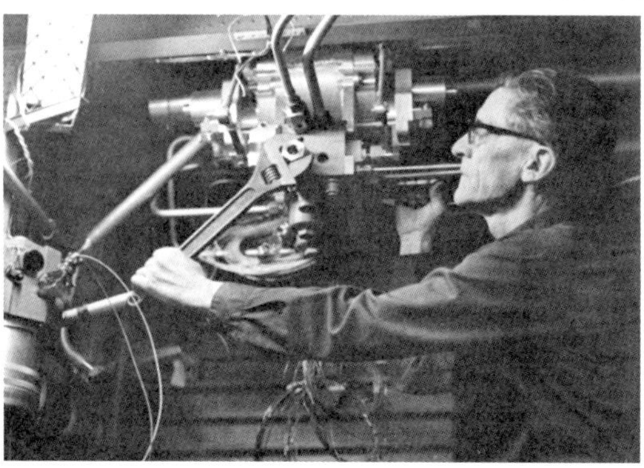

Employees in Building 360, Plant B-6 work on the TriStar fuselage afterbody horizontal stabilizer support assembly, which when complete was sent to the Rye Canyon Research Lab. *(Lockheed)*

before the first production model was airborne. It was intended to show up any potential problem spots in performance of the aircraft or any of its major sub-systems, in time to take action before airline deliveries. 'The VSS encompasses the primary and secondary flight controls, and the electrical, avionics, hydraulics and landing gear systems - and includes the automatic landing system of the TriStar,' explained Loren Harms, VSS program manager, who was a key member of the VSS team since its planning stage in 1967.

'It was designed to accommodate all phases of testing from the component level to complete systems, all to assure TriStar customers the highest levels of performance from their aircraft,' said Forest 'Frosty' Riek, VSS deputy program manager, who had worked on the elaborate system since its conception. It was located in Building 229A, a customised 150-by-150-foot two-story facility at Rye Canyon, to the north of Burbank. Each of the eight major systems and accompanying subsystems was operable from its own TriStar flight station.

The VSS flight station, a functional extension

Stretching its iron wings in Building 229A at Rye Canyon Research Labs is the TriStar Vehicle Systems Simulator. *(both Lockheed)*

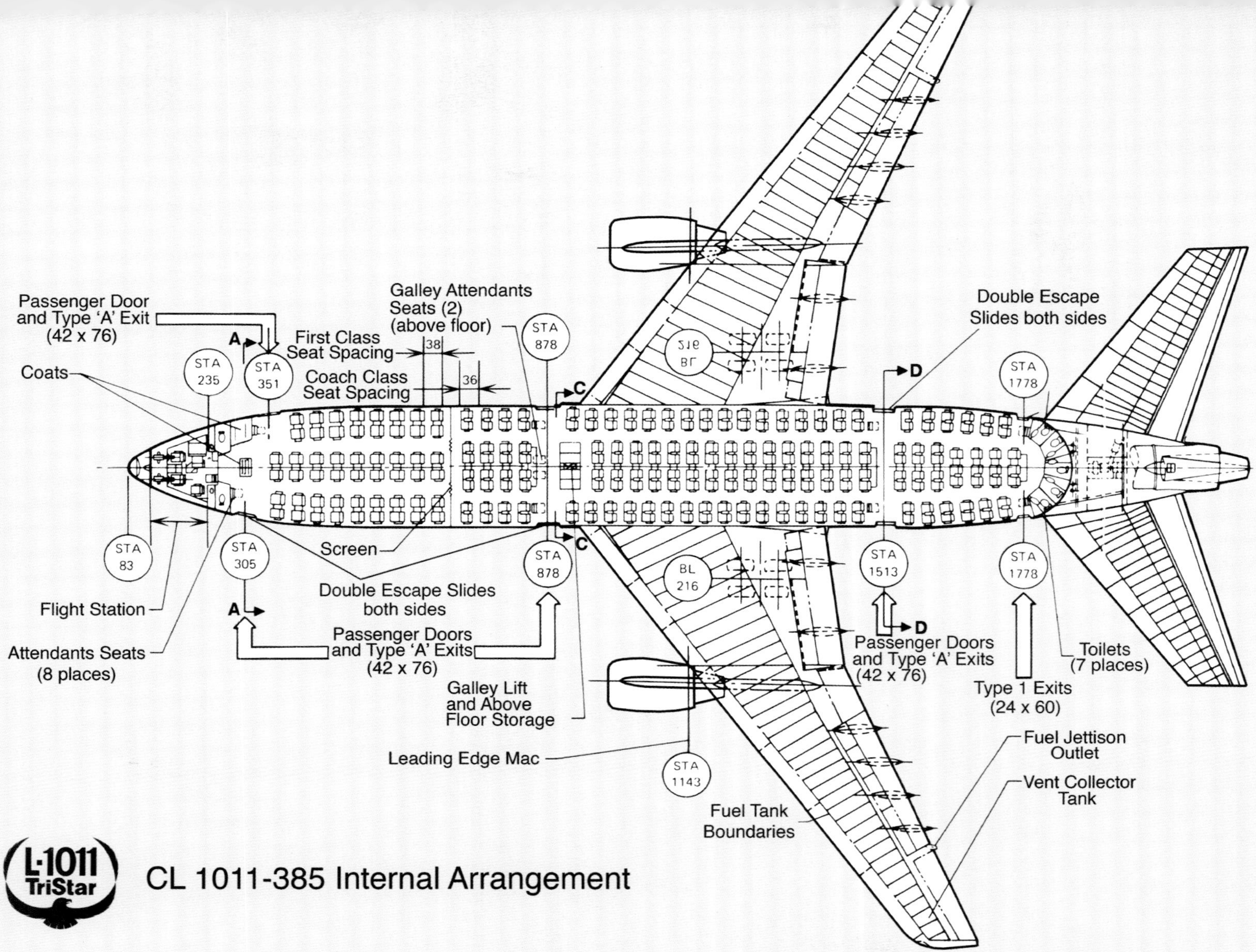

CL 1011-385 Internal Arrangement

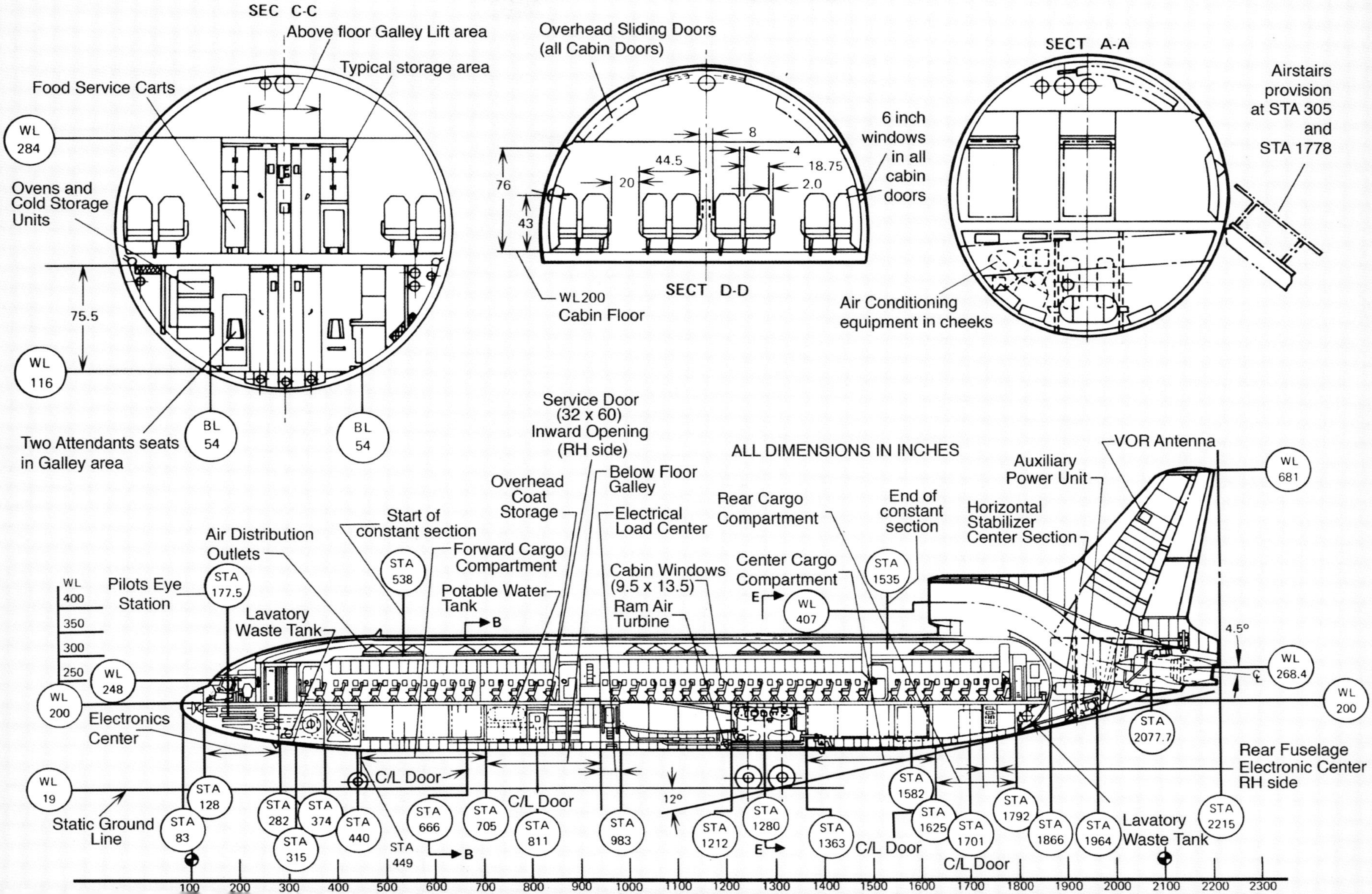

SEC C-C
Above floor Galley Lift area
Typical storage area
Food Service Carts
WL 284
Ovens and Cold Storage Units
75.5
WL 116
BL 54
BL 54
Two Attendants seats in Galley area
Overhead Sliding Doors (all Cabin Doors)
76
43
20
44.5
8
4
18.75
2.0
6 inch windows in all cabin doors
WL 200 Cabin Floor
SECT D-D
SECT A-A
Airstairs provision at STA 305 and STA 1778
Air Conditioning equipment in cheeks
Service Door (32 x 60) Inward Opening (RH side)
ALL DIMENSIONS IN INCHES
VOR Antenna
Auxiliary Power Unit
WL 681
Overhead Coat Storage
Below Floor Galley
Electrical Load Center
Rear Cargo Compartment
End of constant section
Horizontal Stabilizer Center Section
Start of constant section
Air Distribution Outlets
Forward Cargo Compartment
Cabin Windows (9.5 x 13.5)
Center Cargo Compartment
STA 538
STA 1535
WL 400
350
300
250
Pilots Eye Station
STA 177.5
Lavatory Waste Tank
Potable Water Tank
Ram Air Turbine
WL 407
B
E
4.5°
WL 268.4
℄
WL 200
WL 248
WL 200
Electronics Center
STA 2077.7
Rear Fuselage Electronic Center RH side
C/L Door
12°
WL 19
STA 128
STA 83
Static Ground Line
STA 282
STA 315
STA 374
STA 440
STA 449
B
STA 666
STA 705
C/L Door
STA 811
STA 983
STA 1212
STA 1280
E
STA 1363
C/L Door
STA 1582
STA 1625
STA 1701
C/L Door
STA 1792
STA 1866
STA 1964
Lavatory Waste Tank
STA 2215
100
200
300
400
500
600
700
800
900
1000
1100
1200
1300
1400
1500
1600
1700
1800
1900
2000
2100
2200
2300

of the iron bird, had fully operational controls such as flight instruments and systems monitors. Even engine controls were available to test pilots.

The primary purpose of the VSS was to support the L-1011 flight test programme. It was used to spot problems early and correct them, and also to assure TriStar customers that the L-1011 will perform as specified.

From twenty-five to fifty individual tests could be conducted simultaneously. Test data was fed directly into computers, processed and made available to engineers by means of visual replay consoles in the building; this way the data could be evaluated within a matter of minutes.

The VSS represented one of the most comprehensive and totally integrated test programmes in the history of the aerospace industry. Parts and assemblies for the iron bird came from such Lockheed companies as Gelac (Lockheed Georgia), LPC, LAS and LMSC, plus subcontractors such as Avco, Menasco and scores of others.

Some 120 employees were assigned to the Experimental Shops and Services Division in Building 360 at Plant B-6. Employees in Dept. 76-40, under the direction of J S Patton and R C Hartman, assistant division managers, built the enormous VSS Hydro Service Center. 'We have been spending about 1200 hours each week building these large VSS structures, which

Pictures of TriStar serial no. 1000 are rare at the best of times - images of it outside in the sunshine even more so. This airframe was destined never to leave the ground, but simulated some 36,000 flights during its life as a fatigue-test aircraft. This is how it looked as it was rolled out of Bldg. 601, the Palmdale final assembly facility, and installed in Building 602, the flight test facility, to appear on the front cover of Volume 37, No. 21 of *Lockheed Star,* the company house newspaper dated 8 October 1970. The ladder-like attachments on the stabilisers and fuselage were loading frames attached to hydraulic jacks that applied the test loads as the aircraft was cradled in its five-story-high reaction structure test jig. *(Lockheed)*

THE LOCKHEED Star

BURBANK, CALIF., U.S.A.

OFFICIAL PUBLICATION OF THE LOCKHEED-CALIFORNIA COMPANY

LOOK TO LOCKHEED FOR LEADERSHIP

Vol. 37, No. 21 October 8, 1970

In the fatigue-test control room John Thorson, an associate research engineer in 74-42, and L D Canfield, senior electronics research engineer in 74-63, prepare to start a new series of fatigue tests. The test data is recorded on magnetic tape, shown in the background, and subsequently is evaluated by test personnel. Employees working in the control room monitor test results from both the fatigue-test craft and the static-test machine. *(Lockheed)*

actually are prototypes of production articles. It's quite impossible to appreciate the scope of this program until you see some of these enormous structures,' said Dave Hegg, division engineer for experimental shops and services.

We completed the VSS Hydro Service Center, bat wing structures, nose wheel-well structures, leading-edge slat-track rib assemblies and flap-track rib assemblies.

'Because some of these assemblies were so large, we actually had to take down fences at Rye Canyon to get the structures into Building 229A. Other times we've had to disassemble the VSS structures and reassemble them at Rye Canyon' Hegg said.

As well as building the VSS, Lockheed also built an 'almost complete' L-1011, airframe number 1000. After being assembled in Bldg. 601 at Plant 10 it was moved to a concrete stage in Bldg. 602 where it nestled in a five-story-high test jig.

Devoid of the usual highly polished paint and markings, TriStar 1000 was set to 'fly' 36,000 times - each simulated 'flight' lasting from eight to fifteen minutes. Tests included eighty-six different types of flight, covering almost every

Original caption: 'NEWSBUREAU, LOCKHEED-CALIFORNIA COMPANY 1971 PARIS AIR SHOW PRESS BUREAU LE BOURGET. CHALET: C-12 TELEPHONE: 284-7246 AND 833-5332. CAGED TEST BIRDS -- In a hangar at Lockheed's flight-test center at Palmdale, Calif., two L-1011 TriStars in massive test rigs resemble huge birds in cages. At left is a structurally complete L-1011 in a fatigue test rig. Under the force of more than 300 hydraulic jacks, it will simulate some 36,000 separate airline flights. Partially complete TriStar at right is undergoing static tests in which a wing and other major structures eventually will be stressed to ultimate design limits. In flight tests, which began Nov. 16, 1970, other L-l0lls are taking part in proving flights leading to Federal Aviation Administration certification and entry into commercial service in 1972. LA 9256-6'

kind of airline service. Some ninety simulated flights would be flown per day, and approximately 24,000 were concluded by the time the first TriStar was delivered to airline customers.

To inspectors and Lockheed customers, it demonstrated that the L-1011 service life was not fatigue-limited. To prove this, approximately 300 hydraulic actuators applied various load cycles that simulated flight conditions such as climb and descent, while the cabin was being pressurised and depressurised.

The simulated flights also included test conditions corresponding to ground-to-air manoeuvres, low- and high-altitude gust manoeuvres, air-to-ground landing manoeuvres and taxiing procedures. In all, there were forty different fatigue test conditions applied under the direction of the computer-operated load controller. At times portions of the aircraft would be subjected to limit loads, the maximum forces the L-1011 structure was designed to withstand without damage. The limit load on the wing, for example, would cause it to flex across an arc of thirteen feet.

'This will be one of the most comprehensive and realistic fatigue and proof load test programs ever performed in the aerospace industry. The tests will begin in November, and by the first part of January the tests will be conducted around the clock, six days a week,' said Bob Lathrop, group engineer in Dept. 74-42 who was running the tests.

'One of the unique characteristics of this program is that TriStar 1000 will be tested as an entire structural unit. For this reason, Bldg. 602 was specially constructed and reinforced to accommodate the full-scale fatigue test model. During the 1½ years, it will take TriStar 1000 to make the 36,000 simulated flights, she will be subjected to 2.1 million load cycles.'

The test article was instrumented with around fifty strain guages and deflectometers for monitoring the fatigue tests, plus an additional 1000 strain gages and deflectometers at approximately 200 locations for use during the limit load tests.

A Hewlett-Packard 2116B computer controlled the tests, gathered and stored the results. It was programmed to simulate a flight from takeoff to parking at the airliner's destination, actuated hydraulic jacks attached to the test aircraft's exterior. The 2116B was a later development of the 2116A, introduced in 1966 as their first go-anywhere machine. With 4K of magnetic core memory - that was the minimum system configuration - expandable to 32K, the computer cost between $25,000 to $50,000, depending on options used.

Meal service, complete with fillet mignon was carried out. Note the remote controlled TV camera, temporarily fitted to a roof panel during the meal service trials. *(Lockheed)*

Left: Flight Attendants Charlotte Lemons (left) of Delta Airlines and Lucinda Lundberg of Eastern Airlines move carts loaded with food to the elevator in the below-deck TriStar galley.

Below: Diane Kominak, Eastern Airlines flight attendant, pours coffee during the food serving demonstration in the TriStar mockup in Building 360. *(both Lockheed)*

As the jacks exerted loads simulating various phases of flight - such as takeoff and climb - the computer simultaneously recorded the resulting stress patterns in the TriStar structure, as measured by 1700 strain gauges and other sensors installed at 800 strategic locations throughout the airliner. The sensors measured the degree of bending and the directions in which the stress is distributed through the structure.

Lockheed engineers studied the test data, and inspected the airframe each day, using x-ray, ultrasonic and dye penetrant techniques.

Inspectors checked TriStar 1000 daily. Once each week there was a detailed inspection of ten per cent of the airframe, using sonic, x-ray and dye-penetrant crack detection techniques. The entire fatigue model also was examined in detail once every ten weeks, corresponding to approximately 5000 flights.

Another ground-test programme at Palmdale subjected a portion of an L-1011 airframe to static tests that would determine the airliner's ultimate strength by crushing it to destruction.

Testing the meal service

'Never was eating so enjoyable!' This was the reaction of 250 passengers after finishing a full course meal aboard the TriStar cabin mockup in Building 360 at Plant B-6.

'The volunteer passengers last week enjoyed dinner served by flight attendants from four airlines during a ninety-minute imaginary flight.'

'The purpose of the jetliner feast was to demonstrate to a critical jury of airline observers the highly sophisticated food preparation and service equipment built into the L-1011.

'The 250 meals were cooked in unique high-speed ovens in the TriStar's galley, located in the aircraft's belly beneath the passenger deck. Eight stewardesses - a typical number that airlines

expect to use aboard the new trijet—served the dinner using special carts to transport food and beverages from the below-deck galley to the passengers' seats.'

Carts and flight attendants moved between the galley and the passenger deck in two elevators that are part of the aircraft. L W King of the L-1011 passenger accommodations department 73-31 explained that galley equipment and serving carts were designed to permit, in his words, ' gracious, unhurried meal service to 250 or more persons even on brief flights.'

'Because the intermediate-range TriStar will frequently make shorter flights of as little as ninety minutes' duration, we chose that length of time for this demonstration," King said. "We simulated every aspect of such a flight, from the loading of food into the galley and boarding of passengers to takeoff, cruise, descent and landing.'

While stewardesses from the four airlines were at work, their activities were carefully observed

TriStar Sales Center

Lockheed established a sales centre at Burbank, and on 23 June 1970 a team from UK carrier Court Line Aviation and Clarksons Holidays visited Burbank.

Above, left to right: Donald McQueen (Clarksons Director), John Young (Managing Director Court Line Ltd), Ed Posey (Managing Director Court Line Aviation), Tom Gullick (Clarksons Director) and two of the Lockheed Sales Team have the finer points of passenger seating explained to them before (below) trying out the comfort for themselves in the mock-up. *(both Lockheed)*

L-1011 underfloor galley mock-up at Burbank on 18 September 1969. The two lifts to the main deck are behind the Lockheed 'flight attendants', one door open, one closed.

Right: The underfloor galley mock-up had evolved somewhat by the time the Court Line/Clarksons team visited Burbank on 23 June 1970. The TriStar could use ACE, ATLAS or KSSU full and half-cart service trolleys.

Below: from left to right: The Court Line/Clarksons team of John Young, Tom Gullick, Ed Posey and Donald McQueen in what was to become an almost standard pose, demonstrating the width of the TriStar cabin mockup at Burbank. Ed later admitted to me that the look on his face was 'oh no, how cheesy'! *(all Lockheed)*

by Lockheed and airline representatives playing the role of passengers. Twelve closed-circuit television cameras relayed the scene to other observers in a nearby room. Stopwatches clocked the cooking and serving of the 250 dinners.

'Entrees are brought aboard the TriStar in a deep-frozen state', King pointed out. 'Cold-storage units in the galley keep the meats frozen until just before mealtime. With our new ovens, we can have a frozen steak cooked and ready to serve in from eighteen to twenty minutes,' King said. 'Any entrees that are not cooked can be kept frozen instead of being thrown away, as they have to be on older airliners.'

Passengers in the first-class cabin were offered their steak or chicken choice as an entree, as they might be on an actual flight. The first-class dinner also included a choice of cocktails or soft drinks, with toasted almonds, shrimp and tomato salad, dinner wines with the entree, broccoli with polonaise sauce, parsley potatoes, a ricotta eclair for dessert, and a choice of tea, coffee or milk.

In the coach cabin, all passengers were served a grilled filet mignon entree. Also served was a choice of cocktails or soft drinks, hearts of lettuce salad with green goddess dressing, parsley potatoes, broccoli polonaise, apple shalet for dessert and a choice of beverages with the meal.

Flight attendants in the demonstration represented Air Canada, Delta, Eastern and TWA. Other flight attendants from Air Jamaica were on hand as observers.

A Range of Model Numbers

The gross weight of the basic L-1011-1 model, with 42,000-pound-thrust Rolls-Royce RB211-22B engines, was finally established at 43,000 pounds. With minimal structural modifications, the L-1011-100 was later certificated to operate at gross weights up to 466,000 pounds, allowing the addition of centre-section fuel for additional range. The L-1011-200 TriStar had the same structural changes as the Dash 100 but was powered by 48,000-pound-thrust RB211-524 engines.

The L-1011-500 model was the long-range member of the family. Fuel capacity was increased to allow a full 246 passenger load over 6,000 miles. Modifications to the basic TriStar included removing fuselage sections fore and aft of the wing to reduce fuselage length by about thirteen feet; and the addition of wingtips to achieve a nine-foot increase in the wingspan, a change that included the incorporation of active control ailerons. Other modifications included airframe and landing gear strengthening to achieve a gross weight of 496,000 pounds and the installation of 50,000-pound thrust RB211-524B engines.

Lockheed was able to announce a spectacular launch for the L-1011 TriStar with 144 orders and options from Eastern - twenty-five firm and twenty-

Lockheed's Art Department produced a vast amount of L-1011 imagry. *(Lockheed)*

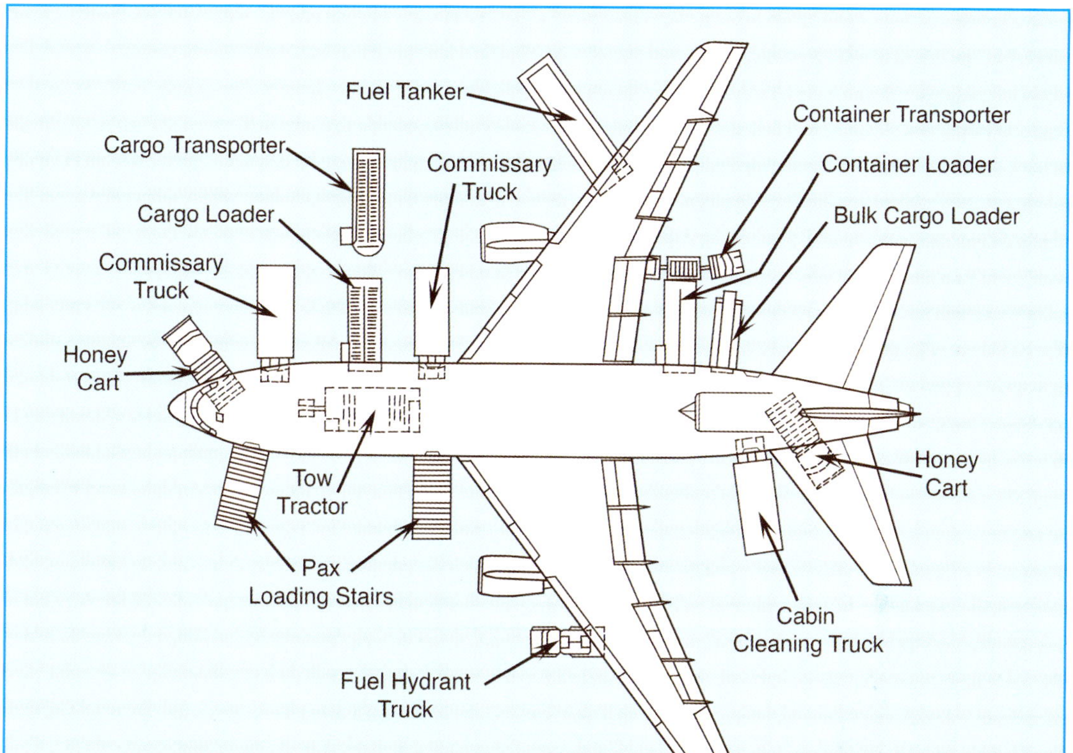

Positioning of ground vehicles during turn-around.

five options valued at £358 million, TWA - thirty three firm and options valued at £313 million, and a total value contract of £300 million from Air Holdings for thirty firm and twenty options.

The Air Holdings order was a clever off-set deal organized by Lockheed and British interests to defuse public and congressional protest in the United States over the selection of the Rolls-Royce RB211 engine in preference to the General Electric CF6 and Pratt & Whitney JT9D. The aircraft ordered by Air Holdings were for resale to carriers in the Commonwealth and, thus, TriStars eventually acquired by Air Canada, British Airways and Cathay Pacific Airways were deducted from the Air Holdings order.

To many outside the UK airline scene, Air Holdings was something of a shadowy organisation. Air Holdings Limited had been formed as a conglomerate out of a trio of other holding companies: Furness Withy & Co. Ltd, Blue Star Line Ltd, Broadminster Nominees Ltd and Guinness Mahon Nomimees; then there was British & Commonwealth Shipping Co. (Aviation) Ltd and Hunting Aviation Management Ltd. Finally there was Peninsular and Oriental Steamship Navigation Co., Eagle Star Insurance Ltd and Cable and Wireless (Holdings) Ltd. Behind these were a large number of British and Irish banking organisations.

Air Holdings had been registered as a company on 3 November 1961, with a capital of £600,000, but was also listed total assets of £20 million and a workforce of over 4000 from companies like Airwork, British United Airways, Channel Air Bridge, British Aviation Services, Manx Airlines, Morton Air Services, and Silver City Airways.

The chairman until his death in 1968 was Sir Myles Wyatt, of Airwork-BUA, Deputy Chairman was Sir Nicholas Cayzer of British & Commonwealth Shipping and BUA. Other directors were Sir Donald Anderson of P&O and BAS, P B Guinness of Mahon Nominees and BUA, Freddie Laker of Aviation Traders and BUA, Sir Brian Mountain of Eagle Star and BAS, G N A Murrant of Furness Withy and BUA, Lord Poole of Broadminster Nominees and BUA, G H Trott of Blue Star Line and BUA and R L Cumming of BUA. Overall, Air Holdings accounted for more than half of all Britain's independent airline activity.

On the strength of these massive orders, to which were soon added orders from Delta, Northeast, PSA and two aircraft leasing companies, the L-1011 was put into production, with final assembly to take place in new facilities built in Palmdale.

If press reports on the DC-10 were glowing, then the British media were ecstatic about the Lockheed/Rolls-Royce announcement. 'In the six days, 29 March to 3 April the Lockheed L-1011 trijet airliner became the subject of the biggest combined civil aircraft contract in history, with customers placing orders for no fewer than 172 aircraft. At the same time, after months of battling by engine firms, it was announced that Rolls-Royce had won the contest to power the L-1011, with their new RB211 advanced technology turbofan. The total value of the orders was £1,075 million, of which Rolls-Royce's share was about £179 a million, the largest single export order ever a gained by the British aircraft industry, or indeed by any British industry.

The flood of orders began on 29 March when Eastern Air Lines (fifty aircraft), Trans World Airlines (forty-four) and the British firm of Air, Holdings Ltd. (fifty) jointly announced their decision to pick the L-1011. The aircraft for Air Holdings (who, among other companies, control BUA) were intended for resale outside the USA. Then, on 2 April, Delta Airlines ordered twenty-four L-1011s and the next day Northeast announced their orderfor four, to be delivered in 1972. The decisions of the other major American domestic trunk airlines - United, Braniff, Continental and National - were awaited. American Airlines, it will be remembered had previously placed an order for twenty-five McDonnell Douglas DC-10s, the engines for Which have still to be selected.

Lockheed stated that, according to their studies, a total of 500 airliners of L-1011 type would be required by 1975, of which 350 would go to US airlines and 150 to foreign airlines. A potential sale of 1,000 by 1980 was conceivable. The L-1011 was expected to enter airline service in 1971, carrying 256 passengers in a twenty per cent first-class/eighty per cent coach-class configuration, or up to 345 passengers in an all-economy airbus configuration

When the orders were announced, Rolls-Royce commented: 'The choice of the RB211 advanced technology engine for the Lockheed 1011 is further recognition of the fact, already established by the choice of the RB207 for the European Airbus and the Trent for the Fairchild 228, that Rolls-Royce has pioneered a unique new concept in the three-shaft principle.' The Trent first ran in December 1967.

Factors which favoured the selection of the RB211 for the L-1011 included economy of operation, ease of maintenance, lower smoke and noise levels, and fewer components, leading to lower costs. To keep pace with the future development of the aircraft, the RB211 had significant thrust growth capability; thrust would initially be in the region of 37,020-40,600 pounds but would be developed to 50,000 pounds eventually. The three-shaft principle gave the RB211 great advantages in permitting, for a given pressure ratio, a shorter, lighter and simpler engine with fewer compressor and turbine stages. It also had an advantage in permitting noise reduction on the approach by the use of a device which slowed the fan.

The first Rolls-Royce project designs for the next generation of subsonic airline engines went back to 1961 and full detailed design of such engines began in 1966. The detailed design of the RB211 began in July 1967 and the programme, including manufacture, is fully underway.

Making it all official - J. Floyd Andrews (seated, left), president of PSA, and Lockheed Board Chairman Dan Haughton (seated, right) sign contract for airline's purchase of TriStars, validating original agreement announced in September 1970. Present were Calac President Chuck Wagner (standing, left) and Dale Wright of the Lockheed commercial sales organization. *(Lockheed)*

'I wish they all could be California Girls!'

Left: PSA Stewardesses pose in front of a Lockheed Electra. Just ten years later they were posing for a TriStar publicity picture.

Original caption: 'HE CALLS THIS WORK? - These 34 girls last week officially were designated PSA stewardesses during graduation ceremonies in the L-1011 TriStar mockup in Bldg. 360. Chuck de Bedts, vice-president for airline industry affairs, who served as Lockheed host during the ceremonies, couldn't resist a chance to show his friends just how difficult his job really is. The 34 graduates join 400 other PSA stewardesses.' *(both Lockheed)*

The media reported that on hearing of the first Lockheed 1011/ Rolls-Royce RB211 orders, James S McDonnell, Chairman of McDonnell Douglas Corporation, said that his company would continue its vigorous efforts to obtain additional orders for the McDonnell Douglas DC-10.

'We are disappointed by the decision made by our friends at Eastern Air Lines and Trans World Airlines, but we are determined to press forward with our own effort for we think that the great big majority of a large world market for our DC-10 type airplane remains' James McDonnell was reported to have said.

Seattle-based Boeing Aircraft also got in on the act. On 22 March William M Allen, Boeing's President, announced that his company had entered the airbus battle with a trijet scaled-down version of the Boeing 747 designated the Boeing 747-300, would be powered by three Pratt & Whitney JT9Ds, the same engines as in the 747, and will seat 275-300 passengers-about 100 fewer than in the 747.

'Span of the 747-300 will be 159 feet 11 inches compared with the 747's 195 feet 8 inches and length 174 feet instead of 231 feet. The Boeing airbus will have a new-design landing gear suitable for asphalt runways and is designed for ranges of up to 1,800

Another view of the interior of the L-1011 interior mock-up, looking in the other direction to the previous. *(Lockheed)*

nautical miles. Boeing state that they are not at present seeking firm orders for the 747-300, but expect to do so between now and early 1969. Deliveries are expected to start early in 1972'.

Pacific Southwest Airlines - PSA - came into being in 1950 as a small flying school, which decided to charter a DC-3, call itself an airline and operate a once-a-week service between Oakland and San Diego. It grew rapidly.

In February 1971 when looking ahead, PSA's Paul C. Barkley, vice-president for finance told The *Lockheed Star* that he estimated an additional fourteen per cent increase in passenger revenue for 1971, even in the face of the national economic uncertainties and high California unemployment.

'1972 will mark another major event in PSA's history as the line accepts delivery of its first two L-1011 TriStars. PSA estimates that each TriStar will be capable of carrying more than 500,000 passengers a year over the line's California routes, which last month saw the addition of service to Long Beach. The airline is currently awaiting PUC permission to add Stockton and Fresno to its routes, thereby completing the link of all major California cities and business centres.'

'The introduction of the L-1011 is going to have a greater impact on our airline than the Electra did,' said Andrews, referring to PSA's purchase of six of the 98-passenger aircraft in 1959.

'At that time, the introduction of the Electras was the signal for a steep rise in the number of passengers carried. The quiet, vibrationless turboprop engines, the above-the-weather flight path, and the higher speed brought new standards of air travel to the PSA system, and the Electras sold their own seats.They remained in service for nine years, until PSA went into the jet age with a fleet of six Boeing 727s'.

According to William R. Shimp, executive, the decision to purchase L-1011's was made only after careful analysis and a hard-boiled look at PSA's future needs and the projected growth of air traffic in California.

Shimp thought that the L-1011 could be phased into the present PSA fleet very easily and with a minimum of training and cost. Commenting on other aspects of the TriStar, he said, 'We'll be able to turn the L-1011 around as fast as our present equipment, and we can operate the aircraft from any of our short-runway satellite airports.

'An additional factor of importance to PSA was our belief that the aircraft can be stretched for future growth with very few modifications. All systems are adequate to handle an increase in cabin size, pressurization, and air conditioning. This could potentially provide for as many as 480 passengers per aircraft.'

Chapter Three

Choice of Powerplant

Lockheed conducted a comprehensive study of the engines available, but the results were not made known until airlines had conducted their own evaluations and had concurred with the choice of the Rolls-Royce RB211.

This selection was based on superior engine characteristics in many areas, including performance, weight, growth potential, installation features, and price. The broad commercial experience of Rolls-Royce was an important factor - with over eighty-five million commercial gas-turbine engine hours at the beginning of 1969 and with gas-turbine engines in service with more than 160 airlines in 75 countries.

Compared with older-generation engines in service, the RB211 high bypass-ratio turbofan engine offered substantial improvements in specific fuel consumption, noise , smoke-levels, maintainability, and reliability.

Chronology of Development

Historically, the derivation of the RB211 can be traced back to two independent lines of development which had their origins in the 1920's. Air Commodore Sir Frank Whittle's work is perhaps more generally known than that of Dr Alan A Griffith, but both had a tremendous influence on the evolution of the aero gas turbine as we know it today.

Following the writing of a thesis in 1928, which discussed jet propulsion, Whittle spent some years of frustration in obtaining support for his gas-turbine proposals. However, forming a new company in 1935, called Power Jets Ltd, with both private and government interests, enabled him to progress with his designs and basic research to develop a jet propulsion engine. This work was crowned by early success, for the WU gas turbine was first run only two years later, in April 1937.

Built by British Thomson Houston for Power Jets, the WU engine was designed to have a pressure-ratio of 4:1 and had a single-stage, double-sided, centrifugal compressor driven by a single-stage turbine.

Above: Group Captain, later Air Commodore Sir Frank Whittle, OM, KBE, CB, FRS, FRAeS (*b.* 1 June 1907, *d.* 9 August 1996).

Left: the first Whittle engine, 'WU' gas turbine, which first ran in April 1937.

The Power Jets W.1X. In 1939, the British Air Ministry placed a contract for the W.1 engine to be flight tested on the new Gloster E.28/39 aircraft. During taxiing tests, the W.1X non-airworthy engine unofficially became the first British turbojet to be airborne when the E.28/39 made short, straight hops. The W.1 flew officially in the E.28/39 on 15 May 1941. The W.1X and drawings of the W.2B production engine were delivered to General Electric on1 October 1941. GE's improved and uprated version, the IA, powered the first US jet aircraft, the Bell XP-59A Airacomet on 2 October 1942.

A distinguishing feature of the WU was the single combustion chamber which ran in a large loop between the compressor and the turbine. On subsequent test engines, this was replaced by an arrangement, subsequently termed as 'tubular', in which many individual combustion chambers were equally disposed around the engine.

This layout - employing a centrifugal compressor, tubular combustion chambers, and single-stage turbine - set the trend for most of the successful gas-turbine designs in the immediate post-war years. The layout was retained in the W.1 'flight' engine, which powered the Gloster E.28/39 experimental aircraft on its epoch-making flights in May 1941. This historic W.1 gas turbine unit had a thrust of 850 pounds at 16,500 rpm and an installed weight of 623 pounds.

Among several engines subsequently developed under the general classification of W.2, was the W.2B engine, which Power Jets Ltd originally designed, and was subsequently built and developed by the Rover and Rolls-Royce companies. This engine was the design from which the Gloster F.9/40 aircraft - the prototype of the Meteor series of fighters - and the Bell P-59 aircraft derived their powerplants, the F.9/40 powerplant having the designation W.2B.23, and the Bell P-59 powerplant, the General Electric Type I-A. After further development by Rolls-Royce, this type became known as the Welland - the first of the Rolls-Royce' river- class' engines.

Another development of the W.2 series of engines was the Rover W2B.26, which used a 'straight-through' combustion system instead of the return-flow system of the classic Whittle design. This engine first ran in March 1942 and served as the prototype of the Derwent 1 engine, which Rolls-Royce subsequently developed for the Gloster Meteor III aircraft.

Based on Whittle's work, another line of development was begun by Frank B Halford in association with the engine division of the de Havilland Aircraft Company. Later this association led to the formation of the de Havilland Engine Company - now a division of Rolls-Royce. However, in January 1941, the design of a turbojet, the H.1, with a single-sided centrifugal compressor and a 'straight through' combustion system, was begun. Subsequently named the de Havilland Goblin, the development of this 3000 pounds thrust engine went

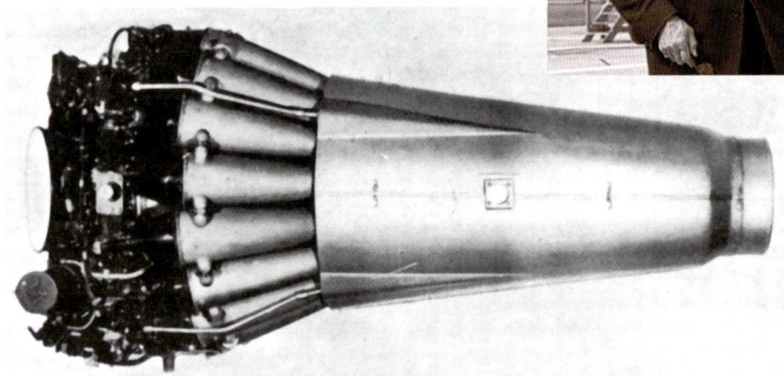

Above left: Major Bernard Halford CBE FRAeS (*b.* 7 March 1894 , *d.* 16 April 1955).

Above: Dr Arnold Griffith CBE FRS (*b.* 13 June 1893, *d.* 13 October 1963) .

Left: the Halford H.1/de Havilland Goblin of 1942.

The Rolls -Royce Nene.

It was designed and built as a result of a 1944 Air Ministry request for an engine of 4,200 pounds thrust, schemed-out by Stanley Hooker and Adrian Lombard as the B.40. Then Hooker visited the US and found that General Electric already had two engines, an axial and a centrifugal, of 4,000 pounds thrust running. On returning to the UK Hooker decided to go for 5,000 pounds thrust and, working with Lombard, Pearson and Morley, a complete redesign of the B.40 resulted in the B.41, later to be called the Nene.

hand-in-hand with the development of the de Havilland Vampire fighter. The H.1 first ran in April 1942, and this engine powered the Gloster F .9/40 prototype on its first flight in March 1943. The Vampire first flew in September 1943, and the Goblin also powered the first prototype Lockheed XP-80 Shooting Star in January 1944. Production versions of the P-80 were powered by the General Electric/ Allison J33 engine.

In April 1943, Rolls-Royce formally took over all the Rover work on gas turbines. Design work was initiated on an entirely new engine but employing the same basic layout as the Derwent 1. The result was the RB41 Nene. It first ran in October 1944 and was rated at 4500-pound static thrust, which soon increased to 5000 pounds. A scaled-down version of this engine actually went into production before the Nene and became the 3500 pounds thrust Derwent 5. This unit was produced for the Meteor IV aircraft, a special version of which set an official world's speed record of 606 mph in November 1945.

Thus, the first five years of this line of development of gas-turbine 'flight' engines produced a steady performance increase - from a thrust-to-weight ratio of 1.36:1 for Whittle's 850-pound thrust W.1 engine to the 3.09:1 figure for the 5000-pound thrust Nene.

In parallel with the turbojet development, Rolls-Royce began, in 1943, the development of turboprop engines. The Trent (the first of two engines to bear this name) was the world's first turboprop to fly. It was basically a modified Derwent 2 engine; the impeller diameter was reduced, and an 8:1 reduction gear, a propeller shaft, and a small five-bladed propeller were added forward of the compressor. This engine delivered 750 shp plus 1300-pound thrust, and it first flew in a Meteor in October 1945.

Another Rolls-Royce turboprop project begun in 1943 not only broke away from the now established centrifugal-compressor design but was the first gas turbine to use a two-shaft configuration. The Clyde, which had both an axial low-pressure compressor and a high-pressure centrifugal compressor, owed much of its design to the second line of development mentioned earlier and to that of Whittle. In 1939, Dr Arnold A Griffith had left the Royal Aircraft Establishment (RAE) to join Rolls-Royce. He developed a contraflow, contra-rotating type of turbojet at the RAE, which he had first proposed in 1926, and several successful axial-flow compressor and turbine units to Dr Griffith's designs had been built and test-run.

A continuation of this work at Rolls-Royce involved various axial-flow engine designs which had annular combustion systems and incorporated multi-stage, axial-flow compressors and turbines. A feature of these designs was that there were no stator rows of blades; the stages rotated freely in opposite directions on a fixed shaft, and each carried an inner row of compressor blades and an outer row of turbine blades. This basic concept was employed in an experimental engine, designated the CR.l, which underwent its first test run in March 1942. This contraflow engine concept was applied as the high-pressure section to several gas-turbine design schemes, which had multi-stage ducted fans and embodied the bypass principle.

The low-pressure, nine-stage, axial compressor

and the high-pressure, centrifugal compressor of the 4000-shaft horsepower Clyde were driven by the same turbine, while another turbine drove the propeller through a reduction gear. However, only eleven Clydes were built. This engine represented a valuable contribution to gas-turbine technology. In particular, it provided valuable experience on axial-flow compressors and problems associated with a two-shaft arrangement. Testing began in 1944, and it was eventually flown in the Westland Wyvern naval fighter, an aircraft for which it was initially intended.

Lessons learned from these two turboprops, particularly the Trent, were applied to the Dart. This turboprop engine was unusual in having a two-stage centrifugal compressor driven by a two-stage turbine. Initially tested in 1946, the engine used a propeller drive similar to that in the Trent turboprop.

Dr Griffith was succeeded at the RAE by Hayne Constant, his assistant for many years. Under Constant, the RAE, in association with the Metropolitan-Vickers Company, continued developing axial-flow gas-turbine engines. This led to the Metropolitan-Vickers F .2 turbojet which was first bench-tested in December 1941 and powered a Gloster F .9/40 aircraft on 13 November I943 - the first British flight of an axial-flow turbojet. Metropolitan-Vickers' aircraft gas-turbine work was later taken over by Armstrong-Siddeley Motors, which, in turn, was merged with Bristol Aero-Engines to form Bristol-Siddeley. The latter became the Bristol Engine Division of Rolls-Royce Ltd.

When the Type 630 Viscount flew on 16 July 1948, it was the first commercial turboprop-powered aircraft in the world to fly with four Darts. More than twenty years later at the time of the design of the TriStar, versions of the Dart were developing more than twice its original power. By then, the latest of that design was in demand for the Japanese NAMC YS-11 transport and the Hawker Siddeley Andover; but, during two decades, the engine powered all of the Vickers Viscount series of airliners and other types of aircraft - including the Fokker/Fairchild-Hiller F-27 and FH-227 series, the Handley Page Herald, the Hawker Siddeley 748, the Armstrong Whitworth Argosy, and the Grumman Gulfstream I - amongst others.

Returning to turbojet development, a new centrifugal engine, the Tay of 6250-pound thrust, had been developed for Pratt & Whitney. This company was building both this engine, with the US designation J48 and the Nene 2, termed the J42 in America under licence. However, even though some experimental work was being done on a large two-stage centrifugal engine - a similar compressor configuration to that of the Dart - it was apparent that the axial-flow compressor showed more promise for the future than the centrifugal in the higher thrust ratings.

Early in 1945, Dr Griffith had been making studies of an engine combining a multi-stage axial compressor and a single-stage turbine. The blade design permitted a small hub-diameter at entry, a high tip-speed, and a large airflow

Above: Metropolitan-Vickers F .2 turbojet.

Right: The Rolls-Royce Avon

capacity. This resulted in much improved values of specific-weight and specific fuel consumption. Design changes for this engine were completed in 1945 and formed the basis for the Rolls-Royce Avon series of engines. Essentially, an axial compressor based on the latest design concepts was applied to an engine bearing all the developed and well-proven features of the Derwent and Nene turbojets.

The RA.1 Avon had a 12-stage axial compressor driven by a single-stage turbine, and eight combustion chambers in a tubular arrangement. It first ran in March 1947 but experienced certain running troubles. The RA.2, which was tested ten months later, retained these basic design features, but the compressor was redesigned to incorporate two-position inlet guide-vanes. Finally, the RA.3 with a two-stage turbine became the first production engine.

With various Marks of this basic Avon design, which were called the 100 Series, the thrust was increased to approximately 8000 pounds. Still, in order to further improve the thrust potential, the RA.14 introduced the 200 Series Avon, a complete redesign of the engine. The principal changes were a new, high pressure-ratio axial-flow compressor with fifteen stages and a new so-called cannular combustion system in which the eight flame-tubes were enclosed in a single annular chamber. The RA.l4 was type-tested in April 1953 at 9500-pounds thrust, and later versions in the 200 Series and in the subsequent 300 Series of engines had thrust-ratings, without afterburning, of well over 12,000 pounds.

The Avon in its various forms has been in large-scale production in the United Kingdom and overseas under license, and it has powered a huge number of military aircraft. The RA.29 was developed from this military family of Avons specifically for airline operation. It was in service with the world's airlines with the de Havilland, later Hawker Siddeley, Comet and the Sud-Aviation Caravelle series of aircraft. It had been in service with the Comet 4 since 4 October 1958 when BOAC inaugurated the world's first transatlantic jet airline service. The RA.29 incorporated features gave long life and low fuel consumption. The engine's mass flow was increased by adding another stage to the compressor, and a three-stage turbine was used. Specific fuel consumption was reduced to 0.785 pounds per pound per hour under maximum takeoff conditions.

In 1946 Dr Griffith proposed that the bypass principle he had introduced into his earlier contraflow engine designs should be applied to the simple axial engine. Using Avon technology and a two-shaft layout similar to that of the Clyde turboprop engine, several bypass-engine projects in the 5000 to 10,000 pounds thrust class were investigated in the next few years and led to the commencement of design of the Conway RCo.2 in January 1950.

The engine first ran in August 1952 and soon achieved its design rating of 9,500 pounds thrust. However, early in 1953, the thrust requirement was changed, and the design of a more powerful version of the Conway, the RCo.3, was commenced. This engine - almost a complete redesign - passed its official type test in August 1955 with 13,000 pounds thrust. This was the highest dry-thrust rating up to that time, and it was achieved at the lowest specific fuel consumption, thus vindicating much of the early work of Dr Griffith. The basic principle of the bypass engine was set down and embodied in several gas-turbine designs by Dr Griffith as early as 1940.

This first bypass engine was also the first production engine employing a two-shaft or two-spool arrangement. Other advanced features included titanium rotor blades, stators, and disks in the high-pressure compressor's rear stages; dovetail blade-fixings; and air-cooled high-pressure turbine blades. The Conway heralded a completely new generation of universally adopted engines. It had military applications and airline service in versions of the Boeing 707 and Douglas DC-8 and in the BAC VCl0 and Super VC10 airliners. One of the last versions of the engine, the RCo.43, was rated at 21,800 pounds thrust and had a specific fuel consumption at a maximum continuous rating of

The Rolls-Royce Conway RCO.43, a 21,800 pounds thrust turbofan.

0.605 pounds per pound per hour.

The success of the Conway led to the development of a family of high- economy, two-shaft turbofans in the 10,000-lb thrust category. The Spey was designed as a commercial engine for broad application to medium-sized, short/medium-range transports from the outset. An earlier engine of similar design, the RB141 Medway, was initially designed for this purpose, but was dropped in favour of the Spey when the engine thrust requirement for the Hawker Siddeley Trident changed.

The Medway was sufficiently advanced in development that several were completed and run while the Spey was still in design and experimental manufacture. Thus the latter engine - essentially an aerodynamic scale-down of the Medway - benefited from early bench tests of the larger engine and the consolidation of Rolls-Royce's extensive commercial turbine engine experience, which by 1960 was approaching twenty million flying hours.

The Spey, in its basic configuration, comprised a four-stage low-pressure compressor, twelve-stage high-pressure compressor, a cannular combustion system with ten flame-tubes, and two-stage high-pressure and low-pressure turbines. The pressure-ratio was 16.821, and the bypass-ratio was unity - the latter being selected based on optimising performance while reducing exhaust noise to a level below that requiring a suppressor. Specific fuel consumption was 0.545 pounds per pound per hour. Bench runs of the 9850 pounds thrust Spey 1 began in December 1960, and the Trident first flew a year later. The subsequent entry of the Trident into airline service with British European Airways soon paved the way to a new generation of turbojet-powered airliners which could compete successfully with propeller-driven transports in the short/medium-haul category. The Trident's basic engine/ airframe concept was followed more than a year later by the larger Boeing 727.

The next version of the engine, the Spey 2, was uprated to 10,410 pounds thrust powered the twin-engined BAC-111 transport, which entered service with British United Airways and Braniff International Airways in April 1965. Other versions of the Spey power later variants of the Trident and BAC-111, the Fokker F.28 Fellowship and the Grumman Gulfstream 2 as well as several military aircraft such as the LTV A-7D and 7E Corsair 2, McDonnell F-4K and 4M Phantom II, and Hawker Siddeley Buccaneer S.Mk.2 and Nimrod MR.Mk.1.

An unusual amount of effort was directed toward saving weight. Blade attachments, bolted flanges, and couplings were eliminated or improved by better design, electron-beam or laser-beam welding, and new bonding techniques. Improved design and casting techniques of the nozzle guide-vanes resulted in their having much reduced sectional wall thicknesses, which enhances the efficiency of the internal cooling system and saving weight. Titanium was used for the turbine disk instead of steel. Glass-fibre laminates are used extensively - their use in the RB162 being the first large-scale application of composite materials to an aero-engine. In the meantime, many uprated versions of the RB162 were under development, and one of these was used as an auxiliary-thrust propulsion engine in the Hawker Siddeley Trident 3B.

The RB211 was the giant High Bypass Ratio engine that the main board of Rolls-Royce finally chose to build. Back in 1958, the Americans, in the shape of Pratt & Whitney, had shown, in meeting the competition of the Conway bypass jet, that it was possible to add on the front of an existing turbojet a large fan, with a diameter much greater than the rest of the engine, driven by extra turbine stages (or an additional turbine driving a separate LP shaft). Such a fan would both supercharge the rest of the engine, called the gas-generator or core, raise the propulsive mass flow and reduce the mean jet velocity.

With the new breed of HBPR engines that came into existence in the first half of the 1960s, the first thing to do was take an existing type of core and add an extra turbine downstream, driving via a long shaft to an enormous fan at the front. This fan, in essence a multi-bladed propeller, ran at a tip Mach number of about 1.5, so most of the area of each blade was supersonic. It had a design pressure ratio of about 1.5, so it supercharged the entire airflow entering the core engine by this amount. Thus, if the core had a pressure-ratio of 16:1, a figure within previous experience, the overall engine pressure-ratio became 24:1 when supercharged by the fan, giving an efficiency higher than ever before achieved.

The third objective was a further major improvement in efficiency gained by running much hotter than ever before. A combustion temperature of about 1,250°C was sought, roughly 150° above the then-current state of the art.

These were the basic objectives of all the new HBPR fan engines pioneered by the TF39 built by General Electric for the Lockheed C-5A Galaxy for the USAF and by the Pratt & Whitney JT9D produced mainly at company expense for the Boeing 747. It was clear that such engines would have an enormous impact, especially on commercial aviation. Their size and power made possible so-called 'wide-body' airliners carrying more than twice as many passengers as their predecessors, for unprecedented long ranges, and with a huge reduction in both specific fuel consumption and noise.

In 1964, an advanced-technology exercise had evolved the RB178, a 27,000-pound thrust, two-shaft turbofan with a bypass ratio of 2.321. This design was seen as a suitable power unit for the stretched BAC Super VC10 or for possible new-generation large transport projects. In 1965, a later version of this engine, the RB178-51, had the thrust increased to 44,000 pounds and a bypass-ratio of 6:1. Intended for the Boeing 747, this was the first three-shaft gas-turbine design.

The basic layout and characteristics of this engine were followed in a series of detail design studies, which were begun in 1966 to evolve a new generation of propulsion engines for subsonic transport aircraft. Primarily, the studies centred on engines of about 10,000 pounds thrust rating for small feeder-line aircraft and larger engines in the 40,000 to 50,000 pounds thrust class for the large 'airbus' type of aircraft. Following on from the RB 178-51 design, the high bypass-ratio and pressure-ratio turbofan employing a three-shaft layout - the fan being driven by its own turbine - was established as the basic configuration for both groups of engines. The first group is exemplified by the Rolls-Royce RB203 Trent, which first ran in December 1967, and the second group by the RB207 design for the A.300 European airbus project and the RB211 engine for the Lockheed L-1011. Bench tests of the RB211 began in 1968. The initial version of the engine gave 40,600 pounds thrust and a specific fuel consumption cruise rating of 0.628 pounds per pound per hour.

By 1967 Boeing's chief rivals, Lockheed and McDonnell Douglas, had offered the airlines large trijets to meet the specifications of American Airlines and other US trunk operators. These needed engines in the 33,000-pound class, compared with 40,000 pounds needed for the C-5A and 747, but the aircraft grew in weight, and more thrust was needed.

Sir Denning Pearson, Managing Director and Chairman of Rolls-Royce, and commercial director David Huddie decided to get into the US wide-body market. The RB178 had been developed for the European Airbus A300 into a very large and powerful engine, the RB207; but this was never built because Sir Denning ordered the entire resources of Derby to be devoted to a smaller engine, the RB211, sized to the requirements of the Lockheed L-1011 TriStar. The final contractual commitment was that RB211 engines would be delivered at a fixed price from September 1971, fully certificated at 42,000 pounds thrust. In March 1968, on this basis, the L-1011 went ahead with large launch orders from Eastern Airlines and TWA, plus a British financial group called Air Holdings, whose purpose was to underwrite fifty of the US jets for sale to non-US carriers.

The three-shaft layout offered advantages over other concepts. Briefly, the fan operates efficiently,

A cutaway of the RB211-22 engine. *(Rolls-Royce)*

Two views of a scale model of a RB211 engine, showing the internal arrangement and method of mounting. *(Rolls-Royce)*

without the need for inlet guide-vanes, and without compromising the speed at which the intermediate-pressure compressor operates. Each compressor runs at its own optimum speed, and the desired pressure-ratio can be achieved with fewer stages. Another important characteristic of the three-shaft layout concerns noise. With the fan on a separate shaft, it can be slowed by reducing the turbine exhaust nozzle area so that noise-levels are well below existing limits during the approach. Also, with the elimination of the inlet guide vanes, a dramatic reduction in the discrete tone of the fan noise results.

An annular combustion system similar to that pioneered in the lift-jets and shorter in length by about thirty per cent than more conventional systems was adopted for this new family of engines. An additional advantage was the small number of compressor stages required by the three-shaft configuration. All this resulted in a relatively short overall engine length. This, in turn, helped to keep the bearings requirement to a minimum. Only eight bearings were used, and these were all located outside the combustion area.

As we have seen, the RB211 turbofan engine came about as the result of a long study carried out by Rolls-Royce in which the main objectives were:

- Substantial improvement on current levels of specific fuel consumption, with a target improvement of twenty-five per cent.
- Low specific weight
- Low noise-level
- Low smoke-level
- Simplicity of construction, leading to better reliability and maintainability at a lower cost.

The rating of engine chosen to power the initial TriStar was the RB211-22 of 40,600 pounds thrust. The RB211-22 had a single-stage fan which was driven by a three-stage low-pressure turbine; the intermediate compressor had seven stages and is driven by a single-stage turbine; and the six-stage high-pressure compressor was also driven by a single-stage turbine (the only cooled rotating blading in the engine). The unique Rolls-Royce lift-jet experience underwrote the choice of an annular combustion system and the use of advanced composite materials in the fan.

The design philosophy of the RB211 was a continuation of a gas-turbine development programme that spanned a quarter of a century, and it encompassed the widespread background and experience obtained in the civil operation of Rolls-Royce gas-turbine engines since 1953.

A programme of scaled component testing was extensively backing engine development. This included running the high-pressure turbine in conjunction with the intermediate-pressure turbine and running the latter in conjunction with the low-pressure turbine, thereby enabling interaction effects to be investigated.

A myriad of configurations was tested, running up thousands of hours of operation. These rigs were invaluable for developing the required performance standard of the engine components, and besides, they provided useful warning of possible aerodynamic vibration problems in the full-size engine.

Bench testing of the RB211 began in August 1968, and a year or so later the total time exceeded 1000 hours across ten test engines.

Bill Hannan, Chief Engineer L-1011 Project: 'Any one of the Big Three engine companies - Pratt & Whitney, General Electric or Rolls-Royce - could have given us a satisfactory engine.'

In 1967, when the engine choice was pertinent, Pratt & Whitney's JT-9 engines were design frozen for Boeing's 747 programmes. Boeing had picked the thrust size, the diameter and even the nacelle

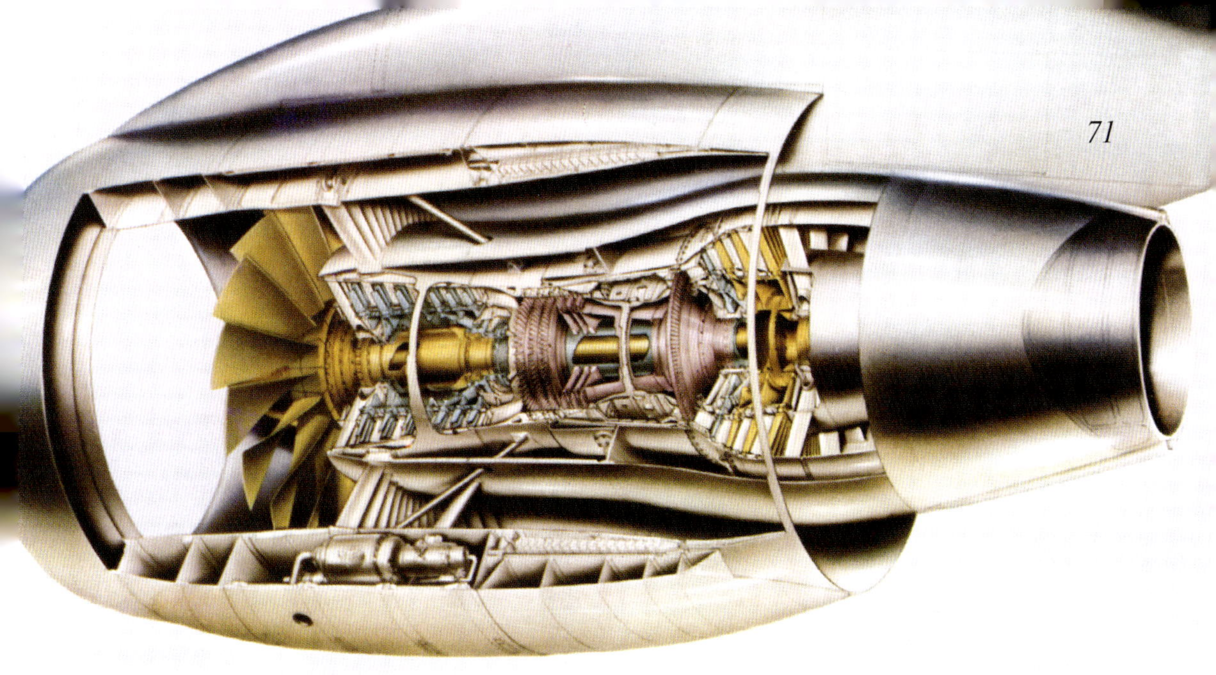

A cutaway showing the cowled installation of the RB211 engine under the wing of an L-1011. *(Rolls-Royce)*

configuration, which had a big effect on the fan cowling and accessory arrangement.

When Lockheed went to P&W in 1967, they were understandably reluctant to change their engine because of tooling already started for the 747 programme. Lockheed wanted certain desired changes. For one thing, they wanted a slightly lower thrust class because of the smaller size of the TriStar. Secondly, they wanted all the engine accessories mounted out on the fan and arranged for better accessibility. Thirdly, Lockheed wanted the engine to meet an acoustic level that was substantially lower than the 747 was shooting for because the L-1011 'Air Bus' concept was going to serve smaller airports and smaller cities.

'You could just see the noise problem coming.' Bill Hannan recalled. 'I remember having meeting after meeting in the corporate conference room with Dan Haughton. Carl Kotchian, 'Kelly' Johnson, Willis Hawkins and Carl Hadden. We had big roundhouse debates over whether we should invest any money at all in making the airplane quiet or whether we should go all out and make it super quiet, or where should we draw the target line. I kept pushing for what I called a 100dB airplane. We knew the turboprop Electra had a noise signature of about 100dB, and it was acceptable - nobody had squawked about it too much. We figured if we could get a big trijet that quiet it would be acceptable'.

'But if we put any more money into it to make it super quiet than we were pretty sure the airline buyers would squawk, loud and clear. It would mean they would have to pay more and they would be carrying around a lot of extra weight. We finally settled for the 100dB airplane for openers.'

All of these factors were included in the specifications that Lockheed sent to the three engine companies. P&W bowed out gracefully, although they left the door open. General Electric which had a similar problem because they were already set with their TF39 engine tooling, did a smart thing. They just clipped the fan down in diameter, reduced the by-pass ratio and the thrust down to just about what was wanted for the L-1011 basic design. The result was a fine engine which later went into the DC-10, the TriStar's competitor.

Rolls-Royce, in the early design stages of the L-1011, really didn't have an engine. They had a prototype they had built to satisfy themselves that introduced a new three-shafted technology, something nobody else had done. In fact, it showed the promise of a big breakthrough in jet engine design. At the time, Rolls was aiming their production of this engine which they called the RB203 Trent for use in the Fairchild/Fokker F-228 twin-jet. But beyond this. Rolls had no commitments.

Bill Hannan: 'When the F-228 programme stopped, Rolls was looking around, and they saw an opportunity to size their prototype exactly to where we wanted it, arrange the accessories the way we wanted them, and do the acoustics the way we wanted it. They did just that. and in this respect, they had an advantage.'

Out of it came the Rolls-Royce RB211, three-shaft, turbofan, high by-pass engine. This, then, was the engine which Rolls proposed to Lockheed and the airlines in 1967 as its entry in the L-1011 engine competition.

Bill Hannan again :'We chose the Rolls engine because we thought it would have three big advantages. Some big technology advantages seemed to start a whole new line of engines that might revolutionize the commercial business. Cost proposals which would let us offer the engine advantageously in the US and, certainly outside the US where it could be bought in pounds sterling.The Rolls-Royce background as the most experienced commercial jet engine manufacturer.'

There probably was another reason: it was like going to a tailor to get your suit fitted instead of buying one off the shelf. Indeed, the development of the engine paralleled the development of the airframe. What Lockheed wanted for the L-1011 was an engine capable of producing 40,000-pound thrust-power, improved fuel consumption over existing engines, a low specific weight, low noise level, improved smoke emission, simplicity of construction and maintenance. It was a big order. But Rolls accepted the challenge.

Above: The RB211 intermediate compressor.

Below: The high pressure compressor.
(both Rolls-Royce)

Basic Design Considerations

Improved mechanical design and more advanced materials played a large part in meeting the initial objectives. Apart from these aspects, the required improvements over the then-current engines in specific fuel consumption, specific weight, and noise-level resulted from increasing the overall pressure ratio, the bypass-ratio, the turbine-entry temperature, and the work-output per stage of the compressors and turbines. As in all engineering solutions, the cycle that evolved was to a large extent a compromise of these particular variables. Because the major contribution that the engine manufacturer can make towards reducing the direct operating costs of an airliner is to improve the specific fuel consumption, the compromise was weighted towards this end.

By varying the thermodynamic cycle, it was possible to improve significantly on current thermal and propulsive efficiencies. Still, it was necessary to define a limit to the increase of bypass-ratio and pressure-ratio. These limits were determined from consideration of engine size, the proportion of the overall pressure-ratio provided by each of the compressors, and the number of stages required.

The third thermodynamic cycle variable that of turbine-entry temperature, was established based on experience gained in service by current Rolls-Royce commercial engines with cooled turbine blades and improvements to cooling techniques and blade materials from Rolls-Royce high-temperature development.

The increased bypass-ratio resulted in higher propulsive efiiciency. This was because the additional air that bypasses the gas-generator section of the engine was exhausted at a lower mean jet velocity than that of the primary jet. The practical upper limit of bypass-ratio was primarily determined by three factors: the number of turbine stages required to achieve a given bypass-ratio; the loss of thrust per unit airflow resulting from increasing bypass-ratio in turn, leading to a larger and heavier engine for a given cruise thrust; and finally, the slightly higher thrust lapse-rate with forward speed associated with an increased size of fan. As a result of a trade-off involving these factors, Rolls-Royce chose a bypass-ratio of 5:1 for the RB211-22, this being selected as the best compromise between specific fuel consumption, weight, cost, installation factors, and the aircraft's mission.

In addition to the improvements resulting from increased propulsive efficiency, it was also desirable to increase the thermal efficiency by raising the overall pressure ratio due to the high bypass-ratio. A ratio of 27:1 at the design point was adopted for the RB211-22 based on two considerations. In the first place, this represented a logical extrapolation of the experience gained at high pressure-ratios by earlier Rolls-Royce engines in commercial operation (the Rolls-Royce Spey engine operated at an overall pressure-ratio of 20:1). The second aspect provided a convenient division of work between the individual compressors of the two-spool gas-generator section of the engine. This allowed the use of two separate, simple compressors, each capable of being driven by a single-stage turbine. A significant temperature drop was associated with each of these turbines, with the advantage that the total temperature of the gas relative to the rotating blades is reduced.

The above outlines the principal considerations that defined the RB211 cycle: a bypass-ratio of 5:1, a pressure-ratio of 27:1, and a turbine-entry temperature level firmly based on the unique Rolls-Royce commercial experience with cooled blades.

A further factor of importance is the work division between the bypass and turbine-efflux streams. For a given cycle with separate exhausts from the fan and turbine streams, the optimum performance is obtained when the energy is transferred from the turbine stream to the fan stream most efficiently.

The Three-Shaft Concept

Commercial jet engines then in service incorporated either a single or a two-shaft gas-generator. The use of two shafts enabled an overall high pressure-ratio to be achieved from two compressors, each operating at a modest pressure-ratio on its own shaft and capable of providing an adequate surge margin for the minimum use of variables. Typically, other designs for a high bypass-ratio engine were also of a two-shaft design with the high pressure-ratio gas-generator driving a fan, the diameter of which was significant concerning the other compressor stages.

Suppose the fan was coupled directly to the forward section of the gas-generator compressor. In that case, it necessitated a reduction in the tip-speed of that compressor to below the optimum value. This is because the forward-compressor tip-speed will now be controlled by the fan tip-speed, which in turn is limited by aerodynamic considerations. The result is design compromises for both the fan and the compressor, the latter usually having additional

The three-shaft design explained.

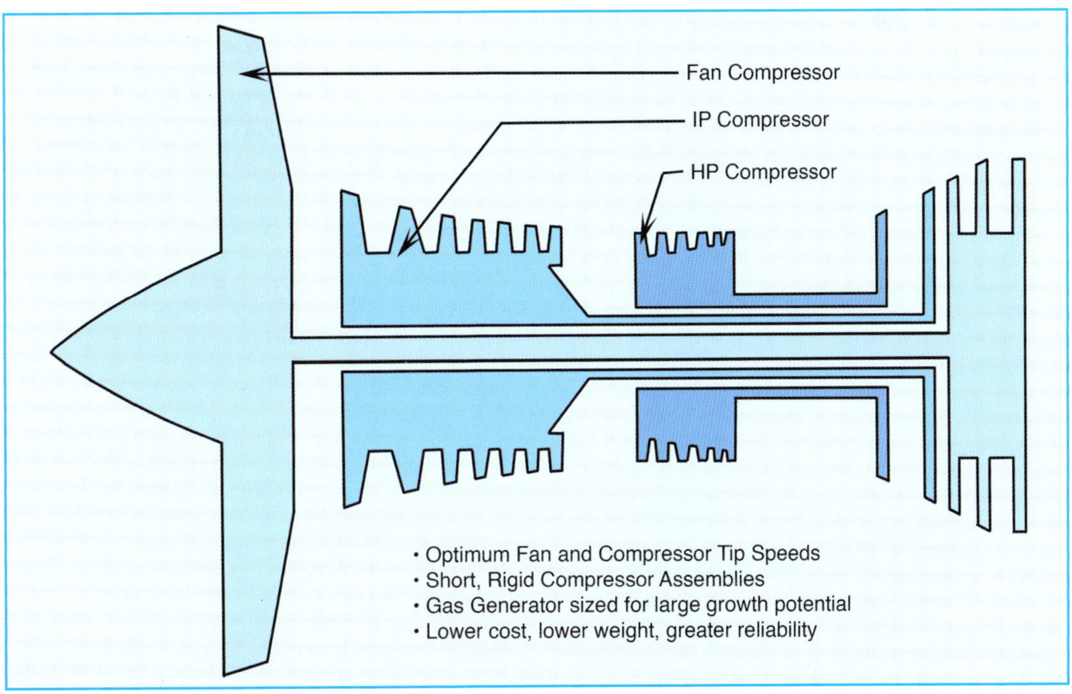

stages which otherwise would not be necessary.

Thus, the provision of the third shaft to carry the fan and its own turbine allowed the fan design to be optimised without any compromise to the gas-generator section of the engine. Or, in more practical terms, the primary advantage of the three-shaft engine, concerning an engine performing a similar cycle with a two-shaft system, is a significant reduction in the number of significant parts needed.

For a defined thrust and turbine-entry temperature, the three-shaft engine was of lower weight and cost compared to the two-shaft alternatives. To express this another way, the three-shaft configuration produced a highly competitive engine, operating at a lower turbine-entry temperature (for a given thrust) than the two-shaft alternatives. Other advantages were as follows:

- Good handling qualities. Because of the mechanical separation of the fan from the intermediate-pressure and high-pressure compressors, throttle response - particularly for accelerations - was exceptional.
- Clean mid-pressure bleed air. Clean air for cabin pressurization could be tapped off, conveniently and efficiently, away from the outside of the annulus between the two compressors. For most flight conditions - particularly cruise - this pressure is adequate, and the need for more wasteful high-pressure bleed air is avoided for these conditions.
- Greater flexibility for development. This is illustrated by the fact that the RB203 Trent - a 3:1 by-pass-ratio turbofan for short-haul operations - was evolved from the two-shaft Rolls-Royce/Turbomeca Adour engine, basically by adding a third (fan)shaft.
- Noise-reduction at the aircraft approach condition by fan slowing. This is described later in the section on noise.

To meet Lockheed's requirement for simplified maintenance, Rolls designed its engine around seven basic modules, each an independent unit. This permitted a very rapid change of engine sections and enabled a service life to be set up for each module rather than for the complete engine. Each module could be removed and replaced individually with the engine still mounted on the aircraft and with minimum disturbance to adjacent engine modules.

This was the engine that Rolls-Royce offered to Lockheed. Lockheed's initial order with Rolls-Royce in 1968 was for 550 engines and spares totalling more than $450,000,000. The engines to be built at the Rolls-Royce Engine Division, Derby England, and sub-assembly plants in England and Scotland with the engine pods and mountings to be built by Short Brothers & Harland Ltd of Belfast, Northern Ireland, under an agreement signed on 21 May 1968. The engine itself was a bold step in advanced technology, but the decision to let Rolls-Royce build it with many international political, technical and economic implications was even bolder. Indeed, for better or worse, it marked the beginning of a new era.

The first RB211 engine ran on the test stand at Derby on 3 August 1968. Subsequent development-type engines were tested on the ground in the high-altitude test facility of the British National Gas Turbine Establishment at Pyestock, England. There the engine was put through rigid tests simulating most of the L-1011 flight envelope.

Rolls-Royce shipped complete engine mock-ups to Lockheed for study and familiarisation by Lockheed and airline personnel. From this, volumes of written information and an interchange of technical personnel - Lockheed people in England, Rolls-Royce people at Burbank - there evolved a commonality of technical language and understanding between individuals which probably more than anything else contributed to the success of the whole programme.

During 1969 and the early months of 1970 TriStar began to take shape in a new factory at Palmdale. California. At Derby, the RB211 engines moved from testbed on the ground to testbed in the sky and onto the production line.

Fan Construction.

Each fan blade was attached to the titanium disk by a dovetail type of fixing. The blade material was 'Hyfil' - a reinforced composite of carbon fibers carried in a resin base. Hyfil had a tensile strength similar to that of high-grade steel or titanium and was lighter than aluminium, having a density similar to that of magnesium.

Obviously, the RB211 was a much greater challenge than Rolls-Royce had ever previously faced. The operating pressures and temperatures were outside the company's previous experience, and the size of the fan blades, casings and rings was more than double anything seen at Derby previously. There were two key features of the RB211 that could be, and were, used by Rolls-Royce to sell the engine to Lockheed instead of a US rival and used by Lockheed to justify their choice to the airlines. One was the use of three shafts, and the other was the Hyfil fan blades,

In the early 1960s, British workers at the RAE at Farnborough had pioneered the conversion of polyacrylonitrile yarn into fibres of pure carbon so strong and stiff, yet extremely light in weight, as to open up a whole new world of structural possibilities. Carbon fibre became all the rage, one of the main planks in what Prime Minister Harold Wilson called 'Britain's white-hot technological revolution'. But actual applications were hard to find until Rolls-Royce decided that carbon fibre material was ideal for the RB211 fan. The fan was huge by previous standards, over 7ft in diameter. Each pound saved in the mass of its blades could be multiplied many times in reducing the weight of the hub, bearings and main engine frame. Aerodynamic calculations showed that with a sharp-edge 'lenticular' profile, the blades could reach surprisingly high efficiencies, at pressure ratios of 1.5 to 1.7 and tip speeds over 1,500 feet per second, or Mach 1.5.

To make each blade, vast numbers of strong carbon fibres, thinner than human hairs, were bonded by resin adhesive into thin flat plies, which were stacked in a pile and bonded after being cut to shape into one solid mass. The blades were smooth, black and amazingly strong and light. They enabled the RB211 to give the TriStar a considerably greater payload than the rival engines with metal fans.

It was thought that this characteristic of Hyfil would permit the use of a simple and reliable test to be used as a means of assessing life remaining in a blade in service: the progressive failure of filaments in a Hyfil blade had a similar progressive effect on the blade frequency so that it was possible to predict the life remaining in a blade by a frequency check.

The shear modulus - or stiffness - was considerably greater to its density in relation to conventional materials. Apart from the obvious advantages of low blade weight, low disk weight, and low containment-casing weight, the favourable relationship between density and modulus resulted in

Above: an RB211 with a Hyfil fan is rigged for test.

Below: on the outside test stand at Hucknall.

Below left: A Hyfil fan in balance test.
(all Rolls-Royce)

a blade design that did not need to incorporate mid-span shrouds. For a blade in conventional materials, such as titanium, it would be necessary to incorporate such shrouds to prevent the blade from being subjected to aerodynamic flutter in the engine running range.

Flight testing of the RB211, prior to its first flight in the L-1011, was carried out in a specially modified VC10 in which the two Rolls-Royce Conway engines on the left side were replaced by a single RB211-22 engine. During its flight-test programme the VC10 simulated typical short-range flight plans extending over a test period of 1000 hours.

Endurance testing of the complete underwing propulsion system was carried out on one of the sea level test cells at Derby. This also simulated short duration flight plans and extended over 1000 hours.

The programme of testing planned for the RB211-22 engine before it entered service in the Lockheed L-1011 TriStar, in November 1971, represented probably the most extensive programme of its sort ever undertaken by an aero engine manufacturer.

Tests on the ground indicated that the Hyfil could save 300 pounds or more and was far less expensive. On test the blades worked well, and an enormous money and effort went into their development and tooling up for mass production.

After some flights in which the VC-10 flew into rain and hail, it was discovered that the Hifil blade tips had a weakness and were affected by erosion. Engineers tried remedying the situation with metal laminations on the blades. When prototype fans and complete RB211 engines were subjected to the

Left: Beside the VC10 used by Rolls-Royce to flight test the RB211 engine for the L-1011 is H Cliff Rogers, (left), chief test pilot of Rolls-Royce, and Henry B (Hank) Dees, project test pilot of the L-1011. On the left of the aircraft is a single RB211, three of which would power the Lockheed airbus. On the other side are two Rolls-Royce Conway engines, four of which normally powered the VC10.

Below: G-AXLR, the partially RB211 powered Vickers VC10 in flight. *(both via Lockheed)*

mandatory birdstrike test, in which chickens from the supermarket were fired at high speed into the engine running at take-off speed, the blades proved to have an Achilles heel. The weak resin plastic could not take the sudden impact on the thin leading edge.

As a fallback programme, an all-titanium fan had been designed, and with great reluctance, this had to replace the new-technology Hyfil construction. At a stroke, this wiped out the engine's weight advantage over its rivals.

Chemical Milling

Rolls-Royce Limited opened a new chemical machining plant at Hucknall to manufacture components for its RB211. The major advantage of chemical machining - Rolls-Royce called it 'chemi-etch' is that it allowed the company to economically form areas of selected jet engine parts that were impossible or impractical to form by conventional machining, forging or casting methods.

Chemical machining is a method of shaping metals by dipping them into an acid or alkaline bath for periods of time that depend on the amount of metal to be removed or reduced and the etch rate of the solution used. In its simplest form, the process uses a chemical solution to reduce the size of metal parts. Selective size reduction can be accomplished by masking off areas of the metal part before dipping it in the solution.

This process made it possible to produce engine components with integral stiffeners, and in these as well as other engine parts, the major benefit is that the method avoids the transferral of machining stresses to the jet engine component. At the time aluminium-based and nickel-based alloys, as well as steel and titanium metals, were worked in the plant. Other significant advantages were that parts having thin cross-sections could be produced without distortion and that some specialised components could be machined on both sides at once.

The new Hucknall machining plant was a suite of sixteen treatment tanks, each measuring eight by eight feet. The facility produced various RB211 components, including the combustion chamber's outer case, the bypass fan casing along with the outlet guide vane assembly, and the rear support flange. In addition, sections of the RB211's engine pod were machined in the new facility.

Noise

Concerns began to arise over aircraft noise. The three major sources of noise in a turbofan engine are the fan, the turbine, and the exhaust jet. In the case of an unmixed-flow turbofan engine, the exhaust provided two sources, one from the bypass stream and the other from the gas-generator stream.

In engines with low bypass-ratios, the predominant noise source is the jet. For a given thrust, increased bypass-ratios tend to reduce the jet velocities, the low-pressure turbine-blade velocities, and mass-flows. At the same time, fan mass-flows and also - with advances in technology - fan tip-speeds, tend to increase. The result is that with by-pass-ratios of the order of 5:1, the noise from a fan with two or more stages would increase the noise level relative to the low bypass-ratio engines.

It is well-known that the noise emanating from turbo-machinery is divided into two types: first, the discrete tones and their harmonics produced by the passage of blade-wakes over the succeeding blade row; and second, the random background noise generated by the reaction of the blade to the passage of air over its surface. Advances in compressor aerodynamic design have enabled the fan duty in an engine of 5:1 bypass-ratio to be achieved in a single stage. In such a fan, the interaction velocities, and therefore noise intensities, are greatest between the inlet guide-vane row - if fitted - and the rotor blades. Deletion of the inlet guide-vane row, therefore, removed this major interaction and substantially assisted the maintainability features.

There remained the interaction effect between the fan rotor and its outlet guide-vanes. If the latter is moved axially downstream, relative to their normal location, the rotor-blade wakes decays' intensity, with a consequent reduction in the noise level of discrete tones. Additionally, if the optimum ratio of the stator to rotor blade numbers was incorporated, further reductions in the basic propagation intensity of the fundamental blade passing tone and its harmonics was possible.

In an engine in which the fan is driven on a shaft separate from that of the gas-generator, the latter's performance is only marginally affected by the changes in the speed of the hub section of the fan. Consequently, the three-shaft configuration allows the required engine thrust to be produced with various combinations of fan and gas-generator speeds. By reducing the hot gas-stream nozzle area, the thrust from the nozzle is increased, balancing the reduction in fan thrust obtained at the lower fan-speed which results from the reduced pressure-ratio across the low-pressure turbine. This lower fan-speed reduces fan noise-level.

However, as the nozzle area is reduced, exhaust velocity - and therefore jet noise - is increased. The nozzle area selected, therefore, is that which provides the lowest overall noise-level. For a given thrust, the reduction in nozzle area requires a higher flame-temperature; consequently, noise reduction by fan-slowing is limited to approach conditions. Another constraint at higher thrusts is the change in bearing end-loads resulting from the modification to engine internal pressures. A further advantage of the variable nozzle is that, in its closed position, it can be designed to form a slot with its major axis vertical, hence further reducing hot-stream noise, as heard from the ground, by preferential radiation.

The above observations were related to the possible means of reducing the basic noise-level of RB211 engine. Further noise reduction is achieved by the use of sound-absorbent linings in the air gap between the lining and backing skin of the exhaust ducts, and by the form of construction being selected to tune-out the most undesirable frequency range.

Because the rear-arc fan noise predominates on a high bypass-ratio turbofan, it was jointly decided by Lockheed and Rolls-Royce that a three-quarter length cowl configuration should be allowed for the fan outlet duct, thus allowing an adequate area of acoustic lining to be incorporated in the duct.

Stopping the beast...

David Lee, who worked for Rolls-Royce for a time before becoming involved with Imperial War Museum Duxford, recalls his involvement with the TriStar and the RB211. 'Having signed the Official Secrets Act, I became a small team member linked to the Stress Office as part of the Design Office at Hucknall. Joe Shaw was the boss, John Ball, who was in a wheelchair, was his deputy, David Lawson and another David (I became D3) and Pete Lygo, who I used to pick up from his home in Linby. I was very much the junior partner, but eventually, my work consisted of assessing the weight and balance of engine projects and production designs. Also, I was responsible for the weight and balance of the entire Rolls-Royce flight test, light, historic and executive aircraft. That was the fun part of my job. At times, the flight test fleet consisted of a Gloster Meteor NF 11 G-ASLW, two YF-4K Phantoms, a Blackburn Buccaneer S2, a Hawker Hunter, three English Electric Lightnings including P1B XA856, a Westland Wessex, a BAC 1-11 briefly hired from Autair and finally G-AXLR/XR809 RB211 VC-10 FTB. The executive fleet was a DH 125, a Heron and a Beagle 206. The historic item was, of course, G-ALGT/RM689, the Spitfire Mk XIV. Finally, as a member of the Merlin Flying Club, I looked after their 2 Auster J4-100s, plus a Jodel G-AWIG. The two Austers were used for training to Private Pilot's licence, which the company subsidised at only 36/- per hour, which is £1.80 in today's money.

But to return to my work. The Weights Department was part of the Stress and Design office then located in a converted hangar in the centre of the Rolls-Royce site. After a couple of years, we moved to a brand new two-storey design block, and our department was on the first floor. Much of my work consisted of calculating the weight of a component from the designer's drawings. I did it by estimating the item's volume and applying the Specific Gravity of the material to get its weight. Slow, rather laborious work, all done with a slide rule and a mechanical calculating machine called a comptometer. Computers were beginning to be used but were mainframe machines filling a whole air-conditioned room as Personal Computers didn't exist. Later, when the component was made, I physically weighed it to see how accurate my calculations had been. As I became more experienced, I was able to assess an outline project drawing and have a calculated guess of the weight of the project.

Much of Hucknall's work then involved the casing or cowling which enclosed the jet engine, which usually had a thrust reverser. Engines were changing their appearance as the turbofan engine began with the Rolls-Royce Conway evolved so that the front fan became very large. The amount of air that bypassed the combustion was expressed as the bypass ratio; in the Conway it was 0.3:1 or thirty per cent of the air passing through the engine was not used for combustion. In the RB211, the ratio was 5:1 so the large fan on the front was passing five times as much air as was being burnt and expelled in the hot exhaust. These engines were much quieter and more efficient than the original turbojet engines.

Some of the work I undertook on the RB211 project was the VC-10 Flight Test Bed. It was not an ideal aircraft for the job since the VC-10 has four engines attached to the side of the rear fuselage and the RB211 was to be underslung under the wings of the Tristar and mounted in the tail. The plan was to replace the port pair of Conway engines with a single RB211. To learn more about the weight and balance of the engines in the VC-10, I visited Vickers at Weybridge. On a very grey 26 March 1969, I boarded G-ASWJ, the companies Beagle 206 at Hucknall, only the fifth time I had flown. We climbed up through the murk and suddenly burst out into glorious sunshine. It was the first time I had flown above the clouds and I was entranced by the spectacle. We first flew to RAF Shawbury to drop off another passenger and then onto Wisley, the Vickers test airfield where I was collected and taken to Weybridge – to the giant Vickers factory in the old Brooklands race track and airfield. After briefing, collecting a lot of documentation and a brief lunch, the 206 flew on to Filton to collect another passenger and we then returned to Hucknall.

Thus it was that XR809 an RAF 10 squadron VC-10 C1 arrived at Hucknall on 17 April 1969 for conversion as an RB211 Flight Test Bed. The work involved removing the pair of port Conway engines and replacing them with a very substantial curved beam which enabled the RB211 to be suspended from its top mounting point. A means of escape was provided in the rear cabin with an emergency exit through the freight hold. All this had significant effect on the aircraft's centre of gravity and although I now cannot remember how much lead weight was required but a large amount was secured on a pallet. Fortunately, the VC-10 was a convertible freight aircraft and there were suitable means of safely securing this heavy item. The military registration was removed and G-AXLR became the identity of what was to be the last Hucknall flight testbed.

Rolls-Royce was in fierce competition with two American companies, Pratt and Whitney, who built the first of the new large fan engines, the JT-9D which powered the revolutionary Boeing 747 and General Electric who were directly competing with Rolls-Royce to provide engines for the slightly smaller three-engined airliners being built by Douglas (the DC-10) and Lockheed (the L-1011 Tristar). Eventually, GE got the Douglas order, and in April 1968 Rolls-Royce won the Lockheed order. There began a close liaison between Rolls-Royce and Lockheed in Palmdale. Many staff from Hucknall went to work at the Lockheed factory for varying periods over the next two years. My Weight Department colleagues all had some time at Palmdale in order of seniority and I was the next to go as, during that period, most of my time was committed to RB211 work. Hucknall designed and manufactured the engine cowlings, the thrust reverser and the hot stream spoiler. The weight and balance of the latter was my particular responsibility.

As you probably know, Rolls-Royce from the 1930s sold their engines as complete packages wherever possible, so I know that Hucknall designed the Thrust Reverser and the Hot Stream Spoiler as my colleagues and I estimated their weights and Centre of Gravity and weighed the finished pieces to

Original captions: Above: First of two Rolls-Royce RB211 engines is unloaded in front of Plant 10 in Palmdale. Both engines arrived from Belfast, Northern Ireland, where pod cowlings and related systems were installed by Short Bros. & Harland.

Left: Employees inside Bldg. 601 at Plant 10 carefully lower Rolls-Royce high bypass ratio turbofan engine. The engines arrived last week at the TriStar final assembly site. *(both Lockheed)*

Both engines shown are in fact 'lying horizontal' and need turning through ninety degrees for installation on the aircraft.

confirm our calculations. I'm not sure about the main cowling as I do remember it was built by Shorts in Northern Ireland but I suspect the original design work was done at Hucknall.

Unlike the Thrust Reverser, which directed the bypass air forward, the Spoiler merely deflected the hot exhaust gases sideways. The HSS is right as the back of the engine and consisted of a pair of doors that made up the cowing around the jet pipe but which translated rearward to deflect the hot engine exhaust sideways when the thrust reverser was deployed. Again, I calculated the weights of the various components, later weighed them and calculated the balance of the whole assembly in the overall cowling. I recall that the whole item weighed about six hundred pounds.

The first engine, the 14th built, was fitted on 6 February 1970. The two spikes protruding at the top and bottom are the stangs on which the spoiler doors translated rearwards.

I was told that the thrust reverser was efficient enough to slow the aircraft. When the HSS was removed, a shorter jet pipe appears to have been fitted which must have saved a lot of weight and money.

Exhaust Smoke

Even in the late 1960s, air pollution was becoming something of an issue. Smoke-producing properties of an engine vary directly with engine size, and have tended to increase as engine pressure-ratios have increased. However, smoky exhausts are solely the result of deficiencies in combustion-chamber design.

The principal region where soot may be formed is inside the fuel spray at the upstream end of the combustion chamber. This concentration of rich fuel/air mixture can be eliminated by injecting into the primary combustion zone, in the form of highly turbulent jets, virtually all of the air required for

The Thrust Reverser - on the left - and the Hot Stream Spoiler - on the rear of the RB211 is deployed on number 2 engine of N1011, the first TriStar. *(Lockheed)*

The 'back end' of an early RB211 showing the 'stangs' holding the operating mechanism of the Hot Stream Spoiler. From this view, it shows they the mecanism was quite bulky. *(Lockheed)*

complete combustion of the fuel. British practice in general, and that of Rolls-Royce in particular, was to use this type of combustion system. In contrast, US practice used less air in the primary zone and introduced the remaining air downstream, thereby operating fuel-rich in the primary zone and so creating smoke.

The advantage of a fuel-rich mixture was to facilitate relighting at altitude. Disadvantages were low volumetric heat - release, the sensitivity of liner-wall temperature to variation in fuel type, carbon deposition on liner walls, erosion of turbine blades, and very smoky exhaust.

Increased engine pressure-ratios reduce the fuel spray's penetration, which tended to remain in the vicinity of the spray nozzle and produce a fuel-rich mixture. Another effect of increased gas pressure was to widen the fuel's burning limits and so permit combustion to take place at the rich-mixture strengths that cause soot to form.

Accordingly, Rolls-Royce developed a new type of fuel injector which provided improved fuel atomization, and a combustion chamber which permited improved wall cooling and combustion efficiency. RB2l1 engine tests demonstrated that there was very little smoke, even at high thrust levels.

Condition Monitoring

To be successful, the provisions made for condition monitoring had to give the earliest possible indication of engine deterioration and check the progress of this deterioration to permit programmed repair. To limit the amount of engine disturbance required during repair, the deterioration area needed to be identified. The above requirements were accentuated by the change in emphasis from scheduled overhaul to on-condition maintenance, and by the modular construction incorporated in the engine. In this type of construction, the engine was built up from a number of major assemblies called modules, each of which is capable of removal with a minimum of disturbance to the other modules. Replacement, either in the repair shop or installed, could thus be confined to one module.

There remained a necessity of detecting the onset of a major failure in time to prevent it leading to a hazardous situation. The monitoring provisions in the engine were used extensively during the engine development programme to provide necessary experience prior to airline service, and to develop the monitoring devices.

An example of the ground indicators fitted to the RB211 engine was those in the oil system. Two master chip-detectors are fitted (one for the gearbox and one for mainline bearings) which sample the total scavenge oil flow.

Provision is also made for fitment of a detector in each individual scavenge line. This arrangement allows the master detectors to be used to indicate the onset of trouble, the individual detectors then being introduced to locate the faulty bearing compartment, or it may be preferred to fit the individual detectors from the start to give the earliest possible warning. The latter procedure is more direct. In the external gearbox configuration, the oil filler, dip-stick, filter, and chip-detectors are grouped together to facilitate access. The oil tank, which is integral with the gearbox, has a remote oil level indicator.

Twenty borescope ports were provided to permit the inspection of all stages of compressor and turbine rotor blades, combustion liners, and the high-pressure nozzle guide-vanes. Rigid borescopes could be used for all these locations.

Nine of the ports were in the combustion chamber, and, as well as providing sight of the combustion liner assembly, enabled the leading edge and concave surface of each high-pressure guide vane to be viewed.

The centre of the low-pressure shaft system was free of obstructions so that an isotope source for radiographical inspection might be introduced with minimal disassembly.

Maintainability

Although the engine could be built in either the horizontal or vertical attitude, it was expected that module replacement was usually carried out horizontally, essential for the maintenance of installed engines, whereas it might be more convenient to build each turbine or compressor module vertically to facilitate seal assembly.

The horizontal assembly of the modules provided the capability of simultaneous strip from either end of the engine, leaving the main engine carcass, with its pipes and accessories, substantially intact.

In practice, the fan, intermediate-pressure compressor, thrust bearings, and internal gearbox were withdrawn from the engine's front. The turbines, combustion liner assembly and high-pressure compressor, were withdrawn from the rear. The remaining structure comprised the fan casing and the entire gas-generator carcass, including the intermediate casing, extending from the intermediate-pressure compressor outer casing front flange to the rear flange of the combustion-section outer casing. Individual fan blades could be replaced from the front of the engine after removal of the rotating nose cone.

The low and intermediate-pressure turbines, together with the turbine-bearing structures form a single module. Access to the low-pressure shaft centre-coupling was provided, from either end of the engine, through the shaft centre. The intermediate shaft coupling was disengaged by a tool inserted radially through one of the intermediate casing struts. Consequently, each coupling could be operated without disturbance of the other shaft system.

The modular build of the RB211 was being used during the development program to facilitate the change of engine units to provide experience for the operation of in-service module changes. Provision was built into the RB211 engine, and into the L-1011 aircraft, to permit operations of this type to be carried out with the engines installed.

Thrust Growth

Rolls-Royce has always been accustomed to the provision of thrust growth once a new commercial engine enters service. A typical example is the Spey turbo-fan engine, which, five years after first entry into service, had increased its takeoff thrust on a hot day by approximately forty per cent.

Thrust growth on the RB211 falls into two categories. Growth of the basic RB-211-22 was obtained by the turbine-entry temperature increase to provide the RB211-40, -41, and -43 ratings. To achieve the higher operating temperature, some modifications to the combustion-liner assembly and to the intermediate-pressure turbine-blade material were required, but the engine was basically unchanged.

Further uprating to a thrust of 55,000 pounds at takeoff was achieved in the dash 56/57 series of engines. The RB211-56 was designed to meet the thrust requirements of the long-range L-1011 TriStar and other aircraft developments, with a substantially improved specific fuel consumption and significant additional thrust-growth potential. This was achieved by using a larger gas generator producing virtually the same pressure-ratio in the same number of compressor stages. The bypass-ratio is maintained at the RB211-22 level by increasing fan airflow, which involves a small increase in fan diameter. The thrust and specific fuel consumption are further improved by the addition of a fourth stage to the low-pressure turbine.

Problems with the big fan

Between 1964 and 1967, Hawker Siddeley Aviation's examination of British European Airways' requirements produced the 160-seat HS.132 and the 185-seat HS.134 both offered the prospect of a twenty-five to thirty per cent reduction in seat mile costs over aircraft then in service. Both designs would have utilised two of the new technology Rolls-Royce RB178 aero-engines of 30,000 pounds static thrust to provide superior operating performance over the first generation three engine contemporaries such as the Trident and Boeing 727.

The roots of the advanced RB178 go back to 1961 when Rolls-Royce officially initiated work on a high by-pass ratio aero-engine as a replacement for the Conway. The company went ahead with the project and under the leadership of Adrian Lombard built the twin-spool demonstrator. Overall development costs of the RB178 was £2.6 million. As a comparison, the GE and P&W companies were awarded nearly $20 million by the US Department of Defense to develop and build the TF39 and STF200 technology demonstrators.

The RB178 was built on the reliable and economic advantages inherent in the Conway and, given that engine's heritage, the new engine's performance looked certain. The RB178 (designated the 16 series) appears to have been the engine proposed for the Vickers Superb DB.265 - later to be called the VC10, with four engines powering the high capacity transatlantic airliner.

There are numerous reasons why the RB178 failed to take off and chief among them was the refusal of Boeing to accept the Rolls-Royce engine on the transatlantic 747. The RB178 was cancelled in May 1966 and in June Rolls-Royce indicated it did not want to go head to head with P&W in a battle to power the Boeing 747. However, in September 1966

Left: a RB211 is placed on its test stand at Hucknall.

Below: an RB211 is about to be placed into a test chamber at the Altitude Test Facility at the National Gas Turbine Establishment at Pyestock in Hampshire UK.

Below: On the outside test stand at Hucknall, without the S-Duct trunking. *(all via Lockheed)*

Rolls-Royce revealed to the world its decision to launch an Advanced Technology Engine (ATE) family covering thrusts ranging from 10,000 pounds with the RB203 through to 60,000 pounds with the RB207. The ATE family introduced new scalable technologies such as the triple-shaft architecture, a high-pressure annular combustor and a structurally integrated power-plant.

Engines were undergoing a period of rapid advance due to the introduction of the high bypass concept, which provided for greater thrust, improved fuel economy and considerably lower noise levels than the earlier low-bypass designs. Rolls-Royce was working on a series of triple-spool designs as replacements for the Conway, that promised higher efficiencies. In this configuration, three groups of turbines spin three separate concentric shafts to power three sections of the compressor area running at different speeds. In addition to allowing each stage of the compressor to run at its optimal speed, the triple-spool design is also more compact and rigid, although more complex to build and maintain. Several designs were being worked on at the time, including a 10,000-pound thrust design known as the RB203 intended to replace the Spey. Work started on the Conway replacement engine in July 1961 and a twin-spool demonstrator engine to prove the HP compressor, combustor, and turbine system designs, had been run by 1966. Rolls-Royce chose the triple-spool system in 1965 as the simplest, lowest cost solution to the problem of obtaining lower fuel consumption and reduced noise levels at a constant power setting. Work on the RB211 as essentially a scaled-down RB207 began in 1966-7 with the first certificated engines being scheduled to be available by December 1970 at 33,260 pounds take-off thrust and at a price of $511,000 each.

In February 1968, American Airlines indicated it had chosen the Rolls-Royce RB211 to power its order for up to fifty McDonnell-Douglas DC-10s. On 7 March 1968, the Washington correspondent of *The Times* wrote of an attempt being made by Congress to block Rolls-Royce's bid to supply engines for the projected United States airbus. Representative Robert Taft had marshalled opposition because of a report

'They are so quiet that the US FAA officially certified the TriStar as the quietest big jet in production. A bonus for the airport resident, on-board passengers and the pilot. Some airports have already eliminated the night curfew for the TriStar. For airline maintenance - good news. The RB211 engines are modular. Built in seven basic modules - each removable and individually replaceable with the engine mounted on the TriStar. They're from Rolls-Royce. Quiet engines. On the L-1011 TriStar.'

that Rolls-Royce had won approval for the engine. On the 9 March 1968, *The Times* reported that President Johnson had received written protests from six senators and five representatives, from Ohio and New Mexico - states that would benefit if a US manufacturer was selected. Their complaint was that 'not adequately balanced information was given during talks between representatives of airlines and the British Government concerning the American Government's position on buying foreign engines'. The US Congress was concerned that the import of foreign engines would result in a United States payments deficit of $3,800 million and the loss of 18,000 to 20,000 jobs.

On 23 June 1967, Rolls-Royce offered the RB211-06 for the L-1011. The new engine was to be rated at 33,260 pounds thrust and combined features of several engines then under development: the large high-power, high-bypass design from the RB207 and the triple-spool design of the RB203. Despite knowing that the timetable was challenging for an engine incorporating these new features, Rolls-Royce committed to getting the RB211 into service in 1971.

Lockheed thought the new engine enabled the L-1011 to offer a distinct advantage over the otherwise similar DC-10 product. However, Douglas had requested proposals from Rolls-Royce for an engine to power its DC-10, and in October 1967 the response was a 35,400 pounds thrust version of the RB211 designated RB211-10. There followed a period of intense negotiation between airframe manufacturers Lockheed and Douglas, engine suppliers Rolls-Royce, General Electric and Pratt & Whitney, and the major US airlines. During this time prices were negotiated downwards and the required thrust ratings were raised. By early 1968, Rolls-Royce was offering a 40,600 pounds thrust engine designated RB211-18. Finally, on 29 March 1968 Lockheed announced that it had received orders for 94 TriStars, and placed an order with Rolls-Royce for 150 sets of engines designated RB211-22.

In 1970 the RB211 for the TriStar was expected to sell for initially over £250,000. There was no way that the RB211 engine could be financed out of existing sales, especially as the company was also developing other engines. However, in order to stay in the civil aero-engine business, it was imperative to bring out new products to match those of the competitors. The problems caused with the weight-saving carbon-fibre fan blades required more time than originally anticipated, resulting in the substitution of heavier titanium blades at an increased cost due to the additional engineering. The British Government had originally agreed to finance seventy per cent of the RB211 development costs, but these were based on a fixed price estimate and did not take account of cost increases in development or escalating costs due to inflation. Any additional RB211 developments for other applications remained shelved due to lack of finance.

Lockheed announced a half-year profit of $8.3 million in August 1970, which was better than expected. However, the C-5A problem remained unresolved with a possibility that production would cease after just thirty-one aircraft were completed, leaving a further fifty in various stages of construction out of the total order for 115 aircraft. This would result in a $1,000 million loss to the US Government, where a $200 million aid payment would provide cash flow until TriStar deliveries commenced at the end of 1971.

Chapter Four

Finance - and Problems

Project Problems

The first year in the most challenging period in the company's history saw Lockheed win the hotly contested C-5 competition in October 1965 when its Marietta division was awarded the contract for the first type of aircraft powered by the new generation of high-bypass-ratio turbofans in the 40,000 pounds thrust class. This award, however, was one of the first under the total package procurement system.

Total Package Procurement, referred to as TPP or alternatively, TPPC was a major system acquisition policy introduced in the US Department of Defense in the mid-1960s by Secretary of Defense Robert Strange McNamara. It was conceived by the Assistant Secretary of Defense for Installations and Logistics, Robert H Charles.

TPP was a method of procuring at the outset of the acquisition phase under a single contract containing price, performance and schedule commitments, the maximum practical amount of design, development, production and support needed to introduce and sustain a system or component in the inventory. The idea was to procure under the influence of competition as much of the total design, development, production and support requirements for a system or component as might be practicable thereby:

- Providing a firmer five-year force structure programme package planning information concerning performance cost and schedules.
- Discouraging contractors from buying in on the design and development effort with the intention of recovering on the subsequent production programme.
- Permitting programme decision and source selection based on binding performance price and schedule commitments by contractors for the total program or major part of it.
- Providing a firmer basis for projecting total acquisition and operational costs for use in source selection and in the determination of appropriate contractual incentives.
- Motivating contractors to design initially for economical production and support of operational hardware which may not receive sufficient emphasis in the absence of productions commitments.
- Requiring contractors to assume more responsibility for program success, thereby permitting the Government to monitor programs more in terms of surveillance and less in terms of detailed management.

Left: Robert Horne Charles (*b*. 14 September 1913, *d*.25 October 2000). He was appointed by President Kennedy as Assistant Secretary of the Air Force and served in that capacity for five years.

Right: Robert Strange McNamara (*b*. 9 June 1916, *d*. 6 July 2009) McNamara and a group of Air Force veterans to work for Ford Motor Company. These 'Whiz Kids'helped reform Ford with modern planning, organization, and management control systems. After briefly serving as Ford's president, McNamara accepted appointment as Secretary of Defense.

Total Package Procurement was not successful and was abandoned shortly after McNamara left office in 1968.

The unworkable application of this novel type of contracting to a high technology programme, combined with a sharp increase in inflationary pressures in the United States and with increased difficulties in obtaining and retaining skilled workers at a time when sharply rising production of military aircraft and jet airliners - due respectively to the intensifying of the Vietnam hostilities and a boom in the air transport industry - forced the manufacturers into a sharp competition for staff, and resulted in substantial cost overruns on the company's programmes, notably that of the C-5A Galaxy. This transporter was being produced under a fixed price contract and was if reports at the time were to be believed, the overruns were as high as $2,000 million. The reduction did not help the reduction in the C-5A production programme from 115 to 81 aircraft, which was announced in November 1969 and gave rise to a legal dispute over the applicability of a repricing formula contained in the C-5A contract. There were also structural problems in the wing of the huge machine.

This cutback in C-5 production had come six months after Lockheed was informed that the US Army, who were alleging default, was terminating the AH-56A Cheyenne Phase III production programme. The development of this advanced compound helicopter had run into difficulties as the AH-56A could not initially meet some of its performance requirements, while its cost rose sharply over the ceiling of 115 per cent of the bid price, forcing the company to absorb substantial losses.

Lockheed Propulsion Company also ran into trouble with developing the solid-fuel engine, which it developed under subcontract from Boeing for the Short Range Attack Missile. Claiming increased costs attributable to unexpected and exceptionally difficult technical challenges encountered in developing the test propulsion motors for the SRAM, Lockheed was forced in December 1969 to submit a $50 million claim to the Boeing Company and asked the Department of Defense for a $25 million provisional payment under this claim pending its resolution. Lockheed and Boeing negotiated an agreement, and Lockheed received $20 million in full settlement of its claim in October 1970. The SRAM engine was then successfully developed but, after this programme, LPC was inactivated.

In the military aircraft business, not all had been bad for Lockheed during 1969, as in August of that year, it had won the VSX competition. The resulting

Pilots Ralph Cokely and Don Moor inspect the L-1011 model on joining the test flight team. *(Lockheed)*

S-3A Viking was first flown on 21 January 1972, but, although it met all of its contractual requirements, the Viking only had a short production life of 187 S-3As, including prototypes. In contrast, the aircraft it replaced, the Grumman S-2 Tracker with its Canadian-built version, and TF-1/C-1 Trader and WF-2/B-1 Tracer derivatives, had a combined production run of nearly 1500 aircraft.

Having opted out of the competition for the first generation of US jetliners, Lockheed did not intend to let its long tradition as a manufacturer of commercial transports lapse permanently. In 1956 the company had studied many configurations for supersonic transports and was thus in an excellent position to answer the requests for proposals. Two versions were proposed, the L-2000-7A intercontinental model, with an overall length of 273 feet 2 inches and accommodation for up to 266 passengers, and the L-2000-7B domestic model, which was larger at 293 feet and could carry up to 308 passengers but had a reduced fuel load.

The two variants were up against the Boeing 2707 and the latter was announced as the winner on 31 December 1966. The selection of the Boeing design, thought by most airlines to be inferior to the L-2000, could be explained by geopolitical considerations. Three equally large contracts were to be awarded in 1965-66 by the US Government. For the Manned Orbiting Laboratory (MOL) Lockheed and Douglas in California competed with Boeing in Washington; for the C-5A the same three companies, but with Lockheed being represented in that instance by its Georgia division, were at odds, while the SST pitted Boeing in Washington against Lockheed in California. The award of the MOL contract to Douglas took care of that company and of the State of California; thus, after the C-5A had gone to

Lockheed and the State of Georgia, only Boeing and the State of Washington remained to be taken care of.

After losing the SST competition, Lockheed somewhat half-heartedly proposed its L-500 - a commercial, civilianised version of the C-5A - but banked its re-entry in the commercial transport market on a 250-passenger, wide-bodied jetliner to meet an American Airlines requirement for a lower capacity, shorter-range, companion to the Boeing 747. This evolved into the TriStar.

The L-1011 programme was to become notorious for the financial problems that caused the near-collapse of Lockheed and the bankruptcy of Rolls-Royce. Both the airframe and engine were launched at a time of high inflation and a reduction in demand for airline seats, making both significant parts of the programme too expensive to finance out of existing sales. The highly competitive market helped the buyers by causing the manufacturers to underprice their products to uneconomic levels to gain what they hoped was a long-term foothold in the market. The gamble eventually paid off for Rolls-Royce but was not a complete success for Lockheed.

The first complete hangar-test engine pod for Calac's TriStar is assembled to a metal mock-up of a RB211 at the Belfast factory of Short Brothers and Harland Ltd. *(Lockheed)*.

Lockheed's profit of £18.5 million in 1968 was followed by a loss of £13.58 million in 1969, the TriStar being a significant factor in this negative figure due to the increasing costs of development. This would not be a problem if the other programmes were profitable, but they were not.

Due to a whole series of disputes between Lockheed and its main customer - and remember, at this time eighty-nine per cent of the company's sales in 1969 were to the US Government - over the C-5A, AH-56A, SRAM engine, and shipbuilding programmes, and of the increased cash requirements to finance the development, testing, and production of the L-1011, it became apparent in early 1970 that the company would require additional borrowings from its bankers. The company had ended 1969 with a loss of $326 million and was anticipating further deficit in 1970 in spite of its record backlog of 5.1 billion US dollars. At that time, it had $230.7 mn in retained earnings and a capital of $90.4 million, but it owed $336.3 million in long-term debt in the form of a Credit Agreement between Lockheed and its lenders, dated 1 May 1969, provided a ceiling of $400 million.

The US Government had several choices, including revising the contracts in Lockheed's favour in the interest of national defence or less attractive alternatives, such as reorganisation of the company, a merger or bankruptcy proceedings. Lockheed maintained that only the four disputed programmes needed finance, all other projects being unaffected, with some $5,000 million worth of advance orders and adequate credit from the banks. The urgent need was for an improvement in the short-term cash flow.

Lockheed's differences with the government on four programmes approached a billion dollars. On 2 March 1970, Board Chairman Dan Haughton wrote to David Packard, Deputy Secretary of Defense, asking for financial assistance to the tune of over $600 million. '...not a hand-out or a bailout, as reported by the press. Simply an arrangement to keep us going on the disputed programs until the corporation gets what we believe is due us.'

'We wrote off $150 million before taxes in 1969 on four programs, and these write-offs were a major factor in our recording a loss in the fourth quarter of $56.3 million or $4.99 a share.'

'For the entire year we reported early in March a net loss of $32.6 million after taxes or $2.90 a share. This was on sales of $2.07 billion for the year. The $150 million in 1969 write-offs brings total losses to $290 million before taxes on the four programs.'

'If these were small amounts we'd be all right - we could wait. But they're not. They're big-

Erection of the 67,000 square feet paintshop hangar at Palmdale nears completion. The skeleton, seen here contained 500 tons of steel. It was built by Butler Manufacturing for completion in the summer of 1970. *(Lockheed)*

especially the C-5A. Over the months and years ahead, we simply won't have the money to pay the bills.'

In his 2 March letter to Packard, Haughton asked for financial assistance - not a hand-out but just fair play.

'It has become abundantly clear to us.' he wrote. 'that the unprecedented dollar magnitude of the differences to be resolved between Lockheed and the military services makes it financially impossible for Lockheed to complete performance of these programs if we must await the outcome of litigation before receiving further financing from the Department of Defense. We consider it imperative that some alternate method of resolution of these differences be immediately and seriously pursued in order to avert impairment of the continued performance of programs essential to the national defense.'

Haughton noted that 'there is a critical need for interim financing.' He also suggested that the way be left open to negotiating settlements' which are within the ability of the corporation to absorb' rather than to pursue the course of litigation.

In a subsequent letter to stockholders, Haughton said: 'Pending a reply in a reasonable period of time there will be no adverse effect on these four programs. Of course. all other military and commercial programs will be unaffected.'

'When the Department of Defense released our letter to the press, it caused a considerable furore. The amount we requested to permit us to continue work on these four programs exceeds $600 million over a period of time.'

The Defense Department apparently recognizes the seriousness of our problem, and Secretary of Defense Packard has explained it to both the House and Senate Armed Services committees. In his testimony to the House committee Packard emphasized the importance of Lockheed to national defense, stressed the fact that all four programs under dispute are important programs. and urged that a satisfactory solution to be found to current problems.'

Packard went on to mention that the press raised other possibilities, including bankruptcy, merger, and reorganization. In response to these questions, he stated that the corporation was not considering merger and bankruptcy was not an issue.

He concluded his House testimony by saying, 'It is an urgent matter that we find a satisfactory solution to these problems. Special teams have been constituted in each of the departments as well as in

Above: The upper half of flight station comes together during early stages of construction. The temporary framework provides structural strenth until the glass is installed.

Below: an almost complete flight station before mating to the main fuselage. *(both Lockheed)*

my office to focus priority attention on the issues involved. We are in continuous consultation with the company officials and with their bankers.'

The first public signs of escalating costs with the RB211 were revealed by Rolls-Royce in May 1970 when the Labour Government-sponsored Industrial Reorganisation Corporation (IRC), loaned the company £20 million to help finance the engine development for the TriStar, the only customer for the RB211-22. Inflation had increased overall development costs more than anticipated, but costs had also been increased by the technical difficulties with the use of carbon-fibre materials. In order to join the competitive big fan engine business against such well established US companies as General Electric and Pratt & Whitney, Rolls-Royce had reduced the price of its engine to level that was both unacceptable and uneconomic. The IRC loan was to provide the cash flow until a positive income could be made on production deliveries, £10 million being available immediately.

A tentative agreement to raise Lockheed's credit limit to $500 million was reached in January 1971 but, before it could be executed, Lockheed was dealt another near fatal blow: Rolls-Royce, the manufacturer of the engine for the aircraft on which the company relied to end its over-dependence on military and space programmes, announced it would not fulfil its contract to develop and produce the RB211 and placed itself in the hands of a receiver. The L-1011 plan, which had entered its flight-trial phase on 16 November 1970, ground to a halt. The new Credit Agreement was held back, and the Lockheed Aircraft Corporation was on the verge of bankruptcy.

The only workable solution to this threat to Lockheed's viability was to revive Rolls-Royce. Weeks of deliberation between Lockheed, Rolls-

A huge jig for a pair of fuselage panels nears completion at Lockheed's Burbank Plant. Much of the TriStar tooling was fabricated in the B-1 Plant there TriStar skin panels were some of the largest in the aviation industry at the time. *(Lockheed)*

Above: The mid-cabin entrance as shown in the mockup.

Much planned use was made of overhead space - coats could be stowed, the equipment being located in the cross-aisles away from general areas frequented by passengers. *(both Lockheed)*

Royce, the British Government, and L-1011 customer airlines, eventually created a possible solution: engine prices were to be revised upward, and large airlines increased their advance payments for L-1011s by $100 million. Nevertheless, Her Majesty's Government desired assurances from the United States Government that it would likewise stand behind Lockheed, for it was evident that the aircraft manufacturer's weakened financial condition would suffer further from the months of interrupted TriStar production.

In February 1971 Lockheed Board Chairman Dan Haughton and other high-level executives of the company went to London to meet with the British government officials and the receiver for Rolls-Royce over the crisis involving Rolls' RB211 engine programme.

'My purpose in being here is a constructive one,' Haughton told British reporters before the meetings. 'I hope that the parties can find a solution that will allow the RB211 program to continue without further delay, so that we can have it to use on our L-1011 TriStar.'

The meetings were the latest in a series of moves on many fronts following Rolls' 4 February announcement that it could not carry out its contract for the RB211 for the TriStar and was voluntarily seeking receivership. Other developments included:

- Announcement by Haughton that he had promised airline customers to 'propose a course of action to them.'
- Announcement of the layoff of 6,500 Calac employees, predicated on a six-month delay in TriStar deliveries.
- Announcement by the British government that it would provide four weeks interim financing to keep the RB211 programme going pending possible renegotiation of the contract with Lockheed.

Haughton's announcement that he would propose a course of action to the airlines on 26 February followed a meeting with airline executives on 9 February when possible alternative courses of action were discussed: whether to continue with the RB211, or whether to seek engines from Pratt & Whitney or General Electric.

But Haughton said that if a satisfactory resolution of the negotiations on the RB211 could be reached, it would be better 'for our two companies and our two countries.'

'I came over here to renegotiate the contract in certain respects,' he told thirty or so newsmen gathered at Heathrow Airport, 'but I did not say I

Even with all the financial problems, construction of the first L-1011 continued unabated.

would pay any more for the engine. I don't want to imply that I came here with my pockets full of money,' *United Press International* reported.

He emphasized that any decision to continue with the RB211 for the TriStar 'must include assurances to our airline customers that we will have a viable program for both the airframe and other systems and for the engine installation.'

'They expect me to provide them assurances on delivery schedules and airline operational support just as we promised them when Rolls-Royce and Lockheed teamed together to sell and launch the L-1011 TriStar with the RB211 engine. The airlines cannot go forward with the program without such unqualified assurances,' he added.

The 6500 layoffs announced by the California Company were predicted on a six-month delay in TriStar deliveries. If there was an appreciable change in schedule slippage, there might be further workforce adjustments.

In a letter to those employees laid off, President Chuck Wagner described the layoffs as 'the most disheartening experience of my thirty-five years at Lockheed,' and assured those affected that the company's management 'is completely dedicated to solving the problems involved in order to turn this situation around in the shortest possible time and get you back to work.'

The British government's decision to provide interim financing for the RB211 until 5 March followed newspaper reports, later confirmed by the White House, of transatlantic conversations between President Nixon and Prime Minister Edward Heath UK concerning the crisis.

It also followed appeals by union leaders, both in the US and the UK, urging their respective governments to do everything possible to prevent the collapse of the RB211 and L-1011 programs and the

Above: the front fuselage section of the first L-1011 were mated with the mid-fuselage section in early March 1970 to make a 115 foot long assembly. When the aft section was mated, it made a fuselage 142 feet long.

Below: the mid-fuselage section of the first L-1011 comes together at Plant 10. *(both Lockheed)*

The first L-1011 is positioned inside Building 10 in preparation for the building dedication ceremony on 20 July 1970 by Governor Ronald Regan. It may be a trick of the camera and light, but the lower cheat-line on the aircraft in this picture looks orange, not red as seen in other pictures *(Lockheed)*

widespread unemployment that would follow.

Both James Quillin, president of Lodge 727 of the International Association of Machinists and Aerospace Workers, Lockheed's biggest union, and Gerald Sklarsky, president of the Lockheed chapter of the Engineers and Scientists Guild, were in the forefront of those appealing to President Nixon for action.

After two sessions on 3 March, Haughton told reporters waiting outside Ministry of Defence in Whitehall, where the meetings were held: 'I feel now as I felt last night. I feel progress had been made, and all of us want to start over tomorrow morning.'

Participating in the London meetings have been Lord Carrington, Minister of Defence; Frederick Corfield, minister of aviation supply, and Lord Cole, Rolls-Royce board chairman, as well as various government and Rolls-Royce technical and financial specialists.

The focus then switched to New York, where Board Chairman Dan Haughton was scheduled to visit New York on 4 March for a morning meeting of 5 March to report on negotiation status with TriStar customers.

In the meantime, Lockheed continued discussions with General Electric and Pratt & Whitney on schedules and terms under which one of their engines might be available for the TriStar. Haughton was also expected to report on these discussions in his airline meeting in New York.

Representing Lockheed with Haughton was Frank L Frain, senior vice-president for finance; Willis M Hawkins, 'senior vice-president for science and engineering, and Roy A Anderson, vice-president and controller.

The British government, which earlier had agreed to fund continued RB211 engine work through March 5 pending completion of negotiations, announced an extension of interim funding.

The tempo increased on both the East Coast and Burbank in the middle of March 1971 as Lockheed, airline, and engine-company representatives converged for additional discussions on L-1011 TriStar engine schedules and costs.

Lockheed Board Chairman Dan Haughton and President Carl Kotchian met on 16 March with several senior airline ofiicials in Washington, DC. No final decisions were reached, as both Lockheed and the airlines continued to analyze alternate engine installations in the TriStar.

Haughton and Kotchian agreed to meet on 19 March with the British government and Rolls-Royce officials. The meeting, held in Burbank, for the purpose of hearing any revisions to the British proposal of 4 March to continue development and production of the Rolls-Royce RB211 engine.

The new developments followed a four-day meeting in Burbank the previous week at which US engine manufacturers presented technical, cost, and schedule proposals to Lockheed and airline technical and financial representatives, and a weekend exchange of messages by Lockheed Chairman Dan Haughton and Lord Carrington, British Minister of Defence.

No deadline was set for a decision on the L-1011 engine selection, which was thrown open when Lord Cole declared Rolls-Royce insolvent and placed the company in the hands of a receiver following the announcment that British government would not finance further RB211 engine development for the L-1011 under terms of the original contract. Unfortunately this came to a head in February 1971 just before Rolls-Royce got an improved RB211 engine on test.

To describe the whole world as being stunned is an understatement. Rolls-Royce was regarded as being no more likely to collapse than the Monarchy or the Church of England. It was, however, a matter of simple arithmetic. After years of massive outgoings, the RB211 was reaching the peak of its cash-flow deficit. If engines, in 1970/71 could have been delivered to Lockheed there would at last have been an inflow of cash, probably enough to stave off disaster.

But the engines could not be delivered because they were deficient in performance and had not yet

The resolution of a small myth!

Images have appeared on other histories stating that this was the day of the rollout, overseen by then Governor Ronald Regan. In fact the event was the dedication of Building 10 at Palmdale on 20 July 1970 and reported in *The Lockheed Star* Volume 37, No. 16 dated 30 July. The picture on the left shows Gov Regan congratulating Calac President Chuck Wagner. Around 4000 people attended the celebrations.

The actual official rollout of the first L-1011 occurred just over a month later. *(both Lockheed)*

Left: Peter Alexander Rupert Carrington, 6th Baron Carrington of Upton, KG, GCMG, CH, MC, PC, DL (*b.* 6 June 1919, *d.* 9 July 2018),

Right: Sir Stanley George Hooker, CBE, FRS, DPhil, BSc, FRAeS, MIMechE, FAAAS, (*b.* 30 September 1907, *d.* 24 May 1984)

passed the tests of the UK or US certification authorities. So the works just went on piling up expensive stocks and work in progress until the cash dried up.

For once, the British government acted with lightning speed. Overnight it purchased, for an unspecified price, all the company's assets, so as to forestall foreign creditors from claiming assets on the basis of first come, first served. The government also dismissed the company's board, with the exception of Lord Cole, Ian Morrow and Hugh Conway, who were left minding the shop.

The purchase was made purely because of the company's importance to defence in Britain and many other countries. The affair thus came under Lord Carrington, who was Secretary of State for Defence in the Heath government. In purchasing the assets the government made one specific exception: it refused to buy the RB211.

He appointed 'three wise men' to give him an appraisal of the technical and financial viability of the RB211. They were Sir William Cook, the former Scientific Adviser to the Ministry of Defence; Sir St John Elstub, chairman of Imperial Metal Industries; and Professor Douglas Holder, who held the chair of Engineering Science at Oxford. Dr Stanley Hooker, formerly of Bristol, was asked to join them at the Ministry of Defence to help prepare the report.

The Cook Report was favourable, and the British government then made Lockheed an offer they could hardly refuse. Either renegotiate the contract, this time under British law, with one year added to the delivery dates and with an increase in engine price, or the programme would be abandoned. Lockheed and their customers were rather relieved, though Lockheed's own financial position was serious and eventually led to an unprecedented decision of support by the US Congress which was carried by just one vote. But more of that later.

Thus, after a long series of negotiations with no historical precedent, Rolls got the RB211 on the road again, and Lockheed went on with the L-1011. The British government formed a new company called Rolls-Royce (1971) Ltd and paid for the day-to-day costs of the RB211 programme. It also restructured the board, inviting Sir Arnold Weinstock and Gordon Richardson to join. Sir William Cook and Sir St John Elstub were also invited, and so Dr Stanley Hooker as Technical Director so that somebody on the board might know about the engineering position.

After a 5 March meeting with airline executives in New York, Haughton told reporters that he hoped to have the question resolved within 30 days. Among developments were:

- Senior executives of US L-1011 customer airlines met in Washington Tuesday with US Treasury Secretary Connally.
- A Rolls-Royce team including Hugh Conway, managing director of the Aero Engines division; Dr Stanley G Hooker, jet engine technical specialist; RB211 program manager Rex Nicholson; and president William Seawell of Rolls-Royce Aero Engines, Inc., a US subsidiary, met with airlines in New York.

The airlines' representatives spent four days in Burbank hearing detailed comparisons of performance, operational economics, product-support plans, and cost and delivery schedules of the General Electric CF-6- 6D-1, Pratt & Whitney JT9D-7, and Rolls-Royce RB211 engines.

Lord Carrington in the meantime notified Haughton that the British government's proposal of 4 March was open to further negotiation. Haughton in his reply stated that the 4 March proposal was not acceptable to any of those concerned and invited the British government to submit any revisions it would like to have considered.

Lord Carrington had reported in Parliament that the 4 March proposal included an engine price increase; British government funding of an additional 60 million pounds for RB211 development, with Lockheed to fund anything above that amount; a plan for a joint Lockheed-British company to carry out the

RB211 programme; and a requirement for Lockheed to arrange that the British government would be repaid its investment if Lockheed should fail to carry through with the L-1011 programme.

Then, on 30 March it was announced that Lockheed and the British Government had reached a conditional agreement on the continuation of the Rolls-Royce RB211 engine programme for Calac's L-1011 TriStar jetliner.

A statement issued by Lockheed and British-government representatives in Washington said: 'Negotiations have reached a stage where it is necessary for Lockheed to hold discussions with its TriStar customers and its banks. Purpose of these meetings is to explore the acceptability of positions which have been conditionally agreed to by Lockheed and the British government.'

The announcement followed two weeks of intensive activity that included negotiation meetings in Burbank and Washington, DC, and transatlantic flights by British negotiators to report to government officials in Washington.

A team of Rolls-Royce and government negotiators headed by Sir William Nield, permanent secretary to the British cabinet, met with Lockheed representatives in Burbank and Palmdale on March 19 and 20. The scene then shifted to the British embassy in Washington, where Lord Carrington, Minister of Defence and principal British government negotiator, joined the talks last week.

President Chuck Wagner and five other Lockheed-California Company executives joined Board Chairman Dan Haughton and Corporate President Carl Kotchian in calling on customer airlines. The Lockheed team called on Air Canada officials in Montreal the same day as the announcement, then travelled to New York for talks with TWA executives on the 31st before moving to Miami and talks with Eastern Airlines executives on 1 April.

Calac members of the team included Jim Clyne, vice-president for commercial marketing; Lloyd Frisbee, vice-president and director of commercial engineering; John Martin, division counsel; Stuart Smith, director of commercial contracts and marketing administration; and Russ Ray Jr., regional sales director for the US and Canada.

Haughton was hoping that the TriStar engine negotiations could be resolved within the next three or four weeks. A combined Corlac-Calac team presentations to L-1011 customer airlines, reporting on the positions tentatively agreed to between Lockheed and British government negotiators in Washington. A corporate team headed by Haughton and President Carl Kotchian then met Lockheed's twenty-four lending banks in New York to review the progress made to date on the TriStar-Rolls-Royce engine programme and also with Treasury Department officials.

'We were encouraged by the tenor of the

No, this is not a fake photograph - it is a special colour slide showing the L-1011 jetliner projected during evenings on the east wall of Building 63 at Plant A-1. The novel photographic concept was conceived by Betty Williams of Dept. 82-22. *(Lockheed)*

TriStar Training Technicalities

When members of the flight or maintenance crews of the various airlines that ordered L-1011 TriStars flicked on their closed-circuit TV tubes to learn just how the TriStar's operating systems operated, they were pleased to discover that all the instructional programs made by Calac's closed-circuit TV people were in full colour.

What's more, the programmes not only complied with the stringent standards set by the Federal Communications Commission, but they compared favourably in quality with those produced by major TV networks.

A mobile colour TV van served as a fully equipped control room. This van enabled Calac technicians, cameramen and producers to put together complete productions on tape in the field.

The van carried three cameras, professional tape recorders and sound-mixing equipment, and motion-picture and colour-slide integration equipment.

The van and a Palmdale-based studio were operated by the closed circuit television group under Bob Ganon as supervisor. This group was part of the motion picture and CCTV department. 82-22, managed by Everett Kelley, and a part of the Financial Operations Branch.

The CCTV group numbered six employees. For additional support, Ganon called on the services of the motion picture group in the same department, which includes five highly skilled cinematographers.

Ganon's group co-produced the maintenance training tapes in close cooperation with the commercial maintenance training department, 63-19, managed by Frank Simmons, and a part of the Product Support Branch. The flight crew training programmes were co-produced with the close cooperation of the flight crew training department, 98-37, managed by Hank Shumway and a part of the Lockheed Flying Operations Branch.

Inside the dimly lighted closed-circuit mobile van, Bob Ganon, left, CCTV supervisor, and Lou Boonshaft, technical director, begin editing videotape that will be used by Calac's flight crew training department. The CCTV group's other colour tapes were utilized by the company's commercial maintenance and flight crew training departments. *(Lockheed)*

Inside the flight station - John Higgins, right, flight engineer, goes over script with Bob Gannon before CCTV cameramen start recording the production titled 'Introduction to the L-1011 Fuel System.' *(Lockheed)*

As was true of any commercial TV production, each programme's success depended on qualified actors and writers, camera operators, technicians, and producers. While he was not a professional actor, John Higgins, an L-1011 flight engineer in Shumway's department, was typical of the actors who would appear in the L-1011 training productions.

Eminently qualified as an authority on systems for modern jetliners such as the TriStar, Higgins was a retired USAF chief warrant officer who served in the Air Force's Presidential Wing for eighteen years.

He was chief flight engineer for President Eisenhower's Super Constellation, *Columbine,* and later served as wing chief flight engineer for Eisenhower until the former President retired.

When Higgins joined Lockheed, he was assigned to help develop the comprehensive training program for customer airlines.

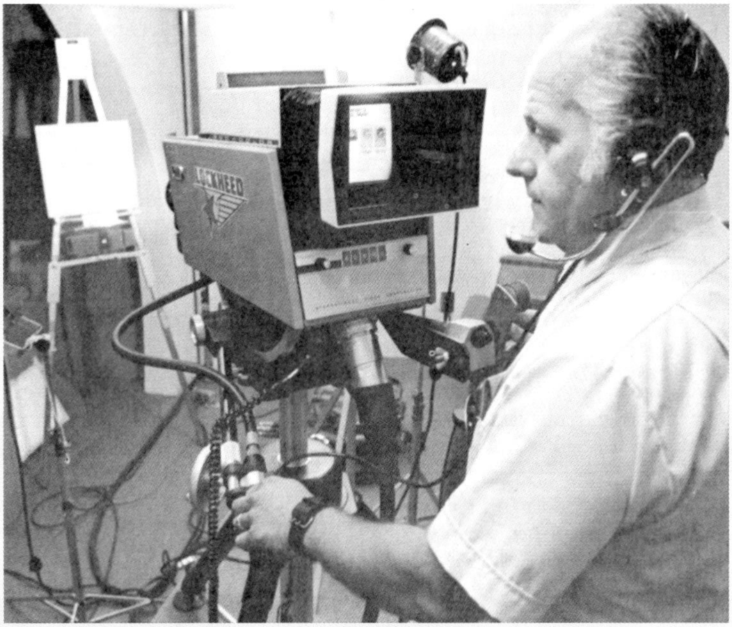

L-1011 Fuel System Tape - Alex Reisman, Lockheed TV cameraman, focuses his closed-circuit color TV camera on chart that details the TriStar's fuel system operation. Description of the L-1011 fuel system is recorded on a video tape and used as a flight crew training aid. *(Lockheed)*

meeting,' a company statement said. 'We believe a long-range financial plan can be successfully worked out. Steps are being taken to expedite a financial agreement and also to arrange for continued financing in the interim.'

Lockheed received positive evidence of continued support from its banks in the form of an additional $50 million loan. Chairman Dan Haughton flew to England for further RB211 conferences with Rolls-Royce (1971), Ltd., and British government representatives.

Haughton also was expected to pay a call on British European Airways, which announced that it was evaluating the Lockheed TriStar and the European A-300B airbus as candidates to fill its fleet re-equipment needs.

Preceding these late developments were the following significant events in the unfolding negotiations to continue the L-1011 TriStar programme with Rolls-Royce engines:

- TriStar customers, banks involved with airline and Lockheed financing, and Lockheed representatives met jointly on 19 April in New York, discussed the conditional agreement reached the previous month by Lockheed, the British government, and Rolls-Royce, and reached important understandings.
  Those present agreed that significant progress was made that would expedite the resolution of the outstanding issues.
- Most of those present at the 19 April meeting went to Washington and met the next day with Treasury Secretary Connally, who said later that he felt progress was being made although perhaps more slowly than he had expected.
- Secretary Connally said that a government-guaranteed loan 'may well be' required to assure the necessary financing for Lockheed to carry through the TriStar programme.

There was press speculation that Connally was nearing a recommendation and was inclined to propose that President Nixon asked Congress to approve a government guarantee for between $200 million and $250 million in bank loans to Lockheed.

Connally met with California Lt. Gov. Ed Reinecke and told him that he did not expect such a request would meet as much opposition in Congress as that for the supersonic transport.

The new $50 million loan was made under Lockheed's existing line of credit and brought total bank borrowings to $400 million, partially secured by the pledge of more collateral. 'We are delighted to have this evidence of continued support from our bankers,' said Frank L Frain, corporate senior vice-president for finance.

Lockheed continued negotiations with the twenty-four banks to arrange further financing to cover its longer-term requirements.

Secretary Connally's remark about a possible government-guaranteed loan brought prompt comment, both pro and con, from several members of Congress.

One of the first to evidence his support was Hubert Humphrey, former Vice-President and now a senator from Minnesota.

'If there's any company that I believe deserves favorable consideration by the government, it's Lockheed,' he said as he attended a county Democratic breakfast in Atlanta. 'I look upon Lockheed as one of our great industries. They've had their difiiculties, not through mismanagement, but actually through many technological changes and the

Left: Richard Milhous Nixon (*b.* 9 January 1913, *d.* 22 April 1994) was the 37th president of the United States, serving from 1969 until 1974.

Right: John Bowden Connally Jr. (*b.* 27 February 27, 1917, *d.*15 June 1993) was an American politician. He served as the 39th Governor of Texas and as the 61st United States Secretary of the Treasury.

problem of the British with the engine.'

California's Senator John Tunney delivered a strong statement on the floor of the Senate supporting a guaranteed loan of $250 million 'providing, of course, that the Treasury department believes such a loan is feasible and seeks Congressional authorization for it.'

Tunney noted that such a loan 'would permit Lockheed to recover from the impact of a $500 million loss because of defense department contracts and the unexpected collapse of Rolls-Royce.'

Negative reactions to the suggestion of a government guarantee were expressed by Senator Mike Mansfield of Montana, Senator William Proxmire of Wisconsin and Congressman Wright Patman of Texas.

Possibly as something of a sop to sharholders and the banks alike, salary cuts for key Lockheed executives were announced 30 April, and annual pay adjustments for 31,000 other salaried employees were deferred.

Board Chairman Daniel Haughton's annual salary was cut by twenty-five per cent. Reductions for other key executives would be on a declining scale averaging twelve per cent.

Earlier, the company had contemplated upward salary adjustments averaging five per cent to reward job performance and reflect economic conditions, effective at midyear. These have now been postponed. Those affected included officers and other salaried employees in the corporate headquarters and in plants located in sixteen states. Wages of hourly workers were not affected by the actions taken for salaried employees.

In announcing this action, Chairman Haughton said the corporation's financial situation made these moves necessary.

Lockheed's overall workforce had declined from 97,700 in early 1970 to about 72,000.

Other steps taken to trim costs and minimize cash requirements included:

- Reduction in capital spending by fifty per cent from 1970 levels.
- Sale of property owned at Newport Beach.
- Sale of other assets not needed for current or anticipated near-term operations.
- Deactivation and mothballing of other properties.
- Reduction in use of short-term leased space.
- Increased transfer of property among Lockheed's eleven operating divisions to improve utilization.
- Substantial reductions in all other discretionary expenditures, including research and development and computer operations.

By all normal banking standards, Lockheed's balance sheet in the spring of 1971 no longer warranted an extension of credit past the previously agreed ceiling of $400 million. To go beyond this limit, the lenders insisted on some unusual form of guarantee and suggested that the company sought assistance from the government. Consequently, to avert Lockheed's bankruptcy and the resultant national economic and defence impacts, legislation was introduced in Congress in May 1971 to provide for a Government guarantee of up to $250 million of commercial loans. These loans would be in addition to the existing $400 million lines of credit and to the $100 million in additional advance payments by customer airlines.

By 12 May 1971 legislation guaranteeing $250 million in private bank loans for Calac's L-1011 programme expected to be introduced in Congress after Lockheed Board Chairman Dan Haughton

Left: John William Wright Patman (*b*. 6 August 1893, *d*. 7 March 1976) was a US Congressman from Texas in Texas's 1st congressional district .

Right: Edward William Proxmire (*b*. 11 November 1915, *d* 15 December 2005)

signed a conditional contract with the newly vested British firm of Rolls-Royce (1971) Ltd. covering the supply of RB211 engines to power the TriStar.

'This is another big milestone in putting back together the whole RB211/1011 program,' Haughton said after the signing. 'The engine is going ahead right now and we have been working on this matter of getting our house in order so that if Congress in its wisdom passes the loan guarantee bill, we will be ready to go ahead.'

Completing the contract, signed for Rolls by Ian T. Morrow, deputy chairman and managing director, followed two days of London conferences involving Rolls, Lockheed and Calac's airline customers which airline spokesmen were quoted as applauding the British effort to keep the programme viable.

Earlier, British Defence Minister Lord Carrington had told the House of Commons that the British government would support the continuing development and production of the engines with an additional $240 million, contingent on Congressional approval of $250 million in loan guarantees for Lockheed.

It was also announced that the Rolls Aero Engine and Marine and Industrial Divisions were being formally transferred from the receiver who took over for the defunct company in February to the new Rolls-Royce (1971) Ltd., 'The transfer of assets referred to above will mean that Rolls-Royce (1971) Ltd. becomes fully operational and arrangements are being made for the employees concerned to come into its payroll," the Rolls-Royce announcement said.

Meanwhile, in the United States, pressures for and against Congressional approval of the loan guarantee continued to build up, following Treasury Secretary Connally's announcement that the Administration would ask Congress to approve such a guarantee.

Despite Connally's statement that, "We do not anticipate any cost to the taxpayer from this loan guarantee," extreme pressure to turn down the legislation or write in hamstringing conditions was being brought to bear on Congress by officials of General Electric, maker of the engines for the rival McDonnell Douglas DC-10 jetliner, and others.

Support for the guarantee came from President Nixon and Secretary Connally, among other high Administration officials, and also from such nationally influential figures as former Vice-President Hubert Humphrey, now a Minnesota senator; Senator Edmund Muskie of Maine; California Senator John Tunney; and the Executive Council of the AFL-CIO.

George Meany, AFL-CIO president, said after a meeting of the council in Atlanta that 'our approach is that here is a company that is in trouble mainly because of the Rolls-Royce Corp. in Great Britain and that this involves thousands of jobs at a time when the unemployment picture is a little more gloomy than ever before.'

Perhaps an editorial in America's largest newspaper, the *New York Daily News,* best expressed the views of proponents of the guarantee. The editorial said: 'At no cost to the taxpayers, the Nixon Administration proposes to provide a $250 million loan guarantee to the Lockheed Aircraft Corp. to save it from possible bankruptcy as a backfire from the financial troubles of Rolls-Royce Ltd. in England.

'The usual 'liberal' squawkers are objecting. Their objections are frivolous because such a loan would save more than 30,000 Lockheed employees' jobs in a period of still-rising joblessness, and keep Lockheed doing business with 35,000 subcontractors, most of them small concerns.

Left: Hubert Horatio Humphrey Jr. *b.* 27 May 1911, *d.* 13 January 1978) an American politician who served as the 38th vice president of the United States from 1965 to 1969.

Right: Edmund Sixtus Muskie (*b.* 28 March 1914, *d.* 26 March 1996) an American statesman and political leader who served as the 58th United States Secretary of State under President Jimmy Carter.

Surprising as it may seem, there were times when pretty girls wearing short skirts were used to promote airliners! Here J Floyd Andrews, president of Pacific Southwest Airlines, places a PSA insignia on the first TriStar in Palmdale, while Calac President Chuck Wagner and PSA stewardess Michele Davis watch. *(Lockheed)*

'Clearly, Congress should OK this loan guarantee without undue fussing and fiddling around.'

Keeping the workforce informed.

The purpose behind all of this was explained to all employees in a two-part special edition of *The Lockheed Star* house newspaper of 20 May.

'Secretary of the Treasury John B Connally - the same John Connally who, on 22 November 1963 was seriously wounded while riding in President Kennedy's car at Dealey Plaza in Dallas when the president was assassinated - announced from the White House on 6 May that the President was requesting congressional legislation authorizing government guarantees up to $250 million for bank loans to be available to Lockheed Aircraft Corporation.'

'The authorization is made necessary by peak financing requirements for Lockheed's new commercial airliner, the L-1011 TriStar, which are beyond Lockheed's ability to borrow through normal commercial credit channels. This $250 million under government guarantees would be in addition to $400 million already loaned to Lockheed by a consortium of 24 US banks and $100 million in prepayments next year by airlines over and above normal progress payments on the L-1011 TriStar.'

'A loan guarantee was made necessary by a series of events that increased Lockheed's need for financing but reduced our ability to borrow. First was the cash drain from losses of more than $500 million imposed on Lockheed mostly through negotiated settlements of legal disputes on four US military programs. These pretax losses had the further effect of severely reducing the company's net worth and its borrowing base. Then there was the increased financing requirement growing out of the five-month delay in planned airplane deliveries, which resulted from the collapse of Rolls-Royce Ltd., producer of the RB211 engine used in the L-1011.'

'The inability to finance the L-1011 TriStar adequately would force its cancellation, and the adverse economic impact would be severe. Well over 30,000 jobs are at stake - and all the human and family problems that would come from unemployment and underemployment. Thousands of

Sound in water reveals all...

Ed Hughes, ultrasonic inspection operator in Dept. 57-14, examines printout of test results during inspection of adhesively bonded TriStar fuselage panels by high speed sound waves transmitted through jets of water. *(Lockheed)*

Calac inspected fuselage panels for the L-1011 TriStar with sound waves transmitted through multiple streams of water.

Charles E. Searles, manager of the materiel and source evaluation department, 57-14, reported that high-frequency sound waves have proved to provide the best method for testing bonded aluminium skin panels for the L-1011.

He said that sonic waves are transmitted at a million cycles per second along ten pencil-thin streams of water splashing against the surface of the fuselage panel. The sonic waves penetrate reinforcing structure bonded to the surfaces of the panel. Water is used to prevent dispersal of the waves into the air.

If a sound wave emerges on the other side of the panel in much the same form as when it entered, no gaps exist in the adhesive that bonds the pieces together. If the wave becomes dispersed or irregular, then flaws, contamination or bubbles exist in the bond line, and the panel is removed from the production line for repair.

Searles described the nondestructive testing method in a technical paper presented before the 1971 Western Engineering and Tool Exposition of the Society of Mechanical Engineers in Los Angeles.

'Chief advantages of the ultrasonic system,' Searles said, 'include its reliability and, when automated in the manner in which we use it, its high production rate. Our new ultrasonic system will inspect the largest TriStar panel in about half an hour, a job that previously required sixteen working hours, using the previous manual method.'

employees are laid off already until continuance of the program is assured and production can pick up.'

'About $1.4 billion in US investments also is at stake, with only minor salvage value if the TriStar is cancelled. The declaration of these investment losses - by subcontractors, banks, and airlines - would mean that reduced tax income to the government over the next several years would be substantially greater than the possible loss to the government if Lockheed had to default on the loan. Added to this would be a huge general impact on the national economy from job losses, disruption, welfare and unemployment expense.'

'Insufficient financing for the L-1011 TriStar would force cancellation of the transport program, and Lockheed would be forced into bankruptcy through its inability to meet the huge obligations it already has incurred on the program. Effects of bankruptcy, beyond the effects of L-1011 cancellation, are uncertain, as legal authorities indicate the one certainty in bankruptcy is uncertainty.'

'In the event of bankruptcy, it is possible but by no means certain that at least Lockheed's more important military programs would be continued and with employees on these projects continued in their jobs. But with the wide powers granted trustees, bankruptcy could cause great confusion, abrogation or alteration of agreements, greatly increased costs on government programs, and displacements and future hazards for Lockheed employees and more than 60,000 shareholders and bondholders.'

'In view of the potential economic effects from L-1011 cancellation, the effects on Lockheed employees, plus the ripple effect on Lockheed subcontractors and their employees, the $250 million loan guarantee was proposed by the Administration. The guaranteed portion of the loans would be drawn down from banks only to the extent needed, and Secretary Connally has said this portion would be on a 'last-in, first-out' basis, thus minimizing the risk to the government.'

'Liens on Lockheed assets would protect the government in the event of default, and the Secretary of the Treasury would have the power to disapprove any disposal of Lockheed assets during the time the government would be at risk.'

'There is no full precedent for this guaranteed loan proposal, although there are many partial precedents. They occur in a wide variety of fields, going all the way back to the Reconstruction Finance Corporation (RFC), which is now abandoned as a single entity but with much of its authority now scattered throughout numerous government agencies. In 1947 the Glenn L Martin Company obtained an RFC loan, against which it made a series of drawdowns reaching a maximum of $26.6 million to alleviate its financial troubles centered around its series of commercial airliners.'

'More nearly related, however, was the 1967 government-guaranteed loan authority for $75 million granted the Douglas Aircraft Company (now merged into McDonnell Douglas) through the V-Loan procedures. At that time Douglas faced financing problems resulting from the DC-8 and DC-9 commercial airplane programs and needed financing to continue its government projects.'

'Also, the US Export-Import Bank frequently guarantees loans for the purchase of US equipment by foreign buyers. Currently, Ex-Im has guaranteed or made credits available for nearly $600 million to finance foreign purchases of seventy-one Boeing 747s and $190 million for twenty-nine McDonnell Douglas DC-l0s. Although Lockheed itself has used Ex-Im assistance on past foreign sales, none has involved L-1011 purchases abroad.'

'Current guaranteed loan authority occurs in areas such as FHA loans, student loans, feeder airline loans, farm loans, the recent Penn Central loan, and many, many others.'

'The British government has agreed to fund fully an estimated $240 million for completion of the development of the RB211 engine, plus financing engine production costs. The US financing plan to continue the TriStar program may be summarized as follows:

- $400 million in bank loans already made to Lockheed.
- $250 million in bank loans to be made and to be covered by government guarantee.
- $650 million provided by twenty-four lending banks to Lockheed.
- $100 million from TriStar customer prepayments over and above normal prepayments.
- This amounts to $750 million total.'

'All the new agreements - with the British, the airlines, and the banks which are either completed or in negotiation, are conditional on the continued viability of Lockheed and the L-1011 TriStar through the $250 million in bank loans that would be guaranteed by the US government.'

'In January 1967 Lockheed turned its attention to the commercial airbus and cargo transport market. It became evident that a move into this market and continued competitiveness for new military programs would require vastly increased expenditures for fixed assets and research and development. In March 1967 an underwriting group offered $125 million in convertible subordinated debentures.'

'Early in 1968, Lockheed re-entered the commercial airliner field with its L-1011 TriStar jetliner, which provided an opportunity to reduce materially the company's dependence on defense contracts. To finance this commercial program and US government programs, Lockheed established a new unsecured bank credit agreement for $400 million, dated May 1, 1969. This was considered to be adequate prior to severe losses on four military programs and the unexpected collapse of Rolls-Royce Ltd. The effects of defense program losses and Rolls-Royce receivership subsequently have made necessary the requirement for up to $250 million in additional bank financing for Lockheed.'

- Military Program Losses: Severe losses imposed on Lockheed through negotiated settlements of the legal disputes on the four DoD programs (C-5A, Cheyenne helicopter, SRAM motor, and shipbuilding claims) resulted in pretax losses for Lockheed in the area of $500 million. Of this amount, $432.3 million came from the area of costs that are allowable under defense contracts and the balance from nonallowable areas, such as interest costs. These losses resulted in a severe cash drain on Lockheed.'
- Net Worth: These losses had the further effect of severely reducing Lockheed's net worth and its borrowing base. Lockheed's net worth in 1968 was almost $371 million and now is about $240 million.
- Engine Delay: The approximate six-months delay in deliveries of Rolls- Royce RB211 engines, of course, results in delay of L-1011 airplane deliveries to airline customers. Consequently, there will be a delay in cash payments to Lockheed upon delivery of airplanes. This, in turn, requires Lockheed to finance inventories for a longer period before receiving payments from airplane deliveries. In short, Lockheed needs more for peak L-1011 funding but can borrow less.'

'The adverse economic effects would be severe in the United States if adequate funds are not provided to meet Lockheed's peak financing requirements. Lack of adequate financing would force cancellation of the L-1011, consequent loss of more than 30,000 jobs, loss of almost all of the $1.4 billion already invested in the program, bankruptcy for Lockheed, and potentially severe ripple effects on thousands of Lockheed suppliers located throughout the US.'

'Jobs: As of Jan. 31, 1971, approximately 17,700 Lockheed employees were attached to the L-1011 program, and just over 14,000 were employed on this program at plants of first-tier subcontractors and suppliers located in 35 states. Layoffs of L-1011 employees at Lockheed have totaled more than 8,000 as of this date, but similar layoffs at supplier plants have been minimal. Some of those laid off would be recalled if the program continues according to present plan. Thus approximately 30,000 jobs in the U.S would be lost if the L-1011 were canceled.'

'If the multiplier effect is taken into account, estimated at a 2.1 to 1 ratio by the UCLA Econometric Model, the total job loss in the US would be approximately 63,000.'

'Such job losses first would result in severe family and human problems from the effects of at least temporary unemployment and under-employment of these skilled workers. Additionally, job losses of this magnitude indicate that up to $68 million would be lost to the government in reduced income taxes from this source alone.'

'Investments: At this time, about $1.4 billion has been invested in the L-1011 program in the US from the private sector - by Lockheed, L-1011 subcontractors, banks, and the airline customers. This investment is in the form of airplane design and development costs, special tools and machinery, and special buildings and equipment for the L-1011. Salvage value would be minor, and the waste from L-1011 cancellation therefore would mean losses of well over $1 billion to the participants in the program.'

'It is difficult to estimate with complete accuracy what the declaration of these losses would mean in net reduced tax income to the US over the next several years. It would seem certain, however, that the lost tax income to the government would be substantially greater than the $250 million loan amount proposed to be guaranteed by the government.'

'If sufficient financing for the L-1011 cannot be provided, the cancellation of the program would follow, and Lockheed would be forced into bankruptcy through its inability to meet huge obligations already incurred on the L-1011. The effects of bankruptcy, other than the direct effects from L-1011 cancellation previously described, are uncertain, for the one certainty in bankruptcy is uncertainty.'

'However, it would seem possible that even in bankruptcy at least Lockheed's more important military programs would be continued and that most employees (other than L-1011 employees) would continue in their jobs. This situation would likely be true at least for several years until products now on order were delivered. But even in the immediate period ahead, bankruptcy could create great confusion, greatly increased costs to the government, and displacements and hazards for Lockheed employees and shareholders.'

'Legal authorities say the trustees would have wide powers: to alter labor agreements; possibly to abrogate Lockheed agreements with DoD including those establishing large fixed losses on military programs, such as the $200 million fixed loss on the C-5A; and to establish new prices for military products. Many subcontractors would have the legal right to abrogate their contracts on military programs and demand higher prices.'

'For example, the possible effects on the US government from a Lockheed bankruptcy were stated rather succinctly in a letter from Elmer B Staats, Comptroller General of the US to Congressman William G. Moorhead. Dated Jan. 25, 1971, the letter was in specific reference to the C-5A, but would apply equally well to other Lockheed government contracts. The last paragraph of that letter said: 'However, we should point out our understanding that the Trustee's obligation would he to protect all of the creditors and that he could not operate the company solely for the benefit of one creditor, even the United States government. Any of the creditors could petition the Court periodically for adjudication of their rights. In addition, there is a serious question whether the company would be required to perform its contracts with the government. Further, there is a question as to the eflect of chapter XI proceedings on Lockheed's subcontractors. The subcontracts were entered into in 1965 and 1966 when lower prices prevailed. If these subcontractors could terminate their agreements, the cost to the government would increase substantially if the C-5A program were to

This 750-hp gas turbine engine is an auxiliary power unit (APU) for Calac's L-1011 TriStar. It provided the power to start the aircraft's engines and to operate such systems as the air conditioning, on the ground or in the air. Here it's being inspected on its arrival at Plant 10 in Palmdale by representatives of Hamilton Standard Division of United Aircraft, for whom United of Canada produced the engine. From left arc E D Berhold, Calac assistant group engineer for APU, of Dept. 73-41, J C Dabek, Hamilton Standard service representative; George Karlis, Calac senior buyer, Dept. 52-31, Unit 35; and R F Farnum, assigned as Hamilton Standard resident area representative. (Lockheed)

The first set of TriStar passenger doors produced at Gifu plant of Kawasaki Heavy Industries in Japan undergoes final inspection by Wayne Lemons, Calac purchasing representative; K Hirano, Kawasaki Aircraft Division general manager; Kawasaki engineer; K Uchino, Kawasaki vice-president and general manager. (Lockheed)

continue.'

'Additionally, if financial stability could not be proved, under bankruptcy, Lockheed could be declared ineligible to bid for future defense business under Armed Services Procurement Regulations. This could destroy the future of the company itself, the career prospects of thousands of Lockheed employees, and at least partially destroy the investments made by more than 60,000 stockholders and bond-holders. This potential future hazard could cause a further severe ripple effect among many subcontractors which have built their own futures around long years of association with Lockheed.'

- Terms: The proposed legislation would provide authority for up to $250 million in bank loans guaranteed by the US government, which would be available to Lockheed. Loans would be drawn down by Lockheed only as needed and to the extent needed. Current cash flow projections indicate the minimum amount needed by Lockheed from this source would be under $200 million, but unanticipated events could require a maximum draw-down up to the full $250 million.

  'Current bank loans made directly to Lockheed now total $400 million, and loans under the $250 million authority would be an addition to that. This $650 million total available financing direct from banks is in addition to approximately $100 million of financing that would be provided next year by the airlines in the form of advances beyond normal pre-payments.'

  'The guaranteed portion of the bank loans ($250 million) would be provided, Secretary Connally has said, on a 'last-in first-out' basis - thus minimizing the risk to the government. The first draw-down of this portion would occur late in 1971. Payback would probably begin in about mid-1973. The guaranteed portion is presently forecast to be paid back completely by the end of 1974.'

  'To further minimize the risk to the government, a lien on Lockheed assets would be granted in the event of default on the guaranteed portion of the bank loans. Additionally, the Secretary of the Treasury would have the power to disapprove any disposal of Lockheed assets during the time the government is at risk.'

- Precedent: There is no full precedent for this particular guaranteed-loan proposal, since the sequence of events in the Lockheed case is unique, and the circumstances that surround the Lockheed situation only developed in recent years.'

  'Precedents do occur in a wide variety of areas, however - going all the way back to the Reconstruction Finance Corporation (RFC), which is now abandoned as a single entity, with much of its authority scattered throughout numerous government agencies. In June, 1947, the Glenn L Martin Company obtained an RFC loan, against which it made a series of draw-downs reaching a maximum of $26.6 million to alleviate the financial troubles centered around its series of commercial airliners.'

  'There are many other partial precedents in areas such as FHA loans, student loans, feeder-airline loans, farm loans, the recent Penn-Central loan, and many, many others. But more to the point are two other guaranteed-loan situations.'

Lighting

Lockheed had long been a pioneer of flight station lighting innovations and developed improved lighting concepts for long-duration aircraft missions. Together with newly developed techniques for integrally lit panels, this background had produced completely new advanced flight station lighting for the L-1011.

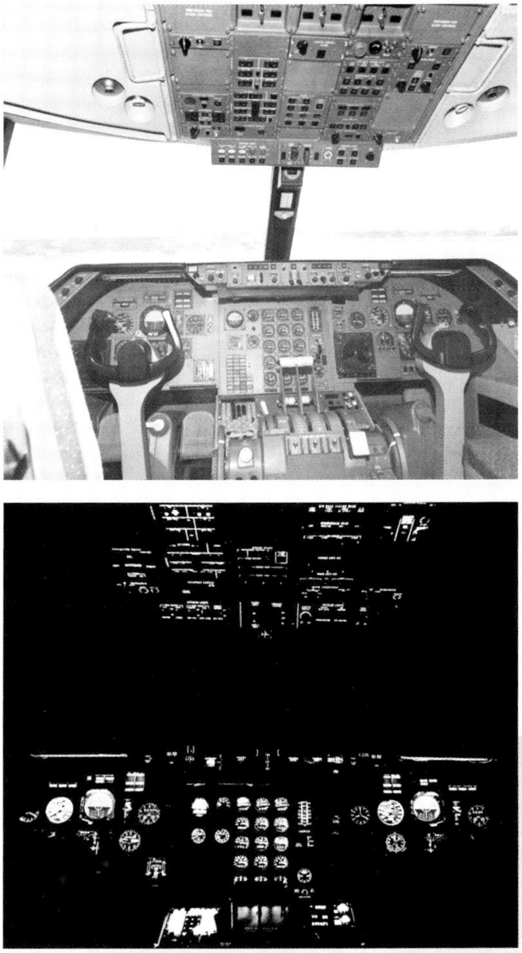

Improved maintainability resulted from the use of solderless lamp replacement, eliminating requirements for special equipment. All instruments, information panels, annunciators, and lighted indicators all were replaceable at the panel fronts. Additionally, the standardisation of long-life lamp types reduced requirements for lamp spares to be carried on board.

A photometric test programme conducted at the Lockheed Rye Canyon Research Laboratory was the most extensive testing programme of its kind ever undertaken for a commercial airliner. Testing encompassed all component types and assemblies. Further evaluation was made on a completed mockup under ambient daylight and nighttime conditions to determine the effects of glare, sunlight shafting, and windshield reflections.

Each instrument application in the flight deck was carefully evaluated to determine the best means for its integral illumination. As a result, it was determined that the many advantages of trans-illumination could be employed for most instruments, while wedge lighting offered its primary benefits in particular applications.

Left: The day and night-time view of the flight deck lighting mock up.

Below: this mock up could be towed around the airport to test the effects of glare and other conditions.

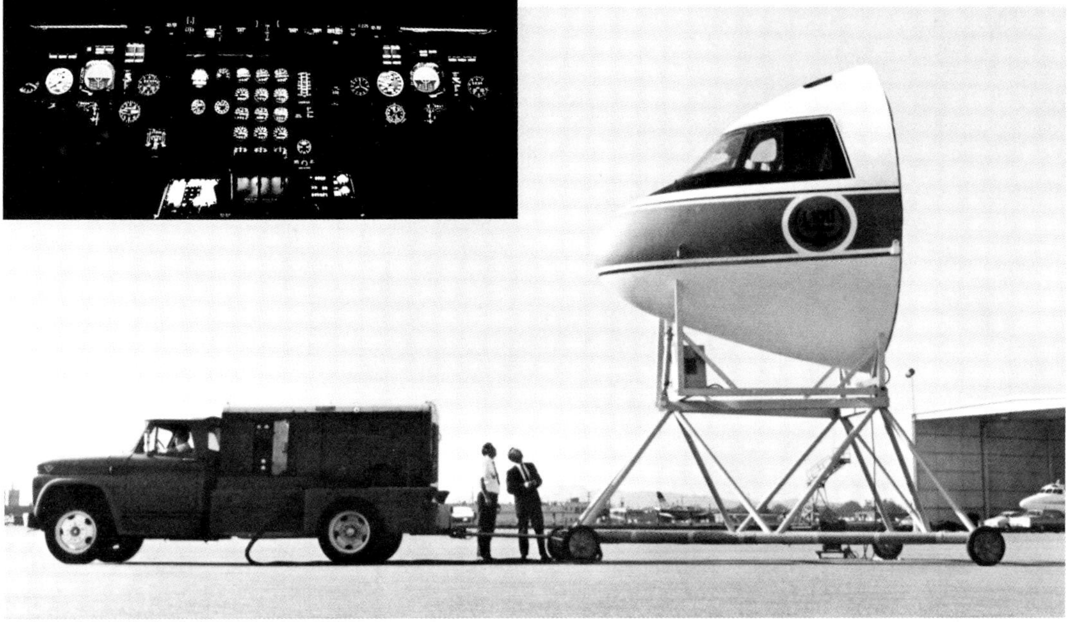

Original caption: Janet Markoe, stewardess consultant in L-1011 passenger accommodations, Dept. 73-41, demonstrates the efficiency of the high-speed infrared ovens used in the TriStar. Here she checks the temperature of a steak that had been frozen to ten degrees below zero before being cooked. The food temperatures were recorded to demonstrate that meals can be cooked more quickly and uniformly in the L-1011 than with convection-type ovens used on all other commercial jetliners. Each TriStar will be equipped with five ovens, and each oven is capable of handling fifty-four casseroles at one time. Bowman/TIC Inc. of Newbury Park, a division of Bowman Instruments Corp., makes the ovens.

- 'First, the US Export-Import Bank frequently guarantees loans for the purchase of US equipment by foreign buyers. For example, guaranteed loans and other direct credits by Ex-Im include nearly $600 million in loans to finance purchases of 71 Boeing 747's by 13 foreign airlines and $190 million to finance purchases of 29 McDonnell Douglas DC-10's by six foreign airlines. Also, Ex-Im assistance has been used to help finance foreign purchases of Lockheed aircraft, although none has involved L-1011 purchases abroad.'
- 'Next is the V-Loan authority granted the Douglas Aircraft Company (now merged into McDonnell Douglas) early in 1967 for $75 million, when it faced financing problems on the DC-8 and DC-9 commercial airplane programs. V-Loan procedures are intended to aid companies with defense business, but the origin of the Douglas problem was clearly stated as being caused by the commercial portion of Douglas activities. Because of new restrictions applied to V-Loans by Congress in 1970, at the time of the renewal of the Defense Production Act, and because of eligibility requirements for V-Loans, this procedure would not fit the current Lockheed financing requirement.'

The second part of the report explained what the company was doing with the TriStar.

'Airline Customers: Lockheed either has completed or is in the process of negotiating new agreements with all L-1011 TriStar customers. These agreements provide for the conditional reaffirmation of airline orders for the TriStar, primarily conditioned on assurances of the continued financial viability of Lockheed and Rolls-Royce (1971), Ltd. and their long-term commitment to L-1011 and RB211 production and future support;

'In such agreements. the airlines agree to an increase in the price of the L-1011 mostly caused by a $180,000 price increase for each of the three RB211 engines for the airplane. Additionally, the airlines agree to aid in the financing of the L-1011 by providing a total of about $100 million next year in prepayments in excess of normal advance payments.'

'Alteration of original airplane delivery schedules also is. made necessary by the delay of approximately six months in delivery of RB211 engines.'

'Banks: Twenty-four US banks have now increased their direct loans to Lockheed from $350 million to $400 million under an amended agreement effective April 26, 1971. Additional Lockheed collateral was provided in the amended agreement.'

'Rolls-Royce: After Rolls-Royce went into receivership unexpectedly on Feb. 4, 1971, its assets were purchased by the British government and it was reorganized as Rolls-Royce (1971), Ltd. With government launching aid of approximately $114 million, commercial loans, plus its own resources, the predecessor company and other British companies had already invested over $400 million in the development of the RB211 engine and for associated components for use in the L-1011. In the period immediately after receivership, there was great uncertainty as to whether the engine would be abandoned, and the original contract was abrogated.'

'However, the British government called its former chief defense scientist, Sir William Cook, out of retirement and began an investigation to determine whether the RB2ll was technically sound and financially feasible to continue.'

'Meanwhile, Lockheed and L-1011 airline customers began immediate evaluation of possible alternate engines manufactured by General Electric and by Pratt & Whitney. Discussions also continued with officials of the new Rolls-Royce company and with British government officials.'

'These discussions took into account all considerations - price, delivery schedules, financing problems associated with engine delay, L-1011 design changes and airframe modifications required to accommodate the different shapes and sizes of the competitive General Electric and Pratt & Whitney engines, and engine performance as it would relate to the L-1011. In effect, Lockheed conducted a new engine competition for the TriStar.'

'The British government investigation did indicate good technical progress on the RB211, although it would be about six months late. Financial uncertainties also were resolved. The British government at this time agreed to pay all further costs for completion of RB211 development, estimated to be about $240 million, and to fund engine production costs, thus requiring no financing subsidy from the US. They did receive agreement from Lockheed and the airlines for a price increase of $180,000 per engine, which is well below what the British were asking but still remains competitive with costs of US engines.'

'These financial agreements mean the Rolls-Royce-powered L-1011 would be priced below the TriStar price if it were adapted to a G.E. or P & W engine and would keep it competitive with the DC-10. Continued use of the RB211 engine avoids losses of about $16 million in prepayments by airlines to Rolls-Royce. It provides better opportunity for foreign sales of the L-1011, with the consequent favorable balance-of-payments effect. And it provides for engine competition as well as airframe competition in the wide-bodied airbus field.'

'But perhaps most important, it avoids an additional delay of about six months, which would result from use of either of the alternate engines. With such an extra delay, cash receipts from delivery of airplanes would be further delayed and more than $100 million more in financing would be required by Lockheed. Lockheed might be forced into receivership unless it could obtain even more loan guarantees than it now seeks.'

'Because of all these considerations, Lockheed signed on May 11 a new agreement with Rolls-Royce (1971) Ltd. In view of the financial commitments of the British government itself, the new agreement does require assurance of Lockheed's financial viability through the US government-guaranteed loan, so as to assure the British that there will be a

A view from the loft, parts come together to make a L-1011. *(Lockheed via Ed Posey)*

The Court Line/Clarksons team are shown around the unglazed flight deck area of an L-1011 on the production line in 1970. *(Lockheed via Ed Posey)*

requirement for their engines when they are delivered.'

'The design of the Lockheed L-1011 TriStar melds airplane and engine to provide optimum performance for a medium-range wide-bodied airliner for US and foreign airlines. The four-year design, development, and integration program for the Rolls-Royce RB211 engine includes design features which bring smoke and noise levels within Federal Aviation Administration requirements.'

'A. Flight Status: Flight-testing of the TriStar has continued pending resolution of final airline, engine, and financing agreements, and now totals over 160 hours.'

'Tests have demonstrated results ranging from routine confirmation of on-target performance of major aircraft systems to surprisingly early full operation of the new automatic landing system. All data continue to point firmly to flight performance and handling qualities equaling or bettering goals, and pilots comment favorably on the stable engine characteristics.'

'Even though they do not incorporate all production refinements, engines have proved to be virtually smoke-free and only about half as noisy on takeoff and landing as earlier jets.'

'B. Market: Lockheed launched the TriStar program in 1968 to fill a key segment of a large market requirement for high-capacity advanced technology trijet transports. Market studies based on the best available economic and population projections continue today to show a free-world airline need by 1980 for 750 such aircraft.'

'While the volume of jet transport orders declined throughout the industry in 1970, a number of factors point to a continuing long-term demand. Passenger-traffic growth continues strong in many parts of the world, and first-generation jet transports, now more than 10 years old, are being phased out of service.'

'In the world airline market, the Rolls-Royce engine tends to promote sales to British and other foreign airlines, and to lessen the chances of their buying transports built overseas.'

Following exhaustive hearings and debate by Congress, the Emergency Loan Guarantee Act, Public Law 92-70 - which provided for the establishment of a Guarantee Board comprising the Secretary of the Treasury as Chairman, and the Chairmen of the Board of Governors of the Federal Reserve System and of the Securities and Exchange Commission, and authorized it to guarantee up to £250 million of private bank loans - was passed on 2 August 1971, and was signed by President Richard Nixon one week later.

The Emergency Loan Guarantee Act gave authority to guarantee or make commitments to insure lenders against loss of principal or interest on loans that met the following requirements:

- The investment is needed to enable the borrower to continue to furnish goods and services.
- Credit not otherwise available to the borrower under reasonable terms and conditions.
- The lender certifies that it would not make the loan without such guarantee.

The Guarantee Board found that Lockheed met the requirements of the Act and committed on 9 August 1971, its entire guarantee capacity to Lockheed.

Enforced re-evaluation

Lockheed and its airline customers twice conducted thorough competitive evaluations of US-built engines as candidates for use in the L-1011 TriStar but each time found sound reasons to favour the Rolls-Royce RB211.

Politics being business - or should that be the other way around? - Dan Haughton reported on 13 May that in response to a General Electric proposal to upset the applecart by insisting that any government-guaranteed bank loans for Lockheed should be made conditional upon changing to one of the two American-made engines.

He described both the GE CF6 and the Pratt & Whitney JT9D as 'fine engines' and said they were seriously considered in joint Lockheed and airline evaluations - first in 1968 and again after Rolls-Royce went into receivership in February 1971. 'In effect, we and the airlines conducted a completely new engine competition,' Haughton said, taking into account all considerations - price, delivery schedules, financing requirements associated with the various schedule delays, airplane design changes and the additional structural - and flight-testing required to accommodate a new engine, and engine performance as it would relate to the L-1011.

From a technical standpoint, any one of the three engines could meet the basic requirements. 'We still believe, however, on the basis of the present development status of the RB211 design, that the advantages of the original concept are still valid,' Haughton said. He also pointed out that there would be added costs and schedule delays involved in changing engines. For example, for the GE CF6, the basic engine cost was substantially equal to the RB211, including duty, under terms of our new conditional contract. But there are added costs for the total GE power package, including nacelles and other

Dwarfed by an L-1011 surrounded by scaffolding, the Court Line/Clarksons team discuss what they have seen on the production line in 1970. *(Lockheed via Ed Posey)*

propulsion system elements.

'And the modification cost of $52 million mentioned by GE in its public statement is based on apparent misinformation,' Haughton said. 'Redesign, re-tooling, additional flight-testing, modification, redundant parts, and added production costs for use of the CF6 would actually exceed $100 million. Obviously, therefore, for the use cost of a GE-powered L-1011 would be greater for Lockheed and for the airlines.'

Among the technical advantages cited for the RB211 were:

- The RB211 combines proven features of the Rolls-Royce Spey and Conway engines now in wide airline use, augmented by the advanced three-shaft design. This results in a short, solid, sturdy engine built to be extremely durable and reliable in airline service.
- The three-shaft design also results in at least twenty per cent fewer rotating parts and greater operational reliability under adverse conditions such as tail-wind starts, cross-winds, high angles of attack, and rough controls handling.
- Its thrust-reversing system has proved uniquely capable of reliable operations down to zero speed.
- From direct measurements in flight, the early predictions that the RB211 would be the quietest engine in its thrust class have now been demonstrated; and, like its competitors, it is virtually smokeless.
- Although the RB211 has increased in weight over that which we originally ordered, the added margins of safety and durability accruing from the added material, plus the engine's relatively low takeoff turbine-inlet temperature, assure substantial thrust growth potential for longer-range or higher-payload versions of the L-1011.

Lockheed's need for legislation to provide a US guarantee of added bank loans results largely from forces outside their control and the negative impact that would be created unless funds are obtained to continue the L-1011 programme justified approval of the proposed measure.

These were among the key points in Dan Haughton's prepared statement submitted to the Senate Banking Committee in advance of his personal testimony.

Risk to the government and taxpayers would be minimal, Haughton pointed out. The guaranteed loans would be the last Lockheed would draw on and the first to be repaid. And a prior lien on company assets would more than amply secure the total amount of the requested $250 million in guarantees.

He noted that continuation of the L-1011 programme would preserve some 30,000 jobs of Lockheed and supplier employees in 35 states. It would prevent the waste of $1.4 billion invested in existing L-1011 inventory by Lockheed, suppliers, and the airlines. And it would provide the airlines with the continuing economic benefits of having a competitive trijet plane-and-engine combination for the predicted air-travel growth of the 1970's and 1980's.

Haughton said that competition had already resulted in savings to airlines of about $1 million per wide-bodied airliner. Numerous advances and refinements would provide improvements in airline operations, and new comfort and convenience for passengers. He projected a requirement by 1980 for nearly 800 basic intermediate-range trijets and that Lockheed would obtain an adequate share of that potential market to result in a viable programme.

Haughton also noted that use of Rolls-Royce engines might be an advantage in sales to the UK and

Plastic fabricators Vivian Blum, left, Olga Pankow, centre, and Mary Lou Tool, all of Dept. 19-36, display TriStar window panels, part of one complete ship set of 120 such panels shipped to Plant 10 from Bldg. 180 at Plant B-1, where the laminated fibreglass panels were made. *(Lockheed)*

Forward end of the main fuselage, the Court Line/Clarkson team are standing where the flight deck will eventually go. Note the size and strength of the temporary formers retaining the shape. *(Lockheed via Ed Posey)*

certain other overseas airlines that might otherwise buy transports built overseas, such as the European A-300 Airbus.

Haughton began by describing the scope of the present overall Lockheed organisation, the variety of its activities and product lines, and its achievements in meeting schedule and target prices in key military programmes between 1951-1971, except for the C-5A Galaxy programme.

First to testify before the committee when it opened its hearings Monday was Treasury Secretary John Connally, who said he had concluded reluctantly that the government must 'act and act quickly' to save Lockheed.

'Just at this time, with the economy moving ahead and unemployment topping out, the failure of the nation's largest defense contractor - with 72,000 employees earning $830 million a year, 35,000 suppliers and $2.5 billion in annual sales - would, beyond any shadow of doubt, generate deep-seated fears,' Connally said.

Connally argued that 60,000 jobs in Lockheed and subcontractors would be lost if the company went bankrupt. The government would have to pay more for weapons it now buys from Lockheed, he said, and the government's tax loss would exceed the $250 million loan guarantee.

The Secretary of the Treasury continued his testimony the following day, rebuking Senator William Proxmire for his charge that the guarantee proposal amounted to a 'welfare' program by pointing out that Proxmire had backed a bill to aid an auto manufacturer in his home state.

Employees take to the streets.

'Lockheed employees, friends and family members, thousands strong, have rallied to the company's support as the Senate Banking Committee recessed public hearings on the bill to guarantee $250 million in private loans to continuance the L-1011 TriStar programme.' The *Lockheed Star* house newspaper reported on 8 July.

In North Hollywood, encouraged by the L-1011 Committee to Save Aerospace Jobs, more than 4000 employees marched on the State Department of Human Resources office - the unemployment office nearest to Lockheed's Burbank plant - to emphasize the unemployment problem that would follow if Lockheed were to go bankrupt. Some 1200 employees and family members followed suit a week later at the unemployment office in Lancaster. In San Jose, approximately 1600 employees of LMSC staged a similar march.

And in Marietta, Ga., more than 10,000 Gelac

The Lockheed-California Company was pleased to show its L-1011 TriStar production and manufacturing facilities in Burbank and Palmdale to members of Court Line Aviation, Ltd., and Clarksons managements on June 23, 1970.

Participating were:

Court Line Aviation, Ltd.

John Young
Managing Director, Court Line, Ltd.

Ed Posey
Managing Director, Court Line Aviation, Ltd.

Clarksons

Donald Mc Quee
Director

Tom Gullick
Director

Thanks to the presentation album given to the Court Line/Clarkson team we have these early images of the L-1011 production line. *(Lockheed via Ed Posey)*

employees, family members, friends, and concerned citizens turned out for a Saturday' Dan Haughton Appreciation Day' rally, to hear Haughton, Georgia Senator David Gambrell, the lieutenant governor, superintendent of schools, the mayor (a Lockheed employee), and other leading citizens point out the need and justification for a loan guarantee for Lockheed. Meanwhile, full-page advertisements telling the Lockheed story began to appear in newspapers throughout the nation, paid for by employees' contributions.

Employees from Burbank, Rye Canyon, Palmdale and Van Nuys, through their volunteer committee, paid for full-page advertisments in the *Washington Post* and *Washington Star* on 29 June.

More such advertisments appeared in other papers in the future, because so far the committee has collected $44,000, with Lodge 727 of the IAM contributing another $2000.

Employees at LMSC paid for a page advert in the *San Jose Mercury* and a quarter-page advert in the eastern edition of the *Wall Street Journal*. Employees at Lockheed Propulsion Company paid for a page advert in the *Redlands Facts*. Gelac employees paid for four full-page ads in the *Marietta Journal*. And employees of Lockheed Aircraft Service Company in Ontario contributed $6000 toward a fund for national advertising during one week of a drive that has reached only about one-third of the payroll so far.

On local legislative and business fronts, resolutions backing the congressional loan guarantee were passed by the Los Angeles City Council (introduced jointly by Councilmen Louis Nowell and Robert Wilkinson of the San Fernando Valley), the Los Angeles County Board of Supervisors, the city councils of Burbank, Palmdale, and Redlands, and the San Bernardino County Board of Supervisors.

Chambers of Commerce which came out in favour of the legislation included Los Angeles, Lancaster, Palmdale, North Hollywood, Sun Valley, Mission Hills, Granada Hills, West Van Nuys, Burbank, Sun Valley and Redlands; the San Fernando Valley Industrial Assn., and the Antelope Valley Board of Trade.

Meanwhile, 'Earned at Lockheed' stickers to go onto cheques employees wrote to pay their bills, were distributed by management club and union representatives throughout most plants, as were 'Lockheed Is Worth Saving' bumper stickers.

This was in addition to the hundreds of thousands of letters, telegrams and phone calls from employees, friends and relatives, to Senators and Congressmen to inform the legislators of the facts concerning Lockheed.

Meanwhile, Board Chairman Dan Haughton told a National Press Club in Washington, DC, luncheon that urged Congress to adopt legislation authorising government-guaranteed bank loans for Lockheed would create a $20 billion aircraft monopoly.

Haughton said the forthcoming congressional decision 'may well be the most important decision

Original caption: Tramp, tramp, tramp, the boys are marching - and so are a lot of the girls - as Lockheed employees demonstrate in front of state unemployment offices in North Hollywood (above) and Lancaster (below) what may happen if Lockheed fails to get loan guarantee from Congress. Number of families added to unemployment rolls in that event has been estimated at from 65,000 to 100,000. *(both Lockheed)*

affecting commercial aviation and air transportation that the Congress will be called upon to make during this year - or perhaps during any other year for quite some time to come.'

Haughton pointed out that the TriStar and DC-10 trijets competed for a major and distinct market segment and said that the monopoly question had been a little-recognized aspect of the public interest in discussing the pending loan guarantee legislation.

'Perhaps people have not understood that there is no way for another company to enter this wide-bodied trijet market, if Lockheed is forced out,' he said. 'Perhaps they have not understood the size of the market. Perhaps they have not understood the long - range economic impact that a monopoly of this market, extending through the remainder of this decade and into the next, would have on the air traveller.'

'Lockheed and others estimated the market for continental and intercontinental trijets would amount to about 1375 airliners by 1980, 'Haughton said. 'For purposes of conservatism, let's say it is only a 1000-airplane market,' he added. 'With escalation plus the cost of spare parts, the price will average out through the decade at about $20 million each. That makes a $20 billion plum - perhaps the largest single monopoly market in the world.'

The Lockheed chairman pointed out that the twin-engine European airbus and the Boeing 747 had their own separate areas in the market, one for short ranges and the other for heavy-traffic long-range flights, with the market segment in between remaining as the prime trijet market. For another company to try at this time to replace Lockheed as a trijet competitor would require the risk of 'several hundreds of millions of dollars' and the gamble of catching up against a competing model that has a four-year headstart, Haughton pointed out.

'It is just not in the cards for any company to accept these huge risks and attempt to produce a viable trijet competitor against the DC-10," he said.

He cited airline-industry leaders statements that trijet competition had resulted in price decreases of at least $1 million per machine - while at the same time providing improved aircraft - and their desires for continued strong competition in the manufacture of commercial transports.

'The question to be considered here, therefore, is not whether this legislation would set a precedent by improperly involving Congress in a competitive commercial market,' he said. 'Rather, it is whether Congress has the desire to establish a more devastating precedent by creating a monopoly.'

Haughton cited other benefits 'from the standpoint of the broad public interest' in approval of loan-guarantee authorisation that would get Lockheed over what he described as a temporary cash flow problem.

He said one of the most important is 'the rescue of tens of thousands of families throughout the nation from the prospective tragedies of unemployment and the already growing welfare rolls.' Haughton cited the testimony of James Quillin, president of Lodge 727, International Association of Machinists and Aerospace Workers , the union representing most of Lockheed's L-1011 workforce, that only one in ten of the 9000 Lockheed employees already laid off as a result of slowdowns in the trijet program has been able to find other work.

'By far the greatest majority of those laid off are collecting unemployment,' he said. 'Some who have used up their savings and are unable to make out on their meagre unemployment benefits already are collecting welfare.'

'How ironic it is,' Haughton said, 'that we have before our government today a precedent-setting program to provide $2.25 billion in cash - that is cash, not loan guarantees - to provide re-training and public-works jobs for already-displaced workers, while we worry about a precedent of $250 million for loan guarantees that would save 60,000 already-existing jobs.

'And that would be the consequence of failure to approve the loan-guarantee legislation - to throw thousands more out of work, bringing disruption and suffering to as many as 60,000 families.'

Elsewhere, action on the Lockheed loan guarantee bill on Capitol Hill was largely taking place behind the scenes, as the Senate Banking Committee prepared to open hearings on a new broader bill that could provide emergency relief for other companies as well as Lockheed. Meanwhile, the House Banking Committee postponed the opening of its hearings on the loan guarantee legislation until 13 July.

Towards the Climax

'To sum up, this guarantee does not constitute a substantial risk to the government. It can prevent the waste of virtually all the $1.4 billion that has been invested in the TriStar. It can mean so much in human terms in preventing personal dislocations and unemployment. It can maintain beneficial competition in the trijet market. It can be an asset to the economy if it continues, rather than a deterrent if it fails.'

So said Dan Haughton, board chairman, battling for the survival of a Lockheed he has served so well for thirty-two years. When he finished his statement to the Senate Banking Committee, Senator Proxmire, a consistent and outspoken critic of Lockheed and foe of the Administration-backed legislation to guarantee $250 million in added bank loans for Lockheed, paid this tribute:

'I have great admiration for your ability as an administrator and as a salesman. Although I have not agreed with you, I think you have been a most responsive witness and you have done an excellent job for your cause today.'

Even TV crews crowded around Haughton to press their congratulations. Reporters who had wanted to seek him out for questioning during earlier committee sessions were astonished to recognize the man who had been quietly seated in the hearing room all week long observing every moment in the proceedings.

As Haughton spoke on 11 June, the small hearing room was crowded with about 150 people, with standees lining both sides and the rear. His four and a half-hour appearance was a dramatic highlight of the Senate committee's hearings. Haughton said that without the help being sought, he knew of no way to save Lockheed from bankruptcy.

Treasury Secretary John B Connally opened the Senate committee sessions on 7 and 8 June ably presenting the Administration's request for the legislation and forthrightly defending it under sharp questioning by Senator Proxmire. The next day Deputy Defense Secretary Packard endorsed the proposed guarantee, cautioning that he hoped it would not set a precedent for other embattled defence contractors.

On 10 June, FAA Chief John Shaffer underscored the TriStar airliner's importance in maintaining competition in the promising airbus market. Later that day, CAB head Secor Browne said the legislation to keep Lockheed in the world airliner market was probably 'the nail to save the horseshoe' in view of the rising competitive threat from consortiums in Europe.

Haughton's appearance on 11 June was followed on 14 June by those of James Kerr, Avco chairman; Charles Tillinghast Jr., TWA chairman; Floyd Hall, Eastern Air Lines chairman; C J Medberry, Bank of America chairman; and William Moore, Bankers Trust chairman.

'We have almost within our grasp the best ship yet produced from an environmental standpoint,' said Tillinghast. 'What purpose would be served by turning all this into junk? The only effect would be to create vast economic loss and unemployment.'

Hall stressed the importance of competition, saying that 'one of the main reasons the DC-10 and L-1011 will each be exceptional airplanes is that the intense competition between the two is producing exceptionally high-quality performance.'

Medberry and Moore emphasised that the proposed guarantee was in the public interest and that it would cost taxpayers far less than the collapse of the company.

First witness the following day was US Senator

N1011 seen parked on the ramp between test flights. *(Lockheed)*

Lowell Weicker of Connecticut, who struck at Lockheed's use of British engines in the L-1011 and at the generous financing arrangements made available to TriStar customers by the British government. Fred Borch, General Electric chairman, pursued the attack on the use of Rolls-Royce engines and lashed at 'the demand of our new competitor . . . that the US government see to it that Lockheed as its customer is capable of paying its bills so as to minimize the competitive risks involved.'

Testimony on 14 June by A Ernest Fitzgerald dealt mostly with his viewpoint on the C-5A Galaxy cost growths.

The next witness was Arthur F Burns, chairman of the Federal Reserve system, who called for the establishment of machinery under which other corporations, as well as Lockheed, could borrow money with a government guarantee.

Jack Vollbrecht, Aerojet-General president, testified in opposition to the proposal, as did Leonard Woodcock, head of the UAW, which represented most of the labour force building the McDonnell Douglas DC-10. Floyd Smith, president of the IAM said the refusal to help the company would destroy 30,000 jobs and throw as many as 90,000 other people out of work.

The House Banking Committee approved a $2 billion emergency loan fund on 21 July that would enable Lockheed to obtain the loan guarantees it needed and reported the bill out to the House Floor.

Prospects brightened a week earlier for the $250 million guaranteed loan Lockheed needed to continue the L-1011 TriStar programne and avert bankruptcy:

- Rep. Wright Patman, chairman of the House Banking Committee, declared himself in favour of some form of aid to Lockheed and said he wanted Congress to approve it before the month-long recess starting 6 August.
- The House committee agreed by consensus to end by 20 July the public hearings that opened 13 July with an eloquent statement by Dan Haughton. The committee planned to immediately start writing a bill.
- The Senate Banking Committee on 13 July approved by a 10 to 5 vote a bill that would set up a three-man board to make up to $2 billion in loans and up to $250 million to one company under conditions Lockheed would qualify.

Purpose of the loans, to be granted for a limited time period, would be to aid solvent businesses suffering from a temporary liquidity problem, who have exhausted their other sources of financing and whose collapse would seriously hurt the national economy or the economy of a region. The Treasury Department has said Lockheed's would be the first application considered.

The board would be made up of the treasury secretary as chairman, the chairman of the Federal Reserve Board, and the Federal Reserve Bank president in the district in which the loan applicant was located. Congress would have veto power starting 1 October over loan guarantees proposed by the board.

Senate Democratic Leader Mike Mansfield scheduled Senate debate on the bill to start that week and said its prospects of passing had improved.

Patman's endorsement of loan guarantee legislation was first disclosed in a news conference

Board chairmen of three of the USA's largest banks were amongst the twenty-four bankers to talk to the House Banking Committee's hearing on Lockheed Aircraft's request for federal backing on a $250 million loan. From the left were Chauncey J Medbury III of the Bank of America, San Francisco; William H Moore of Banks Trust Co, New York, and John M Meyer Jr of Morgan Guarenty Trust, New York.

Ladies and Gentlemen, from the Flight Deck...'

The Captain's and First Officer's main instrument panels were designed according to Federal Aviation Regulations, which specified the conventional T arrangement for the primary flight instruments. The panels contained all of the primary flight and navigational instruments required to operate the aircraft over any airline route in the world. Instruments other than those required to fill the basic T were grouped around the T in accordance with normal priority requirements.

Extensive use of remote sensors and air data computers permitted the use of servoed instruments in those cases where pneumatic instruments were previously used. The servoed instruments exhibited considerable improvements in accuracy and legibility over their pneumatic counterparts, due in part to the use of digital readouts.

The instrument panels were equipped with weather radar indicators. Consideration was given to panel growth for space to be used for other displays and controls. Adequate panel space was available for the future incorporation of pictorial navigation displays. Space provisions were also available on the First Officer's panel for the addition of true airspeed and static air temperature indicators. All instruments were front-mounted and clamp retained for ready removal during maintenance. All sub (control) panels conformed, where practical, to standard Aeronautical Radio Incorporated (ARINC) sizes.

Both pilots' instrument panels include a vertical scale radar altimeter indicator and an Automatic Flight Control System (AFCS) annunciator panel. These panels are so placed that little or no eye movement is necessary, from looking straight ahead, to operate the glare shield mounted AFCS control panel.

The centre instrument panel contained engine performance instruments, the landing gear control, a flap position indicator, a main annunciator panel for alerting trouble in various key subsystems, and the standby flight instruments.

The conventional electro-hydraulic landing gear control was located on the right side of the centre panel. Position indicator lights were located below the landing gear control lever and provided indications of both the nose and main gear and their respective doors.

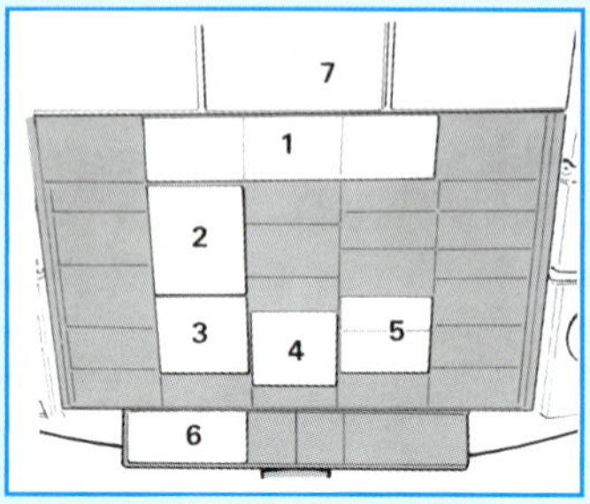

1. Engine Fire Warning and Extinguishing Controls.
2. Stability Augmentation System Panel.
3. Primary Flight Control System Panel.
4. Engine Start Panel.
5. Anti Ice Controls.
6. Exterior Lighting Panel.
7. Overhead Remote Control Circuit Breaker Panel.

The overhead control panel (above) contained the emergency shutdown handles and fire extinguisher discharge controls for the engines, all anti-icing system controls, the flight control electronic system controls, and antiskid system controls, and miscellaneous other controls.

The overhead essential circuit breaker panel was designed with pushbutton type circuit breakers recessed to minimise the possibility of accidental actuation. This panel was primarily accessible to the Flight Engineer but was easily monitored by the pilots.

The centre console was designed to provide the Flight Engineer with a clear view of the engine instruments and to provide all three crew members with access to any of the controls. Space provisions were included for control panels for area/inertial navigation and a pictorial display. Mechanization of instrument and display was being developed in conjunction with the development of the L-1011 Category III all-weather landing system.

A brake system selector switch was located on the center instrument panel and permitted choice of the normal or alternate braking system. A brake pressure indicator was located adjacent to the selector switch.

The annunciator panel provided a warning indication to direct attention to any of the on-board systems, Line Replaceable Units (LRU) or functions which were in an abnormal condition. The legend lights were caused to pulsate for a nominal ten seconds prior to going steady, thus providing an attraction stimulus. A reset button was provided to reactivate the annunciator panel following a warning and subsequent corrective action.

1. Fire and Overtemperature Warnings and Controls
2. Hydraulic System
3. Engine Bleed Controls (Pneumatic System)
4. Cabin Pressure Controls (ECS)
5. Electrical
6. Engine Instruments
7. Auxiliary Power Unit Controls
8. Door Position Annunciator
9. Fuel System
10. Remote Control Circuit Breaker Panel

The Flight Engineer's station arrangement was designed with the following features:

- Critical instrument displays and controls at eye level to provide quick observation and access.
- The overhead control panel and centre console easily reached by the Flight Engineer who could perform all his normal duties without disturbance to the pilots.
- Separate lighting was employed and used without causing annoyance to the pilots.
- Generous workspace for log entries, information checking, and performance of routine paperwork.

All of the Flight Engineer's communications and systems controls remained accessible while he is in a forward-facing position. Thus, he was free to attend to powerplant monitoring and control duties during takeoff, thereafter to operate communications and control, yet supplement traffic surveillance during the initial climb.

Each subsystem of the Flight Engineer's composite panel was arranged as a schematic logical flow diagram. The display of the system source was at the top and users at the bottom. System instruments and controls were located in the correct relative position in the schematic, and where possible, switches displayed an illuminated flow path when actuated.

The significant feature of fault diagnosis offered by the flow diagram concept is illustrated by the Engine Bleed Control panel (centre) which depicts the bleed air and pressurisation systems. The Flight Engineer might identify a fault location down to the Line Replaceable Unit (LRU) level. This is possible from a cross-check of the system function, as visually indicated by the flow diagram section of the panel, and by an abnormal duct temperature as indicated on the monitor section.

Once diagnosed, the fault could be circumvented by proper manipulation of override controls to isolate the bypass the defective unit.

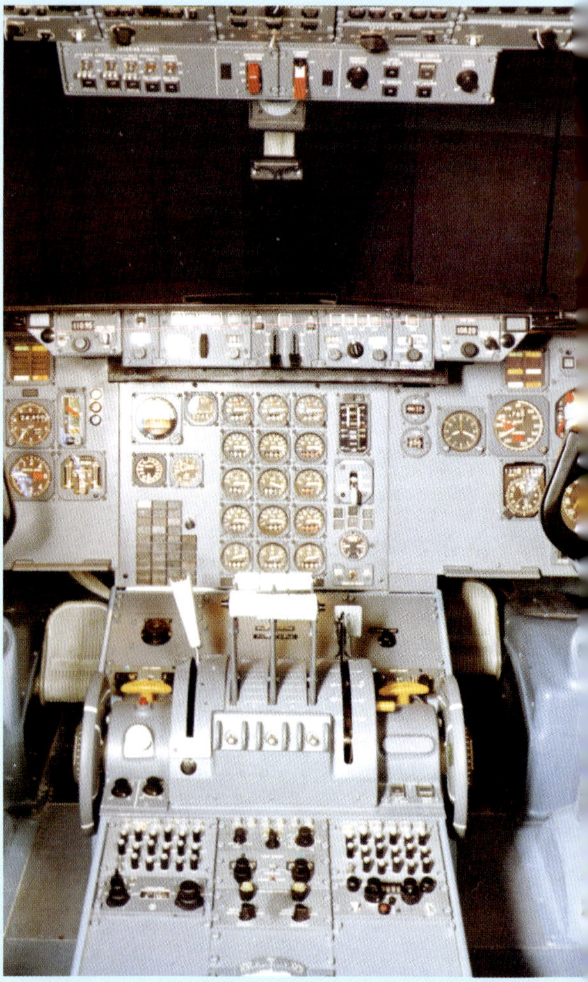

The glareshield panel contained the master/fire warning lights and the AFCS controls. Included in the AFCS control panel were five subpanels:

- Altitude Select (Hold) Panel.
- Heading/Pitch Control Panel.
- Autopilot Flight Director System (APFDS) Control Panel.
- Autothrottle Control Panel System (ATS).
- Navigation System Mode Panel, including Course Select.

At the time the AFCS had the capability for automatically controlled flight through category IIB landings. But, because space was available and wiring was installed, the L-1011 AFCS had a growth capability for category III landings.

Lockheed did offer the L-1011 with a more conventional 'round instrument' centre panel compared to that of vertical 'tape' indicators.

at the National Press Club on the evening of 14 July when he said it was too late to send Lockheed back to private investors for the funding it needed because there was too much sentiment in the House to provide some form of aid to Lockheed. He had opened the House committee's hearing the day before.

Haughton told the committee that 'perhaps the biggest loser of all would be the US government' in case of Lockheed's failure to obtain a government loan guarantee.

'The loss of income tax revenues alone is estimated . . . at more than half a billion dollars," he noted. He then went on to call out several other facts that could adversely affect the government and the taxpayer: 'We must keep in mind that a bankruptcy trustee is required by law to protect equally the interests of all creditors; he cannot favour one . . . even though that one might be the government.

'There is a distinct possibility that a trustee would challenge the settlement under which Lockheed accepted a $124 million loss on the Cheyenne helicopter and a $200 million fixed loss on the C-5A. He might well seek through the courts, and win, a more favourable interpretation of the original C-5A contract - an interpretation that would result in a smaller loss, even a profit.'

He quoted Deputy Defense Secretary Packard's statement that it might cost the government $100 million to $300 million more to complete the C-5A in the event of a Lockheed bankruptcy. And he estimated that 'the failure of Lockheed could involve an overall cost of as much as $1 billion to federal, state, and local governments.'

Haughton hit hard, as he did before the National Press Club on 28 June at the $20 billion monopoly that would be handed to McDonnel Douglas and General Electric if Lockheed is forced out of the wide-bodied trijet commercial airliner market, which he said would be 'perhaps the largest single monopoly market in the world.'

He said official reports filed with the CAB showed price reductions of at least $1 million on both DC-l0's and the L-1011s as a result of competitive pressure. He pointed out that the airlines had received guarantees never before offered on a new aircraft and more favourable payment terms.

Haughton acknowledged that some people tend to blame Lockheed's management 'for its present situation, especially in connection with its disputed defense programs, and declared: before the introduction of total package procurement, Lockheed's management had a very good track record.'

'I could understand people being critical of Lockheed's management if we had comparable problems on our other programs - programs not covered by the total package. But this has not been the case.'

'I could understand such criticism if a total package had been workable for other companies and was an obviously successful form. But this has not been the case either.'

'But I would also say that I am proud of Lockheed's overall record and I am proud of our people. This is not for me that I am speaking, but for our officers, managers, supervisors and employees—who have worked hard through the years and, I believe, have earned the position that Lockheed has occupied as the nation's No. 1 defense contractor in seven of the past ten years.'

President Nixon signed the Emergency Loan Guarantee Act of 1971 into law on 9 August 1971, paving the way for the several additional steps required to qualify Lockheed for federal guarantees authorized under the act for additional bank loans.

Actions were under way in meetings with airline customers, banks, and the government to promptly complete the remaining steps before the guarantees caould be executed. These were:

- Firm agreements with our TriStar airline customers to absorb price increases and reaffirm their orders.
- A firm agreement with the banks to increase Lockheed's credit line from $400 million to $650 million.
- Firm agreements with the three launching TriStar airlines to make additional or accelerated prepayments totalling $100 million. In addition to the bank credit agreement, these agreements were necessary to complete the required total $750 million financing package.
- The British government's final agreement with Rolls-Royce (1971) Ltd. for funding satisfactory to complete development and production of the RB211 engine used on the TriStar.

The loan guarantee act established a three-man board under Treasury Secretary Connally's chairmanship that must pass upon Lockheed's application for a government loan guarantee. A formal application would be ready for review at the first meeting of the board.

Dan Haughton started action on the remaining TriStar steps promptly after the Senate's favorable vote on loan guarantee legislation on 2 August, leaving the very next day for England and two days of talks with Rolls-Royce officials.

After reporting on progress to British Aerospace Minister Frederick Corfield, Haughton told the press prior to his return flight that he expected to have the TriStar programme 'back together in a matter of weeks.'

His answer to a question as to whether recent troubles of Rolls-Royce and Lockheed might deter prospective customers was firm and clear. 'I don't think so. Look at the situation. Rolls is backed by the UK government, and that's as sound as you can get. We've now had our Congress approve a bill to guarantee a loan - not loan us money - with our banks which we think is sufficient not only to finance us during the L-1011 but our defense and other programs.'

'I think there is a reason for prospective customers to have confidence. And, besides, when we get through with this airplane-engine combination, this is going to be the best - and people like to buy the best.'

He also reaffirmed confidence in the overall sales potential. Asked if Lockheed would eventually get orders to break even on the programme, Haughton declared: 'Our economy is picking up, and we think it will pick up some more, which will bring on increased air travel. I'm more optimistic about the long haul . . . We're still forecasting that airline travel will grow by an average of ten per cent a year through the decade of the 70s. We're forecasting that by 1980 we'll get enough orders to more than break even.' He explained he was referring to a breakeven point of 255 to 265 TriStar sales, which Lockheed has previously disclosed.

The contract-signing in New York - where executives of the Treasury Department, Rolls-Royce, twenty-four lending banks and four airlines met Lockheed Chairman Dan Haughton on 14 September 1971 to execute documents ensuring the financing of the L-1011 TriStar programme, had little visible effect on the men and women building and testing the TriStars in Palmdale and Burbank. They were too busy carrying the programme forward.

The news nevertheless proved heartening to those who remained on the job during the previous seven tumultuous months, as well as those recalled from the lay-ofis that followed the collapse of Rolls-Royce the previous February.

Indicative of the British engine-maker's renascence is the fact that the first three service-standard RB211 engines - which arrived from Rolls-Royce over the Labor Day weekend - were immediately put in use on an L-1011 TriStar in the flight-test programme at Palmdale. 'Service-standard' meant a 42,000 pounds thrust engine of the type all the TriStars will be equipped with when they entered airline service the following April.

Three L-1011s assigned to the flight-test programme so far had logged more than 530 hours, and Chief Test Engineer J E Hawkes said the airliner would enter airline service next year meeting or exceeding all of its performance guarantees.

'We are now about one-third through the flight test schedule,' Hawkes explained, 'and testing to date has turned up no requirement for significant changes in the L-1011 airframe or external systems.'

Hawkes said the TriStar had shown exceptional stability in flight and was free of vibration and flutter all the way to its maximum design speed of 660 mph, well above the speed at which the airliner was expected to operate in airline service.

Tests to date, Hawkes said, demonstrate that the TriStar would better its performance guarantees in two areas - its low noise levels and its superior capability for automatic landings. Measurements bore out Lockheed's claim that the TriStar, with its Rolls-Royce engines, was quieter than any commercial jet aircraft then flying or scheduled to enter airline service.

Previously the TriStar had taken off at a maximum weight of 404,570 pounds and had flown at an altitude of 42,000 feet.

'Testing of the TriStar's autoland system continues,' Hawkes said, 'but evaluation of more than fifty automatic landings to date proves that the TriStar's ability to operate routinely from airports under poor weather conditions will exceed the guarantees to airlines.'

Hawkes said formal certification demonstrations of the TriStar for the FAA would begin in mid-November and continue until the aircraft received its type certificate in mid-April 1972.

With three TriStars currently conducting flight tests, a fourth was undergoing a series of extensive ground tests required before the start of formal in-flight demonstrations for the FAA. The fifth TriStar would begin flying late in 1971.

When Air Canada officials announced that they had signed a renegotiated contract with Lockheed for the ten L-1011 Tristars they had on order, they also revealed that they had secured options for nine additional TriStars. The aircraft would be delivered to Air Canada in early 1973 and 1974 and would initially be used on routes in Canada, the US, and the Caribbean.

'We have always believed that the L-1011 was an aircraft which would suit our marketing and operations requirements extremely well,' Yves Pratte,

Air Canada's chairman, said when they made the announcement. 'We are pleased that Lockheed has been able to overcome its financial difficulties and can now go ahead with production of this fine aircraft.'

He said Air Canada had made exhaustive studies of the alternatives available and that in the end this aircraft still stood out as the best for the particular needs of Air Canada.

Air Canada President John Baldwin stated, 'This big new airplane will be extremely popular with our passengers. It combines many features that will make it the most comfortable of the new generation of aircraft. Tests have shown that the TriStar is the quietest commercial jetliner in the air and that its engines are virtually smokefree.'

Picking up the pieces.

The company immediately drew $100 million in guaranteed loans, and its borrowing under the Act peaked at $245 million in September 1974. The last $60 million in guaranteed loans were converted to conventional bank loan on 14 October 1977, and, since then, the company had access to the credit market under traditional terms and conditions without further utilisation of the Government guarantee. Lockheed had been saved.

It is worth noting, however, that the banks were the one's lending funds to the company - the Government only provided its guarantee, and no taxpayers' money was lent to Lockheed. In return for this guarantee, the Government earned over $31 million, net of administrative expenses of slightly less than $1 million, between August 1971 and October 1977.

These earnings, which were transferred to the Treasury to be used as general funds, included approximately $25 million in cumulative guarantee fees (at an annual rate of two per cent) on the borrowings, $2 million in commitment fees on the unused portion of the credit, and $5 mn in cumulative interest on the charges. Furthermore, throughout its guarantee commitment, the Government's position was fully secured by a first lien on Lockheed assets which consistently were valued more than the maximum authorised loan guarantees by both the GAO (General Accounting Office) and the Guarantee Board.

With the implementation of the Emergency Loan Guarantee Act and the assurance that Rolls-Royce (1971) Ltd would deliver the initial batch of 555 engines under a renegotiated contract, Lockheed could again get back to work in earnest on the TriStar programme, and 9,000 employees, who had been laid off at the time of the Rolls-Royce receivership, were rehired. The L-1011 received its FAA Type Approval on 14 April 1972 and entered scheduled service with Eastern Air Lines twelve days later. Other aircraft programmes which could then be continued were those for the Orion and Viking at CALAC (Lockheed-California Company), and for the Hercules, JetStar and Galaxy at GELAC (Lockheed-Georgia Company). The new financing was indeed much needed by Lockheed as, after taking into account a change in accounting practice to charge development costs against current earnings, it reported net losses of $187.8 millon in 1970, $394 million in 1971 and $7.2 million in 1972. Profitability was restored in 1973, with net profits of $18.2 million being reported for that year and of $23.2 million for 1974. Likewise, the following five years brought a total profit of $260.8 mn. As the company's

Lockheed Chairman Dan Haughton, left, prepares to sign documents that provided the company with necessary bank loans to finance L-1011 TriStar programme. With him were Samuel R. Pierce Jr., general counsel for Treasury Department and executive director of the Emergency Loan Guarantee Board authorised by Congress, and Timothy Greene, secretary of the board, right. Officials of twenty-four banks, four airlines and Rolls-Royce (1971) Ltd. also signed documents on 14 September 1971. *(Lockheed)*

management, staff and backers were finally able to breathe sighs of relief, a new calamity struck.

In the post-Southeast Asia War period, the American public and press became increasingly suspicious of big business in general and more especially of the companies from the military-industrial complex. In particular, the so-called questionable practices involving a double standard - one standard of propriety for sales in the United States and a quite different standard for transactions in foreign countries - came under scrutiny. Thus, in June 1975 allegations of improper payments abroad by Lockheed began appearing in the press as a result of a Senate Subcommittee's investigation of similar practices by the Northrop Corporation.

Lockheed's independent auditor, Arthur Young and Company, then requested that certain company officers sign a letter stating that:

- All payments were made following agreements and were duly recorded on the books of Lockheed;
- No employee or official of any foreign government or any director, officer or employee of a customer was a party to any of the agreements;
- No director, officer, or managerial employee of Lockheed or an affected subsidiary knew the disposition of payments made to consultants.

Dan Haughton, the company's Chairman of the Board, did not allow the officers in question to sign the requested letter. This refusal led to a joint investigation of commissions and questionable payments by a special review committee of the Board of Directors and Arthur Young and Company. Investigations revealed illegal bribes and contributions made by Lockheed officials from the late 1950s to the 1970s. In late 1975 and early 1976, a subcommittee of the US Senate led by Senator Frank Church concluded that members of the Lockheed board had paid members of friendly governments to guarantee contracts for military aircraft. In 1976, it was publicly revealed that Lockheed had spent $22 million in bribes to foreign officials in the process of negotiating the sale of aircraft including the F-104 Starfighter, the so-called Deal of the Century. The scandal caused political controversy in West Germany, the Netherlands, Italy, and Japan. In the US, the scandal led to the passage of the Foreign Corrupt Practices Act and nearly led to the ailing corporation's downfall.

As a result, tight controls on the hiring of foreign consultants and the payment of overseas marketing commissions were adopted by the Board in September 1975. Finally, on 13 February 1976, Haughton resigned as chairman of the Board and A. Carl Kotchian, vice-chairman and president, was forced to do so. On the same date a new top echelon, with Robert W. Haack as chairman, Roy A. Anderson as vice-chairman, and Lawrence O Kitchen as president and the chief operating officer took over to implement the new policy and restore confidence in Lockheed. Outside the company, the bribery scandal and related allegations resulted in the fall of foreign government officials and the dismissal of officers from airlines and trading companies.

For Lockheed, the final phase in this unfortunate affair, which also plagued other US corporations and remained a sad fact of life involving non-US companies, came on 13 April 1976, when the Securities and Exchange Commission led a complaint against Lockheed Aircraft Corporation and its two former top executives, Haughton and Kotchian. The main thrust of the claim was that Lockheed had violated the Securities Exchange Act of 1934 by failing to disclose that it had

- Made payments to foreign government officials,
- Used secret funds for that purpose, and
- Hidden these activities by falsifying its financial records and reports.

On the same day, without conceding the truth of the facts alleged, or admitting the illegality of any of its conduct, Lockheed consented to the entry of a permanent injunction and filed an undertaking which together:

- Enjoined it from any activities of the kind described in the complaint;
- Provided for the establishment of a special review committee to investigate the matters alleged in the complaint;
- Provided the procedure under which the committee should make its report to the Board of Directors and the methods under which the directors should transmit it to the SEC and the Court; and
- Provided that Lockheed could seek an order from the Court sealing material, the disclosure of which could injure the interest of Lockheed and its stockholders.

The report and recommendations of the Special Review Committee were transmitted on 16 May 1977.

Chapter Five

Build

When the decision was made to go ahead with the L-1011 programme in mid-1968 the Lockheed - California Company began constructing a manufacturing facility to build the TriStar in an area ideally suited to aviation development. Excellent year-around flying weather and civic-mindedness already oriented toward aviation were major factors that prompted Lockheed to select the city of Palmdale, in Antelope Valley, for what was then the site of one of the world's most advanced technology fabrication and assembly plants to produce the world's most advanced technology airliner.

Lockheed and Palmdale were already no strangers. During the production peaks at the height of the Korean emergency, Lockheed needed a supplemental field for flight testing of the planes as they rolled out of the assembly plant at Van Nuys. To fill the need, the company leased 225 acres at Palmdale Airport and built a $400,000 flight station there which began operations in 1951. The idea was to transfer the sometimes hazardous flight test work away from the growing air traffic, smog, unpredictable weather and the population explosion around the Los Angeles area.

About the same time, the company purchased 677 acres of land adjacent to a $30,000,000 facility the Air Force was building at Palmdale, an isolated spot, where they would build the XB-70 supersonic bomber. At the turn of the decade, and occupying slightly more than one-third of this Lockheed-owned property bordering Air Force Plant 42 and a US Government airport with 12,000-foot runways, TriStars could roll out of the huge final assembly hangar at the rate of about ten a month.

Lockheed's Plant 10 in Antelope Valley, Palmdale. *(Lockheed)*

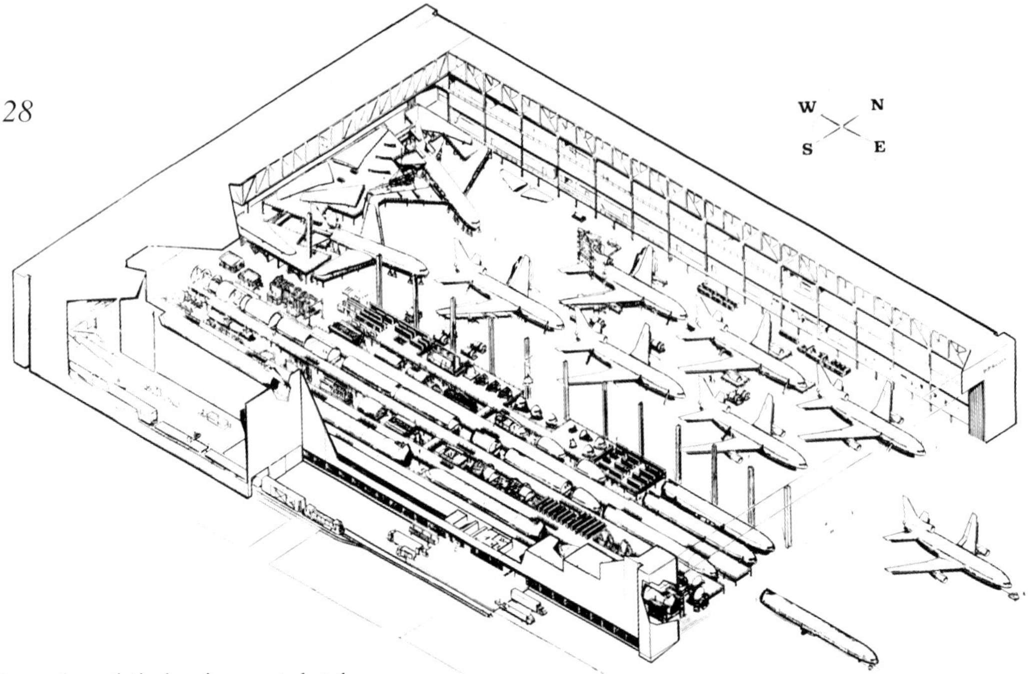

Above: An artist's drawing created at the time of construction shows the interior arrangement of the huge final assembly building at Lockheed-California Company's Palmdale plant. The build-up of L-I011 fuselages is in the foreground with the start of assembly at the lower left. Wing mate is at upper left, and to the right is final assembly. Note: trucks and railroad bringing in materials and various sub-assemblies.

Left: prospective L-1011 flight attendants are given the tour as part of their training. *(both Lockheed)*

Designated Plant 10, the more than $50,000,000 seven-building complex was designed specifically to incorporate the most advanced concepts in aircraft production and logistical support. The Plant, surrounded by the Mojave Desert's Joshua trees and cedars, enclosed nearly 1,300,000 square feet of floor space under one roof. It was located forty-two airline miles north of Los Angeles, twenty minutes flying time, about an hour by road from Lockheed Aircraft Corporation's main office and plants at Burbank. More than 6,000 people would eventually work there.

Indeed, the Lockheed-California Company's Palmdale final assembly and flight test complex changed the whole area's appearance. As someone once said, 'It has turned the desert green!'

The reason that the distance Palmdale was from Burbank was quoted in 'flying time' was simple; Lockheed operated an airborne shuttle service between the two sites. Anyone working in Burbank but had to go to Palmdale on business - either sporadically or fairly regularly - had the opportunity of taking the air-shuttle service flights that regularly operated out of Plant B-6.

As the company explained to employees: 'Have your department manager make your reservation by 3 pm the day before your flight, by calling Howard Gannon on Ext. 75703 (Frank Derby on Ext. 2508, if you're stationed in Palmdale and headed for Burbank).'

'DC-3 flights leave Building 346 in Burbank at 6 am, 8:30 am, and 3:45 pm, arriving in Palmdale 25 minutes after departure; and leave Palmdale at 6:35 am, 11:30 am and 5 pm each weekday for Burbank.

'A 737 jet operated for the company by PSA as a charter flight leaves Burbank for Palmdale at 6:30 am and leaves Palmdale for Burbank at 3:45 pm each weekday for assigned day-shift personnel.'

As they walked up to the Administration Building entrance, visitors would see that the site accommodated offices for Lockheed personnel,

Two views inside Lockheed's Plant 10 in Antelope Valley, Palmdale in early June 1970 as the tailplane, fin and wings start to come together on the first TriStar.

The wing mate began on 20 May, and it was not long before the aircraft was sitting on its own landing gear. *(both Lockheed)*

customer airline representatives, and ground training facilities for future TriStar pilots. The once brown and barren desert floor had been transformed into green grass and flower beds!

The two year transformation was a huge task. Contractors William Simpson Co., Butler Construction Co. and C and I Construction Co. used 20,000 tons of structural steel to frame the buildings. They poured 183,000 cubic yards of concrete for factory floors, parking ramps and taxiways.

TriStar subassemblies and other production materials flowed into the plant by truck, air, and rail. The latter was along a spur line also had to be built directly onto dual sidings inside a wing of the main assembly building. The structure towered 115 feet high, and measured 900 feet by 590 feet, creating a total of 868,522 square feet on the first floor alone.

Lockheed employed Ted Wilson as a dedicated Public Relations representative for Plant 10, giving customers and members of the press tours of the site. There was even a special viewing platform high in the roof on the north wall so that visitors could overlook the factory floor.

Visitors could see at the end of the line, about to move out through the hangar doors was the latest structurally complete L-1011, recently out of the assembly fixtures, engines installed and resting on its own landing gear. After the installation of avionics and flight test instrumentation and checking the functional systems, it was towed over to the Production Flight Test hangar.

To its rear was another machine, the wings and empennage being mated with the fuselage. Further back, fuselage sections were mating. At one station a complete fuselage. At another, wings were being moved into mating position. Here, the empennage, towering rudder and horizontal stabilizer moving into position, there, a nose section complete with Flight Deck. There, the long circular main cabin section was coming together, with workmen swarming over elevated platforms to reach the upper fuselage levels.

As production ramped up, it was not long before more than 1000 employees worked at Plant 10 in Palmdale, and a sizeable number of people assigned to the final assembly facility depended on the efficiency of ten women assigned to the TriStar blueprint control group in Dept. 32-84. This formed part of Calac's

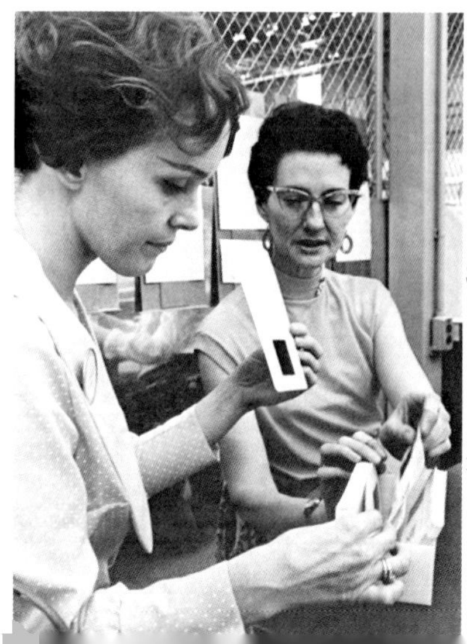

Above: Bonny Sprink, a blueprint control clerk picks up a bundle of drawings ready to file away on the shelves in the background.

Left: file clerk messenger Shirlie Jo Trewin (left) gets instruction on microfilm files from Billie Atkinson.

Right: Using a Xerox blueprint enlarging machine is Janie Maupin, a blueprint control clerk. *(all Lockheed)*

A pair of fuselage panels are prepared on their transport trollies to be placed into the autoclave in the background. *(Lockheed)*

microdata systems organisation in Bldg. 171 at Plant B-1 provided an invaluable service. The specialised unit is part of the photographic and reproduction department, 82-21.

The microdata systems organisation was designed and developed by Marshall Stowell. Employees working in the microdata systems unit reduced mountains of documentation to 35mm microfilm and also transferred statistical and scientific data to microfiche.

Of the maladies peculiar to large corporations in the late 1960s and one that had an impact on major aerospace companies such as Calac was the problem of mushrooming documentation. It is a common saying amongst the aircraft engineering fraternity that an aircraft is not ready to fly until the aircraft's weight is half that of the paperwork that has been generated.

The problem was complicated by the fact that complex technological advances must not only be recorded for history but supporting documentation must usually be reproduced hundreds of times and

Almost certainly a posed picture, but an interesting one nevertheless, for it shows inside the flight station with the temporary window supports in place before the window glazing is inserted. *(Lockheed)*

distributed throughout the company.

The thousands of documents and engineering drawings that detailled every conceivable phase of the L-1011 TriStar programme comprised a case in point. Copies of a single engineering drawing, for example, might be used by hundreds of employees.

By early 1970, members of this group controlled approximately 50,000 TriStar blueprints. And although the facility's L-1011 microfilm files were not completely filled at that time, it was estimated that about 120,000 microfilm cards, 35mm negative copies of engineering drawings, would soon be available.

Although it looks incredibly archaic now, with terrabytes of digital storage available on chips the size of a fingernail, at the time it was cutting edge technology. The decision to use the microfilm system was based on the compactness of the relatively new method, which had been in use a little more than a year. All TriStar engineering drawings were photographed in thirty-four by forty-four inch segments on the 35mm microfilm. Because of the complexity and sheer enormity of the L-1011 programme, it was impossible to maintain blueprint files, as was done on previous Calac programmes. There just was not enough storage space.

Multiple images were generally transferred to microfiche, which was 105mm film. On a single fiche, for example, there are 210 separate frames containing data. What's remarkable was that there were 85 microfiche on each 45 foot roll of film.

'In a single minute, by using our high-speed film duplicator, we can reproduce 133,120 pages of data,' explained one employee. Each week an average of 100,000 microfilm copy cards are distributed throughout Calac's engineering and

TriStar wings in production at Avco Aerostructures Division, Nashville, Tennessee. Six left wings for the TriStar are shown here in the final stages of production. Another six right wings are in a similar stage of completion in the plant area to the right, just out of shot. Jigs in which wing boxes are first built up can be seen in the background. Each wing was 88 feet long, 24 feet at the point of attachment, and tapered to four feet at the tip. Avco Aerostructures Division had a $575-million contract with Lockheed to produce wings for the new wide-bodied jet transport. *(Lockheed)*

Left: Milton McKinney, an instructor in Department 90-25, describes the L-1011 ring assembly technique to Robert Sheers, structural assembler at Building 12. Sheers was a recently gradulated trainee.

Below: Lockheed Board Chairman Dan Haughton, on the left, accepts the first L-1011 wing from James R Keer of Avco on 7 May 1970. *(both Lockheed)*

manufacturing areas. These copy cards represented the equivalent of 1,200,000 square feet of engineering drawings.

One of the busiest areas in Plant 10, the blueprint control booth offered employees use of four microfilm viewers. Since the microfilm was reproducible, a fresh, clean print was always available to each person within a few minutes. Enlarged copies from individual microfilm cards could be made on one of three Xerox machines.

Everything came together, even though some of the sub-assemblies were manufactured thousands of miles distant from the factory in the desert.

The breakdown of these major ones, and the value of contracts - in 1969 dollars - issued during the initial phase was as follows:

Kawasaki Aircraft Co, Japan. Passenger & Cargo Doors - $13.3 million.

Instrument Systems, NYC. Passenger services & Entertainment System - $19.1 million.

Bristol Aerospace Ltd, Canada. Aft Engine Duct - $12.6 million.

Northwest Industries, Canada. Pressure Bulkheads and floors - $27 million.

Bertea Corp, California. Stabilizer Pitch Control System - $13.6 million.

Western Gear Corp, California. Cargo Conveyor System - $10.4 million.

Air Cruisers Co. New Jersey. Escape Chute system - $11.0 million.

Curtis Wright Corp, New Jersey. Trailing Edge Flap Control - $26 million.

National Water Lift Co, Mich. Aileron and Rudder control - $13.9 million.

Aeronca, Ohio, Wing flaps - $30 million.

Menasco Mfg Co. Texas .Nose & Main Landing gear - $95.2 million.

B F Goodrich, Akron Ohio. Wheels, Tyres & Brakes - $5.2 million.

Goodyear Tire & Rubber Co. Ohio. Anti-skid system - $6.9 million.

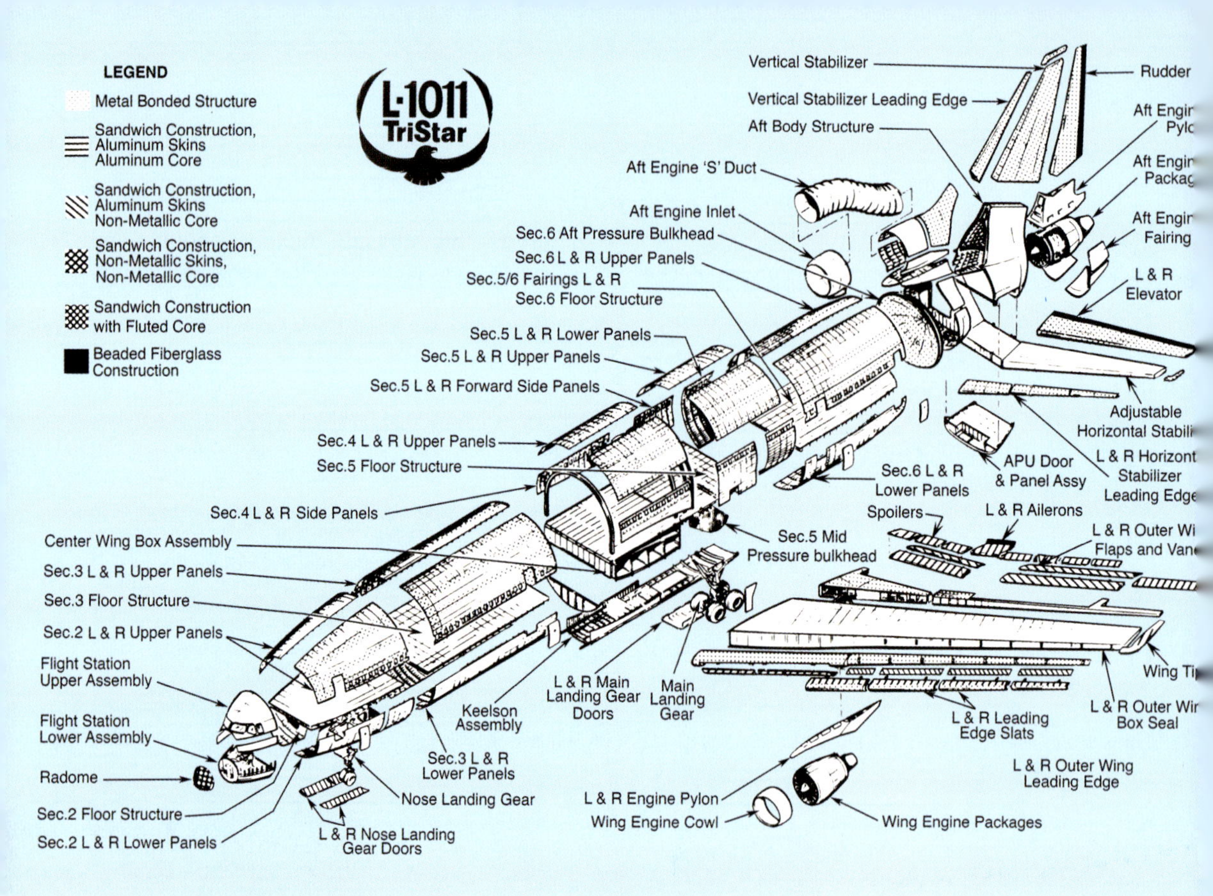

The sub-assemblies of the L-1011, along with details of which were made of composite materials. *(Lockheed)*

Sunderstrand Corp, Rockford, Illinois. Leading Edge Slat Control System, Constant Speed Control, Auxiliary Hydraulic Power System - $46.6 million.
Murdock Engineering Co. Texas. Engine Pylons - $33.8 million.
Sperry Flight Systems, Arizona. Air Data Computer, Flight Instruments - $24.3 million.
Lear Siegler Inc, California. Avionic Flight Control System - $8.8 million.
Collins Radio Co. Dallas, Texas. Avionic Flight Control System, Horizon Director Indicator - $70.7 million.
Sierracin Corp, Sylmar, California. Windshields - $7.8 million.
LTV Electrosystems Inc, Utah. Pitch, Feel & Trim system - $7.9 million.
Hamilton Standard, Conn. Integrated Pneumatic system - $78.7 million.
Grimes Manufacturing Co. Ohio. Interior Lighting, Coffee Makers - $13.7 million.
Avo, Tenn. Wings - $5.75 million.
Heath Techna Corp, Washington. Fairings, Cabin Attendant Seats - $22.8 million.

TriStar items were not only made around the USA and farther afield, but sub-assemblies were also manufactured in and around Los Angeles including at a new site constructed after the infamous Watts riots of August 1965.

The new complex was dedicated at a ceremony on 18 March 1970 as the Watts-Willowbrook Plant 12, Calac's then newest feeder plant.

The change was especially apparent to those officials of school districts, government agencies, and civic organizations who attended the ground-breaking ceremonies at the plant site a year earlier.

At that time the 6 ½-acre site on which Calac's new 104,000 square foot plant was located was a junkyard, which Calac took over as the first tenant of the newly established Watts Industrial Park, built in an effort to regenerate the area.

Those who attended the ceremonies heard President Chuck Wagner say in his dedication address: 'I think I should point out that we are recruiting unskilled, unemployed persons exclusively from this area. It is gratifying that many of our trainees can walk to work. This is exactly as it should be, because this entire project was conceived for the express purpose of helping people of this immediate community.'

'Forty-seven employees are currently being trained at Plant 12, and by the end of the year, approximately 150 persons will have been hired and trained for work on the TriStar program.'

Employees at the Watts-Willowbrook site manufactured TriStar fuselage bulkhead frames, cargo and galley underfloor transversals, insulation batts and numerous other L-1011 sub-assemblies.

Lockheed moved fast, for by the end of April 1970 the first batch of seventy-five fuselage bulkhead ring assemblies had been shipped to Plant B-6 from Plant 12, and production of cargo and galley underfloor support structures was due to start from there a month later. The first batch was delivered in June, with fifty of each making up a ship-set.

Days later - on 4 May 1970 - the first wing for Calac's L-1011 was presented to Lockheed Board Chairman Dan Haughton at Plant 10 in Palmdale by James R Kerr, president and CEO of Avco, which built the huge wings in its Nashville plant.

In a ceremony beside the eighty-eight-foot long, ten-ton left-wing, Kerr told Lockheed officials and newsmen that he believed that the L-1011 'will be the workhorse of the next several decades of commercial aviation.' He described the TriStar as 'big enough, flexible enough and economical enough to meet the needs of aviation into the supersonic era.'

Kerr pointed out that the L-1011 wing was the latest in a long series of Avco-built wings and other assemblies for Lockheed aircraft dating back to the early part of World War Two.

The first L-1011 wing was shipped from the Avco Aerostructures Division plant at Nashville to Palmdale aboard a 'Super Guppy' transport aircraft. The wings control surfaces, high-lift devices and other equipment were attached at Palmdale.

Haughton said the left and right wings would be mated to the first L-1011 fuselage just as scheduled more than two years previously when production of the TriStar was still in the planning stage.

Also present at the delivery ceremonies were Charles S Ames, vice-president and general manager of Avco's Aerostructures Division;

Never one to miss out on putting a pretty face, long legs and short skirt - which today would be called sexist, Lockheed's publicity department went to town showing the strength of their aircraft bonding technique. Here stenographer Judy Tolley points to a one-inch square of bonded aluminium (circled) that holds the entire weight of this car. In the inset picture the size of the bonded piece can be seen. *(both Lockheed)*

Lockheed President Carl Kotchian; Bill Moran, Calac executive vice-president for commercial programs, and representatives of all customer airlines.

Bonding not rivets.

Like other airliner manufacturers, Lockheed made widespread use of metal-to-metal bonding to produce a new generation of lighter, stronger, longer-lived commercial aircraft.

The bonding process was pioneered by Aero Research Ltd (ARL) at Duxford in the United Kingdom under a generic family name of Redux, which was and is a group of phenol-formaldehyde resin/polyvinyl-formaldehyde powder adhesives developed in the 1940s.

Devised at ARL by Dr Norman de Bruyne and George Newell in 1941 for use in the aircraft industry, the adhesive is used for the bonding of metal-to-metal and metal-to-wood structures.

De Havilland used it from 1943 to the early 1960s, on, among other aircraft, the Mosquito, Hornet, Comet and the derived Nimrod, and the Dove, Heron and Trident. It was also used by Vickers on the Viking and by Chance Vought on the F7U Cutlass.

In a meeting with the Society of Automotive Engineers at the Ambassador Hotel in Los Angeles, Jim Hong, manufacturing manager for the L-1011, told them that bonded aircraft structures already had been produced with much greater strength and longer life than is possible using the old method of riveting aluminium sheets together.

'For instance, Lockheed has developed an adhesive so strong that only one square inch of bonding between two straps of metal can hoist a standard American passenger car off the ground.'

As evidence of the strength of bonded assemblies, Hong described the results of tests conducted on production TriStar fuselage assemblies.

'In a typical test, 8000 loading cycles were required to propagate a crack from the edge to the center of a bonded titanium fail-safe strap, whereas only 3000 cycles were required for a crack to reach the same point in an otherwise identical structure with riveted straps.'

Hong said the traditional method of riveting together skin panel assemblies were satisfactory for propeller and earlier jet-powered aircraft, 'but bonding lends itself, especially to design and

A trio of L-1011s inch forward towards completion. Eastern's N313EA (msn 1020) was delivered 15 December 1972, while Eastern's msn 1022 in the foreground was registered as N314EA and delivered 2 Janury 1973. This suggests that the Air Canada aircraft was CF-TNB, msn 1021. *(Lockheed)*

Above: employees wear special dust-free clothing while applying adhesive to titanium straps to fuselage panels before moving into the autoclave for bonding.

Below: Driving a power cart, an employee pushes a loaded carrier into what was then the world's largest autoclave. *(both Lockheed)*

manufacture of the new wide-bodied generation of jetliners, and even more so to advanced aircraft not yet on the drawing boards.'

Hong said research indicated metal bonding could increase the strength of an aircraft structure 'to provide it with an essentially unlimited lifetime in routine commercial service without major repair.'

He predicted that eliminating costly recurring structural repair and the resulting increase in the usefulness of an aircraft to its airline operators would lead to widespread adoption of metal bonding among aircraft builders.

In addition to reducing structural fatigue, Hong said, 'extensive metal bonding contributes substantially toward the elimination of corrosion, a serious maintenance problem for many airlines.'

The TriStar, he pointed out, was produced with fuselage panels assembled through metal bonding. Reinforcing members, such as fail-safe straps and doublers around door and window openings were bonded to the aircraft's skin panels instead of being attached with rivets and other fasteners.

Because of its proved contribution to airframe simplicity and integrity, adhesive bonding of aircraft fuselage skin panels was employed more fully in the L-1011 TriStar than in any other aircraft to that date.

Since the aircraft design and fabrication technique also resulted in a lighter, more

Above: Emerging from this giant forming roll is an L-1011 aluminium fuselage section.

Below: skin panels for the TriStar move through an automatic cleaning system at Plant B. They were washed by a chemical spray to remove dirt and grease before titanium strips and doublers were bonded to them in Calac's autoclave. *(both Lockheed)*

maintainable airliner, TriStar designers sought to utilise the largest bonded panels possible within the then-current state of the art in airframe design.

TriStar fuselage panels ranged up to fifteen by thirty-eight feet, more than twice the size of the largest panels used in any other aircraft then either in service or scheduled for service. Twenty-seven panels were required for each TriStar, and production of the panels proved to be highly successful.

To produce these panels, as well as those of future commercial and military aircraft, Calac established an all-new metal bonding and processing complex in Building125 at Plant B-1. The facility was almost totally automated, with the panels travelling along five-and-a-half miles of mechanised overhead conveyor.

The complex was designed around three major pieces of equipment, each the largest of its type ever built. The forming roll and 500-ton stretch press shaped skin panels to the precise contours of the TriStar fuselage, and the giant autoclave bonded the panels to their underlying doublers and titanium fail-safe straps.

The skin itself was the aluminium alloy 2024-T3 Clad, a tough fatigue-resistant metal with high anti-corrosion properties. Its thickness ranged up to one-tenth of an inch.

Fabrication of a skin panel for the TriStar began in a receiving room where an important step was taken to preserve the aluminium's original gloss. The initial process was to spray a resilient protective material over the skin's exterior side, which remained on the surface throughout the metal bonding phase of production.

From the receiving area, the panels travelled by conveyor to the stretch press or forming roll where they are shaped into precise form to fit the TriStar fuselage.

If a panel was to be located in the tubular, or constant, section of the aircraft body, it was shaped in the forming roll; but if it was a part of the front or rear sections of the fuselage, requiring compound curves, it was processed in the stretch press.

The 500-ton press, built by Cyril Bath, was the largest hydro-mechanical unit of its type in existence. It could handle eight feet by forty feet aluminium skins, stretching them over a die that duplicated the aircraft's particular contour.

The forming roll, capable of handling panels up to thirty-eight feet long, was a pyramid forming machine more than twice as large as any existing precision roll. Built by the Farnham division of Lisk-Savory Corp., the machine consisted of three separate rolls that bent panels under pressure

Five L-1011s for TWA are visible in this picture with N31011. closest to the camera. Towards the rear is a single example for the German carrier LTU.

exerted by two hydraulic cylinders, each developing up to 300,000 pounds-force.

From the press or roll, skins went back onto the overhead conveyor and were transported to a storage area to await further processing. When needed, a skin was removed from storage and sent directly to a Purex-built cleaning line or to a prefit line where correct mating of components in the more complicated panels was conducted.

When fit of the skins, doublers and straps was assured, these tentative assemblies also went through the cleaning line, where a chemical spray washed them free of dirt, grease or other foreign matter. From the cleaning line, all skins and associated parts treated with a corrosion-inhibiting adhesive primer proceeded to clean storage.

With TriStar production at peak rate, thousands of skin panels occupied the storage areas. From clean storage, a panel entered a tape room for application of adhesive and layup of the doublers and straps. The panel was secured to a metal-bond fixture for layup, after which it was enclosed in a sealed plastic bag.

When ready for bonding, the bag was pumped free of air and the fixture inserted on a four-level carrier along with other panels. Air cushions were mounted at the four corners of the carrier to move it from the tape room to the autoclave, which could accommodate two carriers.

The air cushions, inverted pans connected to an air supply, lifted the carriers about a third of an inch off the floor by exerting pneumatic pressure slightly greater than the weight of the carrier and its load. With the air cushions operating, the carrier could be moved by workmen simply pushing it with their hands.

The autoclave operated like a giant pressure cooker. It was twenty-too foot in diameter and sixty feet long. It weighed 600,000 lb, including a thirty-ton door. Under the normal operating pressure of 125 psi, the door carried a load of seven million pounds.

The autoclave burners were capable of generating temperatures of 600 degrees Fahrenheit, but bonding in an atmosphere of inert gas is normally conducted at only 250 degrees. A complete bonding cycle, from heat-up to cool-down, lasted about two hours.

A unique feature of the autoclave was its ability to retrieve and hold for the next bonding cycle, 65 per cent of the heat used in the previous cycle. This advantage greatly speeded up bonding production.

After emerging from the autoclave, the bonded sections of the panel were subjected to ultrasonic inspection for flaws. After inspection, the interior surfaces of the panels were sprayed with a special anti-corrosion paint, and the panels were transported to the jigs where they were assembled into TriStar fuselage segments. At this point, the initial protective coating on the exterior of the panel was removed and replaced with another plastic coating more suited to the drilling and countersinking that took place during assembly.

This covering remained on the metal until the panel became part of a completed fuselage, ready for painting with airline colours.

Extensive use of metal bonding throughout the TriStar contributed toward Calac's goal of unlimited life for the aircraft fuselage in regular airline service. TriStar designers set this goal at the beginning of the programme, and both analysis and continuing structural testing indicated that it would be met.

The TriStar's structural integrity, however, resulted from a combination of factors. These included strength achieved through the combination of bonding, fasteners and riveting and the use of titanium fasteners and rivets of a new and more effective design. The reduced number of fuselage seams resulting from longer skin panels also provided improved integrity as well as reduced weight.

The Paint Shop at LockheedPalmdale contained a moving platform with eight working positions that allowed the entire fuselage to be sprayed at once after it had been masked off.

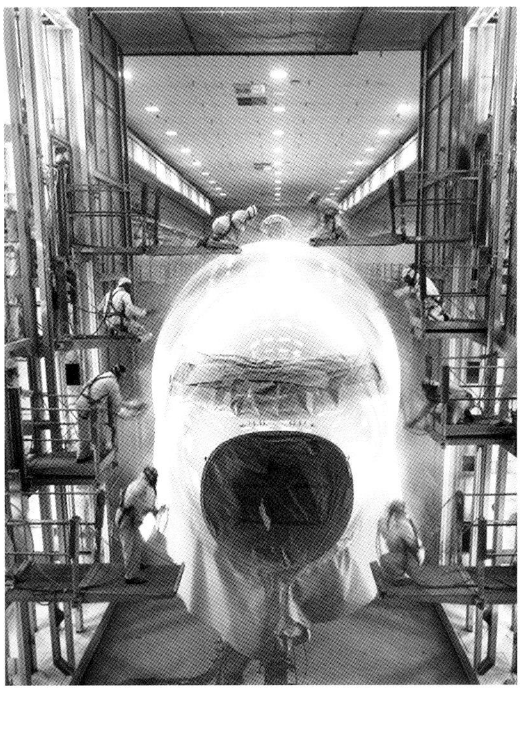

Court Line's G-BAAA's fuselage is moved from the spray-booth back into the assembly shop ready for installation of wings and tail. Note the concrete blocks hanging from the forward fuselage to keep the nosewheel on the ground. The '1024' is the manufacturers serial number. *(via Ed Posey)*

Painting the beast...

A helpful forty-six-ton monster helped paint the bodies of L-101 1 TriStars four times faster than they could be painted with conventional ladders and scaffolds.

The 'monster' was a huge moving paint gantry that carried eight painters and the gantry-operating crew along the L-1011's 178-foot long fuselage so that they could apply one coat of airline colours in just forty minutes. Using older methods, the job would take about four hours, said Bill Larson, manager of the L-1011 Fuselage Mate and Pre-Final Division. Painters sprayed each fuselage with an average of four coats enough to paint approximately one hundred standard passenger cars.

'The new gantry gives airlines higher quality paint jobs on their L-1011's because it's easy for painters to reach any area of the fuselage. It's safer for painters, and we have almost total freedom from dirt,' Larson said.

In the shape of an inverted U, the gantry rolled along the length of the airliner's fuselage under its own power and positioned painters with its own set of elevators, in Bldg. 610 at Plant 10 in Palmdale. The 67,000 square foot building housed the mobile gantry on one side and a large touch-up room on the other.

Even the paint used on the TriStars was new: a polyurethane variety that provided improved resistance to abrasion, corrosion and hydraulic fluids, and adhered better than previous coatings.

Painters stood on eight small elevator platforms as the gantry rolled slowly along the aircraft fuselage, and each painter's spray path blended with those of painters above and below to provide continuous coverage. Fumes and overspray were drawn away by four water-wash exhaust outlets installed in the gantry.

Conditioned air was piped through the gantry to each paint platform, along with hot and cold water for fuselage washing before painting.

In the wash and touch-up area, painters worked from elevator platforms suspended from the ceiling that travelled along the fuselage and across the L-1011's wing.

Dust, the enemy of painters, was kept out by supplying air to the room at ten per cent above the capacity of the exhaust filters. As an added precaution, double walls and ceilings were provided, as well as special seals for building openings.

Even when the paint hangar was not occupied, an anemometer on the roof automatically turned on air conditioning to pressurise the interior against dust when the wind exceeded twenty knots.

They called it Mellow Yellow...

If you were to walk through the L-1011 building you would have observed wing panels being sprayed yellow. They were even shipped yellow. Yet TriStars flying over Southern California were airliners of a different colour - and therein lies a story.

The yellow which you saw on these panels was no ordinary paint. It was a coating called Skinguard. It was tough. It resisted solvents and abrasives. It protected the aircraft part from scratches and stains. It ccould withstand an impact without cracking or chipping.

Skinguard enabled Lockheed and Avco to work the most delicate aircraft part through various assembly areas with little or no damage. The yellow colour was chosen because this particular pigment also acted as a corrosion inhibitor.

As the L-1011 wing panel left anodising, it immediately went to the paint booth where Skinguard was applied. A standard airless gun sprayed a dry film thickness of 0.001 an inch. Thickness was critical since drilling and countersinking - assembly operations which followed - were dependent on the depth of the coating. To hold such a close tolerance of thickness, the coating material had to be thinned down and applied with three separate passes of the spray gun. This required about one and a half gallons of coating per wing panel, or approximately nine gallons per wing.

Skinguard could be hardened by allowing it to age for five to seven days. However, in the case of L-1011 wing panels, it was heat-hardened in an oven at 200 degrees Fahrenheit for one hour. After the coating had completely hardened, the wing panels were removed from the oven and processed through assembly operations.

These operations consisted of drilling, countersinking, riveting, sealing and mating of panels. They all could be performed without damage to the aircraft parts because of resistance properties of this type of coating.

When the wing was assembled and ready for shipping, the coating was cleaned with a solvent to remove any shop soil from its surface.

This was to ensure good adhesion between each coating and an additional coating to be applied next. The additional coating was necessary for shipping protection. Again, a standard airless spray gun was used. About 18 to 20 gallons of uncut coating material was needed for the entire wing. When the final protective coating driedsufliciently for handling, which took about four hours, the wing could be moved. Following assembly of the aircraft at Lockheed-Califomia, this yellow protective coating was taken off by hand peeling.

Skinguard was also used on sections of the C-5 wing. Similar coatings of this nature protected the clad leading-edge surfaces of the L-1011 and clad surfaces of the C-130.

Increasing tempo

The tempo of L-1011 final assembly activity at Plant 10 in Palmdale took an upswing beat in June 1971 with more than 850 employees added to the payroll since 1 March.

Court Line's msn 1032 *Halcyon Breeze* is G-BAAB. Behind it is TWA's msn 1034/N31012, with an LTU machine to the rear.

Court Line's msn 1032 *Halcyon Breeze* is G-BAAB after completion and on its way for its first flight from Palmdale.

The good news was announced by Derk McCardy, assistant director of manufacturing for the L-1011. He explained that the increase in Plant 10 employment was necessary to meet its TriStar delivery schedule - twelve TriStars delivered to customer airlines during the first half of 1972.

'To meet these delivery commitments, we will be adding more employees each week throughout the entire summer to our Plant 10 work force. From this point on, it's go, go, go!' McCardy said.

'The immediate impact of the upswing in employment at the final assembly facility is most noticeable during the swing-shift, which will be in full operation by the end of the month'.

The first employees rehired included structures assemblers, electrical installers and hydro mechanics.

Final assembly work currently was being done on fifteen different TriStars: Ship 1006 already was out of the jigs and into final assembly, while Ship 1004 would be out of final assembly and onto the flightline in July.

'I'm full of optimism about our L-1011 program here at Plant 10, and I'm positive we're going to make the program successful. However, our success depends on each person doing his or her very best. The task ahead is going to be difficult, but so long as everyone has the spirit of getting the job done, our success is inevitable,' McCardy declared.

In the meantime flight-testing of the RB211 engines continued at Plant 10. Already nineteen flight-rated engines had been delivered to the Palmdale facility. Eight of these had a thrust rating of more than 40,000 pounds. Reports from Rolls-Royce at Derby indicated that a number of RB211 engines have been tested to 46,000 pounds of thrust, and 150-hour endurance testing satisfying normal test acceptance standards had been completed.

To date 26 pilots, representing customer airlines and potential airline customers, had piloted one of the three TriStars then being flight-tested. Twenty-two automatic landings had been accomplished.

Chapter Six

Rollout and Flight Test

The first L-1011 TriStar, Serial No. 1001, left Bldg. 602 for the first time to undergo fuel-soak testing 1 September 1970. According to Ernie Joiner, assistant chief engineer for flight test, this test consisted of filling all fuel tanks and lines with kerosene to ensure that there were no leaks in the system.

It would be the first of hundreds of tests that No. 1001 and five sister aircraft underwent during the 1700-hour flight test programme that led to FAA certification in 1971.

Still to be completed before No. 1001's first flight later that year were ground vibration tests utilising specially made 1000-pound electromagnetic shaker units, the ground engine runs, taxi tests, and many others.

When No. 1001 took to the air, its spacious interior did not contain the plush seats and other accommodations that airline passengers would find aboard. Instead, there were seats only for the flight-deck crew and half a dozen engineers.

The rest of the passenger cabin contained banks of electronic test and communications equipment and 29 tanks, each holding 350 gallons of water ballast. The water ballast, weighing up to 58,000 pounds, could be shifted back and forth to change the aircraft's centre of gravity during test flights.

The electronic equipment on board monitored every detail of the jetliner's performance in the air, storing the data on magnetic tape for later analysis by a computer on the ground. Additionally, much of the data was radioed to engineers at Palmdale while test flights were in progress, enabling them to provide an immediate analysis by radio to the test crew on board.

The other five test aircraft contained a variety of equipment to be used in the year-long series of

Serial No. 1001, first of the L-1011 TriStars, rolled out on schedule 1 September 1970, with Lockheed Corporate President A. Carl Kotchian (centre, foreground), California Company President Chuck Wagner, left, and Bill Moran, executive vice-president for commercial programs, leading the way. The airliner immediately entered Bldg. 602 at Palmdale to begin preliminary flight testing. *(Lockheed)*

proving flights.

During the rollout, the 178-foot aircraft, painted white with red and orange stripes, was escorted from the building by Corporate President A Carl Kotchian, California Company President Chuck Wagner, and Bill Moran, executive vice-president for commercial programs.

On-hand to greet the shining new-generation TriStar were stewardesses representing the six airlines that had ordered L-1011s so far: Eastern Air Lines, Trans World Airlines, Delta Air Lines, Air Canada, Air Jamaica, and Pacific Southwest Airlines.

N1011

It is not just coincidence that Lockheed's first L-1011 TriStar bore the US registration N1011.

The chain of events that led to this felicitous designation began more than a year before the rollout, when E E 'Jack' Hansen, assistant division manager for L-1011 Final Assembly and Production Flight, read an account of how an enterprising farmer reserved N707 for his private aircraft, anticipating that someday Boeing might want that number for its first 707.

When his expectations proved correct, the farmer negotiated with Boeing to release his aircraft's serial number to them for a reported $5000.

Hansen was determined that this sort of thing shouldn't happen to Lockheed, so he immediately wrote to the Aircraft Registration Branch of the FAA, asking who had been issued Registration No. N1011. 'They replied that the number was unavailable,' he explained. 'So I wrote to them again, asking who had it. This time I was told that N1011 had been lost.'

'I called the registration branch and was told that some years ago safety inspectors, as well as airplane manufacturers, were issued blocks of numbers, but

Left: Representing customer airlines at the rollout were, from left, stewardesses Fay Huntley, Air Canada; Marty Gutierrez, TWA; Anna Jackson, Delta; Michele Davis, PSA; and Pam Ware, Eastern.

Below: E E 'Jack' Hansen, left, who was issued N1011 for his Piper Apache, relinquished the number to Ed Hefferon for the first TriStar. *(both Lockheed)*

Left: Flight crew project pilot Hank Dees, left Jack Woodman, chief engineering test pilot and Glenn Fisher , flight engineer discuss the upcoming first flight, scheduled for November 1970. *(both Lockheed)*

Below: Key members of the TriStar Manufacturing team. From L to R: Stan Garrow, manager , L-1011 Production Development and Trim Division; Bob Palmer, acting assistant division manager of Production Development and Trim; Bill Larson, manager L-1011 Fuselage Mate and Prefinal Division; Ed Hefferon, director of manufacturing operations; Bob Bell, acting assistant director of manufacturing operations L-1011; Bob Shaffer, acting manager L-1011 Final and Flight Division; and Howard Nelson, manager L-1011 Fuselage Assembly Division.

that some time ago the FAA discontinued this practice and recalled all unissued numbers. N1011 was never turned in, and was therefore considered lost.'

Frustrated, Hansen called Lester G Robinson, chief of aircraft registration, and explained his dilemma. Robinson immediately established a statute of limitations on the original issuance of the number and decreed that N1011 be re-issued to Hansen's Apache.

During the rollout of the first L-1011 Hansen officially turned the number over to Ed Hefferon, director of manufacturing operations, to be transferred to the original TriStar.

Meanwhile, back in Building 601, from which No. 1001 rolled out, eight additional TriStars were in final assembly. Since 1 September the first baggage and cargo loading system, for Eastern's No. 1003, had arrived from Western Gear. The fuselage for No. 1002, the first TWA aircraft, has been painted. Fuselage mate had begun for No. 1005, the first Delta aircraft. And the left wing for TWA's 1002 has arrived.

Following the rollout of No. 1001, Ed Hefferon, director of manufacturing operations, announced the following reassignment of key personnel on the L-1011 program: Sam Fink, the assistant chief manufacturing engineer for the L-1011, returned to Burbank to resume his regular assignment. R E Shaffer, previously assigned to the L-1011 Final Assembly and Flight Division, was reassigned as division manager responsible for manufacturing engineering and planning efforts at Plant 10 in Palmdale. R F Bradford, division manager for L-

1011 Manufacturing Engineering, previously assigned to Plant 10, was reassigned to Burbank. Ray Richter, previously division manager for L-1011 Wing and Empennage Buildup and Mate, was reassigned as manager of the L-1011 Final and Flight Division. C A Deems, assistant manager-nights of the L-1011 Fuselage Assembly Division, was promoted to manager of the L-1011 Wing Empennage Buildup and Mate Division. S R Garrow, manager of the L-1011 Production Development and Trim Division, was assigned to full-time responsibilities for L-1011 interior trim. R D Palmer, previously assigned to the L-1011 production development organization, was given full responsibility for the functional development of the L-1011.

The Lockheed Star reported the first taxi-tests in Volume 37, No. 23, dated 5 November 1970: 'TriStar Crew Jubilant After Successful First Taxi Test'

'Now that's what I call a real good taxi run!' declared Hank Dees, L-1011 project pilot, after the L-1011 TriStar successfully completed its first taxi test last week at Palmdale.

As Dees switched off the power from the TriStar's three RB211 engines, Bill Moran, executive vice-president for commercial programs, entered the L-1011 flight station to congratulate the crew. Recalling some of the jubilation that followed, Moran said: 'Dees was just getting out of his seat, and as he turned around he had this broad grin on his face. He said to me, 'We've got a good one - she's a real winner!'

The first taxi test lasted approximately ninety minutes, during which the TriStar's nose-wheel steering, leading and trailing edge slats and all height controls were tested.

Keeping close watch from inside on how the TriStar responded were twelve employees, including Jack Woodman, chief engineering test pilot; Rod Bray, flight test engineer and team leader on ship 1001; Glenn Fisher, flight engineer; and Walt Hensleigh, Gelac's chief engineering test pilot. Ernie Joiner, chief TriStar flight test engineer, also praised the wide-bodied jet's performance. 'Everything checked out just fine!' he reported.

Two Rolls-Royce employees in separate station wagons followed the TriStar during the runway maneuvers for almost an hour. Their reactions, like those of the Lockheed employees who witnessed the test, were enthusiastic. Mike Goodchild, Rolls senior flight test engineer, described the test as, 'Very smooth; everything seemed to go according to our plans.'

Ron Jackson, Rolls service representative, said, 'I was very much impressed with the results. There was absolutely no indication of any abnormal condition throughout the entire test. All three engines performed very successfully.'

'Next week marks the start of the L-1011 high-speed taxi tests. These tests will reach a climax with the aircraft approaching take-off speeds.'

'Already underway are cabin pressurization tests, performance tests of the TriStar's air conditioning system, and engine instrumentation checkouts.'

What's in a name?

Things were starting to move at an increasing pace. Eastern Air Lines announced 'Whisperliner' as their type name for the L-1011 on national TV in September 1970. Eastern was the largest buyer of the new 268-passenger jet and expected to receive the first of its fifty Whisperliners in the autumn of 1971.

During a sixty-second commercial on NBC's nationally televised 'Today' show, announcer Frank Blair named the five Eastern employees who all submitted the same name for the wide-bodied jet in a company contest.

'We believe this is the first time a major corporation has used network television to talk to its employees,' said Maurice L Kelley, division vice-president for marketing planning and

The prototype Lockheed L-1011 TriStar, N1011,escorted by ground vehicles moves under its own power for the first time

The prototype Lockheed L-1011 TriStar, N1011 at the point of lift-off on 16 November 1970. *(Lockheed)*

advertising. 'It was the fastest and most appropriate way to tell our 32,000 people just who won the contest and announce the official name for this important new aircraft.'

The winners were Harriet N Moran, stewardess, Dwight E Lambert, equipment engineer, and Willard H Weathers, mechanic, all from Miami; Mrs Florence G Wilson, sales and services agent, Toronto; and Orville L. Callahan, ramp services manager, New York.

All five won an all-expense-paid week for two in Los Angeles as official observers at the maiden flight of the Whisperliner. Eastern received more than 2500 suggestions from its employees for naming the wide-bodied trijet during a two-month contest.

Into the Sky!

The first flight of the Lockheed L-1011 TriStar took place on 16 November 1970. Flight station crew consisted of L-1011 Project Test Pilot H B 'Hank' Dees, co-pilot Ralph C Cokely, flight engineer Glenn E Fisher, and Flight Test Engineering Team Leader Rod C. Bray. Takeoff weight was 330,000 pounds, which included 85,000 pounds of fuel and 40,000 pounds of test instrumentation, including the water ballast.

Henry Baird 'Hank Dees, was the co-pilot on the first flight of the C-141 StarLifter transport in December 1963 and the pilot in command on the first flight of the L-1011.

Dees joined Lockheed Georgia Company in Marietta, in 1955 after a career in the US Air Force. At Lockheed, he made the first flight of the C-130BL (later designated LC-130F) Ski-Herk and served as a project pilot on the QB-47 drone, JetStar, C-141, and C-5A Galaxy programmes. He moved to California in 1970 as assistant chief engineering test pilot. He was named director of flying operations at

The prototype Lockheed L-1011 TriStar, N1011,with a North American Aviation Sabre chase.

Lockheed California in 1973, serving until his retirement in 1984.

Takeoff run for the L-1011s first flight was only 5,300 feet, with a lift-off speed of 152 knots. The first flight went very well, lasting two and a half hours. Ground observers were impressed with the quietness of the Rolls-Royce engines. After landing, Pilot Hank Dees remarked, 'It was a lovely flight, we had good control, particularly with the flying tail. The Rolls-Royce engines ran fine. Pilots are going to like this airplane. Handling characteristics were better than our engineering simulations indicated.'

Flying as an extra pair of eyes closely scrutinizing the L-1011 TriStar during its test flights was long-time Lockheed pilot named Arthur Joseph 'Art' Peterson. A veteran of 11,600 flight hours, Peterson took to the air in the role of engineering chase pilot.

'An engineering chase pilot,'said Art, 'is the extra pair of eyes needed by the crew in the experimental plane and those people on the ground monitoring progress of the flight.'

Peterson visually evaluated the operation of the landing gear and flight control surfaces, and examined the engines during aerial shut-down and restart. He jockeyed the old fighter plane into positions above, below and on either side of the L-1011 to maintain close surveillance of the TriStar's external equipment.

The F-86 selected for the TriStar's chase mission was purchased in Canada after being declared surplus by the Canadian Air Force. Equipped with a Canadian-built Orenda engine, the F-86 Sabre 5, registered N8544, was capable of reaching a speed of Mach 0.95 and an altitude of more than 40,000 feet, sufficient to match the flight envelope of the TriStar.

Supporting Peterson's operations were Al Thomale, Lockheed Air Service maintenance supervisor assigned to the F-86, and George Means, a veteran Calac flight test mechanic.

Peterson was assigned as a pilot for the third TriStar earmarked for the flight test programme, and moved into that role as this TriStar approached its first flight.

A JetStar flew backup engineering chase for TriStar flight tests, to carry the photographers

Original caption: First flight crew for Lockheed's L-1011 TriStar pictured in flight station of the new trijet. From left are Rod C Bray, research and development engineering team leader; Hank Dees, project pilot and aircraft commander; Glenn E Fisher, flight engineer; and Ralph C Cokely, co-pilot. *(Lockheed)*

Above: Hank Dees brings N1011 back to the ramp at Plant 10, Palmdale, California, 16 November 1970 after a successful first flight.

Right: First flight crew descends the boarding ladder after a successful first flight of the L-1011. Front to rear are Pilot Hank Dees, Co-pilot Ralph Cokely, Flight Engineer Glenn Fisher, and Flight Test Team Leader Rod Bray. *(both Lockheed)*

necessary to document these flights visually.

Five aircraft were to be used for flight test. L-1011 Number One (msn 1001) did the bulk of the performance and propulsion system testing. Included were takeoff and landing performance, cruise performance, and flying qualities. These tests were done at various center-of-gravity conditions, speeds, and altitudes and at different weights, including maximum gross weight takeoff and landings.

Number Two (msn 1002) was the primary propulsion and AFCS test aircraft, doing a lot of the early in-flight development of the Lockheed Autoland system.

Number Three (msn 1003) was tasked with the certification testing of the Lockheed Autoland system, as well as the evaluation and certification testing of all the major functional systems.

Number Four (msn 1004) was the test aircraft for the navigation, communications, and environmental systems.

Number Five (msn 1005) was in the airline configuration, with seats and galleys, rather than the flight test instrumentation installed on the first four aircraft. This aircraft most closely represented a standard airline configuration and was used for demonstrating the L-1011's general performance and reliability over a large number of operating conditions.

Use of a Simulator

Parallel to test flying the 'real' aircraft Lockheed made use of a flight training simulator for the L-1011 TriStar which had been installed and 'test flown' in Bldg. 608 at Plant 10 in Palmdale.

Hank Shumway, manager of L-1011 flight crew training, said the simulator built by CAE Industries Ltd. of Montreal would become the most important item of ground equipment in training customer airline flight crews to fly the TriStar. Cost of the simulator and related equipment exceeds $2.5 million.

TriStar pilots and flight engineers would spend

N1011 in flight *(Lockheed)*

approximately three hours in the simulator for each hour of training flights in the actual L-1011 while they earn FAA rating on the TriStar. First trainees will be Lockheed pilots, with airline flight crews beginning training this spring, Shumway said.

In describing advantages of the new L-1011 simulator over older systems, Shumway said the goal of the ground simulation was 'to reduce as much as possible the amount of time a pilot must spend in actual flight of a new aircraft type to qualify under FAA rules to fly it. Safety is improved because emergency situations can be programmed into the simulator without using a flying aircraft for this type of crew training.'

The highly advanced simulator could realistically duplicate all modes of L-1011 operation, from taxiing, takeoff and a wide variety of flight conditions to landing and docking at a terminal gate. Heart of the device was the cab, which included a precise duplicate of the L-1011 cockpit with seats for the pilot, co-pilot, flight engineer, an instructor pilot and an instructor flight engineer.

The cab was supported by twelve large hydraulic jacks that provided movement to simulate the manoeuvres of an L-1011 in flight. This six degrees of freedom system provided movement in the horizontal, vertical and lateral axes along with roll, pitch and yaw.

The motion system gave crewmen the feeling of gravity forces in turns, dives and climbs, even though the cab actually moved only about five feet in any direction.

Because the onset of a change in direction is the part of a flight manoeuvre most strongly felt by the pilot, the simulator could duplicate the start of a motion - such as a turn - and then gently halt itself, leaving the pilot with the sensation that the movement wss still underway. The manoeuvre was completed by using the same technique.

To increase realism, cockpit sounds were reproduced from tape recordings and synchronized to aircraft operation. Noises heard by crewmen in the

Lockheed L-1011 TriStar N1011 parked on the ramp at Plant 10, Palmdale, California, 16 November 1970.

President Chuck Wagner, left, and C Douglas Reekie, president and chief executive officer of CAE Industries Ltd. of Montreal, were first to try out L-1011 flight simulator made by CAE, after its installation in Building 608 at Plant 10 in Palmdale. *(Lockheed)*

simulator might included engine sounds, hail, rain, wind, landing-gear actuation, landing-gear touchdown and bounce, and runway rumble.

Attached to the simulator was a VAMP visual system, a film-projection device built by the Link Division of the Singer Company to provide a view of the airport during approaches and landings. The device could simulate all visibility conditions down to zero-zero. Key to the system's ability to simulate all L-1011 handling characteristics was a bank of two Xerox Data Systems Sigma II computers. Linked to the instruments and controls in the cockpit, the computers activated the hydraulic jacks beneath the cab.

The computers activated the instruments and warning devices in the cockpit according to the instructors' panels' signals. Instructors could confront student crewmen with all types of emergencies.

A special feature allowed for an 'instant replay' of up to fifteen minutes of any training manoeuvre. The simulator could record and replay all motions and instrument readings, enabling the student to observe and analyze their performance.

Test Aircraft One

The interior of msn 1001, the first flight test aircraft, was completely different than any aircraft in the airline-delivered configuration.

The special pallet area 'A', in the forward cabin area, was set up to make easy installation changes for special flight test instrumentation for specific testing. This 500-square-foot area had floor attachments for pallets holding a variety of test equipment and included electrical power, cooling air, and interface wiring with the main on-board data centre (diagram item 4).

Dragging the tail on a Velocity Minimum Unstick Speed (Vmu) test designed to determine the absolute minimum speed at which an aircraft, with all engines operating, would take off and maintain a positive rate of climb. This speed was used to determine safe takeoff speed. A protective surface was used on the bottom of the fuselage during this test. *(Lockheed)*

Items 1, 2, and 3 on the interior diagram showed locations of control and display equipment for the flight test engineers running the particular tests.

The main data acquisition centre (diagram item 4) located in the centre of the aircraft contained the instrumentation recording and processing equipment, along with displays, strip chart recorders, and plotters, for real-time flight test monitoring and data analysis (also see photo). The weight engineer station (diagram item 5) had displays for monitoring fuel used for continuous calculation of aircraft weight and centre of gravity.

The main landing gear water fog and pump (diagram item 6) was used for brake cooling, after tests like rejected take-offs (RTOs).

The acoustic chamber (diagram item 7) located near the wing trailing edge was used for developing and evaluating noise reduction treatments, including sidewall structure, window, trim, and seat configurations.

The ballast system was located under the cabin floor and included fixed ballast (diagram items 9 and 10) and 2,000-pound water ballast tanks (diagram item 11). The system had the capability of pumping water back and forth between the forward and aft locations to change the centre of gravity in flight for various test conditions.

The electrical load bank (diagram item 12), located in the aft cargo compartment, was used for applying electrical loads to the aircraft generators, simulating actual and greater loads than would be seen in service.

The second L-1011 TriStar, bearing TWA markings, soared to 10,000 feet on 15 February 1971, achieved a maximum speed of 330 mph, and turned in a first-flight performance that equalled TriStar msn 1001 during its inaugural flight the previous 16 November.

The red and white jetliner lifted from the runway near Plant 10 in Palmdale at 10:58 a.m. and quickly disappeared into an overcast sky. Three Rolls-Royce RB211 turbofan engines powered the L-1011 during the 1 hour and 25-minute flight, during which crew members conducted routine tests on the jetliner's flaps, slats and landing gear. Also, they performed various checks of the TriStar's functional systems.

At the controls were Ralph C Cokely as the pilot and Hank Dees as the copilot. B E Haviland served as flight engineer and L E Sakala as a flight-test engineer. Working as engineer observers were Don Moor and Charles E Wehunt. After the jetliner completed its first flight, crew members reported 'everything checks out just fine.'

Flights continued at Plant 10 with the L-1011's avionics equipment aboard a Convair 240 testbed.

Lockheed L-1011 msn 1001 interior

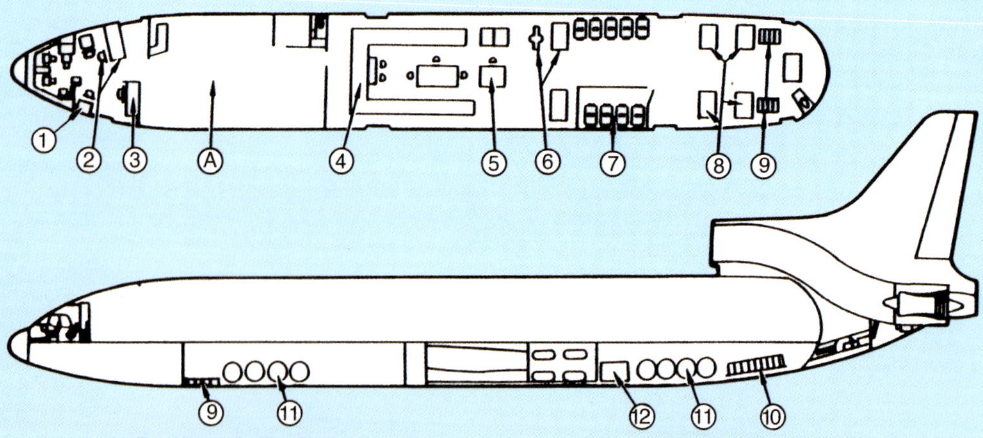

1 Remote Avionics Station.
2 Automatic Flight Controls Center.
3 Flutter and Loads Center.
4 Main Data Acquisition Center.
5 Weight Engineer Station.
6 Mlg Water Fog and Pump.
7 Accustic Chamber
8 Water Ballast Tanks.

9 Fixed Ballast.
10 Fixed Ballast - Aft
11 Water Ballast Tanks - Fwd and Aft.
12 Electrical Load Bank.

A Special Pallet Area (500 square feet) (i.e., Active Contols, Digital Autopilot etc).

The first two TriStars in flight together. Visible on the top of the fin of N31001, the TWA machine is a 'trailing cone'. This device was present on all development aircraft during the first weeks of flight tests. The nylon cable was deployed in flight, generally, 1 to 1.5 times the wingspan length, behind the aircraft to measure the ambient atmospheric pressure - or static pressure - precisely, in the 'free-stream air-flow' outside the disrupted air-flow generated by the aircraft - a key parameter for the pilots. The static pressure was essential to measure the aircraft's exact airspeed and altitude. The static pressure was therefore fundamental to measure the performance of a test aircraft. *(Lockheed)*

Within two weeks, the first two L-1011 TriStars were engaged in simultaneous test flights over the Antelope Valley while work progressed on the other twelve TriStars in final assembly at Plant 10 in Palmdale. Ship No. 3, earmarked for Eastern Airlines, was undergoing functional testing preparatory to its first flight.

Both No. 3 and No. 4, also earmarked for Eastern, were to be used in the engineering flight-test programme leading to FAA certification, before being turned over to their airline owners. Trim work continued on both aircraft.

In addition to Ship No. 4, Ship No. 5, earmarked for Delta Air Lines, was in the final stages of assembly. Ship No. 6. destined for Eastern, was in wing mate, and Ships No. 7 and 8, earmarked for TWA and Eastern respectively, were in the prefinal assembly stages awaiting wing mate.

Ships No. 9 for Eastern and 10 for Delta were in fuselage mate, and Ships No. 11 through 14 were in various stages of structural assembly.

AFCS and Autoland

Created in the mid-1930s with just eight employees, by 1970 the Collins Radio Company was ranked 249th among the top 500 US companies and

First TriStars for each of Lockheed's first two L-1011 customers have rolled out the doors of the final assembly building, 601, at Palmdale. On the left, a typical flight crew greets the first Trans World Airlines TriStar. At right, Gene Pearson, Eastern Airlines manager of factory contracts administration, left, and Jack Neely, Calac senior sales representative assigned to Eastern, congratulate each other as first Eastern TriStar rolls out. They've headed the liaison teams. *(both Lockheed)*

employed more than 20,000 people in plants at Cedar Rapids, Newport Beach (Calif.), Dallas and Toronto. Together they produced more than a thousand different products, which sold for $427 million.

This is the company that, together with Lear Siegler Inc., provided the avionics flight control system for the L-1011 TriStar.

As prime contractor for the avionics package, Collins shared responsibility for the overall system with Lear-Siegler. The avionics flight control system included a fail-operative landing system with new precision and safety standards, a stability augmentation system, a speed control system and a flight control electronics system. System hardware consisted of electro-mechanical equipment installed in the aircraft and control units for the crew to operate the system.

Designed as a fully redundant system combining several systems working as a unit and integrated with the basic airframe, the L-1011 AFCS provided the highest reliability and safety with precise automatic control from takeoff to touchdown in both normal and all-weather situations.

Lear Siegler's work on the L-1011's integrated avionics flight control package was done by the Astronics Division, an outgrowth of operations started by the former Lear Inc. back in 1949 for the development of an automatic flight control system for Lockheed's X-7 ram-jet test vehicle.

The division, which provided three-axis dampers for the F-104 and flight-control components and systems for other Lockheed aircraft, including the U-2, employed around five hundred people at its facilities near Santa Monica Airport.

The Astronics Division with teammate Collins Radio achieved a milestone on the L-1011 programme on 28 May when seven units of first-flight test hardware were delivered to Lockheed's Palmdale facility for TriStar 1001.

Under a separate contract, LSI also developed and produced the TriStar's electric generating system at its Power Equipment Division in Cleveland. The system was a completely new concept which combined the constant-speed drive and the generator into one package called the integrated drive generator.

The IDG, which provided the power to operate all the electrical devices, including flight controls, lights, underfloor galley, navigation and communications equipment, made possible a fifty per cent reduction in weight, compared with conventional generating systems.

When the engineers at Calac and their counterparts at Collins-Lear-Siegler Inc. in Santa

John Gorham, left, Calac chief engineer for L-1011 flight guidance and controls, and Ken Kramer, president of the Astronics Division of Lear-Siegler Inc., set up L-1011 Autoland system before conducting a test that would simulate an automatic approach and landing. The simulator, which was tested by chief pilots of major world airlines, was located at Lear-Seigler Inc. in Santa Monica. *(Lockheed)*

Left: Integrated Circuits - 1970s style! This circuit board was one of thirty similar components located in line electronic "black boxes" that made up the Autoland system. They incorporated some 4000 integrated circuits.

Below: During preliminary design work on the L-1011 Autolond system, employees at Lear-Siegler Inc. linked this computer console shown in foreground, to the Autoland simulator, shown in background right via the computer, background left. Work on the Autoland project, started in 1968, was done by 120 LSi and 40 Calac engineers.

Monica designed the Autoland system for the L-1011 TriStar, they were challenged by the prospect of bad weather.

Their assignment: develop an all-weather landing system that would enable the L-1011 TriStar to land safely, routinely, and on time in both good and foul weather.

The job was tackled by forty Calac design engineers, headed by John Gorham, chief engineer for L-1011 flight guidance and controls, and by 120 design engineers of the Collins Radio Company of Cedar Rapids, Iowa, and Lear-Siegler Inc. (LSi) of Santa Monica. In charge of the Collins-LSi team was Ken C. Kramer, LSi vice-president and Collins-LSi L-1011 program manager for Autoland.

When work on the Autoland system first began in 1968, Gorham was confident that the Lockheed - Collins - LSi team would achieve a basic objective meeting and exceeding FAA criteria for landing the L-1011 under Category II weather conditions (100-ft ceiling; at least 1200-ft horizontal visibility). This was accomplished, but more important, the L-1011 Autoland system had the inherent capability of qualifying under Category IIIB criteria. This meant that the pilot need have only 150-ft visibility along the runway surface.

'When we started this work, both our engineers and the Collins-LSi people realized that anyone with enough technical know-how could design and build an Autoland system. However, not everyone can build an Autoland system that airline pilots actually like and feel completely safe in using,' Gorham explained.

The L-1011 TriStar made its first two fully automatic landings on 27 April 1971 in Palmdale, using advanced avionics systems that permitted routine operation at airports under very poor visibility.

The first test of hands-off landing with the big trijet went off 'without a hitch,' according to Ernie Joiner, the TriStar's chief flight test engineer.

'It was phenomenal for such a sophisticated system to perform so perfectly on the first try. Our first landing this morning included manual control of the engine throttles, but the second and third were fully automatic, including the rollout after touchdown.'

'Joiner' said the pilot, Ralph Cokely, just pushed a button 'and the plane did the rest.'

Some two dozen Lockheed flight test crewmen and engineers were aboard during the flight, including John Gorham, who directed design and development of the TriStar's avionics systems including the automatic landing equipment. On board was Kenneth Kramer, president of the Astronics Division of Lear-Siegler, which developed the new system with Collins Radio Company.

'Prior to today's flight, we had made thousands of automatic landings with our system installed in simulators,' Gorham said. 'Today's successful landings confirmed the findings we had obtained with the simulation.'

Additional praise came from J E 'Elly' Hawkes, chief engineer for commercial engineering testing. "When you consider the sheer complexity of such a system, coupled with the fact that it worked perfectly the first time, why, it's almost a miracle. As a result of this first successful autoland, the company will be able to save substantial development costs."

As an example of the complexity of the Autoland system, it was made up of more than 4000 integrated circuits. Nine electronic boxes contained approximately 30 individual circuit boards, and there were more than 12,000 interconnecting electrical and electronic points throughout the system.

Why did the L-1011 Autoland system deliver such a superior performance? 'Teamwork,' said Gorham. 'From the beginning and right through the entire development and testing of the system, we worked as a closely-knit team. We were able to eliminate a lot of paperwork because we always had open lines of communication with all the key team members. In effect, we were able to respond like 'Lee contributed to the success of this program in a great way. He had incredible experience. Before he joined Calac he worked at Gelac as a design and development engineer for the C-141 and C-5 Galaxy automatic landing systems,' said Gorham.

Other members of the Autoland team at Calac included E 0 'Jack' Throndsen, senior research and development engineer in charge of avionic and flight-control analysis; Tom Mahone, group engineer of the Plant 2 L-1011 servo and electrical systems department; Harvey E Worden, manager of the commercial engineering flight-test systems integration department; Richard A Moore, manager of the L-1011 avionics procurement department; and William F Smith, engineering test pilot.

'From this team we were able to achieve quick-reaction results,' explained Gorham. He added that he put to use the following principle: 'We told our team members what we wanted to achieve, and then we exploited their potential by giving them enough freedom to utilize their talents.'

These talents were put to good use both at Calac and at Collins-LSi. At the Collins-LSi facility in Santa Monica, the Autoland system was tested more than 100,000 times - each test representing a simulated landing. Contributing to the success of the program was the fact that chief airline pilots of the major world airlines participated in the testing, evaluation and criticism of the L-1011 system after trying out the Autoland simulator at the Collins-LSi plant in Santa Monica.

Thousands of automatic landings also were conducted in the integrated test facility known as ALSTAR (automatic landing systems test and analysis rig) at Rye Canyon Research Laboratories. ALSTAR was used to test individual black boxes and actual aircraft sensors, including the radio altimeter, instrument landing system (ILS), and attitude and heading gyros.

The Vehicle Systems Simulator (VSS), also at Rye Canyon, enabled engineers to simulate the L-1011's landing operation. This was accomplished by using a closed-loop configuration that connected the automatic flight control system hardware with primary flight controls. Sensors and a computerized mathematical modelled the jetliner's aerodynamics.

'The thousands of automatic landings on the Collins-LSi simulator, on ALSTAR and on the VSS, together with actual flight test results, will establish the high confidence level required for the system and provide the evidence of fail-operative operation essential for certification,' said Gorham.

In addition to 'Autoland', there was a new radar device under development for Lockheed's new L-1011 TriStar jetliner that allowed pilots' see' runways through fog would also be useful to many other types of aircraft, members of the Society of Automotive Engineers learned in Atlanta. John Gorham, the assistant chief engineer in charge of flight guidance and controls for the L-1011, described the TriStar's independent landing

The first Eastern Airlines pilots to fly the L-1011TriStar, from left, are Wyatt Alexander, EAL chief development pilot; Gaspar Garcia, assistant chief development pilot; and John O'Neill, chief pilot and vice-president of operations, as pilot.

monitor (ILM) system in a paper co-authored with Gerald Holliday, Lockheed research and development engineer. The paper was presented at the Society of Automotive Engineers' National Air Transport Meeting. Gorham, who also was appointed chairman of the forum on air navigation, said the new ILM system is a joint development of Calac and Texas Instruments, Inc.

'The purpose of the device was to give a pilot an electronic picture of a runway during an automatic landing approach when the runway was obscured by weather conditions. Although the pilot may not be able to see any of the airport through his windshield, the ILM's electronic image, displayed on his instrument panel, shows him exactly where the runway is throughout the landing approach, touchdown and rollout.'

Gorham said the system operated with a Ka-band radar using a horizontal antenna forty inches wide. In-flight testing has been conducted with the system installed in a Convair 240 flying test-bed operated by Texas instruments.

Other pilots fly on tests.

Within the test-flying schedule, customer airline pilots began to test-fly the jetliner, and their reactions were enthusiastic. Three Eastern Airlines captains were first to fly the L-1011 on 7 May. John H O'Neill, vice-president of operations; Wyatt H Alexander, chief development pilot, and Gaspar Garcia, assistant chief development pilot, made these comments following the flight: 'This was a very good demonstration. We feel we have a very good airplane.'

'L-1011 attitude and speed stability and approach manoeuvring is outstanding, and stability at ten per cent above stall speed is rock solid.'

'Dutch roll damping is good, wheel brake performance is outstanding, and thrust reverser operation is excellent.'

'The autoland capability is absolutely outstanding.'

'This is a beautiful cockpit. Visibility is excellent, even in a nose-high attitude.'

The Eastern pilots also witnessed five landings and four take-offs while beside the runway and were complimentary about the low noise levels.

L-1011 test aircraft had, by this point, logged more than 154 hours. A third aircraft, in Eastern Airlines striping, was scheduled to make its maiden flight 14 May 1971.

Three Air Canada pilots praised the TriStar's performance Tuesday following their first test flight, which lasted approximately two and a half hours.

On board were Capt. Ron J Baker, director of flight operations-engineering for Air Canada; Capt. John Wild, director of flight operations-technical development; and Capt. W O 'Hoagy' Hoagland, chief instructor. The pilots, were accompanied by Bob Christie, Air Canada's plant representative at Lockheed. Their comments included:

'I like the aircraft's lack of pitch trim change during the use of flaps and speed brakes. This isn't the case with all airplanes, and this feature will be welcome to our pilots during air traffic control approach.'

'We gave the L-1011 a very hard braking test, and it showed good response with no tendency to swing at all - even with the nose wheel barely on the ground. It was very smooth.'

'I consider the flight deck (flight station) layout very well designed. It offers clear panoramic visibility, as well as over the nose. Furthermore, the instrument presentations are well placed. At no time did I notice instrument reflections in the windshield. It will be a nice plane to fly.'

Colonel Frank Borman, the former astronaut, piloted the L-1011 TriStar for 21/2 hours on 22 May and called it 'a real winner.'

Borman, who was senior vice-president-operations group for Eastern Airlines, declared the TriStar 'a real pilot's airplane' after putting the TriStar through a wide variety of test manoeuvres.

'From the pilot's standpoint, the flight station is well laid out, and the visibility is excellent. From the passenger's standpoint, I think our customers are going to find this airplane spacious and quiet.'

It was Borman's first time at the L-1011 controls, and he took the plane to 30,000 feet altitude as he made systems checks, stall approaches and stability analyses. He also made one touch-and-go landing with one of the Rolls-Royce RB211 engines deliberately shut down. 'The Rolls engines performed magnificently,' Borman said.

Eastern Airlines was the largest customer for the L-1011 with fifty on order. Borman was commander of the Apollo 8 spacecraft which was the first manned vehicle to escape Earth orbit and circle the moon.

'This is an extremely fine airplane and will meet the needs of the world's airlines for the foreseeable future. I hope we can make the necessary accommodations to continue its production," he said, in a reference to a Government loan guarantee for Lockheed.

'The Rolls-Royce engine is a very fine engine. We evaluated very carefully the engine options we had when Rolls went into receivership. But the unanimous recommendation of our people was to stay with the RB211.'

Riding as co-pilot with Borman during the test flight was chief L-1011 project pilot Hank Dees. Borman flew the No. 2 TriStar, but later toured the No. 3 aircraft, the first to bear Eastern Airlines colours, and the first to contain seating in the coach compartment.

New Records

'The L-1011 TriStar has again reached new highs in speed and altitude', said Ernie Joiner, chief flight test engineer. 'N1011, the No. 1 TriStar reached a true airspeed of 660 mph, or Mach 0.95, in a descent from 40,000 to 28,000 feet during a flight that lasted 4 hours and 9 minutes on 25 June 1971.' On 1 July it reached maximum operating altitude - 42,000 feet. In a different test, the L-1011 achieved a new low-altitude speed of 440 knots calibrated airspeed, representing five knots beyond the TriStar's maximum design speed. This means that the TriStar had flown at its maximum design speed during both high and low flights.

Normal cruise speed of the L-1011 is Mach 0.82 to Mach 0.85. "We have now flown as fast as we'll ever have to go to prove the airplane," Joiner said.

L-l0l1 Project Pilot Hank Dees reported that at ninety-five per cent of the sound speed, the TriStar experienced no buffeting or other adverse aerodynamic effects.

By this date, the total flying time of the three L-1011's in the test program has exceeded 290 hours.

Chapter Seven

TriStars on Tour!

It was time to take the TriStar on tour, so L-1011 No. 1003, decked in the brilliant two-tone blue and white of Eastern Airlines, set out eastwards.

Until almost the last minute, as *Aviation Daily* pointed out, the appearance of the TriStar had been doubtful. But, as Calac President Chuck Wagner told a cheering crowd at Montreal International Airport when the L-1011 arrived there en route to Paris and the Salon international de l'aéronautique et de l'espace de Paris-Le Bourget - the Paris Air Show. 'We made it!'

More than 250 Canadian government officials, airline guests and members of the Canadian press attended ceremonies commemorating the first international flight of the L-1011 TriStar from Palmdale to Montreal.

The wide-bodied jetliner touched down at Montreal International Airport at 4:25 pm 29 May on its way to the Paris Air Show. It was the first time the L-1011 had landed on foreign soil. On hand to greet the crew members was Walter McLeish, Canadian director of civil aviation.

President Chuck Wagner, who arrived in Montreal before the L-1011 landed, presented McLeish with a plaque commemorating the L-1011 international flight. Wagner told McLeish and guests at the airport that it was especially fitting that the TriStar's first landing on foreign soil was in Canada since the airliner was piloted by Jack Woodman, Calac's chief engineering test pilot, a former Royal Canadian Air Force pilot. Wagner added that more than $100 million in L-1011 subcontracts had been awarded to Canadian industry.

On arrival over Paris, the big jet twice swung low over the field at Le Bourget, for the Paris Air Show before landing exactly as scheduled at 10:15 am on 1 June 1971.

An audience composed of virtually every visitor in attendance at the air show gave her a standing ovation amid shouts of 'Bravo!' and the *Paris Air Show Daily* the next day reported: 'Regardless of what the official schedule said, yesterday was

TriStar N301EA seen at the 1971 Paris Air Show, in the company of a C-5 Galaxy and N2241, a Lockheed JetStar in Eastern Airlines markings. A film crew seems to be hard at work at the bottom of the steps. *(Lockheed)*

Walter McLeish, right, Canadian director of civil aviation accepts a plaque representing the first international flight of the TriStar from Calac President Chuck Wagner. *(Lockheed)*

Lockheed Day at the Paris Air Show. Appearance of the L-1011 with its Rolls-Royce RB2l1 engines was much more than the arrival of just another airplane. It was the demonstration of a spirit which has kept the 1011 project going despite obstacles which at times have seemed insurmountable.'

Thank God you're here!' one airshow official reportedly told a crew member. 'It would have been a Russian show without Lockheed's C-5, L-1011, P-3, JetStar and C-130.'

A lot of people said we couldn't take this plane to the Paris Air Show- but they forgot to tell us!' At a press reception inside the TriStar on the day of arrival, Lockheed President Carl Kotchian told reporters, 'This airplane is living proof of the progress that has been made in California since February, when Rolls-Royce went into receivership. Flying this airplane to Paris also supports an important Lockheed marketing effort. We believe some of our best prospects for future L-1011 sales are here in Europe.' He added that Lockheed had 'identified about sixty airlines and inclusive tour operators that are potential customers for the L-1011 - Lockheed sees a total market for approximately 800 basic L-1011-type trijets.'

Others participating in this opening press conference included Calac President Chuck Wagner; Floyd Hall, board chairman of Eastern Airlines, who hosted the reception; Robert Rummel, TWA vice-president for technical development; Geoffrey Fawn, managing director of the Rolls-Royce Derby Engine Division; and Dr. Stanley Hooker, Rolls' technical director.

Much of the applause accorded the TriStar wherever it went undoubtedly resulted from the crowd's admiration for the courage and perseverance of the people - employees of Lockheed, the airlines, and our subcontractors - who forged ahead to prepare the aircraft and fly it to Paris, regardless of difliculties.

Immediately upon arrival, Lockheed issued a lengthy press release extolling the virtues of the new machine. In many respects it was the first time the general public heard some of the details.

'Newsbureau, Lockheed-California Company
1971 Paris Airshow Press Bureau
Le Bouget. Chalet: C-12
Telephone: 284-7246 and 833-5332

Lockheed's new L-1011 TriStar to enter airline service in 1972

'Lockheed's L-1011 Tristar jetliner, powered by Rolls-Royce RB211 engines, will go into airline service beginning in April of 1972.'

'The new wide-body trijet will seat from 250 to 345 passengers in a variety of airline interior configurations. It will provide passengers with new levels of comfort, convenience and spaciousness. A special configuration designed for the economic operations of inclusive tour operators will seat 400 persons.'

'Flight crews will welcome provisions in the flight station for their comfort, as well as airplane features such as the L-1011's flying stabilizer, and all-weather landing system, designed to reduce their workload and contribute to ease of operation.'

'Reduction of engine noise has been one of the primary design goals for the Tristar, and Lockheed and Rolls-Royce engineers predict the L-1011 noise levels will be well below new FAA requirements.'

'Maintenance features such as an emphasis on corrosion prevention and design for unlimited fatigue life through use of adhesively bonded structure will add to the already favorable economics of the aircraft in other areas that will allow it to make a profit for its operators, even at reduced load factors.'

'Design of the L-l0ll was begun in 1966, choice of the Rolls- Royce advanced turbofan three-spool engine was made early in 1968, and the Tristar production program was launched April 1, 1968 after record-breaking orders of 144 aircraft - by Eastern. TWA and Air Holdings of Great Britain - were announced. Orders now total 178.'

'The basic version of the Tristar, now in production, is designed to fly a full load of passengers and cargo over distances of more than 3,500 statute miles (5,600 km) at a cruising speed of more than 600 mph (965 kph).'

'Production of the first L-1011 components began in December 1968 at Burbank, Calif., where an extensive modernization of production facilities was initiated. Included in this modernization has been installation of machinery and equipment that enables Lockheed to use, for the first time on a large scale in commercial aircraft, adhesive bonding to join large (up to eight feet by thirty-eight feet) fuselage panels with supporting structure.'

'The reduction in weight and increase in strength achieved by this method is believed to set a pattern for future construction of large aircraft.'

'At Palmdale, Calif., 60 miles from the main Lockheed-California Company plant in Burbank, Lockheed built a new $50 million final assembly and flight test center designed exclusively for the production and test of large aircraft.'

'After the rollout of the first L-1011 September l, 1970, the first aircraft made its maiden flight on November 16, 1970. The second Tristar flew on February 15, 1971, and the third airplane entered the flight test program in May, 1971.'

'Supporting the production of the Tristar has been a worldwide network of suppliers in 45 states of the United States and seven countries sharing about $2 billion in subcontracts.'

'Lockheed's L-l0ll test program includes approximately 1600 hours in the air and 36,000 equivalent flights or a lifetime in airline service in ground tests.'

'Certification of the TriStar by the Federal Aviation Administration is anticipated April 15, 1972, with airline deliveries to begin the same month.'

'Lockheed looks on its present intermediate range Tristar as the first of a family of wide-fuselage trijets, with a longer-range version now in the planning stage.'

Contributing equally to the TriStar reception was its appearance, both inside and out, and the fact that it was the only one of the new wide-bodied trijets at the show that was opened to tours by the general public. In all, more than 25,000 people inspected the TriStar's interior during its Paris stay. About half of

At Paris, literally thousands of people patiently queued to see the TriStar for the first time. *(Lockheed)*

these were members of the general public. The others included government officials, press members, executives, and employees of potential customer airlines, who toured the aircraft by appointment.

'People from almost every airline I ever heard of - plus some I hadn't heard of - expressed interest and admiration after seeing the plane, said Bill Moran, executive vice-president for commercial programs. 'The trip provided an unparalleled showcase for our L-1011, and our salespeople are tremendously cheered by the response it received.'

'Many visitors were surprised at how spacious the plane was when they got inside,' Moran added. 'Apparently, it's so well dimensioned that it doesn't look as large from the outside as it really is.'

The largest number of employees from a single airline to tour the aircraft came from British European Airways; more than 400 - pilots, stewardesses, flight crew members, ground crews and airport employees - trooped through the airliner at Paris.

Both Wagner and Moran praised the Calac crew members and the cooperating Eastern Airlines stewardesses who helped conduct visitors through the airliner. 'Both our people and the Eastern girls pitched in as though the aircraft belonged to them personally,' Wagner commented. 'They did their own thing, and then they pitched in to do whatever else was necessary, like cleaning up after the crowds, and so on.'

'When people expressed surprise that we had been able to make the trip with the L-1011 in view of our difficulties, I told them we had every confidence in our people and in the plane and the

Above: Colonel Frank Borman, senior vice-president - operations for Eastern Airlines, fields questions asked about L-1011.

Above: Lloyd Frisbee, left, vice-president and chief engineer for Lockheed Commercial Aircraft, and President Chuck Wagner posed for this historic photograph taken shortly after the TriStar landed at Le Bourget airfield near Paris on 1 June 1971.

The two number on the nose of the aircraft are of interest. '301' is the Eastern Airlines fleet number and the '162' is the Paris Airshow number. All participating aircraft carried a unique number to aid identification. *(Lockheed)*

Below: Geoffrey Fawn, managing director of the Rolls-Royce Derby Engine Division, discusses performance of RB211 engine. At left is Bob Rummel, TWA vice-president for technical development. *(both Lockheed)*

engines; otherwise, we wouldn't have tried it.' Wagner said.

'I believe our interior attracted the most praise from visitors, but many also told me that they thought our plane was much better looking than its competitors from the outside, and much better balanced,' he added.

In all, reporters from more than one hundredh major newspapers and magazines and five television networks previewed and photographed the TriStar during its Paris stay.

Before returning to the USA, N301EA made a three-day stay at East Midlands Airport near Derby, England, home of its Rolls-Royce RB211 engines, where it evoked equal enthusiasm from crowds as large as those in Paris. Bill Moran: 'When we flew over the British countryside and saw field after field of parked cars waiting for us to land, Wagner said, 'It looks like Le Bourget all over again.'

More than 20,000 Rolls-Royce employees and their families stood in long lines in the mist and cold rain awaiting their turns to walk through the airliner as it sat on the ramp at East Midlands Airport. Most of them managed to see the inside of the airliner, whilst others walked beneath the wings and around the landing gear and peered into the huge fanjet engines as they windmilled in the cold winds.

'We wanted the people who worked on these engines to have an opportunity to share the pride we have in the TriStar,' declared Calac President Chuck Wagner, who flew aboard the TriStar with the forty-two member TriStar crew on the flight from Paris to East Midlands, a modern airport at Castle Donington, a few miles from the Rolls headquarters at Derby.

Wagner spoke of the complete re-evaluation of all possible engines for the TriStar made by Lockheed and its airline customers earlier this year. He said he wanted Rolls-Royce employees to know that as a result there was 'unanimous agreement that the Rolls- Royce engine was the best one for this particular airplane and in the long run was the best of all the engines.'

The L-1011 had been welcomed on Saturday by batteries of television cameras, photographers and reporters from throughout England, Scotland and Belfast, as well as by the thousands of Rolls-Royce families and their neighbours whose vehicles choked the approach roads to the airport. TriStar's first trip to Britain was an unquestioned morale booster for the thousands of Rolls-Royce employees involved in the RB211 programme.

Geoffrey Fawn, managing director of the Rolls-Royce Derby Engine Division, said during a joint press conference with Wagner, 'We want to welcome the largest aircraft ever to land at East Midlands. And we want to show Lockheed that we are fully behind this programme. Our future task is to advance the running time on these engines which now have about 6000 hours. This is the aircraft of the future. This is an ecological engine. It is quiet and clean. We are confident it will meet all of the regulations for noise and cleanliness.'

Fawn praised the team spirit of the people involved in the programme and declared that 'We have no doubt about the job Lockheed is doing.'

Lloyd Frisbee, Calac vice-president and director of commercial engineering, who participated in the press conference with Wagner, Fawn, Bill Moran, executive vice president for commercial programs, and Ernie Joiner, chief flight test engineer, answered several press questions on noise and smoke, explaining that the RB211 engine was slightly lower in noise levels, compared with Brand X in all areas. He said that the TriStar on approach produced 102.5 Db, compared with 105 Db by the opposition airliners.

Pilot Jack Woodman, who flew the TriStar to Europe with Co-Pilot Ralph Cokely, called the TriStar 'an easy airplane for pilots to adapt to, an easy airplane to fly.'

Woodman made three low and slow passes over

TriStar N301EA made a stop-over at East Midlands Airport so it could be inspected by Rolls-Royce staff and the media. *(Lockheed)*

Right: President Chuck Wagner, left, and Geoffrey Fawn, center, managing director of the Rolls-Royce Derby, interviewed by a BBC newsman shortly after the TriStar landed at East Midlands Airport. More than one million people in Great Britain and Northern Ireland got a chance to see the L-1011 during low flights over Derby, Glasgow and Belfast.

Below: thousands queue to see N301EA at East Midlands Airport. *(both Lockheed)*

the airport and around the town of Derby on Saturday, before landing to the cheers of thousands gathered for their first glimpse of the aircraft, which was important to their future.

The lines of people filed through the cabin from the landing at about 3:45 pm on Saturday until 9:45 pm and continued from 7:30 am to 1 1:45 am Sunday until Joiner closed the airliner to prepare it for the homeward trip.

As the aircraft taxied out for takeoff Monday, hundreds of spectators at the airport and hundreds more lined along the automobile-clogged roads which curve over the green rolling landscape dotted with clumps of trees and hills that are characteristic of the land of Robin Hood.

Some 1500 workers at the Rolls-Royce Test Establishment at Hucknall, England, stood in a cold drizzle on the runway on Monday to form a human 'Good Luck, TriStar' as Calac's L-1011 ended a triumphant European tour and headed for home.

The outbound TriStar crew were touched by the employees' message, which symbolized the warm welcome accorded them throughout their two-day visit to East Midlands Airport.

As the blue-and-white TriStar disappeared into the haze, to be greeted en route to Shannon by hundreds of thousands of well-wishers at Glasgow and Belfast Airports, an employee at East Midlands supposedly declared: 'She's truly a beautiful bird. We hope it won't be too long before she comes back here in regular service.'

More than 20,000 persons toured the No. 3 TriStar interior when the aircraft visited San Juan, Puerto Rico, Miami, Fla., and Marietta, Ga. During the 8000-mile roundtrip, the L-1011 became the first of the wide-bodied trijets to visit the Caribbean, Florida and Georgia.

It was the second journey outside the continental

United States for the No. 3 TriStar. Some 600 Eastern Airlines officials attending a marketing conference were on hand to welcome the L-1011 when it arrived at the Puerto Rican capital. In the blue and white markings of Eastern, the aircraft made a low pass over the runway at San Juan with Chief Engineering Test Pilot Jack Woodman at the controls. A large crowd of spectators, including a delegation of Puerto Rican newsmen, marvelled at the Rolls-Royce RB211 engines' quietness as the TriStar passed low overhead and then circled for its landing.

Following the landing, a press conference was held on board. Jim Clyne, Calac's vice-president for commercial marketing, answered questions from the press along with Eastern Board Chairman Floyd Hall and Tom McFadden, the airline's senior vice-president for marketing.

Hall told the newsmen that San Juan would become a major destination for Eastern's fleet of L-1011 Whisperliners when the big trijets joined the airline in 1972. Eastern was celebrating its 25th anniversary of service to Puerto Rico, Hall added.

Clyne assured the reporters that their ears had not deceived them when the TriStar passed overhead. 'Extensive noise measurements of the L-1011, compared with data published about other aircraft, indicate that the TriStar is quieter than any jetliner now in airline service,' Clyne said.

Also on hand were officials of the San Juan Port Authority, who told the Eastern and Lockheed executives that they believe the quietness of the L-1011 will go a long way toward relieving their community relations problems in the vicinity of the San Juan airport.

Following the press conference, the L-1011 was opened for tours by the public. Despite intermittent rain showers, an estimated 15,000 visitors walked through the TriStar during one afternoon and evening at San Juan.

The following day the L-1011 flew to Miami, site of Eastern's operational headquarters. Another low-altitude flyover preceded the landing, and then Clyne and Eastern's Capt. Mike Fenello, vice-president for operational coordination, met with Florida journalists on board the aircraft.

'Eastern's commitment to the Whisperliner has its roots in the people of the airline who will fly it, maintain it, service it and - as a team with our public contact people - realize its full potential as the superior passenger aircraft we know it to be," Fenello told reporters.

At Miami, where the TriStar was parked near the massive steel skeleton of a vast new hangar under construction by Eastern for L-1011 maintenance and overhauls, some 4000 employees of the airline walked through the aircraft in a two-hour period.

For most, it was their first look at the airliner with which they will become intimately familiar beginning next spring, when Lockheed starts delivering the fifty L-1011's Eastern has ordered.

Later that day the TriStar paid a visit to the Lockheed-Georgia plant at Marietta, where its wing was designed and where its empennage is built. Gelac President Bob Furhman welcomed the L-1011 and its crew. After another onboard press conference, several thousand Gelac employees and invited guests toured the airliner.

Touring the L-1011 at this stop was a delegation of executives from Delta, which had twenty-four Tristars on order. Included were Charles H Dolson, chairman of the board for Delta; Robert Oppenlander, senior vice-president for finance and treasurer; R W Allen, vice-president for administration; D P Hettermann, assistant vice-president for engineering; W L Miller, assistant vice-president for material services; J F Nycum, assistant vice-president for flight equipment development; and Julian May of the engineering staff.

The visitors saw the TriStar's interior equipped with a data-gathering centre for the test-flight

During the TriStar's 8000-mile round-trip journey, with stops at San Juan, Miami and Marietta, the flight test crew, headed by Ernie Joiner, conducted an extensive series of tests and evaluations of various TriStar systems. Flight test crew members included, from left, Harry Meyer, instrumentation engineer in Dept. 59-15; Alan Dippel, autoland representative for Collins/Lear-Sigler; and Len Macy, electronics technician in 59-13. *(Lockheed)*

programme as well as a first-class lounge, and first-class and coach seats representative of Eastern's interior design.

Throughout the four-day journey, a Calac flight-test crew headed by Ernie Joiner, chief flight-test engineer, conducted an extensive series of tests and evaluations of the TriStar's various systems.

Testing included the hydraulic system and the automatic pilot in cruise and autoland mode Joiner pointed out. On its return to Palmdale, the aircraft made an automatic landing with a system recently installed in the No. 3 TriStar.

'This was our first flight to an area with high humidity and temperatures, and it gave us a good opportunity to evaluate our cabin air conditioning and other parts of the environmental control system under those conditions,' Joiner said.

Cockpit crew members on the flight, in addition to Woodman, included A J Peterson and Bill Smith, co-pilots, and Dick Watson and Warren Grossklaus, flight engineers.

1972 saw TriStar N305EA, destined for Eastern Air Lines, appearing at Transpo 72 in the company of a Boeing 747 and Douglas DC-10. Officially called the US International Transportation Exposition, this was a trade show held on 300 acres of land at Dulles International Airport outside Washington, DC for nine days from 27 May to 4 June 1972.

N305EA then went on a demonstration tour as the sales battle continued between the two tri-jets, and both were demonstrating at the same time in Japan in July 1972. The TriStar flew into Osaka and the DC-10 into Tokyo on 23 July. Next day each aircraft

Left: Ernie Joiner Calac chief flight test engineer on the left, and Jim Clyne, centre, Calac vice-president for commercial marketing, greet Gelac President Bob Furhman who was followed by several thousand Gelac employees and invited guests who toured the TriStar.

Below: More than 4000 Eastern Airlines employees had an opportunity to walk through and inspect the L-1011 TriStar during its brief stay at Miami, site of Eastern's operational headquarters. *(both Lockheed)*

made two demonstration flights, followed by each aircraft changing places, flying along Japan's major trunk route. These demonstrations were part of a major world tour of both types to generate further customer interest.

Low noise level of the Lockheed TriStar and its ability to perform automatic landings were the two major features of the Far East's fourteen-day tour by the sixth TriStar built. The aircraft began and ended its tour at the Lockheed plant in Palmdale. A party of Lockheed and Rolls-Royce executives flew on tour, and six Eastern Airlines stewardesses also accompanied the aircraft. It had the standard Eastern seating layout for 256 passengers.

During its tour, the TriStar flew more than 26,000 statute miles and made eleven demonstration flights at Taipei, Singapore, Hong Kong, and three cities in Japan - Osaka, Tokyo, and Kagoshima.

More than 1600 people flew in the TriStar at the points it visited on its tour. They represented a wide cross-section of airline personnel, government officials, journalists, bankers, and other prominent local people and, in the case of the visit to Japan, many local people associated with anti-noise groups.

The TriStar was demonstrated to executives and pilots of China Airlines, Malaysia Singapore Airlines, Cathay Pacific Airways, All Nippon Airways and Japan Air Lines. A wide range of pilots flew the aircraft and commented favourably on its handling, good flight deck visibility, advanced autopilot and ability to make fully automatic landings. Eight automatic landings were made during the tour, including the first-ever to be made in Japan.

Although the tour took in a number of airports never previously visited by a wide-bodied trijet, no ground handling or other problems were experienced. Nor did any technical difficulties arise with either the airframe or the Rolls-Royce RB211 engines. All departures were made on schedule apart from minor delays for air traffic reasons.

Explaining aircraft noise

Aircraft noise was a growing community relations problem wherever there were airports, but the most noise-conscious country visited during the tour was Japan. Measurements of aircraft noise were made by a wide range of bodies such as the Central Government through its agency, the Japanese Civil Aeronautics Board, local government authorities, and individual anti-noise groups. In the case of Osaka, a number of local city authorities within the conurbation took readings. The internationally accepted unit for noise measurement is the Effective Perceived Noise Decibel (EPNdB). It is used to specify noise certification limits for new aircraft by the International Civil Aviation Organization (ICAO) and the US and British airworthiness authorities.

This unit makes allowance for the response of the human ear to noise level and for the character and duration of the noise. It compensates for the fact that the various types of noise produced by an aircraft have different effects on the human ear. Thanks to the quietness designed into its RB211 engines, the TriStar had been certificated at noise levels well below the stringent new limits. As the quietest of the wide-bodied airliners, it had a certificated take-off noise level nine EPNdB below the Federal Aviation Administration limit. At approach, it was four EPNdB below the limit and its sideline noise is twelve EPNdB below. Due to the logarithmic basis of the EPNdB scale, a three EPNdB reduction lowers the annoyance level by twenty per cent and a ten EPNdB reduction by fifty per cent.

When N305EA arrived at Osaka it made much less noise than local journalists had anticipated. Demonstrations clearly established with the Japanese public that the aircraft was quieter than smaller jet airliners than in service. It was also accepted that the noise produced by the RB211 engine was much easier on the ear and more acceptable.

The aircraft was flown under conditions that did not make for the lowest possible noise level. No power cutback was used after take-off. Although this could reduce the noise level at a particular measuring point, less annoyance is produced for the areas under the take-off path as a whole by climbing the aircraft steadily without cutback. The aircraft was flown from Osaka at a take-off weight equivalent to that which would be used for flying 300 passengers to Tokyo. Temperatures were high when the take-offs were made - over 90° F was typical - and thus take-off and climb performance would have produced lower noise levels at more typical temperature conditions.

Two demonstration flights were made at Osaka. There were 262 passengers and crew on one of them. The invitation list for this flight had been decided in close consultation with the Japanese CAB and included a wide cross-section of local residents and members of anti-noise groups. Nearly thirty per cent of those aboard were making their first flight; they included small children and old ladies in kimonos.

Pilots who flew the TriStar during its demonstrations commented favourably on a number of features. One reaction was that there were 'acres of glass,' giving the pilots a better view than from earlier-generation airliners. This also permitted the TriStar to climb at angles up to twenty degrees - a feature demonstrated on a number of flights. The visibility from earlier aircraft tended to limit their permitted climb angle to about fifteen degrees.

Pilots were also impressed with the TriStar's handling. One particularly appreciated feature was its flying tail, which enabled a pilot to cope easily with a mistrim condition while still taking off in the same distance as when the trim was correctly set. It also enabled a trim runaway to be handled easily. The proportional trim system used on the aircraft was popular because it allowed the aircraft to be trimmed very precisely and at any desired rate.

Another feature that impressed pilots was the TriStar's direct lift control system. This DLC system comprised four spoilers on each wing, which were extended to an angle of approximately eight degrees whenever the flaps were lowered thirty degrees or more. They were used in both manual and automatic approaches. In the case of a manual approach, the spoilers were coupled in with the control column and any control input in pitch raised or lowered the spoilers from the eight-degree position to give a rapid change of lift before the flying tail took effect and changed the aircraft's attitude.

This gave the pilot an effective and rapid means of tracking the approach glide slope without changes in aircraft attitude, which would affect the cabin floor angle and thus be noticeable to passengers. As soon as the aircraft's main wheels touched the ground on landing the spoilers were automatically extended to the sixty-degree position to reduce wing lift and to act as air brakes. The automatic landing capability of the TriStar was demonstrated on eight occasions during the Far East tour and never failed to impress both pilots and passengers, who applauded on several occasions as the aircraft touched down.

The TriStar was certificated for Category IIIA automatic landings; that is Decision Height twelve feet and Runway Visual Range 700 feet). In order to land in conditions of such poor visibility, appropriate ground facilities are required. These consist mainly of a Category II ILS beam, one cleared for aircraft landing when the visibility is 100 feet, and the runway visual range is 1200 feet.

The TriStar's autoland system relied on a radio altimeter to give it the primary height guidance, with secondary guidance from the ILS glide slope. The advanced techniques used could, in effect, make a rough ILS beam a smooth one, thereby providing an autoland capability even with a poor beam.

Two views of TriStar N305EA seen during the sales tour of the Far East, both thought to have been taken at Kai Tak Airport, Hong Kong. *(both Tenmil Soket Collection)*

Noise was a subject much discussed and keenly monitored in Japan. Here, local technicians measure the sound generated by TriStar as it takes off from Osaka. Reactions of journalists in this city were favourable to the aircraft's noise levels. *(Tenmil Soket Collection)*

During the initial approach for an automatic landing, the pilot set the TriStar's autothrottle system to maintain the desired speed. The aircraft had a very smooth autothrottle that acted symmetrically on all three engines. Another of the system's features was its ability to compensate automatically for gusts. Accelerometers sampled the size of a gust and provide a computer input that enabled the autothrottle to compensate for its effect.

On a typical approach, the aircraft captured the ILS localizer beam at about ten to twelve miles from the airport. The aircraft then continued under automatic control by the autopilot until it intercepted the ILS glide slope beam. Before this happened, the pilot extended the landing gear, and when the glide slope was intercepted, the landing flap setting was selected. At this stage, the angle-of-attack system took over and controlled the autothrottle to hold the speed at 1.3 V_S - the stall speed or minimum steady flight speed for which the aircraft was still controllable.

The direct lift control system was also coupled in automatically when the flaps were extended to assist in tracking the glide slope, with the radio altimeter providing the master height inputs to the system.

These heights were measured at the lowest point of the aircraft, which was the bottom of the main landing gear. When the height reduced to one hundred fifty feet, the aircraft was put into the alignment mode to compensate for the effect of any crosswind. If the wind was from the left, say, this involved rolling it slightly left wing down and applying opposite rudder, so that the actual touchdown would be made with the aircraft's centreline correctly aligned with that of the runway.

At the height of fifty feet, the aircraft entered the flare mode. It was pitched up in order to reduce the sink rate, and the autothrottle cut the speed at a fixed rate of 0.9 knots per second. In this way, the sink rate was reduced to provide a smooth landing at a value of two feet per second.

Meanwhile, when the aircraft was at the height of five feet the autopilot prepared for rollout guidance after touchdown. This was provided via the localiser signal and input from yaw rate accelerometers to ensure that the aircraft did not follow a zig-zag course down the centerline of the runway.

After the main gear touched down, the autoland system changed the fuselage attitude at a rate of two degrees per second so that the nosewheel touched down approximately five seconds later. All the pilot then must do was to brake and apply reverse thrust.

A wide range of safety features was incorporated in the L-1011's autoland and autopilot systems and these were demonstrated during the Far Eastern Tour.

The autoland was a 'dual-dual' system to provide a safety back-up. It consisted of two autopilots, each with two channels. Even if one were to fail completely the other could take over with no change in the flight path. During an autoland, both autopilots were engaged, with one on standby. A sampling procedure eliminated any of the systems that were outside the desired tolerances.

The Collins-Lear Siegler autopilot provided automatic go-around capability. This permitted the TriStar to abort a landing when it was only ten feet above the ground at the end of its approach. The pilot selected the appropriate switch and opened the engines to full thrust, at which point the autopilot took over. It also demonstrated its ability to compensate for the loss of a critical engine either on the approach or take-off.

On completion of the Asian tour, the TriStar returned to Palmdale for maintenance in preparation for its European tour, starting in mid-August and finishing at the Farnborough Air Show. This aircraft was in the basic Eastern colours, with the airline titles changed as appropriate.

N305EA arrived in the UK during August bearing Court Line's name, and visited a number of UK regional airports including Luton, Manchester and Newcastle.

The imminent arrival of N305EA was reported in issue 4 of *Court Line News,* the staff newspaper published in April 1972. 'After much speculation, it has now been confirmed that a Lockheed TriStar will visit Court Line at Luton Airport this summer. The aircraft will stay for three days en route to the Farnborough Air Show where it will be on general public display. This aircraft will be in the Eastern livery but with our 'Court' insignia. For those of you who wish to view the arrival of the first wide-bodied jet into Luton, the ETA will be approximately 1400 hours on Sunday 13 August 1972.'

'During its three day visit, the aircraft will make several flights in and around the UK for

TriStar safety card! The safety card as provided in the Court Line/Eastern Air Line flight from Luton to Majorca.

The safety card shows a number of things. The airline was called 'Court Line Aviation Ltd', so as to differentiate between the parent shipping group, and that already the company was preparing material in the tri-colour design. *(Ed Posey/Autair-Court Collection)*

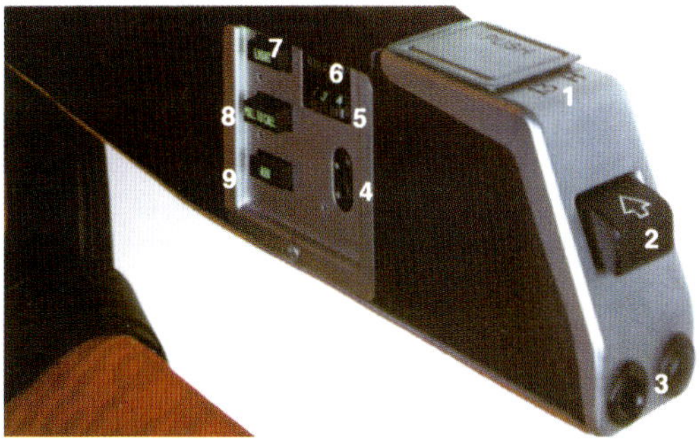

L-1011 Seat Controls - Court Line Style!

1. Seat Number
2. Seat Recline
3. Table Slots
4. Plug for Headset
5. Channel Selection
6. Volume
7. Reading Light (Press)
8. Pull to call
9. Ventilation (Press)

Court Line. These movements will take into account the evaluation required by various departments who will be concerned with the handling of the TriStar. During the visit, the aircraft will be available for Court Line personnel to inspect. The TriStar will leave Luton on Wednesday evening 16 August 1972.'

This 'familiarisation' visit to the airline's base included a celebration dinner in Palma, Majorca, as Doug Bennison of the British Airline Pilots Association, who was one of the guests, recalls: 'The event, billed as the inaugural flight by Lockheed TriStar to Palma, Majorca, was intended to mark the publication of the first Clarkson inclusive tour programme to feature this new aircraft. We were requested to be at a special marquee by the Court offices at Luton Airport by 1530hrs on 14 August, for a 1600hrs departure. The flight out to Palma was aboard the Eastern Airlines aircraft flown by a Lockheed crew under Captain J D Wells. Having been wined and dined to perfection, we were back at Luton by 23.30. A better aircraft could not have been chosen, for the demonstrator was only fitted with 230 seats - spaciousness indeed!'

All the guests were invited to inspect every aspect of the new aircraft, including open access to the Flight Deck, where an etched notice on a panel at the Engineers Station was brought to everyone's attention by the flight deck crew. It read 'Achtung alles lookenspeepers! Das machinen is nicht fur gefingerpoken und mitten grabben. Is easy schnappen der springenwerk, bloen fusen, und poppen corken mit spittsensparken. Is nicht fur gewerken by das dummkopfen. Das rubbernecken sightseeren keepen hands in das pockets - relaxen und watch das blinken lights'.

The L-1011 then went down to London Heathrow, for a rapid paint job before being seen at the SBAC show Farnborough from 4 to 10 September with BEA's logo on the nose and their Union Flag marking on its fin. The airliner quietly opened the flying display - by intent, it seems - and then reappeared later in the programme, so giving visitors a double chance to appreciate the quietness of this American airliner's Rolls-Royce RB211s.

During the sales tours, the aircraft flew 91,000 miles in 138 flights and logged 198 flying hours. On the intensive European part of the tour, which included the Farnborough appearances, three sorties per day were averaged, carrying 8,500 passengers in fifty-two flights from thirty-five airports. Both the aircraft and engines performed well, resulting in a departure regularity of ninety-nine per cent.

The TriStar's British type certification was

N305EA on it's way to dinner in Palma Majorca for an evening meal. *(Ed Posey/Autair-Court Collection)*

Same aircraft, different markings!

Above: N305EA especially named *Halcyon Days* for the occasion, comes in to land at Luton for demonstration to Court Line employees.

Left: Court Line girls, Eastern Airlines aircraft and BOAC aircraft steps - oh, and the location is Manchester! *(Ed Posey/Court Line Aviation Collection)*

Below N305EA *Halcyon Days* is stocked at Luton prior to the evening jaunt to Majorca
Opposite page, top: Taken at the same time, the photographer has caught a tiny, but fascinating detail. About the R2 door are the words 'Provisional Airworthiness' - this special FAA airworthiness certificate is issued to conduct special purpose operations of aircraft with provisional type certificates. Two classes of provisional type certificates may be issued. Class II certificates are issued for transport category aircraft only and have a duration of 12 months. *()*

It was then time N305EA to make a quick trip into BEA's then-new aircraft serving hangar at London Heathrow on 19 August for the removal of the Clarksons' C' from the fin, the application of the stylised Union flag on the tail and BEA titles replacing the Court name.

A few days later N305EA was the 'opening act' at the 1972 Farnborough Air Show. *(John F Hamlin)*

TriStar G-BAAA for Court Line Aviation comes together at Palmdale.

achieved in July 1972, culminating in about thirty hours of test flying, including a proportion of automatic landing development work. Very few adjustments needed to be made to the aircraft, especially as the British registration authorities had been working with Lockheed for about three years in preparation.

A major sales boost for Lockheed occurred on 7 August 1972 with an announcement by the British Government of BEA's approval to buy TriStars. BEA's preference for the TriStar was no secret, although it was in no hurry to place the order. The initial authority was for six standard TriStars with options on six more, which could be extended-range models. The order was worth £60 million, with a further £20 million allocated to supporting service, the initial delivery being in the autumn of 1974 for services commencing in 1975.

Although technically a BEA order, the selection closely involved the British Airways board in integrating BEA and BOAC. BEA could see a possible need for up to eighteen aircraft by 1980, but any extended range versions would be more suited to the longer haul BOAC routes. It was also expected that BEA Airtours would use some of the TriStar capacity. As BA's Marketing Director Henry Marking said 'Because of the fuel crisis and the world economic situation British Airways, like the rest of the airline industry, will face serious traffic and financial problems in the next year or so and there is great uncertainty about the rest of this decade. So, for the time being, we are restricting our commitment to the number of aircraft for which we can foresee a positive requirement towards the end of the 1970s. These TriStars will be replacing our older, noisier and less economic aircraft, which will by then have to be retired from service. We shall negotiate flexible delivery arrangements so that we can adjust to the demands of the market the dates on which these aircraft are to be delivered.'

At the time of the formal signature for the six TriStars for BEA on 26 September, the options were increased from six to twelve aircraft. Particularly useful to BEA was the low noise level of the RB211 engines which allowed round the clock operations without noise disturbance to surrounding communities. The autoland system would provide economic and operational gains.

The TriStar was to enter service with Court in the Spring of 1973 and BEA in September 1974. During the show it was announced that Pacific Southwest Airlines had ordered five more TriStars bringing sales and options at that time up to 169.

By 1973 the TriStar was starting to become a common sight and with two of the type starting to operate in Europe, Lockheed did not send over a demonstrator, instead preferring to use a Court Line aircraft. Court Line was not slow to show off its new aircraft to the public; on 18 May 1973 'Alpha Alpha' was demonstrated at the Biggin Hill Air Fair, and also at the Paris Air Show two weeks later where it shared duties with G-BAAB, both machines carrying passengers to and from the show when not on display. Lockheed themselves made good use of the charter by using the airliners presence at Le Bouget to display it to the public and aviation industry alike.

Spring Bank Holiday Monday found Luton Airport reeling under the impact of 400 passengers - one of which was this author - for the Ian Allan Travel TriStar flight to Le Bourget. The car parks were incapable of digesting vehicles at the rate they wished to enter and the airport lounges bulged. Passenger check-in was efficiently done, a number of desks being allocated by Court Line exclusively for this particular flight. Such was the Paris Air Show's popularity that year, that the tour organisers found it necessary to put on no fewer than three TriStar and one BAC One-Eleven flights from Luton, plus a Northeast Trident and Viscount from Heathrow. This type of excursion was conceived some six years previous by Trevor Bailey, a Director of Ian Allan Travel.

OU4133 was scheduled to depart at 0940 by which time all the passengers had been transported to the waiting *Halycon Days* and installed therein with the minimum of fuss and bother. At this point, French Air Traffic took command, which meant a half-hour delay. Eventually, G-BAAA was allowed to taxi slowly out to Runway 26 for a smooth take-off into what had become a murky sky. By this time, most of the passengers were investigating the contents of the cardboard box they had found waiting on each seat, their curiosity if not hunger being satisfied at the sight of some dainty sandwiches and a choc roll. The supplies for the TriStar's round trips weighed two tons, made up with food, drinks and other goods for sale on board which included 150,000 cigarettes. The captain informed his captive audience that the Paris weather was cloudy and rainy, which proved to be an accurate description! He also mentioned that a fully automatic landing would be made and proceeded to read off heights, speeds etc. continuing the commentary until reverse thrust was selected and brakes applied. This proved a fascinating experience and was appreciated by his passengers, who were, after all, aviation enthusiasts. No one could be blamed for thinking the arrival of the TriStar surprised the French authorities since it was some time before one inadequate pair of steps arrived and even longer before a coach materialised. Excited voices called out registrations of airliners seldom seen in the UK until the first batches were allowed to disembark and scatter.

Although not open to the public until 13.30, Ian Allan Travel had succeeded in acquiring entry tickets to the Show which were issued during the flight by Mrs Jean Dare and her assistant, the two company representatives on board. As a result of

The 1973 Le Bourget Air Show is largely remembered for the spectacular crash of the first production Tupolev Tu-144 supersonic transport. After a violent downward manoeuvre, the aircraft broke up and dived into the ground, destroyed fifteen houses and killed all six persons on board, as well as eight on the ground. Not unnoticed, however, were the appearance and demonstration of the new Lockheed L-1011 TriStar widebody airliner with two aircraft coming from Court Line, Alpha Alpha seen here taxiing back after its display flight.

'The Pink Lady', G-BAAB, taxies in at Le Bourget. The number '80' aft of the flight deck-glazing is the so-called 'aircraft type number' that was put on the TriStars so as to aid readers of the Salon international de l'aéronautique et de l'espace brochure. *(Ed Posey/Autair-Court Collection)*

this early admission, crowds absence was a great advantage for the photographers. Persistent rain made certain that only the British were paddling around the dripping static exhibits!

During the afternoon, the TriStar was demonstrated to the visitors before going off for an hour-long flight to benefit a Russian delegation and other VIPs. Apparently, the Russians were busy measuring distances between seats while airborne! Certainly, once loaded, those not beside an aisle found it difficult to move. The existence of eight conveniences could be of little comfort to them; although so near they are so far!

Later in the day many of the damp enthusiasts sported one Franc to ascend to the viewing gallery for a final spotting sortie. By the time the party was due to report for the return flight, the rain had ceased. This was fortunate since the long queue from the solitary desk wound its way through a set of automatic doors (which eventually gave up trying to close) and along the outside of the terminal. Mrs Dare and her colleague were trying to keep a check on numbers as their flock filed through Customs - by no means a simple task with 400 people to marshal in one spot at the right time.

Complications arose, such as the odd body which presented himself at Customs minus boarding card, those who couldn't find the right desk etc. A fleet of three buses took the first load off on a tour of the airport to where the TriStar had been parked after its demonstration flight. It took a further five busloads and fifty-five minutes to get the remainder on board. Were they all present? But no! 399 heads were visible and one empty seat. It was learned then that number 400 had decided to stay!

Demonstrating in the Far East

With a pair of 400-seat TriStars to keep busy, the Sales Department was on the look-out for any methods of soaking up the spare capacity. Already a series of 'Hadj' flights (carrying devout Muslim pilgrims to Mecca) had been flown for Royal Air Maroc between Rabat and Jeddah, the airport closest to Mecca. John Begg was Court Lines Sales Executive. 'I was in charge of selling the TriStars for long-haul charters - quite a challenge as they were fitted with short-range tankage!

After long negotiations, I concluded a deal for a series of charters between Bandar Seri Begawan in Brunei, Singapore and Kuala

The interior of G-BAAA.

Lumpur for 'Hadj' pilgrims to Jeddah. On 29 November 1973 G-BAAA departed Luton for Kuala Lumpur via Dubai two days earlier than was required for the 'Hadj' flights, for Lockheed had asked me if we would go out early so that Lockheed could demonstrate the L-1011 to Malaysian Airline System (MAS). I charged Lockheed $25,000 per day for the two-day demonstration, and they agreed without quibbling.' It was the easiest and the best charter I ever got for Court Line.' Alpha Alpha operated two flights for MAS locally from KUL, and Lockheed put a huge effort into it, including having their President, Carl Kotchian, fly out to meet us from LAX. We then positioned to BSB and were the first widebody to land at Brunei. Thousands of people turned out to meet us, and we did a low-level pre-landing flypast for them.

Here I was introduced to the Prime Minister of Brunei, and we picked up 200 pax for Jeddah, and a further 200 boarded us at Singapore. That in itself created a bit of a mystery. The TriStar was fitted with Weight and Balance and could weigh itself. As we were preparing to depart Singapore, the readout came up that we were about four tons under the estimated weight. Then we realised that our Far Eastern passengers were of a much slighter frame than the average European passengers our load charts and calculations were prepared for. The skipper promptly called the fuel tanker back, uplifted extra Jet 1A to put us near max allowable weight, and we managed to miss out a tech-stop!'

Midnight in Moscow

The appearance of the TriStar - be it a yellow or a pink one - in European skies was still a very novel event - for one to appear at a Soviet air show, deep behind the Iron Curtain was probably regarded by members of the Politburo as a perfect example of Western decadence!

Being a high-profile company - and one with an excellent safety record - it was not surprising that Court Line announced their co-operation on a Lockheed and Rolls-Royce charter to present the TriStar to the Soviet Union in Moscow, the first time a wide-bodied airliner had been seen in Russian skies.

The task - to show off the aircraft to the best advantage - was planned with military precision, with people gathering in Moscow from all points of the globe. On board *Halcyon Days* was a delegation of nearly sixty people; including Lockheed personnel, headed by George Prill, President of Lockheed International with their own interpreters; a team from Rolls-Royce; a number of Court support personnel - Michael Bell, Fred Kozo, John Margrave, Kenneth Nicholson and Gordon Wright; and, of course, the Flight Crew.

On the Flight-Deck were Captain Michael Williams, Captain Peter Hogg, First Officer David Walker, Flight Engineer Michael Albone and Flight Engineer David 'Danny' Duffain. In the cabin were Angela Abrahams, Barbara Alexander, Maureen Ashton, Kathleen Atkinson, Patricia Dalgleish, Linda John, Patricia Knights, Ann

The crew with Alpha Alpha at Kuala Lumpur. Captain Freddie Fox is fourth from the left, Captain Dave Hampson is on the far right. John Begg, from Court TriStar Sales is seventh from left, next-but-one to a Lockheed test-pilot. *[via John Begg]*

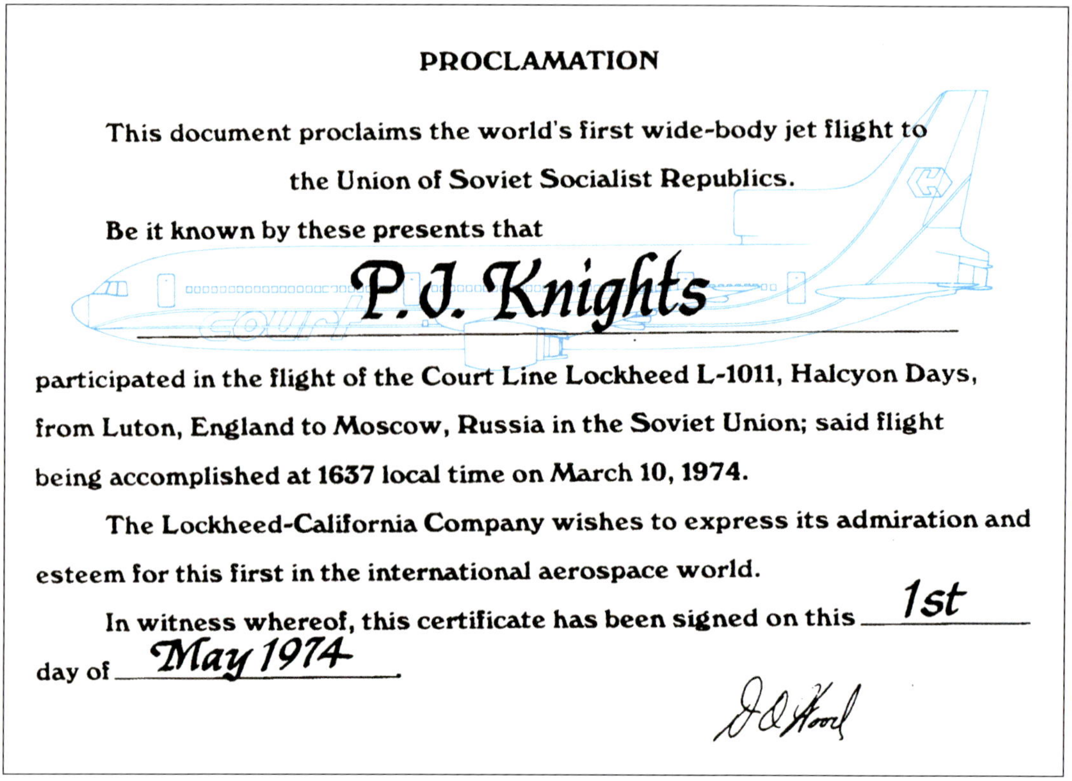

PROCLAMATION

This document proclaims the world's first wide-body jet flight to the Union of Soviet Socialist Republics.

Be it known by these presents that

P.J. Knights

participated in the flight of the Court Line Lockheed L-1011, Halcyon Days, from Luton, England to Moscow, Russia in the Soviet Union; said flight being accomplished at 1637 local time on March 10, 1974.

The Lockheed-California Company wishes to express its admiration and esteem for this first in the international aerospace world.

In witness whereof, this certificate has been signed on this 1st **day of** May 1974.

McNulty and Margaret Royffe.

Alpha Alpha departed Luton, arriving at Moscow at 1637hrs local on 10 March 1974. Whilst there, the aircraft gave demonstration flights to officials from the Soviet Ministry of Aviation Industry, and representatives from Aeroflot, the State airline. The aircraft was also open for inspection on the ground, until departure on 16 March. From all accounts the aircraft had a 'major check' during its stay: the majority of removable parts were removed; the aircraft was photographed from the outside, inside, upside and downside. People were seen scurrying about with pads and pencils on which appeared little diagrams and sketches of ice tongs, trays, seatbelts, food trolleys and oxygen masks. The questions kept on coming: 'Can you really board in fifteen minutes?' 'Can you drop the oxygen masks?' 'Does it really seat 400 people?'

So successful was the tour, that afterwards George Prill, President of Lockheed International wrote to Edward Posey, Court Line Managing Director...

'On behalf of the Lockheed/ Rolls-Royce team, I wish to express our appreciation for the absolutely outstanding cooperation and assistance rendered by the Court Line personnel during our recent successful flight demonstration of the L-1011 in Moscow.'

'As you well know, the demonstration of an aircraft is heavily dependent upon the attitude and competence of the crew. Captain Hogg and Captain Williams and the other members of the flight crew acted as front-line Lockheed salesmen.'

'All had a special effect on the Ministry of Aviation Industry and Aeroflot officials.'

'The young ladies of the cabin crew, led by Ann McNulty, did particularly valiant work, both during the demonstration flight and the ground displays. They received plaudits not only from the Lockheed /Rolls team but also from our Soviet guests. The fact that the airplane performed perfectly, and all the operations in Moscow went smoothly throughout was a testimonial to Michael Bell and his ground crew.

'I can make no better comment about the success of the charter from our point of view than to say that if we had to repeat it, we would immediately seek the same charter airline, the same arrangements and the same crew.'

'I think the Press coverage was good both in the United States and in the UK. In summary, I trust you were as satisfied with the endeavour as we were.'

Chapter Eight

On Board the L-1011

The L-1011 interior had the atmosphere of spaciousness, made possible by a fuselage almost twenty feet in diameter. The main cabin ceiling was ninety-five inches high, with no overhead racks or projections in the centre. The wide double aisles were also an important feature, which resulted from the large cabin diameter. Advancements were made over existing transports of the time in the areas of interior lighting, environmental control, interior decor, storage for passenger belongings, and food service arrangements.

Early cabin interior colours were very much 'of the time'. Everything tended to be a sea of brown or orange hues, with even the flight attendants wearing tan uniforms.

Lockheed wasted no time or effort in extolling the new airliners virtues: 'The interior of the TriStar is designed for people. To please passengers. To make them comfortable.'

'Two large, 26½-inch wide aisles traverse the cabin (20 inches in coach) for passenger ease and casual mobility.'

'Typical First Class seating is arranged for six persons across in three-seat pairs. Typical coach seating is four-seat pairs interspersed by two aisles, so no passenger is ever more than one seat from an aisle.'

'Entryways are double - type doors, a good 42-inches wide - three on each side of the cabin, and

TWA's First Class zone on their L-1011s featured swivel seats. *(TWA via Lockheed)*

a smaller emergency exit in the aft section.'

'Wide cross aisles between each pair of double—width entry doors make boarding and deplaning easier. Closets - storage - the L-1011 TriStar has it. Self-locking, over-window cabinets for carry-on luggage. Retractable clothes closets just inside passenger doors to store coats and garment bags. And baggage retention cages under seats. Lavatories, five aft and two forward, are large and well lighted'

The L-1011 interior was readily converted between configurations. Seats could be moved in one-inch increments throughout the cabin length and the class divider could be located anywhere in the constant section of the cabin. Passenger service modules could also be positioned at one-inch intervals to suit variations in seat locations. Individual reading lights and air outlets were adjusted to suit seat locations. These features enabled customer airlines to obtain the interior seating arrangements most suited to their particular operation and provide the flexibility to vary arrangements at any time. Aisle seat rows in the economy section were staggered so that passengers entering or leaving their seats on either side of the aisle did not interfere with each other. Basic to the TriStar interior were seven lavatories, two at the front of the cabin and five at the rear.

TWA L-1011s were equipped with carry-on luggage compartments in the main cabin. *(TWA via Lockheed)*

TWA L-1011s had a stand-up bar area in their Coach lounge. *(TWA via Lockheed)*

A ten/ninety per cent mix of first-class and economy class passengers accommodated 273 passengers. Seating was six-abreast at a forty-inch pitch for twenty-eight passengers in first class, and eight-abreast at a thirty-four-inch pitch for 245 passengers in economy class. All seats were extra-wide doubles, with no passenger more than one seat away from an aisle.

A twenty/eighty per cent mix accommodated 256 passengers. Seating was six-abreast at a thirty-eight-inch pitch for fifty-two passengers in first class, and eight-abreast at a thirty-six-inch pitch for 204 passengers in economy class.

All economy class seating could accommodate from 330 to 400 passengers. A typical one-class economy seating arrangement accommodated 330 passengers, with nine-abreast at thirty-four-inch pitch throughout the constant section of the cabin. Triple seats were installed along the left side of the cabin, with double seats in the centre of the cabin and on the right side.

With short extensions to seat tracks in the forward cabin, 345 passengers could be accommodated in a nine-abreast arrangement at a thirty-two-inch pitch. This interior represented the maximum number of seats that could be installed in order to meet emergency evacuation requirements with three pairs of Type A doors and one pair of Type 1 exits.

Left: L-1011 main cabin doors retracted up into the roof space when open.

Below left: After boarding the flight attendants slid them down...

Bottom: ...until they were completed closed, and plugged up the hole. *(Lockheed)*

With the installation of an additional pair of Type A doors at the rear of the cabin, in place of the existing Type 1 exits, and right and left side outboard triple seats with quad seats in the centre, a total of 400 passengers could be carried in a ten-abreast seating at thirty-inch seat pitch.

Airstairs

Some of the airports TriStar operators planned in flying into had far fewer facilities available than airports like London Heathrow, New York or Los Angeles. Either complete lack of or just shortages made it imperative to make sure facilities were available for getting the passengers swiftly on and off the aircraft. The answer was to bring along your own stairs!

The self-contained, power-operated airstairs were designed to provide a wide, stable, two-abreast boarding and deplaning stairway. The airstairs were installed in the centre cargo compartment, immediately behind and below the Number 3 right-hand passenger door.

The airstairs, when stowed, occupied the threshold area of the centre cargo compartment. Normal actuation of the airstairs was controlled from the control panel, located on the inside of the passenger cabin aft of the Number 3 right-hand door or from the external control panel located in the lower part of the fuselage below the wing. An additional control panel was located on the airstair carriage, within the cargo compartment.

Stairs had a heavy-duty, non-slip surface, and each step was illuminated. The time required to deploy or retract the stairs, including opening or closing the cargo door, was less than one minute. Installation of the airstairs precluded the use of LD-3 cargo containers in the centre compartment. However, space forward of the airstairs was usable for either bulk cargo or baggage. Total installed weight of the airstairs was approximately 2,500 pounds.

Court Line was one of the L-1011 operators that had the airstairs installed on its TriStars.

One of the additional equipment options offered to customer airlines was the self-contained airstairs. This concept was used previously on narrow-bodied airliners to assist with passenger ingress and exit at airports lacking vast amounts of passenger-handling equipment.

One of the airlines that ordered them was Court Line, the UK airline that flew into many lesser-known, smaller airports in Europe. In order to thoroughly test and demonstrate the self-contained airstairs, Lockheed built a fully functioning test rig at Palmdale even going to the extreme of painting it in Court Line colours!

As can be seen, the system was installed under the main floor, and when required was extended first out, and then moved to the left into position under the door before fully extending outwards. Once in the correct position, the handrails rose upwards. *(all Lockheed)*

The Lower Deck Galley

A unique feature for an airliner was the L-1011 underfloor galley. The galley occupied an envelope 238 inches long, 164 inches wide, and 74 inches high and was located under the cabin floor, forward of the wing box. It was equipped with refrigerators, ovens, bun warmers, work counter, storage areas, waste disposal areas, and interphone system. The galley compartment was air-conditioned, lighted, and provides restrained parking areas for twenty food and beverage service carts. The entire compartment was sealed so that any spillage or leakage was retained and observable for easy cleanup.

Location of the main galley facilities below the passenger cabin offered important advantages:

- Increased available space in the main cabin for additional passenger seats (up to 16 more),
- Eliminated food preparation odors from the cabin, and
- Eliminated the noise and confusion associated with conventional galley operations.

The food and beverage cart system provided rapid and high-quality service to large numbers of passengers by relatively few attendants. Three service centres located in the passenger cabin supplemented the underfloor galley. Refreshment services could be performed quickly, either during or between-meal service, from the cabin level.

The two galley lifts were fully independent and could be operated simultaneously. Each lift was designed to transport either one service cart or one

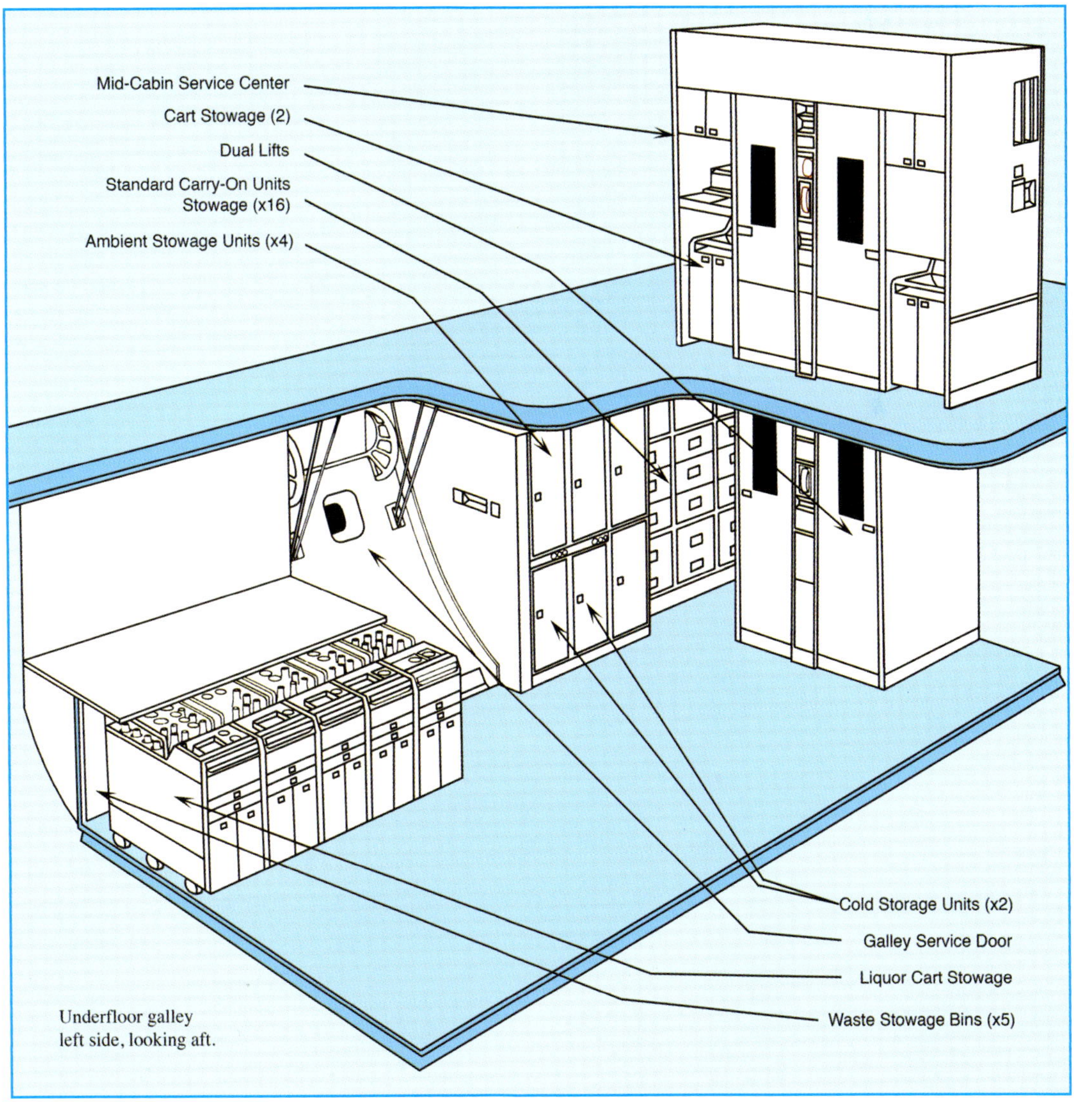

Underfloor galley left side, looking aft.

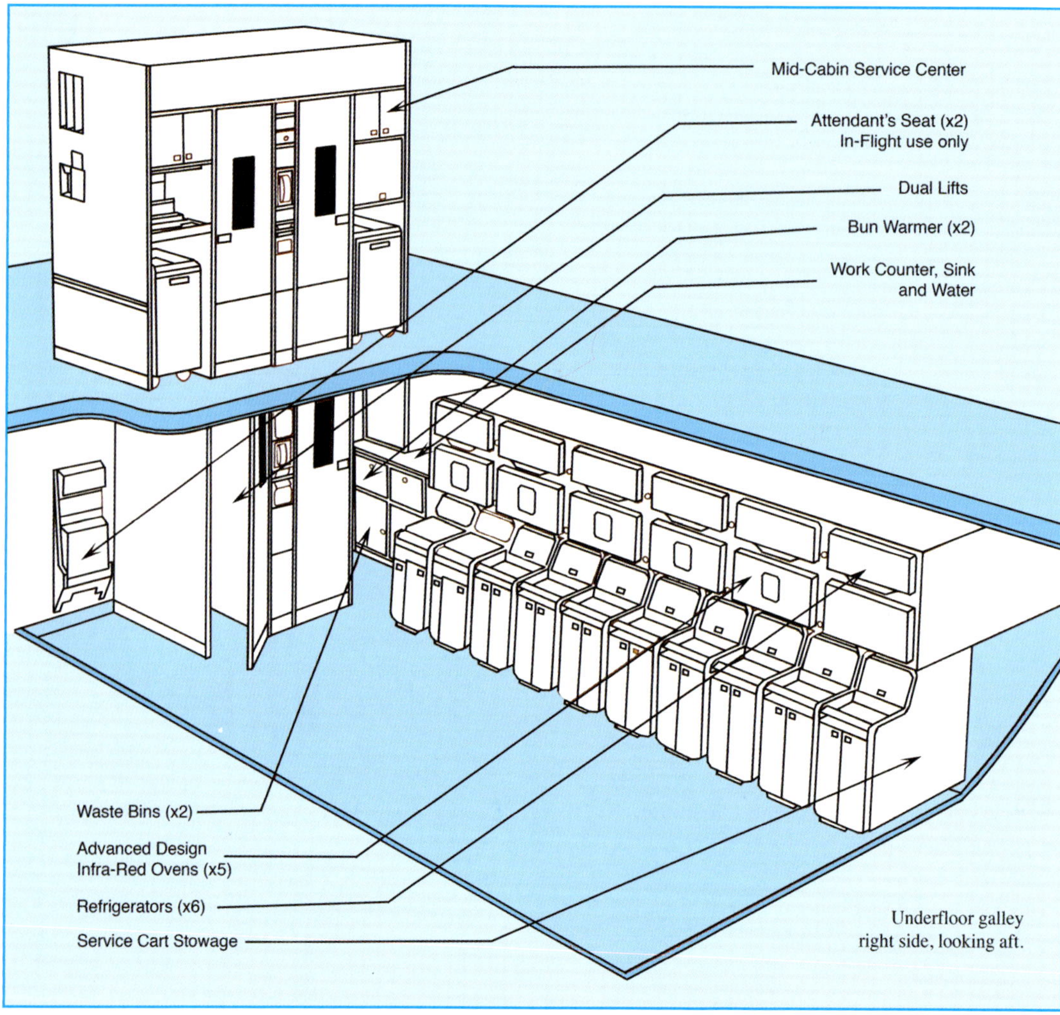

For the passenger, the commotion, the noise, the hurry-conversations of flight attendants, and the food odours were all gone on the early L-1011s. Now the food and beverage service by cart - transported by two enclosed lifts - speeded up the service.

Ground servicing of the galleys was through a separate galley service door. Five quick-cooking, infra-red ovens cooked 270 meals in twenty minutes - each oven handled up to fifty-four standard casseroles at one time. The TriStar below-deck galley allowed space in the cabin for ten to nineteen additional passenger seats, or a lounge, depending on the seating arrangement.

Below: the location of the underfloor galley is shown in orange.

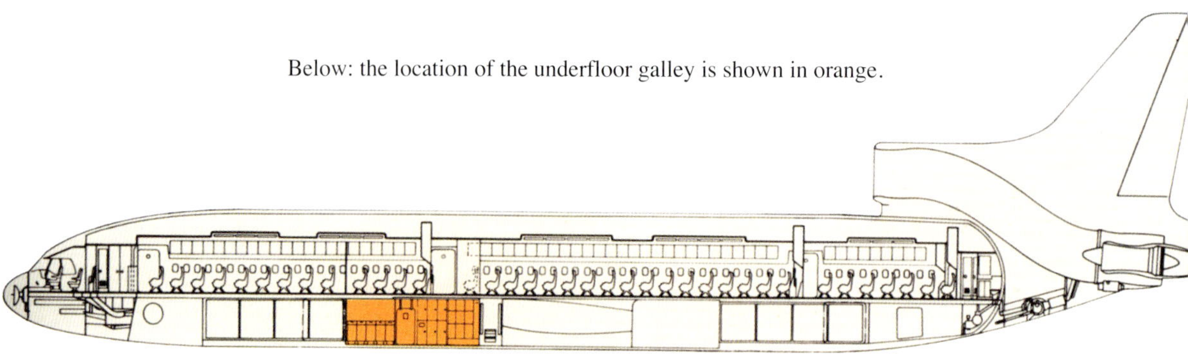

attendant travelling in either direction between the underfloor galley compartment and the main cabin. The electro-mechanical lift system might be operated from either of the external control panels, located at the cabin and galley level, or by switches inside the lift. Emergency stop buttons, at cabin and galley level, overrode the control inside the lift. When an attendant rode the lift, both hands were required to operate interdependent switches. Releasing either switch will stop the lift.

The doors are provided with safety interlocks that stopped the lift if the doors were opened. The normal one-way travel time of the lifts was eight seconds. Each lift was equipped with two independent, motor-driven systems. If one motor failed, the remaining motor would continue to operate the lift at half speed. The design of the power train was such that should any failure occur the lift would not fall free; however, it could be manually lowered to the galley level.

Incidentally, Lockheed deliberately referred to the system as a 'lift' - using the English phrase, rather than the American terminology of 'elevator', to avoid any confusion with the flight controls elevator during communications on the intercom.

Above: A typical flight attendant seat and communications centre on TWA L-1011s. *(TWA via Lockheed)*

Lounges, Baggage and Cargo Compartments

The L-1011 lower deck lounge provided operators with a unique passenger-appeal feature. The early 1970s was at a time when cabin level lounges were

Below: the lower deck lounge area, looking aft. The relatively low headroom and lack of windows made the space slightly oppressive. *(Lockheed)*

Above: the lower deck lounge area, looking forward. The half-bubble seats and sofas had seat-belts and could be used for take-offs and landings.

Below: the lounge area is shown in green. *(both Lockheed)*

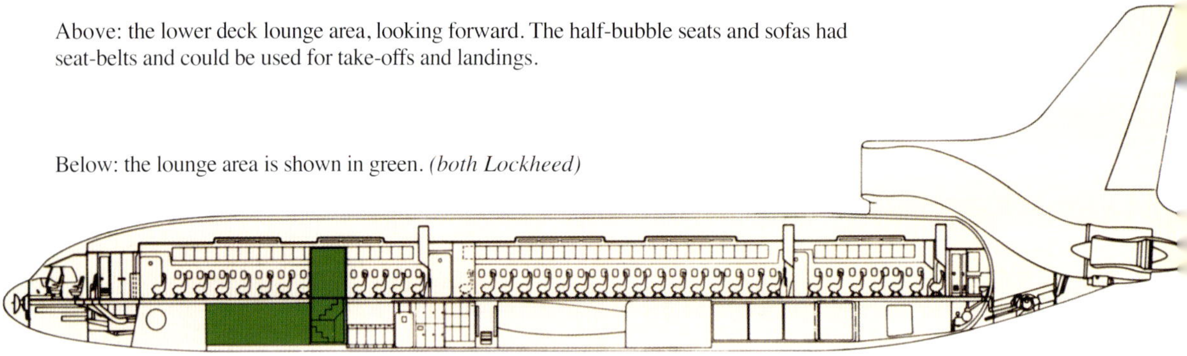

becoming popular among wide-body operators. The lower deck lounge offered the operator an economic advantage over conventional cabin-level lounges by displacing a smaller number of revenue passenger seats. Cabin-level lounges could substitute as many as twenty-eight revenue seats, but the lounge below the cabin only displaced revenue seats in the area occupied by the stairway connecting the two compartments.

Two basic configurations were offered: a non-saleable seat lounge for in-flight use only and a combination lounge and carry-on baggage compartment, utilizing both the forward cargo compartment and the underfloor galley area, with seats certified for use during takeoff and landing.

The non-saleable seat lounge was located in the forward cargo compartment area immediately ahead of the underfloor galley. This lounge was twenty-one feet long, thirteen feet seven inches wide, and had a clear ceiling height of six feet four inches. To achieve this, Lockheed lowered the cargo floor by nine inches. Access from the main cabin was provided by a 'U' shaped stairway that eliminated the narrow tapered treads associated with spiral stairways used on other airliners such as the Boeing 747.

A wet bar was provided and included a coffee maker, coffee warmer, ice storage, and associated

Passengers aboard this Air Canada TriStar had fingertip controls built into the seat arms with plug-in pneumatic headphones for the on-board entertainment system. These rubber hoses were used instead of traditional electromagnetic transducer headphones for two main reasons; first, the hoses were much cheaper than a decent pair of traditional headphones at the time, and to an extent, they were washable so that airlines could provide a pair for everyone at a much lower price than traditional headphones. Second, the hoses were more or less useless without the driving system aboard the aircraft, largely removing the incentive for passengers to walk off with them, again reducing costs of providing the system to passengers! *(Air Canada)*

electric, water, and drainage services. The bar was located at the rear of the lounge to the stairway's left, with access to the galley through a service door in the dividing bulkhead. The lounge's lighting was provided by pinhole ceiling lights and concealed sidewall lights similar to the main cabin.

The lounge was also available with saleable seats certified for take-off and landing. This configuration required the installation of two emergency exits.

The alternative was a combination lower deck lounge and carry-on baggage compartment that consisted of a lounge arrangement in the forward cargo compartment in conjunction with a carry-on baggage compartment. It was located in the area generally used for the underfloor galley.

The main door that incorporated folding boarding stairs was located at the forward end of the carry-on baggage compartment on the fuselage's left-hand side. Passengers could board the aircraft through this door and deposit their baggage or other personal belongings in the racks provided along either side of the carry-on baggage compartment. Passengers then proceeded forward through a door into the lounge area to their seats.

Lounge seats were certified for use during take-off and landing. Swivel seats locked in a forward-facing position for take-off and landing and rear-facing fixed seats were provided with retractable headrests. An additional exit was required to satisfy emergency evacuation regulations. This exit was a modification of the existing galley service door, from an upward-inward opening door to a downward-outward opening door, incorporating an emergency Type 1 escape slide.

I never have been quite sure what was happening in this Air Canada publicity picture! Snoopy appears to be having his seabelt fastened in the event that this TriStar is about to go into combat with the Red Baron! *(Air Canada)*

The forward cargo compartment and galley area lent themselves to other alternate uses and at various times some of the following were considered by the airlines:

- First class dining room.
- First class sleeping berths.
- Duty-free store.
- TV room or theatre.
- Children's nursery.

Above: high class dining aboard Air Canada. *(Air Canada)*

Below: TWA centreline modules *(TWA)*

Below left: Push-button operated clothes closets aboard Air Canada. *(Air Canada)*

Three baggage/ cargo compartments were located in the lower fuselage below the cabin floor. The compartments were pressurised and heated to a minimum of fifty degrees Fahrenheit in flight. The compartment lining and floors were sealed to limit air volume available to support combustion and prevent the propagation of a fire. The three compartments were lined with fire-and impact-resistant materials.

Cargo floors in all compartments were provided with bulk cargo tie-down hard points to restrain heavy cargo against flight loads. The floors were sealed against spillage of liquids and equipped with drains leading to overboard-draining sumps.

Compartment ceiling and sidewall surfaces were white. Recessed light fixtures were installed to provide adequate levels of overall illumination. Lights were automatically controlled by door-operated switches. In addition, manually operated override switches were provided in each compartment near the loading door.

Cargo doors for three compartments were located on the right side of the fuselage. They were arranged to permit simultaneous loading of the compartments without interference with galley servicing or passenger boarding.

They were of were the outward opening plug type, solidly seated against the inside of the

fuselage when pressurised. They swung outward and upward when opened to allow maximum clearance for loading cargo. All doors were electric power-operated, normally from control panels adjacent to each door. Doors could be operated manually if electrical power was not available.

The forward and centre compartments were

used for containerised baggage and/or cargo. Each compartment was equipped to carry eight LD-3 containers, or four double-width containers, which could be carried interchangeably on other wide-bodied jet transports. A floor-mounted ball mat and roller system were installed, and an electrically-powered drive system provided powered container handling, which was remotely controlled to permit one-man loading operations.

Each compartment was fully lined, and sidewalls, floor, and ceiling were designed to withstand flight and ground handling loads from bulk cargo and containers. The floor and ceiling provided vertical restraint of the LD-3 containers, which eliminated the containers' requirement for certification.

The aft compartment was used only for bulk cargo loads. Tie-down points were provided in the floor and sidewalls to restrain heavy or dense packages, as required. A restraint net was installed to protect the access door from cargo loads and provisions were made to install a transverse divider net aft of the access door, if required. The aft compartment was provided with positive conditioned airflow of ten cubic feet per minute and was suitable for carrying pets or other live animals.

A major advantage of containerisation was the time saved in the loading operation. The controlling element in loading time, for all practical purposes, was the cycling time of the ground equipment. With a loader capable of handling one complete delivery cycle per minute and handling a pair of LD-3s back to back, either the forward or centre compartment could be completely loaded or unloaded in approximately five minutes. Since each compartment was entirely independent, it was possible to load the forward, centre, and aft cargo compartments simultaneously. The normal operation of the containerised system, and the ease with which the LD-3 containers were handled on the ground,

Two LD-3 cargo containers are loaded in the forward underfloor cargo compartment. This compartment held eight LD-3 containers did the centre compartment. LD-3 containers could be carried interchangeably on other wide-bodied transports making it easy to transfer cargo loads between airlines. The lift shown could handle double-width containers. *(Lockheed)*

Right: the stages of operation of the Polarised window light control system.

permitted rapid handling of the passenger's checked baggage. There were other advantages offered by containerization. Baggage was well protected from the weather and was less subject to damage than when hand loaded into old-style cargo pits.

All of the checked baggage, for 316 passengers, could be carried in either of the containerised baggage/cargo compartments. This was based on an average of four cubic feet of checked baggage per passenger. The remaining 1,264 cubic feet of containerised cargo space, plus 700 cubic feet of bulk cargo space, could be used for revenue-producing cargo.

Polarised windows

As early as 1957 Lockheed Aircraft Corp applied for patents to use polarised light to lighten and darken aircraft windows, based on 1943 patents by Edwin H Land of the Polaroid Corporation. Lockheed saw this as a way of lightening airframes - especially when airliners became larger and larger, requiring more and more windows. With the advent of pressurised aircraft, double-paned windows were used, and these were, of necessity, heavy in weight, requiring duplication of pane supports and seals that were costly to manufacture, install and maintain. In addition to the double-paned pressurised windows it was the general practice to provide each window with drapes, or curtains, so that entrance of sunlight could be controlled at will. These curtains required brackets, mouldings and the like for installation and adjustment. They materially complicated the overall assembly, weight and increase the initial cost and maintenance cost.

The windows - 126 per ship-set - were made by Fortin Plastics, of nearby Valencia Industrial Park. They operated by simply rotating one of the polarising shades (inner/rotator) against the other (outer/fixed). The window would then become progressively darker and darker until it was virtually black. In addition, not only did the polarised windows reduce the amount of glare, but they blocked harmful UV radiation exposure and helped the interior remain cooler longer.

Chapter Nine

Into Service!

It was not long after the initial launch two more US domestic trunk route carriers joined the customer list, Delta and Northeast. The Delta order was initially for twenty-four aircraft worth £150 million, twelve to be delivered in 1972 and the remainder in 1973. The Northeast order was for four aircraft plus four options to be delivered in 1972, in a contract worth £25 million. This brought total orders within less than one month of the TriStar launch to 152 aircraft, worth £1,035 million, including £160 million earned by Rolls-Royce.

Northeast Airlines was born on 19 November 1940 when the railroad owners of Boston Maine/Central Vermont Airways decided to change the name and corporate identity to prepare a public stock offering. Fast forward to 1970 and the airline employed well over 3500 people using a mixed fleet of forty-one aircraft.

The airlines were enthusiastic about introducing this new TriStar, with its high passenger capacity to match the expected growth in travelling numbers, and the wide-bodied interior to be more attractive to the occupants. Its range flexibility was a particular advantage flying economically from US coast-to-coast nonstop, or the shorter segments such as New York to Chicago or Phoenix to Los Angeles. Seat-mile costs would be lower than any of the jets operating at the time. The TriStar would also be compatible with the Boeing 747, particularly in terminal facilities. Northeast planned to use the TriStars initially on its Boston to Florida and New York to Florida routes, with 40 first-class seats and 227 tourist-class, eventually linking Montreal, Baltimore, Washington and Philadelphia with Florida. Northeast added two more firm TriStar orders in mid-1968, bringing total sales to 174 aircraft.

In the Air Holdings contract, it was understood that Lockheed would only sell to airlines in the USA, leaving Air Holdings as the worldwide sales distributor responsible for arranging any financial needs, including credit arrangements, through the City of London merchant bankers, Lazard Brothers. Overseas sales predictions by Lockheed were 175 aircraft by 1975 and could even reach 500 by 1980.

The first TriStar sale out of the Air Holdings batch was for ten aircraft for Air Canada, ordered in December 1968 with nine more options. This was followed in April of the same year by an order for two aircraft by the newly formed Air Jamaica, worth £12.5 million, also as part of the Air Holdings allocation, although it seems the contract was placed with Lockheed direct. The Air Jamaica's announcement came in April 1969, at a time when their fleet consisted of two DC-9s and one DC-8 which provided a daily flight between Jamaica and

What might have been: artist's impressions of Air Jamaica and Northest Airlines L-1011s. *(Lockheed)*

New York and thrice daily Jamaica-Miami. Planned route extensions were to Puerto Rico, the UK and Canada.

An indemnity from Rolls-Royce supported the Air Holdings order, and the British Government underwrote half the commitment up to a maximum of £5 million. If Air Holdings sold no aircraft, the total potential liability was estimated to be £15 million. With the sale of TriStars to Air Canada and Air Jamaica, the liability was reduced to £10 million, and the British Government received a rightful share of the profits. Additional orders in December 1968 for lease to airlines were three aircraft for Air Finance and two for the Haas-Turner investment group.

Air Canada

Air Canada's predecessor, Trans-Canada Air Lines (TCA), was created by federal legislation as a subsidiary of Canadian National Railway (CNR) on 11 April 1937. The Department of Transport under Minister Clarence Decatur Howe desired an airline under government control to link cities on the Atlantic coast to those on the Pacific coast. Using $5 million in Crown seed money, two Lockheed Model 10 Electras and one Boeing Stearman biplane were purchased from Canadian Airways and experienced airline executives from United Airlines and American Airlines were brought in.

Passenger flights began on 1 September 1937, with an Electra carrying two passengers and mail from Vancouver to Seattle, a $14.20 round trip, and, on 1 July 1938, TCA hired its first flight attendants. Transcontinental routes from Montreal to Vancouver began on 1 April 1939, using twelve Lockheed Model 14 Super Electras and six Lockheed Model 18 Lodestars. By January 1940, the airline had grown to nearly six hundred employees.

Canadian Pacific Airlines suggested in 1942 a merger with TCA. Prime Minister William Lyon Mackenzie King rejected the proposal and introduced legislation regulating TCA as the only airline in Canada allowed to provide transcontinental flights. With the increase in air travel after World War Two, CP Air was granted one coast-to-coast flight and a few international routes.

Originally headquartered in Winnipeg, which was also the site of the national maintenance base, the federal government moved TCA's headquarters to Montreal in 1949; the maintenance base later also moved east. With the development of the ReserVec in 1953, TCA became the first airline in the world to use a computer reservation system with remote terminals.

By 1964, TCA had grown to become Canada's national airline and, in 1964, Jean Chrétien submitted a private member's bill to change the name of the airline from Trans-Canada Airlines to Air Canada, which TCA had long used as its French-language name. This bill failed, but it was later resubmitted and passed, with the name change taking effect on 1 January 1965.

During the 1970s, government regulations ensured Air Canada's dominance over domestic regional carriers and rival CP Air. Short-haul carriers were each restricted to one of five regions and could not compete directly with Air Canada and CP Air. CP Air was subject to capacity limits on intercontinental flights and restricted from domestic operations. Air Canada's fares were also subject to regulation by the government.

Air Canada's L-1011 C-GAGH in the Singapore '85 livery with number 553 on the nose door and tail lands at London Heathrow. *(Richard Vandervord)*

Air Canada's L-1011 CF-TNB with number 502 on the tail. *(Air Canada)*

The TriStar deal, at the time unique was somewhat complicated. Air Canada arranged with a US investment group to lease two L-1011s. Under the agreement, the Haas-Turner investment group would lease the two aircraft to Air Canada during the summer months, and in the winter they would be leased by Eastern Airlines. The contract was to run for a fifteen-year period. This arrangement, where one Canadian airline and one United States airline share aircraft, each for half a year, was the first of its kind in the industry.

The agreement provided both airlines with additional capacity during their peak traffic periods - the summer months for Air Canada and the winter season for Eastern. By leasing the aircraft rather than purchasing equipment outright, both airlines realised substantial financial savings over the lease period.

Air Canada was to take delivery of the two leased aircraft in May 1973, to be operated until October when they were turned over to Eastern, who used them from November to April.

To give the TriStar a transatlantic capability, Air Canada commenced modification of three of its aircraft to L-1011-100 standard to increase the take-off weight by 36,000 pounds and make available the centre-section fuel tank capacity of 19,000 pounds of fuel. This extended the range with 257 passengers by 900 miles. Routes to be served were from Toronto and Montreal to London, Frankfurt and Paris. The first of the three Air Canada TriStars retrofitted to the L-1011-100 standard commenced transatlantic operations at the end of April 1977. The range was increased to 3,660 nautical miles and the gross weight rose to 466,000 pounds for a modest increase in empty weight of 1,400 pounds. With the RB211 thrust remaining the same, the field length was increased from 8,350 feet to 11,200 feet, so they were a bit of a ground-hugger. Air Canada also fitted duplicate Litton Inertial Navigation Systems to the three converted TriStars to assist on the long over-water navigation.

After many years of good service, in June 1990 Air Canada also decided to sell its TriStar fleet, phasing out the eight L-1011-100s before the end of the year and replacing them with high-density Boeing 767s on leisure market routes. The remaining long-range TriStar 500s used on international routes were due to remain in service until being replaced by new 767-300EBs from 1993. Still, three were brought out of desert storage and painted in the latest colours in mid-1994 to make up for a shortage in capacity.

Eastern Air Lines

Also colloquially known as Eastern, this was a major American airline from 1926 to 1991. Eastern was one of the so-called 'Big Four' domestic airlines created by the Spoils Conferences of 1930.

It was a composite of assorted air travel corporations, including Florida Airways and Pitcairn Aviation. In the late 1920s, Pitcairn Aviation won a contract to fly mail between New York City and Atlanta, Georgia, using Pitcairn Mailwing single-engined aircraft. In 1929, Clement Keys, the owner of North American Aviation, purchased Pitcairn and in 1930, Keys changed the company's name to Eastern Air Transport. After being purchased by General Motors and experiencing a change in leadership after the Airmail Act of 1934, the airline became known as Eastern Air Lines.

In 1938 World War One flying ace Eddie

Eastern's N301EA in the white hockey stick livery is captured in flight. *(Eastern via Emma Dayle Collection)*

Rickenbacker bought Eastern from General Motors. The complex deal was concluded when Rickenbacker presented Alfred P Sloan with a certified check for US$3,500,000. In March 1939, Eastern had fifteen-weekday departures from Newark, six to Washington, five to Miami and one each to Richmond, Atlanta, Houston and San Antonio, two from Chicago to Miami, one from Tampa to Atlanta and one from Tallahassee to Memphis. Those flights and their returns were Eastern's whole scheduled operation. Later, Eastern was the fourth-largest airline in the country by passenger-miles: 103 million in 1939. It had a near-monopoly in air travel between New York and Florida from the 1930s until the 1950s and dominated this market for decades afterwards.

Rickenbacker pushed Eastern into a period of growth and innovation; for a time, Eastern was the most profitable airline in the post-war era, never needing state subsidy. In the late 1950s, Eastern's position was eroded by subsidies to rival airlines and the arrival of the jet age. On 1 October 1959, Rickenbacker's position as CEO was taken over by Malcolm A MacIntyre, a brilliant lawyer but a man inexperienced in airline operations. Rickenbacker's ouster was largely due to his reluctance to acquire expensive jets as he underestimated their appeal to the public. A new management team headed by Floyd D Hall took over on 16 December 1963, and Rickenbacker left his position as Director and

The two protagonists at Eastern during the TriStar years!

Left: former NASA astronaut Frank Frederick Borman II (b. 14 March 1928).

Right: US businessman and corporate raider Francisco Anthony Frank Lorenzo (b 19 May 1940).

Eastern's N319EA in the silver hockey stick livery-lands at Miami. *(Eastern via Emma Dayle Collection)*

Chairman of the Board on 31 December 1963.

In 1960, Eastern's first jets, Douglas DC-8-21s, started to take over the longer flights, like the non-stops from Chicago and New York to Miami. The DC-8s were joined in 1962 by the Boeing 720 and in 1964, the Boeing 727-100, which Eastern - along with American Airlines and United Airlines - had helped Boeing develop. On 1 February 1964, Eastern was the first airline to fly the 727. Shortly after that, 'Captain Eddie' Rickenbacker retired, and a new image was adopted, which included the famous hockey stick design, officially Caribbean Blue over Ionosphere Blue.

On 30 April 1961, Eastern inaugurated Eastern Air Lines Shuttle. Initially, ninety-five-seat Lockheed Constellation 1049s and 1049Cs left New York-LaGuardia every two hours, 8 am to 10 pm, to Washington National and to Boston. Flights soon became hourly, 7 am to 10 pm out of each city. Shuttle emphasised convenience and simplicity - revolutionary in an era when air travel was

Eastern's pristine N310EA taxies past the camera. *(Eastern via Matt Black Collection)*

196

Bare metal!

Eastern went through a period of using what was termed the silver hockey stick scheme - claimed to be an economic weight-saving attempt. Left: an inidentified Eastern L-1011 with a company DC-9 in front.

Below: Eastern 319 seen at the gate, about to pushback.

considered a luxury.

Internationalisation began as Eastern opened routes to markets such as Santo Domingo and Nassau, Bahamas. Services from San Juan, Puerto Rico's Luis Muñoz Marín International Airport were expanded. In 1967, Eastern bought the Lockheed L-1011 TriStar, which would soon become known in the Caribbean as El Grandote (the huge one).

In the late 1970s and early 1980s, during the deregulation, labour disputes and high debt loads strained the company under former astronaut Frank Borman's leadership.

In 1975, Eastern was headquartered at 10 Rockefeller Plaza in New York City. After Frank Borman became president of Eastern Air Lines in late 1975, he moved Eastern's headquarters from Rockefeller Center to Miami-Dade County, Florida.

Eastern's massive Atlanta hub was in direct competition with Delta Air Lines, where the two carriers competed heavily to neither's benefit. Delta's less-unionised workforce and slowly expanding international route network helped lead it through the turbulent period following deregulation in 1978.

In 1980, a Caribbean hub opened at Isla Verde

Eastern's '309' in the white hockey stick livery with a sticker by Door 1L stating 'Operated by TWA'.*(Eastern via Emma Dayle Collection)*

International Airport near San Juan, Puerto Rico. Two years later Eastern acquired Braniff's South American route network. By 1985, Eastern was the largest IATA airline in terms of passengers and operated in twenty-six countries on three continents. During this era, Eastern's fleet was split between their bare metal hockey stick colour scheme and their white-colored hockey stick livery.

Eastern began losing money as it faced competition from no-frills airlines, such as People Express, which offered lower fares. In an attempt to differentiate itself from its bargain competitors, Eastern began a marketing campaign stressing its quality of service and its rank of highly experienced pilots.

Frank Lorenzo acquired Eastern in 1985 and moved many of its assets to his other airlines, including Continental Airlines and Texas Air. He was well known for his management of Continental Airlines and Texas International Airlines, between 1972 and 1990, through airline deregulation. Lorenzo also led the creation and management of the holding company for the group, Texas Air Corporation, through which New York Air was formed in 1980 and Eastern Air Lines was acquired in 1986, as well as Frontier Airlines and People Express Airlines.

As an airline manager, he gained a reputation of union acrimony, stemming from his management during the 1983 bankruptcy of Continental. He utilised bankruptcy law to abrogate union contracts and seize employee pension funds - a practice that subsequently became illegal. Continental survived until its merger with United Airlines in 2010. Lorenzo unsuccessfully facilitated a similar scenario at Eastern Airlines, a strike and bankruptcy, which led first to Lorenzo being stripped of his authority at Eastern Airlines and seeing a trustee named to oversee the carrier, then to that airline's permanent shutdown in 1991. Lorenzo's airline history is contentious, as he is both 'despised by unions and admired by airline strategists.' In 1990, after Lorenzo liquidated his holdings after eighteen years in the airline industry, Alfred E Kahn, claimed by some as the 'main architect of airline deregulation,' offered this perspective on Lorenzo's leadership: 'I don't think there is any question that he saved Continental, but his tactics didn't work when he took over Eastern.'

After continued labour disputes and a crippling strike in 1989, Eastern ran out of money and was liquidated in 1991.

Some ground was lost on the order book progress when Northeast Airlines decided to merge with Northwest Airlines in early 1970. Northwest already had orders for fourteen long-range DC-10-20s with options on a further fourteen. However, Northeast eventually merged with Delta on 1 April 1972.

The loss of this modest order was largely replaced by a new order when the prototype TriStar was officially rolled out at Palmdale.

Pacific Southwest Airlines

The first order in over a year came from Pacific Southwest Airlines (PSA). They issued a Letter of Intent for two TriStars on 1 September 1970, with reservations on three additional delivery positions. PSA, the Californian airline, was the largest US intra-state carrier. The first two aircraft were planned for the high density 284 nautical mile Los Angeles - San Francisco route from 1972, with the other aircraft

A Californian smile comes in to land! *(Matt Black Collection)*

being delivered from 1973. The expected configuration was between 250 and 300 seats to cope with the route's heavy anticipated growth over the following six years. The confirmation of the order was subject to satisfactory financial arrangements, although the airline was weathering a tight economic period, with aircraft overcapacity at the time. The RB211 was particularly suited for the more frequent cycling of the engines, with a large number of take-offs and landings characteristic of PSA operations.

As the provisional airworthiness certificate was granted to the TriStar at the end of 1972, the PSA order was in some doubt. The reported cancellation of the two TriStars and three options was caused by a failure to agree on the renegotiated contract following the Lockheed financial crisis. PSA intended to re-evaluate the TriStar choice, and talks continued with Lockheed.

PSA confirmed its choice of the TriStar in September 1972 by ordering five aircraft, following a successful contract renegotiation. The first two aircraft were due for delivery in the spring of 1974 and would seat between 250 and 300 passengers with

Pacific Southwest Airlines' slogan was 'The World's Friendliest Airline'. Its recognisable trademark was a smile painted on each plane's nose and an advertising campaign declaring 'Catch Our Smile'.

Above: posing before delivery. Right main cabin colours. Below: 'Catch Our Smile' *(PSA)*

PSA was an airline of the times - psychedelic colours, girls in short shorts and micro-dresses posing in engine intakes; sexist and surreal it may have been, but it certainly was a time when flying was fun!

Top: The forward cabin.

Above: PSA had a lower deck seating area with seat-belt equipped loungers and half egg chairs that could be used by paying passengers sitting their during take-offs and landings.

Right: a company L-1011 at San Franscico. *(PSA)*

a downstairs cocktail lounge as a feature. To suit the aircraft for quick turn round commuter operations on the intra-California trunk routes, several special features were developed including the facility to exit the maximum number of passengers through four wide doors, and the boarding of more than 100 passengers with carry-on baggage through an auxiliary entrance. The first PSA aircraft was delivered on 2 July 1974 and featured a lower deck entrance door into a passenger lounge.

In September 1971, British & Commonwealth Shipping assumed the worldwide TriStar sales responsibilities when it increased its share of Air Holdings from forty-six per cent to a full takeover. While the players were locked in negotiations on the aircraft's future and engine, All Nippon Airways of Japan placed an option for six TriStars in early March 1971, but no money changed hands. This was later increased to a total of twenty-one - six first buys and fifteen on a follow up second buy order.

On 20 October 1971, Lockheed clarified the order situation on the TriStar. There were a total of 103 firm orders, with forty-six second buys, for which non-returnable deposits had been paid. The commitment for fifty with Air Holdings still stood, but the airline had failed to meet the 1 October deadline for the progress payments on twenty-nine aircraft unallocated to customers. Lockheed reduced its previous seventy-five second buys.

This adjustment was a bookkeeping exercise since the actual order book was not affected. Air Holdings was still expected to take the aircraft as part of the RB211 offsets. The terms of the contract stipulated that if the 1 October payment was missed, Lockheed could waive the contract, retain the money already deposited until 31 July 1977, and use it to finance the production programme. Refunds would be made to Air Holdings as each of the twenty-nine aircraft were sold, all the outstanding funds being returned by July 1977. The deposits paid by Air Holdings on the first twenty-one aircraft, ten plus nine for Air Canada and one plus one for Air Jamaica, had been refunded as the airlines made their own progress payments. The Air Jamaica order was later cancelled.

Lockheed retained the responsibility for selling the aircraft with Air Holdings as a marketing partner. It appeared that it was more profitable for Air Holdings to part with the money already transferred to Lockheed for an extended period, than to continue to make payments on aircraft which were not selling. The production order for 555 RB211 engines from Rolls-Royce was unaffected.

The continuing fuel crisis in 1975 and a recession in the air transport industry particularly affected the US markets. Both Eastern and TWA had an excess of capacity equal to about four TriStars each and in March PSA grounded its two TriStars, replacing them with Boeing 727-2003 following a ten per cent decline in traffic. The TriStars were reintroduced in June.

After the Airline Deregulation Act of 1978, PSA expanded to cities in other western states and eventually to several cities in Mexico.

In 1986 PSA became the first of two airlines that merged into the existing USAir, followed by Piedmont Airlines in 1987. The PSA acquisition was completed in 1988.

Court Line Aviation

Within a few days of the Lockheed announcement, Court Line, a Luton-based British tour operator, ordered two TriStars with three more options. The two initial aircraft were due for delivery in time for

Court's *Halcyon Days* climbs the hill from the terminal area at Luton, on it's way to another departure.

the 1973 summer season, with the optional aircraft due for delivery at the rate of one per year from 1974. Court Line became the first inclusive tour operator to order a wide-bodied jet and the first European TriStar customer. The initial order, worth £19 million, was placed in association with Clarkson's Holidays, with which Court Line had just signed a new five-year contract providing a high utilisation.

The TriStar gave Court Line a range of up to 2,700 miles, bringing every major holiday centre in Europe, North Africa and the Eastern Mediterranean within nonstop range, and increasing the ability to boost winter utilisation. The aircraft were 400-seat single-class aircraft in a 3-4-3 configuration. The only visible external change from the basic aircraft was a wide double door to cut down delays in passenger boarding and disembarkation. Each TriStar would be staffed by twelve cabin crew, the first aircraft being painted in an orange livery, and the second one pink. Integral airstairs and baggage handling conveyors eased operations at remote airports without ground handling facilities. The Court Line order was finally signed on 12 August 1972 when the financial arrangements had been confirmed. Airlease International was technically the purchaser, leasing the aircraft to Court Line. The first Court Line TriStar made its maiden flight in late January 1973.

The introduction of the Court Line TriStars brought new low levels of noise to Luton Airport and the destinations. The TriStar was permitted a full annual allowance of 340 night movements, even before the normal quota was divided up amongst Luton's operators.

Court Line Aviation has a somewhat convoluted history - it came out of Autair International Airways, itself a division of Autair Helicopters, a helicopter operator established in the early 1950s by William 'Bill Armstrong. It began public transport operations with an ex-British European Airways Douglas DC-3, used on contract work for other airlines. More DC-3s and Vickers Vikings were bought. The first of the latter joined the fleet in 1962. Both types operated freight and passenger services, including a growing number of inclusive tour flights.

In the days before e-mails and Instant Messaging, if a document needed to be sent long distances almost immediately, companies used Fax Machines. These created the most transient and most poor quality of facsimiles, using telephone lines and being printed on thermal paper, which rapidly faded the image. Therefore, it is remarkable that the two Aircraft Delivery Certificate of Conformance Export for both G-BAAA and 'AB survive. Both provide a myriad of detail. *(Lockheed, via Ed Posey Court Line Aviation)*

LOCKHEED-CALIFORNIA COMPANY
A DIVISION OF LOCKHEED AIRCRAFT CORP.

AIRCRAFT DELIVERY CERTIFICATE OF CONFORMANCE EXPORT	BUYER AIRLEASE INTERNATIONAL	MODEL L-1011-385-1	SERIAL NO. 193K-1024	REGISTRATION NO. G-BAAA

SALES CONTRACT NO. CLX-216 DATED 8/17/72 AS AMENDED

BETWEEN THE LOCKHEED AIRCRAFT CORPORATION, COURT LINE AVIATION LIMITED

AND AIRLEASE INTERNATIONAL

ONE EACH, THREE ENGINE AIRPLANE TRANSPORT MODEL L-1011, CONSTRUCTED IN ACCORDANCE WITH CONTRACTORS SPECIFICATION REPORT NUMBER LR20111-12 DATED 7/30/71 REVISED 10/1/72 AND FURTHER AMENDED BY CERTAIN SPECIFICATION CHANGE STATEMENTS, IS DELIVERED PURSUANT TO CONTRACT NO. CLX-216.

THE UNDERSIGNED HEREBY CERTIFY THAT THIS AIRPLANE CONFORMS WITH THE SPECIFICATION AND IS EQUIPPED AS SHOWN ON THIS AIRCRAFT DELIVERY INVENTORY, WITH EXCEPTION AS NOTED ON APPENDIX (A) OF THIS CERTIFICATE OF CONFORMANCE.

Dan Harrison — 2-28-73

LOCKHEED AIRCRAFT CORP.—AUTHORIZED QUALITY ASSURANCE REPRESENTATIVE — DATE

EXECUTION OF THIS DOCUMENT BY BUYER WILL CONSTITUTE, (1) ACKNOWLEDGEMENT THAT AIRPLANE MANUFACTURING SERIAL NO. 193K-1024 COVERED BY CONTRACT NO. CLX-216 HAS BEEN INSPECTED BY AN AUTHORIZED TECHNICAL REPRESENTATIVE, OF COURT LINE AVIATION LIMITED, AND (2) ACCEPTANCE OF DELIVERY OF SAID AIRPLANE AT PALMDALE, CALIFORNIA.

2-28-73 — 8:09 am PDT ~~PST~~

AUTHORIZED REPRESENTATIVE — DATE — TIME

COURT LINE AVIATION LIMITED

CLAC Form 3376W

LOCKHEED-CALIFORNIA COMPANY
A DIVISION OF LOCKHEED AIRCRAFT CORP.

AIRCRAFT DELIVERY CERTIFICATE OF CONFORMANCE EXPORT	BUYER AIRLEASE INTERNATIONAL	MODEL L-1011-385-1	SERIAL NO. 193K-1032	REGISTRATION NO. G-BAAB

SALES CONTRACT NO. CLX-216 DATED 8/17/72 AS AMENDED
BETWEEN THE LOCKHEED AIRCRAFT CORPORATION, COURT LINE AVIATION LIMITED
AND AIRLEASE INTERNATIONAL

ONE EACH, THREE ENGINE AIRPLANE TRANSPORT MODEL L-1011, CONSTRUCTED IN ACCORDANCE WITH CONTRACTORS SPECIFICATION REPORT NUMBER LR20111-12 DATED 7/30/71 REVISED 3/30/73 AND FURTHER AMENDED BY CERTAIN SPECIFICATION CHANGE STATEMENTS, IS DELIVERED PURSUANT TO CONTRACT NO. CLX-216.

THE UNDERSIGNED HEREBY CERTIFY THAT THIS AIRPLANE CONFORMS WITH THE SPECIFICATION AND IS EQUIPPED AS SHOWN ON THIS AIRCRAFT DELIVERY INVENTORY, WITH EXCEPTION AS NOTED ON APPENDIX (A) OF THIS CERTIFICATE OF CONFORMANCE.

LOCKHEED AIRCRAFT CORP. - AUTHORIZED QUALITY ASSURANCE REPRESENTATIVE

April 30, 1973
DATE

EXECUTION OF THIS DOCUMENT BY BUYER WILL CONSTITUTE, (1) ACKNOWLEDGEMENT THAT AIRPLANE MANUFACTURING SERIAL NO. 193K-1032 COVERED BY CONTRACT NO. CLX-216 HAS BEEN INSPECTED BY AN AUTHORIZED TECHNICAL REPRESENTATIVE, OF COURT LINE AVIATION LIMITED, AND (2) ACCEPTANCE OF DELIVERY OF SAID AIRPLANE AT PALMDALE, CALIFORNIA.

AUTHORIZED REPRESENTATIVE

April 30, 1973
DATE

22:30 pm G.M.T.
TIME.

The Aircraft Delivery Certificate of Conformance Export for AB show its true owner, Lockheed Model Number, date of export and other contractual aspects. *(Lockheed, via Ed Posey Court Line Aviation)*

One of the earliest charter customers for Autair's DC-3s was ex-naval officer Tom Gullick, who would later head Clarksons. Clarksons began its relationship with Autair by contracting the airline's Vikings to ferry day-trippers between up to ten UK departure points and Rotterdam during the Dutch bulb fields season.

1964 saw the formation of Clarksons Tours (later, Clarksons Holidays) with Tom Gullick as managing director. Over the next few years, Clarksons would become Autair's and its successor Court Line's most important tour operator customer.

In April 1965, Court Line - a shipping company that could trace its history back to 1905 - purchased Autair's entire share capital.

Autair became a jet operator in 1968 when three

G-BAAB *Halcyon Breeze* touches down at Luton after another flight from the sun.

brand-new BAC One-Eleven 400 series joined its fleet. The new jets mainly operated IT flights.

By spring 1969, five One-Eleven 400s operated Autair's IT flights, primarily under contract to Clarksons Tours. These carried the bulk of the airline's half-a-million annual charter passengers, which far outnumbered the 66,000 using its scheduled services each year.

In summer 1969, Autair announced its decision to withdraw all scheduled services. On 31 October 1969, scheduled services were stopped and all turboprop aircraft sold. This was followed by an order for seven of the larger 119-seat 500 series One-Eleven.

To coincide with the arrival of the first BAC One-Eleven 500, the airline changed its name on 1 January 1970 to Court Line Aviation with Edward 'Ed' Posey as its Managing Director and introduced a new corporate look and strategy that focused exclusively on the then fast-growing package holiday market. As the larger One-Eleven 500s were delivered, all but one of the smaller, former Autair 400 series One-Elevens were retired.

The corporate look was an all-over colour design by Peter Murdoch. In keeping with the holiday mood, One-Elevens were painted in distinctive, eye-catching pastel colour combinations. The flight attendants wore trendy uniforms designed by Murdoch's wife, Julia.

The TriStars were concentrated on the Luton to Palma and Rimini routes and trips to Athens and North Africa. The TriStar's shorter routes economics were comparable to the company's BAC One Elevens, but it became increasingly competitive over longer ranges. The new aircraft would allow Court Line to expand its destinations to the Caribbean, where it had hotel interests and owned Leeward Island Air Transport, a regional operator.

The second Court Line TriStar, *Halcyon Breeze*, was delivered to Luton nonstop from Palmdale on 3 May 1973. This 5,500-mile great circle route was the longest flight by a TriStar to date and was flown automatically from take-off to touchdown.

For further details of Court's L-1011 operations, see *Colours in the Sky* (Air World) by the same author.

Court Line went bankrupt on 15 August 1974, and the entire airline was grounded. After more than a year on the ground at Luton, the ex-Court Line TriStar G-BAAA flew on 28 August 1975, followed by Alpha Bravo. The owner, Airlease International, was renewing the certification of the aircraft. Both aircraft departed Luton for Palmdale in late November 1975 for updating and onward use by Cathay Pacific.

Trans World Airline

The airline was formed as Transcontinental & Western Air to operate a route from New York City to Los Angeles via St. Louis, Kansas City, and other stops, with Ford Trimotors. With American, United, and Eastern, it was one of the 'Big Four' domestic airlines in the United States formed by the Spoils Conference of 1930.

Billionaire Howard Hughes acquired control of TWA in 1939, and after World War Two led the expansion of the airline to serve Europe, the Middle East, and Asia, making TWA a second unofficial flag carrier of the United States after Pan Am. Hughes gave up control in the 1960s, and the new management of TWA acquired Hilton International and Century 21 to diversify the company's business. As the Airline Deregulation Act of 1978 led to a wave of airline failures, start-ups, and takeovers in the

Left: Howard Robard Hughes Jr. (b. 24 December 1905, d. 5 April 1976) was an American business magnate, investor, record-setting pilot, engineer, film director, and philanthropist, known during his lifetime as one of the most financially successful individuals in the world.

Right: Carl Celian Icahn (b. 16 February 1936) is an American businessman. In the 1980s, Icahn developed a reputation as a corporate raider after profiting from the hostile takeover and asset stripping TWA.

TWA's L-1011 N31001 seen on a test flight. *(Lockheed)*

United States, TWA was spun off from its holding company in 1984. Carl Icahn acquired control of TWA and took the company private in a leveraged buyout in 1988. TWA became saddled with debt, sold its London routes, underwent Chapter 11 restructuring in 1992 and 1995, and was further stressed by the explosion of TWA Flight 800 in 1996. TWA was headquartered in Kansas City, Missouri, and planned to make Kansas City International Airport its main domestic and international hub, but abandoned this plan in the 1970s. The airline later developed its largest hub at St. Louis Lambert International Airport. Its main transatlantic hub was the TWA Flight Center at John F. Kennedy International Airport in New York City, an architectural icon designed by Eero Saarinen and completed in 1962.

The first two TriStars were handed over to

N31024 seen in the original 'arrow' TWA TriStar livery at John F Kennedy Airport, New York. *(Richard Vandervord)*

Eastern and TWA at the beginning of April 1972 for crew training before certification in mid-April, to be ready for passenger operations. Eastern received the first delivery on 6 April with N306EA, with three of its captains were already qualified to fly the aircraft. This allowed Eastern to commence services from Miami on 26 April, departing at 07.00 for New York with 123 passengers. It was not an official inaugural, as the aircraft was substituted for a DC-8 and was one of the two aircraft delivered to the airline by that time.

The first TriStar was delivered to TWA for crew training in early May, to prepare for service entry on daily nonstop flights from St Louis to Los Angeles and Chicago to Los Angeles. Each TWA aircraft had a 206-seat layout. On Sunday 25 June 1972 at 17.00 TWA TriStar N31001 pushed back at St Louis at the start of the inaugural flight to Los Angeles. There was a full complement of thirty first-class passengers, and

A pair of TWA airliners at the gate. The L-1011 is boarding through 1 and 2L while the 747 is using 1L and the overwing jetway.

On finals! N81025 comes in to land at London Heathrow. *(Ruchard Vandervord)*

in the economy section, only ten of the 176 seats were unoccupied. For the 1,527-mile flight, some 87,000 pounds of fuel had been loaded, giving a take-off weight of around 378,000 pounds. The take-off was entirely automatic from the point of lining up on the runway, and the whole flight was completed automatically until turning off the runway at Los Angeles. This was a remarkable achievement for the advanced avionics so early in the career of a new aircraft. The aircraft operated at 31,000 feet and a cruising speed of Mach 0.87 gave a true airspeed of 520 knots. Out of the total flight time of three hours ten minutes, take-off to cruising altitude had been twenty-two minutes, with fuel consumption was 6,800 pounds per engine, per hour.

On 28 September, 1972 TWA commenced their own US transcontinental daily services with the L-1011 between Philadelphia and Los Angeles via Chicago. Since the 206-seat aircraft introduction, the operations had gradually expanded linking Chicago with Los Angeles, San Francisco and Phoenix. In October for the TWA TriStars to operate in Category 3A weather conditions, the US FAA approved the first aircraft to be FAA approved. The TriStar had quadruple redundancy of the major components, and the operation included closing the throttles after touchdown, extending the spoilers and steering on the runway.

One of TWAs TriStars - N11002 - caught fire during take-off from New York Kennedy on 30 July 1992. The take-off was abandoned at the point of flight, and the airliner turned off the runway on to the soft ground, where the 274 passengers and twelve crew evacuated the aircraft safely before it burnt out completely. The cause of the accident was a combination of an incorrect stick shaker operation during rotation, followed by a crack in the rear spar caused by the overweight landing, spilling fuel from the integral tanks, which then ignited.

In late 1977 TWA converted four of its thirty L-1011-1s to the -100 configuration, with 256 seats, and more conversions followed to allow transatlantic services to start in the spring of 1978.

All Nippon Airways

ANA's earliest ancestor was Japan Helicopter and Aeroplane Transports Company - also known as Nippon Helicopter and Aeroplane -, an airline company founded on 27 December 1952.

Nippon Helicopter and Aeroplane began helicopter services in February 1953. On 15 December 1953, it operated its first cargo flight between Osaka and Tokyo using a de Havilland Dove, JA5008. This was the first scheduled flight flown by a Japanese pilot in postwar Japan. Passenger service on the same route began on 1 February 1954 and was upgraded to a de Havilland Heron in March. In 1955, Douglas DC-3s began flying for NH as well, by which time the airline's route network extended from northern Kyūshū to Sapporo. In December 1957, Nippon Helicopter changed its name to All Nippon Airways Company.

ANA's other ancestor was Far East Airlines. Although it was founded on 26 December 1952, one day before Nippon Helicopter, it did not begin operations until 20 January 1954, when it began night cargo runs between Osaka and Tokyo, also using a de Havilland Dove. It adopted the DC-3 in early 1957, by which point its route network extended through southern Japan from Tokyo to Kagoshima.

Far East Airlines merged with the newly named All Nippon Airways in March 1958. The combined companies had a total market capitalisation of 600 million yen, and the result of the merger was Japan's largest private airline.

ANA grew through the 1960s, adding the Vickers Viscount to the fleet in 1960 and the Fokker F27 in 1961. October 1961 marked ANA's debut on the Tokyo Stock Exchange as well as the Osaka Securities Exchange. 1963 saw another merger, with Fujita Airlines, raising the company's capital to 4.65 billion yen. In 1965 ANA introduced jets with Boeing

The initial ANA colour scheme involved a light blue roof, with banding down to a cheat line. Early examples carried a large fleet number in the same blue visible in the ANA publicity picture on the bare metal below the flight deck windows, Not all ANA aircraft carried the number as the picture on the left shows.

727s on the Tokyo-Sapporo route. It also introduced Japan's first homegrown turboprop airliner, the NAMC YS-11 in 1965. In 1969, ANA introduced Boeing 737 services.

As ANA grew it started to contract travel companies across Japan to handle ground services in each region. Many of these companies received shares in ANA as part of their deals. Some of these relationships continue today in different forms: for instance, Nagoya Railroad, which handled ANA's operations in the Chūbu region along with other partnerships, maintains a permanent seat on ANA's board of directors. By 1974, ANA had Japan's largest domestic airline network.

While ANA's domestic operations grew, the Ministry of Transport had granted government-owned Japan Airlines (JAL) a monopoly on international scheduled flights that lasted until 1986. ANA was allowed to operate international charter flights: its first was a Boeing 727 charter from Tokyo to Hong Kong on 21 February 1971.

ANA bought its first wide-body aircraft, six

Lockheed L-1011s following a lengthy sales effort by Lockheed, which involved negotiations between US President Richard Nixon, Japanese prime minister Kakuei Tanaka and UK prime minister Edward Heath, who was lobbying in favour of engine maker Rolls-Royce. Tanaka also pressed Japanese regulators to permit ANA to operate on Asia routes as part of the package. The aircraft entered service on the Tokyo-Okinawa route in 1974. The carrier had ordered McDonnell Douglas DC-10s but cancelled the order at the last minute and switched to Lockheed. It was later revealed that Lockheed had indirectly bribed Prime Minister Kakuei Tanaka to force this switch: the scandal led to the arrest of Tanaka and several managers from ANA and Lockheed sales agent Marubeni for corruption.

The All Nippon Airways TriStar interest was confirmed in October 1972 by an initial order for six aircraft worth £55 million with deliveries due in November 1973 for Japan's busy domestic trunk routes. All Nippon Airways (ANA) had had a tremendous passenger-mile growth rate over five years of thirty-five to forty-five per-cent. It was the largest domestic Japanese airline with fifty-nine routes served in 1971, 420 daily round trips and well over 28,000 seats offered daily.

This was more than JAL and Toa Domestic Airlines combined on these routes. In 1970 ANA carried 7.61 million passengers and flew 2877 million passenger-miles over average stage lengths of around 370 miles. This made it the sixth-largest domestic airline globally, with Tokyo-Osaka probably the world's second most dense air route. ANA confirmed its order by signing the contract for six TriStars in January 1973 and took out options for another fifteen aircraft, bringing the overall eventual value to around £200 million.

In September 1973, ANA took up eight of its TriStar options worth over £120 million, bringing its firm orders for the type to fourteen aircraft. Another two were confirmed in October 1974. Although ANA was primarily a domestic operator, with the arrival of the TriStars, the airline planned weekly charter flights between Tokyo and Manila in the Philippines. ANA ordered pylon attachments for four of its TriStars to enable them to ferry spare RB211 engines. The pylon was attached to the right-hand wing between the engine and the fuselage.

ANA had to ground its six TriStars on 4 September 1974 due to two occasions when two engines were shut down on approach to Tokyo. The problem was found to be oil loss due to cracks in a pressure casing around a drilled oil-scavenger aperture. Services were restarted on 8 September by changing the faulty modules for a later standard model. This relatively minor problem did not stop ANA from signing an agreement for seven more TriStars in September 1974, conditional upon the Japanese Government allowing wide-bodied aircraft into Osaka Airport. Even without Osaka, at least two more TriStars were required.

ANA confirmed its options for three more TriStars in April 1977 bringing its total fleet size of the type to twenty aircraft.

All Nippon Airways' L-1011 JA855 poses for it's portrait, with Mount Fuji in the background top right. (ANA)

All Nippon Airways' L-1011 JA855 comes into land. *(Tenmil Soket Collection)*

LTU

Simultaneously, as the ANA order was placed, the Dusseldorf-based airline LTU signed a Letter of Intent for two TriStars for delivery in May 1973 and the spring of 1975. Each aircraft would carry 330 passengers in an all-economy layout with a minimum seat pitch of thirty-four inches. LTU planned to use the airliner on tourist flights from Dusseldorf to Mediterranean resorts and the Canary Islands.

LTU was established in May 1955 as Lufttransport Union and started operations in Frankfurt. It adopted its present name in 1956 when it operated charter flights. The initials LTU stand for the German phrase LuftTransport-Unternehmen which translates to 'air transport enterprise'.

LTU had been headquartered in Düsseldorf since 1961. Over the years, LTU rose to become one of the biggest and most renowned German leisure time airlines and operated worldwide charter flights from many German airports, but mainly from its traditional main hub at Düsseldorf.

LTU purchased an Eastern TriStar in July 1975. Just over a year later, in October 1976 LTU, came to an agreement with Lockheed to return its two TriStar L-1011-1s, and buy the three TriStar L-1011-1s built for PSA but never delivered. This would give LTU the advantage of a high-density layout common to all three aircraft, instead of adding a new aircraft to a later standard of modification, without full commonality with the earlier two. The first of the three new TriStars were delivered to LTU in mid-March 1977 ready for the airline to become the first

D-AERP of LTU allows a sister L-1011 to land before entering the active runway to take off.

LTU TriStars were so popular they even made the Rf8.00 stamp of the Republic of Maldives.

D-AERP seems to have been a well-photographed LTU TriStar. This was the former Eastern Air Lines N337EA.

Rolls-Royce RB211s were somewhat prone to smoky starts on cold days, as shown here.

regular transatlantic TriStar operator on 4 April. The services were advanced booking charter flights between Dusseldorf and New York. The LTU aircraft featured the lower deck passenger lounge as specified by PSA and had a door with airstairs fitted for lower deck entry just forward of the wing leading edge. The second new TriStar was delivered in May and the third in December 1977. TriStar No 3 was cleared to the 466,000lb maximum take-off weight of the L-1011-100 but without the extra fuel capacity. LTU had no interest in carrying freight, so the lower deck lounge's extra capacity would allow 330 passengers to be carried, nine abreast at a thirty-four inch pitch. Triple Internal Navigation Systems were fitted to assist on the long over-water flights with Omega added later.

In 1983, a Munich-based subsidiary called LTS Lufttransport Süd was founded, which had a similar livery, but with blue instead of red. It was renamed LTU Süd in 1987 and received a new livery closer to the familiar red LTU livery. In 1998 LTU Süd was completely incorporated into LTU.

LTU also operated sister companies in Spain (LTE, 1987 - 2001) and Austria (LTU Austria, 2004 - 2008). Their traditional red and white livery barely changed over the years, thus becoming a recognisable trademark in the German charter flight business.

In 1983 LTU was the air company featured in the CBS video of the Wham! hit record *Club Tropicana* featuring George Michael and Andrew Ridgeley as

D-AERC of LTU in a virtually bare metal scheme.

TriStar heaven! The dawn scene at Palmdale as new L-1011s are prepared for delivery. *(Lockheed)*

air crew. It disposed of the last of its L-1011s in 1996 and was taken over by Air Berlin in 2007.

Meanwhile, back at Palmdale...

By November 1972, the TriStars had completed their first six months of commercial service. Both Eastern and TWA had six aircraft each in service. The RB211 engines had worked well, and the predicted removal rate of the engines of 1.1 per 1,000 hours had been slightly bettered. This term had been somewhat outdated by the modular construction of the engine which was maintained 'on condition', a more realistic parameter being a basic inflight shutdown rate of 0.55 per 1,000 hours. The engine entered service on an eight hour daily utilisation with three hours average stage lengths with Eastern and later on ten hour daily utilisation with three and a half hour average stages with TWA. Any problems encountered with the engine were relatively minor and the cure was provided rapidly. TWA and Eastern also operated a reciprocal TriStar leasing programme, designed to spread capacity more economically between their different peak seasons.

There had however been some problems with the RB211 engines. On 28 December 1972, an Eastern Airlines TriStar suffered a complete loss of the number three engine's titanium fan. There were no injuries to passengers or crew, and the fan fell into the Atlantic. A second similar incident occurred on 10 January 1973 to the number one engine on a TWA TriStar flying from Chicago to Los Angeles, again with no injuries. The fan fell into the desert but was not recovered. The fan inspection period was reduced to 150 aircraft cycles, the Eastern aircraft having completed about 250 cycles were replaced by new units and some evidence of cracking was found in the discs removed from the older engines. The investigation's main concentration was on fatigue failure of the titanium-alloy forged fan disc, allowing several blades to separate. At Lockheed, a flight test programme was operated with an RB211 engine fitted with strain gauges to assess stresses in flight.

After a detailed investigation on both sides of the Atlantic, Rolls-Royce announced the engine problem analysis results. Stress levels were reduced during the material manufacture for the fan discs. All discs were spun up on additional quality control test to a rated speed before final inspection, disc component thickness was increased as an interim procedure, and in the long term, a definitive standard disc would be developed, possibly using a new titanium alloy.

In its first year of commercial airline service, TriStar carried more than 1.3 million passengers and covered more than 2,000 million passenger-miles. Eastern, TWA, Air Canada and Court Line accumulated nearly 30,000 flying hours on more than 11,000 revenue-earning flights. Twenty-five TriStars had been delivered, about a dozen behind schedule, but future deliveries included the first for LTU, Delta and ANA. The first LTU aircraft was delivered on 29 May 1973 to Dusseldorf.

The fuel crisis starting in late 1973 brought further financial problems to Lockheed, mainly due to deferment of orders and options due to overcapacity with the airlines. Eastern Airlines deferred the delivery of nine TriStars, a subsequent slow down in production being a very costly exercise. Lockheed had healthy orders and options for 199 TriStars, of which fifty-six had been delivered up to the end of 1973. Plans allowed for thirty-five to be delivered in each of 1974 and 1975. The lack of cash would affect any long-range developments, restricting the overall market. If arrangements could not be made with the banks, a possible alternative was a merger with another company, talks later being held with Hughes and Textron.

Lockheed's cash flow problems were eased by Delta, TWA and ANA asking for a total of seven TriStars to be delivered early. With the worsening fuel crisis, rationing allocations to ninety per cent of that used in 1973 in some cases, the fuel-efficient RB211-powered TriStars were more economical than the aircraft they were replacing.

Lockheed's financial troubles still plagued the TriStar programme, aggravated by the fuel crisis giving a significant drop in demand for new aircraft, despite their greater fuel efficiency. To make a profit, it was necessary to sell three hundred of the basic L-1011-1 version, but the decrease in production rate gave less efficient use of the tooling. Programme costs were also increased by even minor developments of the existing airframe. In April 1976, firm TriStar orders stood at 157 plus 50 options, covering the three variants then available, the standard L-1011-1, the extended-range L-1011-100 and long-range RB211-524-powered L-1011-200. Lockheed had delivered 127 TriStars, but the 1976 rate was expected to be between nine and twelve aircraft, due to the scarcity in orders which was one option confirmed by Delta. Eight of the thirty aircraft backlog were for British Airways, which needed its deliveries spread evenly up to 1982. The TriStar was not unique in its lack of sales, as the medium-range DC-10-10 had not achieved any sales over the same period, but at least a long-range version could already be supplied, and more DC-10s had been sold overall.

Lockheed was openly looking for an acquisition partner to help it through financial difficulties and had not achieved the conditions required for a Textron merger. They also had rejected one well-heeled candidate - Howard Robard Hughes. For a time in 1973 there was a plan that would have allowed Hughes' wholly-owned Summa Corporation of Encino, California, to acquire nearly ten per cent of Lockheed's stock, making it Lockheed's largest stockholder, by offering a $100 million financing package that included loans and rights to $10 million in twenty-year, six per cent convertible subordinated debentures. However, the plan lapsed.

The Lockheed bribes scandal reported widely at the time had not helped credibility in a market place where only the Airbus was collecting orders.

Orders for new aircraft were not encouraged by the number of second-hand aircraft available. The first two PSA aircraft were grounded at the airline's base, and the other three remained undelivered. Eastern had disposed of three of its current fleet and was interested in selling more, either from service or

Surrounded by TriStars for Delta, a pair of British airways aircraft in the Negus scheme come together at Palmdale. *(Lockheed)*

off the production line. TWA was disposing of aircraft from the production line, and ANA threatened to cancel three deposit-paid options.

Lockeed's engineers - in the shape of Kelly Johnson and thermodynamicist Benjamin 'Ben' Rich - had been investigating the use of liquid hydrogen as an aircraft fuel since 1956. Suntan was the code-name of a prototype reconnaissance aircraft programme, intending to create a much faster and higher-altitude successor to the U-2, enabled by the use of liquid hydrogen. The programme was cancelled in 1958.

Towards the end of 1979, Lockheed California announced the development of an experimental airline using liquid hydrogen-fuelled aircraft for cargo flights between the US, West Europe and the Middle East.

The company's latest proposal envisaged using a modified L-1011 to demonstrate the feasibility of liquid hydrogen as an alternative to petroleum fuel in aviation. The hydrogen-fuelled TriStar would be similar to the aircraft currently in production, with the same wings, tail, fuselage diameter and landing gear. Fuselage length would be increased by some thirty-five feet to install liquid hydrogen fuel tanks forward and aft of the cargo compartment, but only minor modifications would be needed to the engines.

Lockheed expected that the development of hydrogen fuel technology would take two to three years and it would need a further four years to modify aircraft and construct ground storage facilities for the fuel.

By the middle of 1976, the first signs of the move out of the world depression were appearing. Airlines were beginning to see passenger growth returning and could consider expanding their fleets again. However, one of Lockheed's problems was the stock of hardly used bargain TriStars awaiting a new owner. An encouraging sign was the confirmation in August 1976 of two options by Delta for delivery in May and December 1978.

Into service with British Airways.

In 1972, British European Airways (BEA) was looking for a new technology high-capacity wide-bodied jet airliner for its European and Near East destinations. The three major contenders were the McDonnell Douglas DC-10, the projected British Aircraft Corporation BAC211, which was never to leave the drawing board, and the Lockheed TriStar. The latter became the winner of this order when a contract was signed for nine L-1011-1 TriStars with options on a further six. They could carry between 346 and 398 passengers on medium-range routes up to 3,000 nautical miles. Power came from three RB211-22B engines developing 42,000 pounds thrust each.

The TriStar was probably the most significant catalyst for the effective merging of the European and Overseas Divisions of British Airways into one major airline because it was the only aircraft operated by the two divisions.

In mid-1974 British Airways was well advanced in its preparations for the first of its nine TriStar 1s, all of which featured a forward freight door large enough to accept standard containers. The

G-BEAK in the original as delivered British airways Negus scheme, seen at a very different-looking Stansted Airport in 1978. *(British Airports Authority)*

Typical of the view from the Roof Gardens at London Heathrow is this of a British Airways TriStar in the Negus colour scheme. *(Alan Conberry Collection)*

preparations cost around £36 million, which was more than one-third of the aircraft's purchase price. British Airways engineers had liaised closely with Court Line on the introduction of its two TriStars, which helped in the provisioning plans. An engine test cell was built capable of handling engines of over 80,000 pounds thrust and capable of adaptation to any of the large engines. Redifon supplied a flight simulator and was complemented by an engineering simulator capable of reproducing 385 engineering faults. For additional training, a cockpit procedures simulator, systems trainers and passenger cabin mock-up were ordered, the latter for cabin crew training. Ground support equipment had to be bought, and the departure gates had to be adapted at Heathrow. Lockheed had already trained fifty-three maintenance personnel and twenty-eight aircrew.

The first three BA TriStars were due for delivery towards the end of October 1974 commenced with G-BBAE in October 1974. This aircraft made its maiden flight from Palmdale on 3 September 1974. The aircraft was configured with twenty first-class seats and 300 economy seats. It was delivered to Heathrow on 21 October 1974, but service entry was delayed by industrial action. It finally made its first revenue flight two months later to Malaga under the command of Captain Charles Owens.

In November 1974 British Airways increased its order by six more standard TriStars, bringing its total to fifteen. By December, the first points to be served were Malaga, Palma, Madrid and Brussels, increasing to Paris Orly.

That same year BEA formally merged with

BOAC, and since the nine BEA TriStars were under-utilised, four of the L-1011-1s were operated by the Overseas Division on the Middle Eastern routes.

During late December 1974 and early January 1975, British Airways carried out a series of proving flights with the three TriStars delivered to the airline. This cleared the aircraft for the first London to Paris service to start on 12 January, followed by Brussels and Madrid the next day, and Malaga and Palma soon after. With five aircraft in service by the end of February, TriStars were phased into sorties to Amsterdam, Tel Aviv, Faro, Alicante and Athens in time to meet the start of the summer schedules on 1 April.

The British Airways 'Negus' livery which was used between 1974 and 1984. As BEA and BOAC merged to become British Airways in 1974, elements of both of their liveries were incorporated together to create this new livery, designed by creative agency Negus & Negus. The modern and fresh design was based on the British national colours of red, white and blue. It featured a streamlined evolution of the BOAC and BEA insignia by way of a quartered Union Flag with a red tip on the tailfin and the Speedbird symbol on the nose.

It now became clear that a longer-range version of the TriStar was required, initially designated as the L-1011-250 powered by RB211B4 (improved) engines developing 50,000 pounds thrust. However, the L-1011-500 with a shorter fuselage and extended span wing was chosen, and the six earlier options were converted to a firm order, the power coming

British Airways TriStar G-BBAE *The Stargazer Rose* in the Negus colour scheme. BA dropped the word 'Airways' for a while, although they were certainly painted with the full name at Palmdale and it appeared as such on adverts. *(Kim Bolton Collection)*

British TriStar G-BBAH *The Scottish Rose* swoops in to land at Athens after another flight from London Heathrow. *(Richard Vandervord)*

from three RB211-524 BO/2 engines, each giving 50,000 pounds thrust. Meanwhile, an Eastern Airlines L-1011-1 N323EA was leased to British Airways from October 1978 for a twenty-month period to be used on the European routes.

The later L-1011-500 introduced a flight management system (FMS) which gave an area navigation capability using an inertial platform updated by the distance measuring equipment (DME) and (VOR) as described in a later chapter. It also controlled lateral navigation and controlled the climb, cruise, and descent to give the best fuel economy. Originally this involved much throttle movement of the engines, which Rolls-Royce predicted would dramatically shorten engine life. To overcome this problem and give the engine smooth operation, the TriStar would climb gradually to reduce speed or go into a shallow descent to increase. The passengers would not detect the change of altitude. The cost of £0.75 million to retrofit the L-1011-1 fleet with FMS was saved every three to four months reducing fuel costs.

All BA TriStars had a full autoland capability built-in from the start. The Collins triple autopilot flared the aircraft at thirty feet, but instead of using kick-off drift which could cause the aircraft to drift too far to one side, one wing was automatically trimmed slightly low to overcome any crosswind component. The TriStar was the first aircraft to be certificated to land in zero visibility and with a zero decision height. Direct lift control used spoilers to maintain a stable approach in pitch. The FMS was introduced on all BA TriStars, and in 1978 the European and Overseas Divisions' TriStars were finally combined into one fleet. The L-1011-1 aircraft were modified for common crew operation, all aircraft wired for triple INS, although only one was fitted for short-range operations. The triple

G-BBAH *The Caroline Davison Rose* lines up to take off from London Heathrow. *(Richard Vandervord)*

G-BBAG in full British Airways Landor Associates colour scheme lands at London Heathrow. *(Richard Vandervord)*

installation was reserved for long overwater flights on the -200 and -500. With other changes on the flight deck, common crew operation was introduced, one of the major problems resolved was the relevant crew seniority.

In 1980, BA needed to operate the L-1011-1 to the USA, but it was range limited. However, it was found that the last three aircraft in the batch, G-BEAK to G-BEAM, featured additional structural modification built-in on the production line, giving them the designation L-1011-50. All BA Engineering needed to do was to change the wheels and axles - literally an overnight job - and the aircraft could carry an additional nine tons of payload, allowing an easy operation to the East Coast of the USA. The L-1011-50 was powered by 42,000-pound thrust RB211 22B engines giving a range of 3,300 nautical miles. However, the L-1011-200 were used more regularly to and from New York, where their autoland capability was particularly appreciated during the winter months, allowing TriStars to operate into Heathrow when other aircraft often had to divert to other destinations.

With the amalgamation of the TriStar fleet in BA, further long-range high capacity aircraft were required. Orders were placed for eight L-1011-200s with options on four more, which were not taken up. The '-200' was a high capacity aircraft powered by three 50,000 pound thrust RB211-524 BO/2 engines giving a range of 3,600 nautical miles. This mid-range aircraft could fly to the Middle East or any part of the US East Coast down as far as Miami. Depending upon the configuration, the -200 could carry between 250 and 400 passengers. The first acceptance of the -200 was G-BGBB on 5 March 1980 by Captain Terry Lakin, which was delivered five days later ready for service entry soon after: The last two -200s were leased across to British Airtours at Gatwick, the charter subsidiary of BA.

British Airtours - formerly BEA Airtours - was formed on 24 April 1969 as a division of BEA to provide it with a low cost platform to participate in the then rapidly growing inclusive tour holiday flights market, which until then had been the exclusive domain of wholly privately owned airlines independent from the government-owned corporation BEA and BOAC. BEA saw this as a necessary counterweight to the independents' rapidly growing scheduled activities that began encroaching on what BEA and BOAC had traditionally regarded as their sole preserve. BEA Airtours' formation was in line with one of the recommendations of the Edwards Report on the future of the British air industry – that the corporations should enter the inclusive tour and charter market.

The independent charter airlines were suspicious of BEA's motive to enter the IT market and feared that the operator held a hidden agenda to destabilise this market by undercutting the independent carriers, none of which could match the corporation's financial resources and access to capital at the time. Moreover, the independents thought that BEA Airtours was meant to take on the corporations' excess staff and absorb aircraft that were surplus to their requirements. They feared that this would lead to significant market distortions, creating excess capacity and further depressing the already low charter rates in a highly competitive market.

BEA's new charter division had a startup capital of £250,000 and selected Gatwick Airport south of London to serve as its base, where it took over the former Transglobe Airways hangar to provide engineering support for its Gatwick fleet. During 1970, the airline commenced commercial operations out of Gatwick, initially using a fleet of seven second-hand ex-BEA de Havilland Comet series 4B aircraft which seated 109 passengers in a single-class configuration. On 6 March 1970, the first revenue flight departed Gatwick.

Following the Falklands campaign in 1982, the RAF realised that it urgently needed long-range high capacity tanker/transport aircraft. The six L-1011-500s were withdrawn from service with BA during 1983, the last flight with an airline crew being on 12 December when Capt Terry Lakin flew the aircraft from Boscombe Down on a formation exercise with RAF fighter aircraft to assess the compatibility for flight refuelling. The ex-BA TriStar 500s were chosen and bought from BA to help the airline with a shortage of cash flow, the aircraft being initially delivered to RAF Brize Norton, where following crew training, they were used on long-range trooping flights, often with BA flight and cabin crew members, pending delivery of the aircraft to Marshall at Cambridge for conversion to tankers.

With the amalgamation of the TriStar fleet in BA, further long-range high capacity aircraft was required. Orders were placed in January 1979 for eight L-1011-200s with options on four more, which were not taken up. The '-200' was a high capacity aircraft powered by three 50,000 pound thrust RB211-524 BO/2 engines giving a range of 3,600 nautical miles. This mid-range aircraft could fly to the Middle East or any part of the US East Coast down as far as Miami. Depending upon the configuration, the -200 could carry between 250 and 400 passengers.

In January 1979, British Airways ordered its first two TriStar 200s for delivery in March 1980. These aircraft, powered by the RB211-524 engines, were initially to supplement the similarly-powered TriStar 500s on the Gulf route, releasing the TriStar 1s back to the European Division.

British Airways ordered six more TriStar -200s in September 1979 with deliveries commencing, six months later. This order was valued at £127 million and brought BA's total TriStar commitment to twenty-three. At this time Lockheed claimed over 300 TriStar sales, consisting of 270 firm orders and 71 options. Lockheed had sold twenty-three TriStars worth £560 million in two months, including fourteen to unannounced customers.

The first acceptance of the -200 was G-BGBB on 5 March 1980 by Captain Terry Lakin, which was delivered five days later ready for service entry soon after. The last two -200s were leased across to British Airtours at Gatwick, the charter subsidiary of BA.

The iconic British Airways 'Landor' livery was designed by Landor Associates and used between 1984 and 1997. Landor is a brand consulting firm founded in 1941 by Walter Landor, who pioneered some research, design, and consulting methods that

An airliner with many names! British Airways' G-BBAF - seen here in full Landor livery - was originally called *The Coronation Rose*, then *Babbacombe Bay* and finally, when in service with Caledonian, *Loch Fyne*.

are still in use by the branding industry.

Headquartered in San Francisco, the company maintained offices around the globe, including China, France, Germany, India, the United Kingdom, Mexico, Singapore, Australia, Japan, South Africa, and the United States. Landor is a member of the Young & Rubicam Group network within WPP plc, the world's largest advertising company by revenue. Landor's work includes brand research and valuation, brand strategy and architecture, brand purpose and green design, corporate identity and packaging design, innovation, naming and writing, branded experience brand equity management, employee engagement, and digital branding.

As British Airways prepared for the privatisation that would take place in 1987, a new livery and fresh corporate identity was created. A key part of the design was incorporating the best of British Airways' past while being innovative and recognisably British. The quartered Union Flag on the tailfin was retained from the previous 'Negus' livery and the addition of the Coat of Arms against the midnight blue was promoted as a 'touch of class'. The Speedbird symbol, that had been ever-present on British Airways and aircraft, was stylised to create the new red Speedwing; which was designed to become an integral part of the livery and synonymous with British Airways.

In early 1985, politics decreed regional route exchanges with British Caledonian, and BA regretted disposing of its TriStar 500s. Two machines were subsequently leased from Air Lanka and reregistered G-BLUS and G-BLUT for the newly acquired South American routes to Bogota, Caracas, Rio and San Paulo. These continued in operation at least until early 1988.

The TriStar-500 and, following their disposal, the -200s were widely used for long-range Royal flights. The first one was under the command of Captain Terry Lakin in -500 G-BFCA, carrying Her Majesty

TriSar *The Elizabeth Harkness Rose*, G-BBAJ, in the Negus British airtours scheme awaits clearance to enter the runway at London Gatwick.

G-BEAM *Swansea Bay* in full Landor scheme with British Airtours titles. It had previously been named *The Silver Jublilee Rose*. *(both Richard Vandervord)*

the Queen to Fiji, leaving Heathrow on 1 November 1982. A year later, a TriStar took Her Majesty to Nairobi via Geneva and Akrotiri, then on to Dakar and Delhi before returning to Heathrow. Other Royal tours in the TriStar have included Amman, Portugal, the Caribbean and Belize, Australia, New Zealand and China. For these flights, the first class cabin was fitted with a particular layout, including a large centrally placed table with four first-class seats around it and a couch along the side of the cabin. To the rear was a bedroom and dressing room, and behind that in the business class cabin was located fifty to sixty first-class seats for the Royal household. In the rear cabin, tourist class seats were retained for BA staff and any additional passengers, such as accompanying media.

British Airways undertook all major maintenance of the TriStar airframe and engines at Heathrow. They were awarded maintenance contracts for the TriStars of Gulf Air, Saudia, the RAF and British Airtours.

The maintenance cycle of the TriStar consisted of a number of checks. A transit check - little more than the First Officer walking around and kicking the tyres - was completed at every stop. A Ramp Check 1 was completed once every calendar day and largely consisted of topping up all the consumables such as oil, water, hydraulic fluid and tyre pressures. A Ramp Check 2 was completed not more than 150 flying hours, the Ramp Check 3 up to 300 flying hours and Ramp Check 4 up to 600 flying hours.

Major base maintenance started with a Service Check 1 to be completed not exceeding 850 flying hours, subject to satisfactory samples being taken at 750hr. A Service Check 2 was up to 1,600 flying hours with samples at 1,300 hours and a Service Check 3 was up to 3,100 flying hours. Inter Check 1 was completed up to 4,000 flying hours and inter Check 2 was up to 8,000 flying hours. These checks covered full structural audit and repairs where necessary of the airframe, replacement of life-expired items, the overhaul of equipment and incorporation of modifications.

BA maintained high utilisation - the L-1011-1 short-haul aircraft achieving five to six hours a day on up to six round trips from London to Paris, the low hours being due to the many turnaround times on the ground. The TriStar -200s averaged around ten hours per day, and the -500s achieved between fifteen and twenty hours per day.

Normal BA TriStar crewing was with two pilots and a flight engineer, while British Airtours sometimes used three pilots. Most of the captains were trained at Hamble, while others were ex-RAF aircrew. Promotion usually came from captains of narrow-bodied jets to the wide-bodied TriStar. Crew training and conversion was completed on a pair of simulators covering the L-1011-1 and L-1011-200. These simulators were also used for refresher flying, instrument rating renewals and any special development flying. A captain and copilot were trained to the same standard, flying forty hours on the simulator and a maximum of one and a half hours on-base training covering three circuits. These circuits, often made at Stansted or Prestwick where at the time the air space was not too busy, and the landing charges were lower, usually consisted of a normal

TriStars could - and occasionally did - carry spare RB211s on a pod under the wing.

The 'spare' in this picture is the one closest to the main landing gear leg and had an external brace strut between the pylon and the wing. *(Lockheed)*.

G-BBAJ *Loch Rannoch* of Caledonian at London Gatwick. *(Richard Vandervord)*

take-off, an engine failure, a two-engine go-around and a landing. This qualified the crew for a Group 1 endorsement.

In April 1988, British Airtours adopted the popular Caledonian Airways brand when the newly privatised British Airways had completed the takeover of its former Gatwick-based rival British Caledonian. By the 1980s, it leased on average three TriStar-1s and the three TriStar -50s from the BA main line fleet, although the fleet size depended upon seasonal demand. As an additional measure to signify the change, the airline also adopted a modified Caledonian livery which had been adapted from the contemporary, Landor Associates-designed British Airways livery. The newly rebranded Caledonian Airways transferred its Gatwick operation from the airport's South Terminal into the then-brand-new North Terminal, thereby concentrating the majority of the British Airways group's Gatwick services within the new terminal.

Shortly thereafter, Caledonian Airways commenced the replacement of its Boeing 737 narrow-bodies with additional ex-British Airways L-1011 Tristar widebodies as well as with a number of brand-new Boeing 757s sourced from the large 757 orders placed by its parent company.

In addition to operating charters in its own right Airtours also operated the BA mainline services from Gatwick to Malta and Spain on wet lease back to the parent organisation. With the failure, and subsequent takeover of British Caledonian Airways in December 1987, the TriStars operated in Caledonian Airways' colours, the new charter division of British Airways.

During 1995, British Airways decided to leave the short- to medium-haul package holiday market; accordingly, the airline sold Caledonian Airways to British-based tour operator Inspirations, which was then a part of the American-owned Carlson group, along with the firm's core fleet of five Tristars. Following Caledonian's sale to Inspirations, the Boeing 757s were returned to British Airways. During 1999, Inspirations became part of the Thomas Cook group when Caledonian Airways was merged with the Flying Colours airline to form JMC Air Services, which in turn became the British arm of the Thomas Cook Airlines. It all became very confusing for a while! Following Inspirations' takeover by Thomas Cook, the remaining former Caledonian Airways Tristars were withdrawn from service as they had suffered increasing and widely publicised reliability problems which had resulted in a generally poor perception of Caledonian amongst the travelling public.

With the economic downturn caused by the Gulf

The Gulf Air Golden Falcon livery was very attractive, but there were considerable variations in delicacy, especially in the Arabic writing. On A40-YV as seen here, it is particularly chunky. *(Richard Vandervord)*.

War, a number of major airlines had to find ways of reducing costs. BA had already disposed of its TriStar 500s to the RAF for conversion to tankers, and decided to withdraw the nine TriStar 1s from service by the middle of 1990 due to a twenty per cent fall in traffic. This left eight TriStar 200s in operation with the airline.

Gulf Air

In the late 1940s, Freddie Bosworth, a British pilot and entrepreneur, began an air taxi service to Doha and Dhahran from Bahrain. Bosworth later expanded service and, on 24 March 1950, registered Gulf Aviation Company Limited as a private shareholding company. This makes its current operating company, Gulf Air, one of the oldest carriers in the Middle East. The early fleet contained seven Avro Ansons and three de Havilland DH.86B four-engine biplanes.

In October 1951, BOAC became a major shareholder in Gulf Aviation, holding a twenty-two per cent stake through the BOAC subsidiary company BOAC Associated Companies. (see

In 1973, the Emirate of Bahrain, the State of Qatar, the Emirate of Abu Dhabi and the Sultanate of Oman agreed to purchase the BOAC Associated Companies holding in Gulf Aviation. The Foundation Treaty was signed on 1 January 1974 and gave each government a twenty-five per cent shareholding in Gulf Aviation, which became a holding company. The operating company was now branded as Gulf Air and became the flag carrier for the four states.

Gulf Air signed a contract for four extended-range TriStar 100s, in December 1974, the first two to be delivered in January and February 1976. The contract included four options. These aircraft had 18,000 pounds of additional fuel in the wing centre-section and a maximum take-off weight of 466,000 pounds. They were initially fitted with RB211-22B engines, but options were open for a later retrofit of more powerful engines.

Gulf Air took delivery of its first TriStar at the end of January 1976, so as to prepare for the start of its Bahrain to London service in April. These aircraft had the most luxurious layout of any airliners then in service, with only 171 economy-class and 40 first-class seats. Also in January, Delta increased its order by one aircraft, to a total of twenty-two aircraft, this being the first sale for over one year, none having been achieved in 1975. However, Cathay Pacific cancelled two of its options in February and two new TWA aircraft were sold straight off the production line to Saudia.

On 17 March 1976, Gulf Air demonstrated its Golden Falcon TriStar, G-BDCX, to the press and travel agents with a forty minute flight from London to Amsterdam. This was one of two aircraft delivered with two more arriving in May and June. The seating was plush and roomy, the first-class seats being at forty-inch pitch and the economy-class at thirty-four inch pitch. The centre pair of seats in the first-class cabin could be swivelled to face a table, forming a four-place conference or dining area. There was no surcharge for the extra luxury, as the long-term passenger appeal was expected to justify the extra fittings' investment. The introduction of the TriStars doubled Gulf Air's capacity from London to the Gulf, the major competitor at the time being the newly introduced Concorde. The regular Gulf Air TriStar services were inaugurated on 1 April 1976.

With leased Lockheed L-1011 Tristar and Boeing 737 aircraft joining the fleet, by 1976 Gulf Air had expanded its route network to include Amman, Amsterdam, Athens, Baghdad, Bombay, Bangkok, Beirut, Cairo, Colombo, Delhi, Dhaka, Hong Kong, Jeddah, Karachi, Khartoum, Larnaca, Manila, Paris, Ras al-Khaimah and Sana'a. The fleet comprised four Vickers VC10, three BAC One-Elevens, two Lockheed L-1011 Tristar 200s and five Boeing 737-200s. In 1978, the airline doubled the Tristar fleet to

Golden Falcon A40-TY of Gulf Air sweeps in for another landing. *(Emma Dayle Collection)*

replace the VC10s. Meanwhile, the airline increased the Boeing 737 fleet to nine and phased out the One-Elevens.

Gulf Air ordered two TriStar -200s in August 1979 to add to its fleet of four -100s. The new aircraft were scheduled for delivery in February and March 1981 and were fitted with the Flight Management System (FMS) similar to those offered on the later -500s.

The 1980s saw an increase in air travel and growth for Gulf Air. In 1981, Gulf Air became an IATA member. In 1985, Emirates, the startup national carrier of Dubai, began operating. During their first year of operations, Gulf Air profits fell thirty per cent, prompting the airline to drop its privatization plans. In 1986, Gulf Air posted a loss.

In 1988, Boeing 767s joined the fleet, and the airline launched service to Frankfurt, Istanbul, Damascus, Dar es Salaam, Fujairah and Nairobi, and resumed service to Shiraz and Baghdad.

In April 1989, Gulf Air, one of the early customers for the TriStar, ordered an additional six extended range Boeing 767s, with some options, to start the replacement of the eleven TriStars of various marks, commencing with the withdrawal of the first two in June 1989.

Gulf Air celebrated its 40th anniversary in 1990. The light-blue and peach Balenciaga-designed uniform was introduced. Services to Singapore, Sydney and Thiruvananthapuram were launched, Gulf Air thereby becoming the first Arab airline to fly to Australia. Gulf Air added services to Johannesburg and Melbourne in 1992, becoming the first Arab airline to fly directly to these cities. By mid-1992, Gulf Air still had eight TriStars in the fleet, due to the economic problems caused by the Gulf War. In 1993, it opened a flight-simulator training centre in Qatar and introduced services to Casablanca, Entebbe, Jakarta, Kilimanjaro, Madras, Rome, San'a', Zanzibar and Zürich.

In 1997 Gulf Air was still experiencing economic problems and disposed of some of the 767s for much-needed cash and brought out of storage three of the TriStars, which it had been unable to sell.

At the same time as the start of the Gulf Air TriStar operations from Bahrain to London, British Airways Overseas Division started to replace its VC10s and 707s on Abu Dhabi's services Dubai, Dhahran and Kuwait. This was achieved with two TriStar L-1011-1s on a three-year transfer from the European Division. The BA TriStars were not as luxurious as the Gulf Air aircraft, but had been configured with thirty-eight first-class seats and 202 economy-class. The use of these TriStars helped

Gulf Air Golden Falcon TriStar N92TA looks stunning in the sunshine. *(Kirk Smeeton Collection)*

utilise the excess capacity experienced by the European Division; although the range was on the L-1011-1 limits with the possibility of technical stops on hot days. Whereas the problem with much of the world's airline routes was overcapacity, the Gulf routes were experiencing exceedingly rapid growth, the BA share having grown to forty-five per cent of the market, although the TriStars were not used to compete with Concorde to Bahrain.

Saudia

In March 1974 Saudia ordered two TriStars for delivery in mid-1975, with options on a further three aircraft. The order was for L-1011-100s fitted with increased wing fuel tankage, but without the centre-section tanks specified by Cathay Pacific. Take-off weight of Saudia's aircraft was raised by 20,000 pounds to 450,000 pounds, and they were able to carry 259 passengers over a range of 4,000 miles.

The first order for what became known as the L-1011-200 was for two long-range TriStars from Saudia on 19 September 1974. The last of what was then a total of four aircraft was due for delivery in 1977, powered by the uprated RB211-524 engines. These developed 48,000 pounds thrust each, an increase of 6,000 pounds over the earlier engine. The remaining three aircraft were to be retrofitted with the new engines making them all to the -200 standard. The new aircraft was expected to have a range of 4,700 miles with full reserves which gave it a transatlantic capability.

In May 1978 Saudia further increased its fleet of TriStars to thirteen, by ordering three more aircraft.

Saudia, formerly known as Saudi Arabian Airlines, is the flag carrier of Saudi Arabia, based in Jeddah. The airline's main operational base is at King Abdulaziz International Airport in Jeddah. King Khalid International Airport in Riyadh and King Fahd International Airport in Dammam are secondary hubs.

When US President Franklin Delano Roosevelt presented a Douglas DC-3 as a gift to King Abdul Aziz Ibn Saud in 1945, the event marked the kingdom's gradual development of civil aviation. Saudia, the nation's flag carrier, was founded as Saudi Arabian Airlines in September 1945 as a wholly-owned government agency under the Ministry of Defence's control, with TWA running the airline under a management contract.

Saudia's HZ-AHQ turns on to Runway 33L at Athens Ellinikon Airport. *(Richard Vandervord)*

It was rumoured that following the attack on Iran Air Flight 655 - an Airbus A300 scheduled passenger flight from Tehran to Dubai via Bandar Abbas - shot down on 3 July 1988 by a surface-to-air missile fired from USS *Vincennes*, a guided-missile cruiser of the US Navy, many Middle Eastern airliners were discreetly fitted with anti-air-to-air missile devices. One machine was this Saudia TriStar with the equipment highlighted on the rear of the engine pylon.

Saudia TriStar Hotel Foxtrot on finals. *(Kirk Smeeton Collection)*

The now-demolished Kandara Airport, close to Jeddah, served as the flag carrier's main base. Among the airline's early operations was a special flight from Lydda (Lod) in Palestine to carry Hajj pilgrims to Jeddah. The airline used five DC-3 aircraft to launch scheduled operations on the Jeddah-Riyadh-Hofuf-Dhahran route in March 1947. Its first international service was between Jeddah and Cairo. Service to Beirut, Karachi and Damascus followed in early 1948.

In 1962, the airline took delivery of two Boeing 720s, becoming the fourth Middle Eastern airline to fly jet aircraft. On 19 February 1963, the airline became a registered company, with King Faisal of Saudi Arabia signing the papers that declared Saudia a fully independent company. DC-6s and Boeing 707s were later bought, and the airline joined the AACO, the Arab Air Carriers Organization. Services started to Sharjah, Tehran, Khartoum, Mumbai, Tripoli, Tunis, Rabat, Geneva, Frankfurt, and London.

In the 1970s, a new livery was introduced. Boeing 737s and Fokker F-28s were bought, with the 737s replacing the Douglas DC-9. The airline operated their first Boeing 747s service in 1977 when three Jumbo Jets were leased from Middle East

Saudi Arabian Airlines' L-1011 HZ-HM5 seen at London Heathrow. *(Richard Vandervord)*

Saudi Arabian Airlines' L-1011 HZ-HM6 being towed by a tug at Heathrow. *(Richard Vandervord)*

Airlines and deployed on the London sector. The first all-cargo flights between Saudi Arabia and Europe were started, and Lockheed L-1011s and Fairchild FH-27s were introduced. Saudia's first TriStar, an extended-range L-1011-100 was delivered in July 1975 ready for services to start on 15 August.

The buoyant Middle East market became apparent to Lockheed, when on 25 May 1976, after eighteen months with only one TriStar sale, Saudia ordered three more RB211-524-engined L-1011-200s for delivery starting in September 1977. This order's value was $98.6 million, and the two ex-TWA TriStars were to be re-engined with the newer Rolls-Royce engine. However, the order for new TriStars was reduced to two aircraft less than two months later due to a revision of fleet requirements.

The airline kept changing its identity from one name to another. It reverted to its abbreviated English brand name Saudia - from 1 April 1972 to 1996 - from Saudi Arabian Airlines, the historic name in use until 1971 and reintroduced in 1997. Then on 29 May 2012, the name was changed to celebrate the company's entry into the SkyTeam airline alliance on that day, and it was a part of a larger rebranding initiative.

New services, including the Arabian Express 'no reservation shuttle flights' between Jeddah and Riyadh. The Special Flight Services (SFS) was set up as a special unit of Saudia and operated special flights for the royal family and government agencies. Service was also started to Rome, Paris, Muscat, Kano, and Stockholm. The Pan Am/Saudia, joint service between Dhahran and New York City, started on 3 February 1979.

By the end of 1993, Saudia was beginning to look at the long-overdue requirement for the modernisation of the entire fleet, including the replacement of the TriStars. Economic difficulties caused delays within Saudi Arabia due to the large purchases of military aircraft, a contract for the new Boeing and McDonnell aircraft being signed in October 1995, with deliveries commencing in 1998, again with delays caused by financial problems.

Cathay Pacific

Cathay Pacific Airways Ltd. (CPA) is the flag carrier of Hong Kong, with its head office and main hub located at Hong Kong International Airport. The

TriStar alley at Kai Tak. Cathay Pacific's L-1011s became synonimous with the original Hong Kong airport. *(Kirk Smeeton Collection)*

airline's operations and subsidiaries have scheduled passenger and cargo services to more than 190 destinations in more than sixty countries worldwide including codeshares and joint ventures.

The airline was founded on 24 September 1946 by Australian Sydney H de Kantzow and American Roy C Farrell. It celebrated its 70th anniversary in 2016; and as of March 2018, its major shareholders are Swire Pacific, with a forty-five per cent stake and Air China, with a twenty-nine per cent stake.

In the 1960s, the Boeing 707s had carried Cathay into the wider world. Success fed ambition, and the company's thoughts turned towards a genuine wide-bodied, intercontinental aircraft - ideally, the Boeing 747, which was undoubtedly the aircraft of the age. The trouble was that the 747s were designed to carry about 450 passengers, and several airlines, including Cathay, were not sure that they could fill these monsters. There were., however, two other wide-bodied aircraft came onto the market with a 300-passenger capacity: the Douglas DC-10 and the Lockheed TriStar, both three-engined aircraft. Engines made by General Electric powered the DC-10; the TriStar's engines came from Rolls-Royce. There seemed little to choose between them, so a team from Cathay set out for America to investigate both at close quarters. They arrived at a time of desperate competition between Douglas and Lockheed with the big, long-range DC-10 well out ahead - in fact, already flying. Lockheed had also produced a superb aircraft - indeed, the TriStar was something of a technical miracle - but was lagging behind Douglas in production.

The Cathay team returned to Hong Kong with their recommendations and, on 29 January 1974, John Bremridge, Cathay's Managing Director and his directors unanimously agreed to go for the Douglas DC-10. And that normally would have been that. But

Cathay Pacific was proud of its British connections, and were happy to show of it's links with Rolls-Royce.

Here a company TriStar poses alongside one of thre engine and car-makers products..

Below: Company L-1011 VR-HOA seen at Osaka airport. *(Temil Soket Collection)*

Cathay's SuperTriStar VR-HHW taxiing at Kai Tak. *(Richard Vandervord)*

something quite unexpected occurred.

It had been agreed to defer for thirty-six hours any announcement of the Board's decision in favour of the DC-10 to allow time for the British Government to be informed of it. This was an unusual procedure, but the involvement of Rolls-Royce with the TriStar had created a special circumstance. For Rolls-Royce was in crisis. Swires in London had an idea that the official reaction to their choice of the rival DC-10 with American engines might be somewhat, shall we say, 'adverse'? Indeed it was. So adverse in fact that the Minister responsible, Michael Heseltine, telephoned in person to request the earliest possible meeting with John Swire, Adrian being away in Hong Kong. When they met, the Minister was upset and did not attempt to hide it. He felt let down by Cathay's decision, he said, indeed he had been 'flabbergasted' by its suddenness.

Why had he not been given a chance to bring pressure to bear on Lockheed to provide Cathay with a better deal? Or 'to have a word' with Rolls-Royce, who was admittedly going through a difficult patch but who could no doubt be prevailed upon by government to provide cast-iron guarantees of all-out technical support in the future?

As John Swire later reported, there was no table-pounding; there was more sorrow on the Minister's part than anger. Calmly fingering his Brigade of Guards tie, Mr Heseltine was all 'urbanity and sweet reasonableness'. He just made it very plain indeed that he and his advisers needed an answer to one question: 'Why, oh why, with nothing to choose between the two aircraft, had Cathay come down unanimously in Douglas's favour?'

John Swire agreed that all other things being equal, Cathay would have preferred an aircraft with a British component. Heseltine nodded. Nevertheless, the British government was very concerned to look after the interests of both Cathay Pacific and Rolls-Royce. 'It would be much less embarrassing for me if those two interests had dovetailed.' The Minister kept his most telling point to the last. Walking Swire to the lift, Heseltine gently slipped a final word into his ear: 'I should perhaps tell you that one of my embarrassments is persuading other Asian airlines to buy British equipment at a time when one of the most successful operators in the area - British, at that - has gone elsewhere.' He hoped Cathay would hold up their final decision to give him time to encourage Rolls-Royce to improve the package they and Lockheed were jointly offering.

John Swire was puzzled. For a Minister to take such an interest was most unusual. Cathay Pacific had been making its own decisions about buying aircraft for over twenty years, and this was the first time Her Majesty's Government had intervened. Was Cathay being leaned on? John Swire was not sure, but a further meeting with Sir Peter Thornton, Permanent Secretary at the Department of Trade and Industry, clarified matters. Sir Peter spelt it out: the deteriorating British balance of payments; the need to keep employment at Rolls-Royce; the desirability of giving an encouraging lead to the other airlines in South East Asia at that very moment, undecided

'Gear Up!' SuperTriStar VR-HHY climbs out. *(Richard Vandervord)*

whether to order the TriStar or the DC-10. These were pressing British concerns. Of course, Sir Peter hastened to add, Her Majesty's government would not be putting pressure on Cathay Pacific if it did not believe the TriStar was a good aircraft, but as it was, the government hoped and expected - that Cathay would take all these British concerns into account.

Cathay's interpretation of all this was that a 'patriotic' decision in favour of the TriStar and Rolls-Royce would ensure, for any plans Cathay Pacific might have in the future, a sympathetic attitude from the Department of Trade and Industry.

Cathay and Lockheed went back to the negotiating table, and Lockheed undertook to provide an improved aircraft at a lower price, thus achieving a considerable edge over Douglas. For its part, Rolls-Royce promised to keep producing the RB211-22B engine and to come up with an even better one very shortly.

Slightly shaken but with a good conscience, in March 1974, Cathay Pacific signed a Letter of Intent for two TriStars plus two options. These were the first aircraft fitted with a centre-section fuel tank, and the maximum take-off weight was increased to 46,000 pounds.

The first Cathay TriStar, VR-HHK, arrived from Palmdale, California, at Kai Tak on 2 September 1975, flown in by Captian E B 'Bernie' Smith and Captain Lawrence 'Laurie' King to be officially welcomed by Hong Kong's Governor, Sir Murray Maclehose, and the Hong Kong police band.

The TriStars' arrival coincided very neatly with a boom in Asian air travel, and thus it was that at the end of 1978, John Bremridge was able to announce to the Board an operating profit six times larger than that of the year before. By May 1979, the Cathay fleet consisted of eight 300-seat TriStars and eight 707s, a tremendous increase in both traffic and capacity.

Cathay Pacific was a major operator of the TriStar from its Hong Kong base on Asian regional services but placed orders for ten Airbus A330-300s powered by Rolls-Royce BB211-524L engines in 1989 to replace the fleet of TriStars eventually. The Cathay fleet consisted of fourteen TriStars with additions purchased from the bankrupt Eastern Airlines fleet.

Delta's L-1011 N729DA taxies past the camera in this chilly winter snowscape. *(Gary Baldie Collection)*

'751 Rolling!' Delta's N751DA departs London Gatwick, with 747 'Big Orange' of Braniff International behind on the taxiway. *(Richard Vandervord)*

The aircraft was flying about seven hours a day due to restrictions with night time curfews at a number of airports in the region. The first of two Cathay TriStars was leased to Dragonair from 1 July 1990 for services to Shanghai and Beijing, eventually being replaced by A330s in May and September 1995. In mid-1990, Cathay announced that the eighteen-strong TriStar fleet had been sold to Airfleet Credit Finance, the aircraft being withdrawn from 1995 onwards, as the A330s were delivered. After twenty-one years in service, Cathay operated the last TriStar revenue flight on 15 October 1995 between Nagoya and Taipei. The last Cathay TriStar flight was flown by VB-HHY, which had been with the airline since 1978, had flown 39,754 hours and made some 20,100 landings.

Delta Air Lines

Delta Air Lines' history can be traced back to what is alleged to be the world's first aerial crop dusting operation called Huff Daland Dusters, Inc. The company was founded on 2 March 1925, in Macon, Georgia before moving to Monroe, Louisiana in the summer of 1925. It flew a Huff-Daland Duster, the first true crop duster designed to combat the boll weevil infestation of cotton crops. Collett Everman Woolman, general manager and later Delta's first CEO, led a group of local investors to acquire the company's assets. Delta Air Service was incorporated on 3 December 1928 and named after the Mississippi Delta region.

Passenger operations began on 17 June 1929, from Dallas, Texas, to Jackson, Mississippi, with stops at Shreveport and Monroe, Louisiana. By June 1930, service had extended east to Atlanta and west to Fort Worth, Texas. Passenger service ceased in October 1930 when the airmail contract for the route Delta had pioneered was awarded to another airline, which purchased the assets of Delta Air Service. Local banker Travis Oliver, acting as a trustee, Woolman, and other local investors purchased back the crop-dusting assets of Delta Air Service. They incorporated them as Delta Air Corporation on 31 December 1930.

Delta Air Corporation secured an airmail contract in 1934 and began doing business as Delta Air Lines over Mail Route 24, stretching from Fort Worth, Texas, to Charleston, South Carolina. Delta moved its headquarters from Monroe, Louisiana, to its current location in Atlanta in 1941. The company name officially became Delta Air Lines in 1945 and by 1946, the company commenced regularly scheduled freight transport. Three years later, in 1949, the company launched the first discounted fares between Chicago and Miami. The company launched its first international routes in 1953 after acquiring Chicago and Southern Air Lines. In 1959, it was the first airline to fly the Douglas DC-8. In 1960, it was the first airline to fly Convair 880 jets. In 1964, it launched the Deltamatic reservation systems using computers in the IBM 7070 series. In 1965, Delta was the first airline to fly the McDonnell Douglas DC-9.

By 1970, Delta had an all-jet fleet, and in 1972 it acquired Northeast Airlines. Trans-Atlantic service began in 1978 with the first nonstop flights from Atlanta to London. In 1981, Delta launched a frequent-flyer programme. In 1987, it acquired Western Airlines, and that same year Delta began trans-Pacific service (Atlanta-Portland, Oregon-Tokyo). In 1990, Delta was the first airline in the United States to fly McDonnell Douglas MD-11 jets. In 1991, it acquired all of Pan Am's trans-Atlantic routes and the Pan Am Shuttle substantially, rebranded as the Delta Shuttle. Delta was now the leading airline across the Atlantic.

During Lockheed's financial troubles, Delta ordered five DC-10s as an insurance against a failure of the TriStar. In mid-1972, Delta confirmed its wish to have TriStars, and transferred its rights on the DC-10s to United Airlines. The arrangement was that on delivery to United, the DC-10s would be leased to Delta for about two and a half years pending delivery of sufficient TriStars and then returned to United.

The first Delta TriStar, N701DA was rolled out at Palmdale ready for its first flight on 7 September 1973 and was delivered to the airline on 3 October. In December, services started covering New York, Philadelphia, Atlanta, Houston, Miami, New Orleans, and Tampa.

Delta, having introduced the TriStars to replace its leased DC-10s, converted three of its twelve options into firm orders in November 1974, bringing their total orders to twenty-one L-1011s.

Delta confirmed a further option for a TriStar in February 1977, with five options remaining. This brought the total Delta fleet to 25 TriStars in service by the end of 1978. Two more were ordered in August 1977 for delivery in 1979. In October 1978, Delta ordered five more standard L-1011-1 TriStars with options on a further 15 aircraft. The aircraft on order were for delivery in 1980 to 1981 and the options covered delivery positions between 1982 and 1984. This was the largest order for the TriStar for over four years.

In 1978 Delta headquarters focused chiefly upon preparations for the opening of the London route. After careful study of the options available, management decided that the best airliner to provide the new transatlantic service was the long-range L-1011-500. On 23 January Delta placed an order for five of these, becoming the first US carrier to do so. Deliveries, however, would not begin until May 1979. As a temporary substitute, the company leased two L-1011s from TWA, which lacked the L-1011-500 series's payload capacity, they had a more extended range than Delta's regular TriStars.

The marketing division completed scheduling plans for the new route. Initially, Delta would provide one daily round-trip flight to London; originating at New Orleans in mid-afternoon, it would proceed to Atlanta for an early evening departure and arrive at London's Gatwick terminal at breakfast time the following day. Travellers could then attend morning business meetings or make various connections to Europe, Africa, and the Middle East. The return flight would depart from London in the afternoon and be back in Atlanta by suppertime, continuing to New Orleans for an early evening arrival. The beginning and end of each round trip were designed to mesh with many connections to southeastern and midwestern points through Delta's famous hub-and-spoke system.

The advertising and public relations departments devised a series of displays featuring a 'Peachtree to Piccadilly' theme. They then prepared information useful to tourists - an impressive glossary of British colloquialisms for travellers who might not otherwise appreciate the vast difference between the meanings of different words in the two countries. Along with it went a sheet explaining the idiosyncratic nature of English terminology for certain types of food or public accommodations. Meanwhile, dining service officials planned choice menus for passengers, including smoked salmon, Pheasant Galantine, Filet of Beef Wellington, and Cornish Game Hen Veronique.

In *Delta News*, the airline's staff newspaper, later to evolve into the *Delta News Hub*, the reporter waxed lyrical about the innuaguration.

'Perhaps nothing in Delta's fifty-year history captured its staff's imagination more than the opening flight to London, which took place on 30 April 1978. Traditional ribbon-cutting ceremonies were held at New Orleans, after which the newly leased TriStar with its partial complement of passengers flew on to Atlanta for a more elaborate celebration. As official hosts Vice-Chairman of the Board and Mr Richard S Maurer gathered with 159 revenue passengers in one of the VIP' Crown Rooms' at Atlanta's Hartsfield International Airport - it all then got slightly surreal. Stilton cheese and Scotch whiskey were served in the lounge while bagpipes droned and a young lady danced in Highland costume. Georgia Governor George Busbee entrusted to Maurer an intricate glass dogwood sculpture by Atlanta artist Hans Frobel, to be presented at the other end of the flight to the Lord Mayor of London. Then the party proceeded to gate 51-A while the bagpipes struck up 'Scotland the Brave.' Before they boarded the L-1011-100, resplendent in its Delta insignia, Maurer and Busbee took part in yet another ribbon-cutting ceremony, assisted by two Delta employees, one dressed in a beefeater costume and the other in the uniform of a

'Align the airplane with the runway, advance throttles to approximately 60% N1, and command the copilot to "Set T.O. power". During the takeoff roll, maintain light forward pressure on the yoke and maintain directional control with thew rudder pedal steering.'

Delta flight DL37 starts its take-off roll from a very misty London Gatwick on its way to Cincinnati/Northern Kentucky International Airport. *(author)*

London bobby.'

'Many off-duty employees were on hand to see the flight off; they began cheering as the TriStar was tugged away from the embarkation gate. As the airliner moved down the finger toward an exit lane, it passed between two rows of Delta tugs, whose drivers had lined them up in a formation similar to that of cheerleaders greeting an athletic team as it takes to the field.'

'In the captain's seat on the left side of the cockpit was Delta's most senior pilot, Elmer Bennett, who had joined Chicago and Southern as a reserve copilot in 1939.'

'Under the flight plan, the TriStar flew across the Carolinas crossed the Virginia line and departed the American mainland in the vicinity of Norfolk. Despite some open patches through which the dark ocean could be glimpsed far below in the waning twilight, the craft was now flying mostly over a cloud cover which blotted out the surface of the water. Dinner was served at about 8:30 PM, and a motion picture was shown for the entertainment of the travellers. Then, while the passengers slept or mused upon the adventure they were taking part, the airliner continued to speed through the night toward its destination. As the sun came up the big jet passed over Land's End, England's westernmost tip, and proceeded eastward over the English Channel with Plymouth and Brighton on its left and the French coast on the right. Hot towels were provided to freshen the travellers up, and a continental breakfast was served. Because of a low ceiling over Gatwick, Bennett decided for an automatic landing. With its sophisticated electronic systems operating correctly, the ship broke through the clouds a few hundred feet above the ground in exact alignment with the runway. At 7:30 AM GMT, eight hours after departing from Atlanta, the plane was on the ground, just as its schedule had specified. It was drizzling, but this did not lower the group's spirits that participated in more ribbon-cutting ceremonies at Gatwick's gate 18, including Sir Kenneth Keith, chairman of Rolls-Royce, and David Garrett, Delta's president and chief executive officer. The company's inaugural flight to London thus passed successfully into history.'

As well as using the shorter-range TriStars domestically, Delta used the L-1011-500 for transatlantic flights to Gatwick, and then on to Frankfurt from November 1993, where a European hub had been established. This was achieved when Delta took over the PanAm routes in November 1991 with the demise of that airline, which also allowed the take over of a number of the old Pan Am worldwide routes from Germany.

Delta Air Lines continued to top up its TriStar fleet when it converted two options to firm orders for L-1011-1s in March 1980 for delivery in December 1981 and January 1982. This brought Delta's total to thirty-two TriStars in service, eight on firm order and a further thirteen options. Gulf Air added a seventh TriStar with an order in the spring of 1980. Delta added another TriStar in July 1980, a further one in the following month, another in November and one more in early 1981. Two more options were converted into firm orders for TriStar 1s by Delta in April 1981 for delivery in April and May 1983. Delta planned to have forty-four of the type in service by mid-1983, with ten still scheduled for delivery over the following two years and seven options remaining.

Delta was later to open another hub at CVG - Cincinnati/Northern Kentucky International Airport. At its peak, CVG became Delta's second-largest hub, handling over 670 flights daily, to numerous transatlantic destinations including Amsterdam, Brussels, Frankfurt, London, Manchester, Munich, Paris, Rome, and Zürich, many using their L-1011s. Indeed, the Delta DL37/36 service between Gatwick and the tri-state airport was one I regularly used to catch.

Delta and Lockheed formed a strategic alliance to provide maintenance and technical support for the TriStar in December 1995, using the airline's Atlanta engineering base for light maintenance of the world fleet. Lockheed Martin offered heavy maintenance at Greenville, North Carolina. At its peak, Delta had fifty aircraft of all versions used both domestically and on international flights. However, Delta began the rundown of the TriStar fleet in February 1996 with further orders for 767-300ERs to replace the trijets on the North Atlantic routes, the long-range aircraft eventually replacing earlier TriStars on domestic services. In 1997, Delta placed the launch order for the stretched Boeing 767-400, which finally decided the ultimate replacement for the TriStar with the airline.

Chapter Ten

Later Models and 'Active Control'

To put the L-1011 - for which Lockheed initially projected a market totalling up to 800 units - into perspective, it is worth recalling that the TriStar was launched in 1968 based on a specification that included three 40,000 pound static thrust engines, a gross weight of 380,000-409,000 pounds and a range of 2,650-3,250 nautical miles with 250 passengers. Later, the basic L-1011-1 - the initial production version - was operated at a gross weight of 430,000 pounds with 42,000 pounds static thrust RB211-22B engines and a range of 3,570 nautical miles with layouts available for 256 up to 400 passengers.

To increase the range of the basic aircraft, Lockheed obtained certification at increased gross weights during 1975; successive steps in this process were weights of 440,000 pounds, 450,000 pounds and 466,000 pounds, all of which could be associated with a centre section fuel tank that increased the capacity by 19,000 pounds. Designated the Dash 100, this TriStar variant used the same RB211-22B engines as the Dash 1. The L-1011-100 entered service with Cathay Pacific and was also ordered by others that included Gulf Air and Saudia; Air Canada, Delta, LTU and TWA converted some of their Dash 1s to this standard.

When Rolls-Royce developed the RB211 engine to the 50,000 pounds static thrust bracket, Lockheed was quick to take advantage of the extra thrust to offer improved payload/range and/or airfield performance in the TriStar. Using the RB211-524B - flat-rated, as in the Dash 500, to 48,000 pounds ststic thrust up to ISA plus 196 deg C - in the Dash 100 resulted in the Dash 200, with the same three gross weight and two fuel capacity options. The first order for the Dash 200 came from Saudia in mid-1974, serving to launch the -524 version of the RB211 then on test, but the government did not authorise production until an airline had committed itself to a firm order.

Flight testing of the RB211-524 series began on 10 April 1976 when one engine was flown in Lockheed's N1011, first on one wing and then in the centre engine position, RB211-22s being retained in the other positions. During August, N1011 flew with three -524 B2 engines, and the first production TriStar 200 with these engines for Saudia flew on 8 October 1976. This aircraft was delivered in June 1977; Saudia meanwhile had received three TriStar 100s, the first on 15 July 1975, and subsequently converted these, plus two TriStar 1s purchased from TWA, to

Artists impression of the L-1011-400

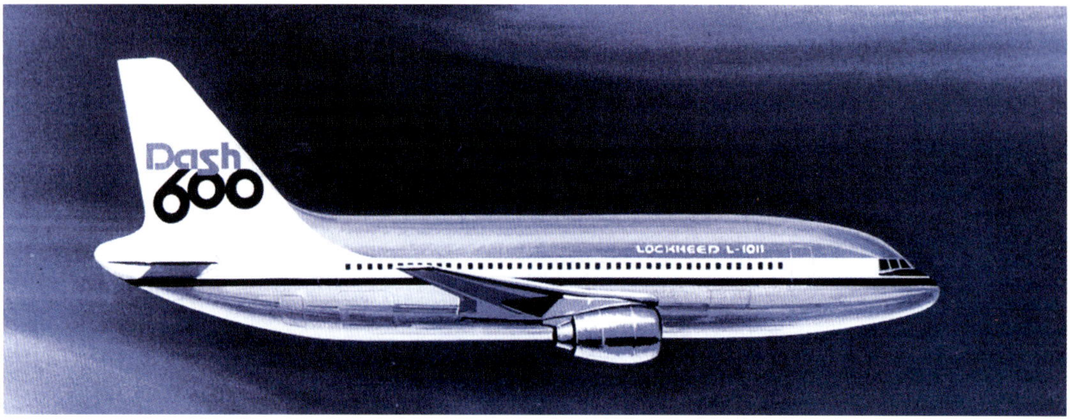

How Lockheed's artists saw the twin-engined L-1011-600

Dash 200 standard.

In 1980 the development of a stretched-fuselage Dash 300 version of the TriStar remained a long-term prospect. Previously, in 1979, Lockheed indicated that stretches of fourteen feet or thirty feet one inch were under consideration. Development of a Dash 300 would have required considerable investment and would proceed only if a substantial market was identified. The timescale was likely to be such that the smaller tailplane could be used in a full active control system, together with advanced aluminium alloys and composites for secondary structure. More powerful variants of the RB211, such as the 55,000-pound static thrust -524G might be required, to match weight growth up to as much as 600,000 pounds. At this weight, the Dash 300 would probably have required six-wheel main undercarriage bogies, which in turn led to a new, enlarged wing centre section with the gross wing area going up to about 4,000 square feet.

More readily available were variants that combined features of TriStars already certificated.

The differences in wingtip and aileron between the -1 series (left) and -500 series.

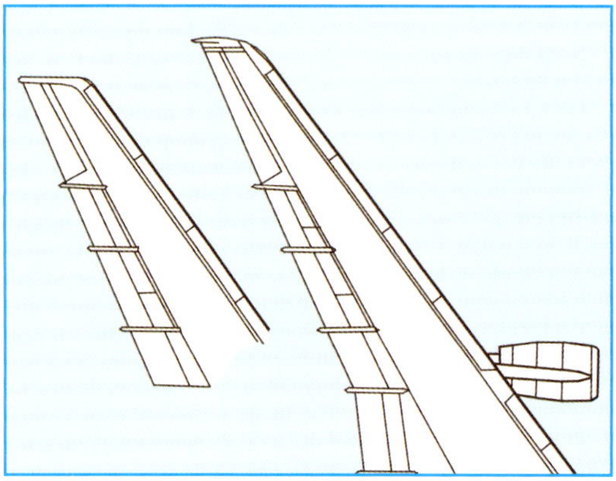

Lockheed had already offered and would produce a TriStar 250, a Dash 200 with the extra fuel capacity and higher weights of the Dash 500. This, like the L-101 1-1, -100 and -200, had a passenger capacity in a typical mixed-class of 302 with underfloor galleys or 284 with main cabin galleys, and the ranges with full passenger payloads would be 4,540 nautical miles and 4,602 nautical miles respectively. Active controls would be used, as on the Srs 500.

Going in the other direction, the lower-rated RB211-22B engines could be used in the Dash 500 airframe to produce a TriStar 400 offering even better fuel economy if extreme ranges were not required. The centre-section fuel tanks could be eliminated and the aircraft flown at lower weights to match the reduced power. This was a more attractive variant than the twin-engined TriStar 600 that Lockheed publicised in 1978 but in the shorter term, most interest was likely to focus on new variants of the TriStar 500 itself. These included a 500LR, in which extra fuel would be carried in an extended wing centre section - as in the Dash 300LR - to stretch the range to more than 7,500 miles; and a series of all-freight and combination possibilities. The L-1011-500F, with a forward side freight door, would have a max cargo payload of up to 146,400 pounds over short ranges, while the L-1011-500HB and -500QC combi and quick-change versions would have a convertible rear main deck, with the cargo door aft of the wing.

Incidentally, the 'BiStar' was studied as early as 1972 as a twin-engined RB211-22X-powered 200 - 250 seater with Japan as full partners. The airliner would have had a reduced wing area and a gross weight of 276,000 pounds. It would have returned seat/mile costs comparable with the TriStar, with aircraft seat/mile costs twenty to twenty-five per cent lower. Development costs were estimated to be $290 million and would need to have been approved by the US Government.

While most interest centred on developments of the later TriStar variants, the original L-1011-1 was also the basis for further improvement, as Lockheed demonstrated when it proposed the L-1011-ISF short-field version. The objective was to allow operation of the basic aircraft from 6,560-fiit runways with a commercially viable payload, and could be achieved, Lockheed suggested, by introducing full-span ground spoilers on the wing, increasing the authority of the standard direct lift control system, using automatic braking as specified for the -500s with brake cooling fans, and recertificating the approach speed to a lower value. The proposal was made primarily for All Nippon Airways, which was looking for a replacement for a part of its Boeing 727 fleet from 1983 onwards.

Early versions of the TriStar 500 - for British Airways and Delta - were powered by the RB211-524B2 whereas the 211-524B3 engine powered at least the first six for Pan American. As further improvements in fuel consumption became available, uprated thrust engines were offered. In 1981, the RB21 1-524B4 replaced the B3, with the same thrust but a reduction of up to four per cent in cruising fuel consumption; this engine featured a larger diameter fan and larger-diameter IP/ LP turbines in what was referred to as the 05 module. Uprated versions which could be adopted were the -524D with a take-off thrust of 53,000 pounds static thrust became available from 1981, along with the -524G at 55,000 pounds static thrust. Destined initially for use in the Boeing 747, these new versions had lower specific fuel consumption and lower powerplant weight.

The concept of the short-body, very long-range version of the L-1011 emerged during 1975, after earlier discussions with the airlines of long-range versions of the standard TriStar and the so-called Mini-Trijet, a short-range version with the shortened fuselage. The 'unstretch' planned for the mini-trijet was twenty feet two inches and proposed to the airlines in 1975, the Dash 500 had this same reduction; by using the uprated RB211-524 engines offered by Rolls-Royce for 1979 service at a minimum rating of 48,000 pounds static thrust, Lockheed was able to plan much higher gross weights and therefore larger fuel capacities with the same payload. The idea was to offer an airliner suitable for use on the 'long thin routes' where there was not enough traffic to make the full-size L-1011, DC-10 or 747 viable but was able to replace the 707s and DC-8s that were getting long in the tooth.

At a gross weight of 490,000 pounds, this early Dash 500 version would carry 212,000 pounds of fuel, giving it a non-stop range of up to 6,200 miles with 231 passengers in mixed-class configuration.

In 1976, British Airways and British Caledonian

The reduction in fuselage length between the L-1011-1 and the -500 series.

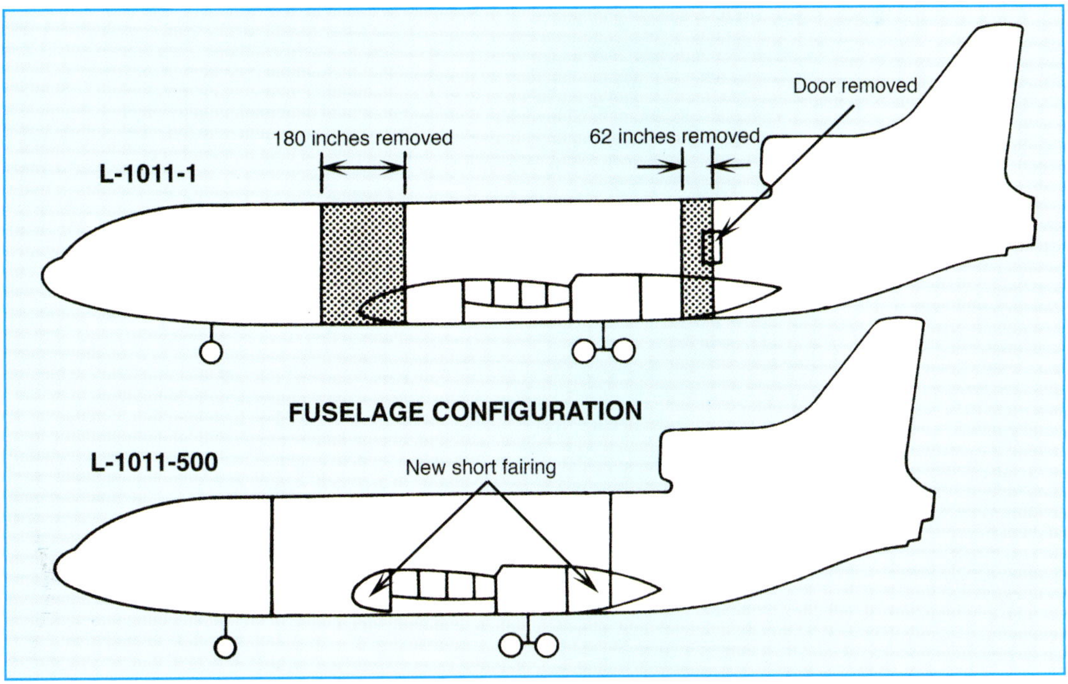

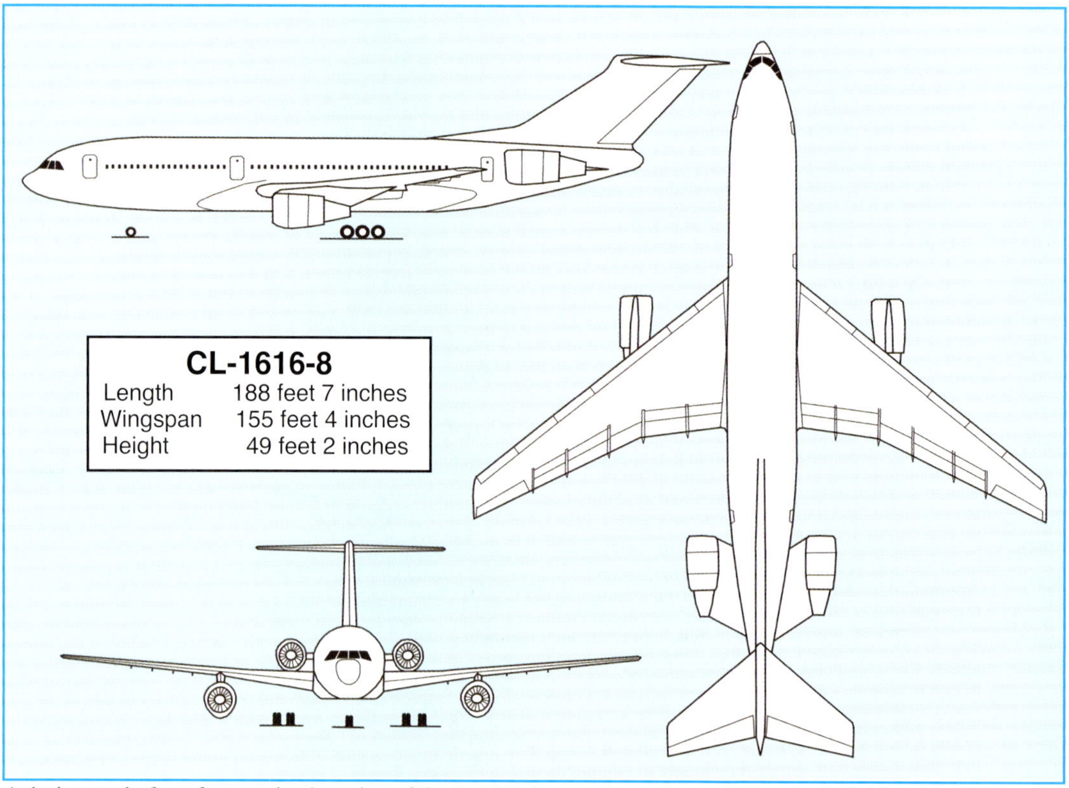

A design study for a four-engined version of the L-1011 that used two General Electric CF6-6D engines under the wing and two podded engines on the aft fusaelage.

emerged as prime candidates for launching orders for the TriStar 500. The BCal decision, in June 1976, to buy DC-10s was a blow both to Lockheed and to Rolls- Royce. Still, two months later, on 6 August, British Airways eliminated the DC-10 from its deliberations, despite the handsome offer made by McDonnell Douglas to develop a new version with RB211 engines. Before the end of the month, the airline confirmed its order for six TriStar 500s. Since the airline had inherited the original BEA fleet of nine TriStar 1s and had others on option, its selection of the TriStar 500 had seemed to many to be a foregone conclusion. Indeed, it gave Lockheed a strong base from which to launch the Dash 500 as well as confirming British Airways as a significant future operator of the TriStar.

By April 1976, the L-1011-500 had changed slightly as the fuselage shortening was reduced to thirteen feet six inches and the capacity was increased to 246 passengers to reduce seat/mile costs. The L-1011-250 had been dropped in favour of the '-500'. The maximum take-off weight had been increased to 496,000 pounds, 400 pounds of weight being used in strengthening the wing and landing gear. The wing centre section was provided with 54,000 pounds more fuel capacity, the two tanks feeding the main wing tanks. The range with the new RB211-524 engines was 5,310 nautical miles with a full passenger load. The aircraft would be suitable for such routes as London to Los Angeles, New York to Buenos Aires or Sydney to Hong Kong.

When finally launched by a British Airways order in August 1976, the configuration was eighteen first-class and 217 economy-class seats in a fuselage shortened by one hundred inches ahead of the wing and sixty-two inches aft.

In the autumn of 1976, Lockheed was investigating other TriStar configurations for future applications. The stretched TriStar 300 would be capable of carrying 410 passengers on the main deck and 45 in a lower deck cabin. This variant was dropped when All Nippon Airways decided to buy high capacity Boeing 747SRs. By the mid-1980s, Lockheed could see a need for a reduced energy version, the TriStar RE, using extended wingtips, active controls and improved RB211 engines. Later an advanced TriStar could have a new high technology wing. Short- and medium-haul developments could be a -500 short fuselage version with the L-1011-1 wing and derated RB211 engines.

Studies continued on a twin-engined 200—seater with new wings and tail on the existing fuselage.

As launched, the TriStar 500 was larger than the original proposal, the reduction in length finally having been set at thirteen feet six inches with a one hundred inch plug removed ahead of the wing and a sixty-two-inch plug aft. The weight was increased to 496,000 pounds including the 54.000 pounds of extra fuel in two bays in the wing centre section. The fuselage was large enough to seat up to 300 passengers with British Airways specifying a mixed-class layout of 202 plus 30 with galleys on the main deck rather than underfloor as in the original TriStar versions.

With the 48, 000 pounds static thrust RB211-524B engines, the Dash 500 was calculated to have a full-passenger range of 6,056 miles and a maximum space-limited payload range of 4,857 miles. To allow the increased gross weight, the Dash 500 had strengthening to the fuselage. wing and tail unit as well as the landing gear which made use of new tyres and heavier duty brakes and a reinforced axle and bogie beam.

The reduction in length and passenger capacity meant that two passenger doors could be deleted; the aft passenger doors' design was also changed to enlarge them. Relocating the galleys on the main deck made it possible to enlarge the forward cargo compartment, accompanied by an increase in the size of the forward cargo door to allow pallet loading.

The Dash 500 additionally benefited from some general drag-reducing improvements designed over the years for the TriStar including revised wing-to-fuselage fairings, the so-called Frisbee fairing on the fuselage centre line ahead of the third engine intake that reduced noise in the cabin as well as drag, revised wing-engine inlets based on those for the RB211 engines on the Boeing 747. with sharper lips than hitherto and the improved fifteen-degree engine afterbody that Rolls-Royce adopted towards the end of 1975.

The -500 entered flight testing on 16 October 1978. This and the second aircraft flown in January 1979 was part of the British Airways order and were used to obtain certification for the new variant - a milestone achieved after some 350 hours of flight testing in April 1979 when both the FAA and CAA issued airworthiness certificates. BA was able to put the new variant into revenue service on 7 May 1979. initially on the London-Abu Dhabi route and later on other destinations to the Middle and the Far East, including Singapore.

The design study for the L-1011-300 that added two fuselage barrel sections to the basic L-1011. It was never built.

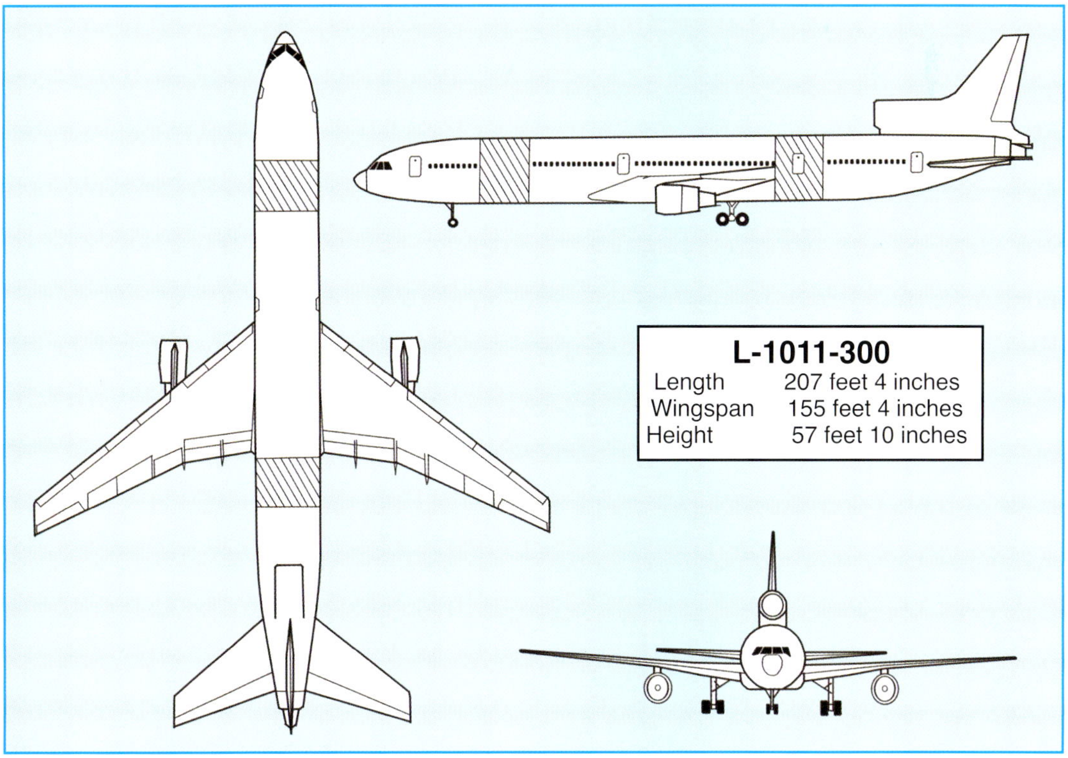

Above: The Advanced TriStar configuration developed on the prototype included the extended wingtips with active controls. The aircraft is seen flying over the Lockheed plant at Palmdale.

Left: Lockheed's advanced TriStar prototype also tested cathode ray tube (CRT) displays in the cockpit, fitted to the first officer's position, replacing the original analogue instruments. *(both Lockheed)*

In the spring of 1977, Lockheed announced a range of new projects based on the TriStar, and aimed at the medium capacity, short- to medium-range market. The projects were a trijet L-1011-400 and the twin-jet L-1011-600. Advances in technology meant that both versions could provide noise reduction and fuel economy. The concepts included the use of composite materials, improved aerodynamics and active controls. The -400 was optimised with a maximum take-off weight of between 350,500 pounds and 374,500 pounds, seating 200 to 250 passengers depending upon fuselage length. The range would have been 2,700 nautical miles covering the US transcontinental routes and the RB211-22B engines were to be derated by ten per cent to improve economy and overhaul life.

The L-1011-600 was to be powered by a pair of 50,000 pounds thrust RB211-524B engines mounted on the existing TriStar wing. Seating, depending on fuselage length, was to be for between 174 and 200 passengers, maximum take-off weight up to 297,000 pounds and range between 2,000 and 700 nautical miles.

Active Control...

As delivered, BAs Dash 500s lacked the active control system, described below, that made the 1980 model, when it entered service with Pan American, the most advanced of any of the then-current production airliners. Another major innovation applicable to all TriStar 500s was the Flight Management System (FMS), an extension of the system that Lockheed first introduced in TriStar 200s delivered to Saudia. FMS was a flexible system that could be customised to specific customer needs and preferences that allowed the aircraft to be flown more accurately, in terms of speed - meaning Mach number - for best specific fuel consumption than conventional manual control by the flight crew.

Lockheed had been co-operating with NASA on a programme that investigated the use of active controls in the Lockheed L-10ll for increased energy efficiency. The tasks involved active wing load alleviation for extended span, increased aspect ratio, and active stability augmentation with a smaller tail for reduced drag and weight. Tests included flight tests of active wing load alleviation on the baseline aircraft and moving-base piloted simulation that developed criteria for stability augmentation.

Cruising at the precise Mach number for the best specific air range is an obvious way of achieving the lowest possible fuel consumption, but is less easy to achieve than might be thought. When the TriStar was cruising at its best economy speed of 0.83 Mach, tiny engine thrust variations through throttle movement could cause significant speed variations. This, along with the aircraft held on a constant altitude as would be customary, by the autopilot, it was necessary for the crew to make almost constant, minor, throttle corrections to hold the Mach number precisely on the desired figure.

Unfortunately, using a cruise autothrottle system tended to cause excessive throttle activity and reduced engine life, so the more usual practice was for the aircraft to be cruised at a higher, but more fuel expensive Mach number of about 0.85-0.86, where it was less susceptible to speed variation with engine thrust. Lockheed estimated that the difference between a Mach 0.83 cruise and Mach 0.85/0.86 on transcontinental US flights could cost £50,000 a year per aircraft in extra fuel in 1979 values whilst saving only a few minutes on each journey.

Right: Rosalind 'Roz' Hanby, the face of British Airways in their *Fly the Flag* advertising campaign during the 1970s and 80s.

L-1011-500 G-BFCA *Princess Margaret Rose* in the full Negus scheme. *(Richard Vandervord)*

-500 G-BFCB *The Harry Wheatcroft Rose* at London Heathrow. *(Richard Vandervord)*

The solution from Lockheed was a fully-automatic flight management system that was an integral part, and extension, of the aircraft's avionic flight control system (AFCS), using the digital computer already used for the TriStar's area navigation (RNAV) system. It sounds archaic now, but an additional 24,000 'words' of memory was added to the device redesignated the FMS computer and accepted for processing data from the engines, the central air data system (CADS) and the navigation receivers. General aircraft and engine performance data were stored in the computer, which supplied control signals to the autopilot and auto-throttle; information available from the computer was displayed on a CRT control and display unit in the cockpit.

Although the cruise portion of the flight was the most important for fuel-saving, an important contribution could also be made during the climb and descent. The FMS had three principal operating modes. The climb controlled flight speed with great precision following any IAS/Mach climb schedule commanded. It directed the engines very accurately through the autothrottle systems to any selected climb schedule, with five levels of derated engine thrust available to cater for the optimum thrust versus gross weight selection. In the cruise, the problem arose from the fact that at the optimum cruise Mach number, the thrust-speed relationship was almost neutral. Simultaneously, the exact setting of the throttle required to maintain 0.83 Mach varied continuously as fuel was burned off and the aircraft weight decreased. It also changed at random during encounters with turbulent air.

Early experience with prototype FMS showed that the automatic system was no better than the flight crew in holding the 0.83 Mach cruise by means of throttle variation, so Lockheed opted instead to control the speed by pitch coupling. Within a narrow band of plus or minus just fifty feet, the aircraft was pitched up or down by FMS-instigated commands to the autopilot. This interchange of kinematic and potential energy was sufficient to hold the speed with great precision. Mach number excursions of less than 0.002 in smooth air and 0.01 in turbulence were sufficient to call for the seatbelt signs to be switched on whilst throttle motion was barely perceptible to the flight crew. The pitch changes were imperceptible to the passengers.

As a standard feature, there were five cruise options, allowing the captain to select minimum cost, minimum fuel or maximum endurance programmes that were fully automatic, or to select a given Mach or IAS, as was be necessary under ATC. The third FMS mode was used for descent when the system flew the aircraft along a flight-idle descent profile to reach any predetermined geographical destination at the correct altitude and speed.

Other advanced technology features fitted to, or available for the TriStar 500 included a digital autopilot, digital central air data computer, digital automatic flight control system including fault isolation data display system (FIDDS), automatic take-off thrust control and an automatic braking system that used a 'g' sensor and applied the brakes in accordance with any one of three pre-selected rates. From the earlier TriStar models, on which they were already well tried, the Dash 500 inherited the flying tailplane, direct lift control fromautomatic spoiler operation to achieve the best glide-slope precision on the approach, and an autoland system for Cat IIIA operations at approved airports.

All of this made the TriStar a very technologically advanced aircraft, but there was more.

In common with other companies, Lockheed was interested in the application of active control systems.

Early studies were concerned with the theoretical usefulness of active controls to achieve high reliability and precision in flight-critical applications. With the original L-1011 established in production, attention was switched in 1974 to the possibility of adopting active controls to allow higher gross weights to be used without major structural changes.

While this work was in hand, an even more valuable potential benefit emerged: that of improved fuel economy, made possible by using active controls to increase the wing's aspect ratio without counter-productive increases in structural weight. Since fuel consumption is a direct function of drag, and since induced drag is inversely proportional to the aspect ratio, an immediate reduction in fuel consumption is derived from increasing the aspect ratio. However, any extra span moves the lift distribution outwards on the wing, increasing the bending moment at the wing root and reducing the margin available for gust and manoeuvring loads.

Strengthening the wing root is expensive in production terms and adds weight and therefore reduces aircraft economy. The other alternative to lowering the 'g' loadings by limiting airspeed and reducing manoeuvring limits, is unacceptable; but having a system that alleviated gust loads on the wing as they were encountered was attractive. This was what lay at the heart of the L-1011's active control system.

Fully automatic, it was a system that deflected the outboard ailerons symmetrically upwards in response to measured vertical accelerations, to give instantaneous relief of wing root bending moments. The 'up aileron' movement's effect was to redistribute the wing lift inboard, into a pattern resembling that of the original, unextended wing to achieve root bending loads compatible with the original structure's strength. Lockheed was fortunate in that the original L-1011 wing structure design was so stiff in torsion that it was unnecessary to 'dwell' the outboard ailerons in high-speed flight. Thus, the ailerons were available for use as active controls, whilst maintaining differentially for roll control throughout the flight envelope.

After extensive laboratory investigation of active control systems, in 1977 Lockheed gained a research contract under the NASA Aircraft Energy Efficiency programme, to perform a flight test evaluation of a breadboard system. Using TriStar N1011, Lockheed initially tested the control system applied to the original wing and ailerons, before adding the definitive four-foot six-inch extension at each wingtip, with lengthened outboard ailerons and outboard leading edge flap sections. Earlier, in late 1975, three-foot wingtip extensions had been flown on N1011, without an ACS, as part of the general research into drag and fuel consumption reduction. The horizontal tailplane, an all-moving surface, was also included in the active control system for testing, but as applied to the TriStar 500, the system used only the ailerons. Triple vertical accelerometers in the wings and the forward cargo compartment were the system's sensors, together with a Q sensor in the cockpit, providing data for computer processing; the computer was programmed to give the required output voltage commands to the outboard aileron actuators.

On initial operations, it was found that the -500 was not achieving its guaranteed range performance. To overcome the around nine per cent shortfall, the RB211-524B4 engine was retrofitted, providing the same thrust but improved fuel consumption. The wingspan was increased by nine feet giving greater lift, allowing the aircraft to fly from London to Los

Delta's Lockheed L-1011-385-3 TriStar 500 N765DA. This aircraft passed through several operators before finishing up with Yes Linhas Aereas Charter of Portugal, after which it was broken up. *(Al Conberry Collection)*

Angeles with a full load. The increase in span raised the gust loads on the wing main spar, and therefore active controls were fitted to reduce these loads and avoid any structural problems. Another problem found was that at high Mach number and high gravity forces, the wingtips caused a pitch up, resulting in buffet and probable loss of control. This very remote situation was only likely to happen with an aft loaded centre of gravity, and precautions were taken on overall operations to keep the critical flight condition clear until suitable permanent cures could be developed. The American FAA specified a high-speed stick shaker to warn of the approach of the critical Mach number, but the British CAA insisted on a rather more costly recovery speed brake to avoid the pitch up.

The first flight of a production TriStar 500 with the full active control system and the extended wing was made on 16 November 1979, this being, of course, the first of the Pan American aircraft.

If the horizontal tailplane was brought into the active control system - as it already experimentally had been on N1011 - the TriStar took a further big step toward being a control configured vehicle (CCV). Plans were in hand for a smaller, active tailplane to be introduced, with estimates showing a reduction in area from 1,280 square feet to 800 square feet with a saving of 1,680 pounds in weight, giving a further three per cent reduction in fuel consumption. Additional weight savings might be made in due course using composites for some structural components in the TriStar.

Delta Air Lines, which had become the second customer for the Dash 500 in January 1978, was the first to specify active control systems. However, delivery of its first two aircraft was scheduled to be made in May and June 1979, a year or so before Lockheed expected to obtain FAA certification for the ACS; consequently, the Delta aircraft were delivered with wing and structural provisions for the system to be retrofitted during 1980. British Airways subsequently decided to adopt the system, but this called for substantial modification of its first four Dash 500s during 1980/81, since the appropriate provisions were not made during manufacture.

The Pan American aircraft entered service with the ACS fully operational and certificated, and the system was also specified by the other Dash 500 customers.

By September 1980, Lockheed had shelved plans for the L-1011 freighter and concentrated its plans on a modern-technology stretched TriStar 500. It was to have the -200 fuselage with strengthened -500 wings and active controls. This aircraft would have a transatlantic or transcontinental range. A hot and high TriStar 500 was proposed in the spring of 1981, powered by the Rolls-Royce RB211-524D4 engines developing 53,000 pounds thrust, an increase of 3,000 pounds thrust over the existing engines.

-500 G-BLUS *Laggan Bay* at London Heathrow. The airliner went to Air Transat before being broken up. *(Al Conberry Collection)*

Lockheed also developed composite ailerons and fin, the carbon-reinforced plastic ailerons being each sixty-five pounds lighter than the metal equivalents. The fin, which weighed 630 pounds, a twenty-seven per cent reduction on the metal equivalent, was the largest composite structure produced at that time but was not flown on the aircraft. However, the fin was subjected to static testing to destruction, and a number of components were environmentally tested.

With the cessation of the TriStar programme, all significant development halted, and the original prototype was dismantled to be used for spares.

Lockheed has continued to offer modest product improvements to existing operators, mainly aimed at better fuel consumption, greater range, improved reliability and easier maintenance.

As part of this programme, Lockheed and Rolls-Royce offered a package in October 1985 that gave the earlier TriStar a long-range capability. This involved re-engining with upgraded RB211-524B4 engines and structural modifications to boost the nominal maximum range from 2,700 nautical miles to 4,500 nautical miles. Structural strengthening concentrated on critical areas of the wing, fuselage and undercarriage, increasing the maximum take-off weight by fifteen per cent to 496,000 pounds and the fuel capacity from 150,560 to 213,640 pounds.

The modified aircraft became the L-1011-250, and Delta was the first customer for six conversion kits. All TriStars from 52 onwards could benefit from these changes apart from the L-1011-500, which already incorporated the improvements. Each conversion required between five and eight weeks to complete at a total investment of $35 million per aircraft, including the change of engines. While Lockheed and Rolls-Royce provided the conversion kit, it was expected that

Pan Am's advertising claim - assuming this is one - was based on the fact that their -500s were slightly more advanced than those of British Airways and Delta.

A short-lived, if typical for the time scene at John F Kennedy Airport New York. A Pan Am series 500 taxies out in front of a company 747. *(Matt Black Collection)*

Pan Am's N503PA *Clipper Flying Eagle* comes into land at London Heathrow. This aircraft was later converted to C2A standard for the RAF, and was withdrawn from use at Cambridge in 2013. *(Richard Vandervord)*

the operator would undertake the work on its own premises with the manufacturer's assistance where necessary.

Pan Am's short-lived Tristar Adventure

Pan American was the third airline to order the Dash 500 version of the TriStar and the third to put it into service, albeit at a more advanced standard than adopted by the two earlier customers, British Airways and Delta Air Lines.

As it was once known, Pan American Airways System was on a long, slow, inevitable decline from the golden years of ownership by Juan Trippe. Pan Am had been on a long downward slide since the early 1970s, and by 1985 the situation was becoming desperate. It had managed to lose $762 million between 1980 and 1985, including $206.8 million in 1984 alone. The huge debt from overspending on Boeing 747s, inefficient operations, an ageing fleet, the disastrous National Airlines takeover and industrial action had all contributed.

On the other hand, United Airlines was on the up, having recorded sizeable profits in both 1983 and 1984. It had long desired an expanded international network and was in an excellent position to take advantage of Pan Am's weakness.

In keeping with the airline's general malaise of its last fifteen years or so, Pan Am's dalliance with widebody three-holers was not an entirely happy one. In 1978 the airline caused some consternation by ordering twelve of Lockheed's L-1011-500s.

By 1984 the Tristars were used on routes to Miami and Chicago and South American services, but between the end of that year and the sale of the Pacific division, all would be sold. Three went straight to Delta, and three others joined the RAF. The remaining six all passed to United in 1986 and

Pan Am's N513PA *Clipper Wild Duck* went to Delta. *(Adam Brookes Collection)*

found themselves at Delta by 1989.

In April 1985, Pan Am announced it would sell its entire Pacific operations to United for $750 million. At the time, the sale was praised for being good for both carriers, but its hard not to see it now as being just another of many bad decisions by Pan Am. The Pacific routes were one of the few profitable areas the airline had left, but the sale amount seems very small considering the size of the network and the inclusion of eighteen aircraft! On the flip side, despite the profits, Pan Am's share of Pacific operations had reduced from twenty-three per cent in 1975 to only fourteen per cent, and with National's old Eastern seaboard-centric operation, they were struggling to feed the West Coast-based Pacific network. Still, the Pacific network was about a quarter of PA's whole. It was just the first of what would become a gradual fire-sale of assets, reducing the mighty Pan Am to a shadow of its former self by the time of its final death in 1991.

United got a bargain, including routes to New Zealand, Hong Kong, Singapore, Taiwan, Korea, Thailand and the Philippines. Previously it had only had two Pacific routes; Hong Kong and Tokyo from Portland and Seattle, respectively.

United Air Lines

United Airlines, Inc. - commonly referred to as United - is a major American airline headquartered at Willis Tower in Chicago, Illinois. United operates a large domestic and international route network spanning cities large and small across the United States and all six continents.

United traces its roots to Varney Air Lines (VAL), which Walter Varney founded in 1926 in Boise, Idaho. Continental Airlines is the successor to Speed Lanes, which Varney had founded in 1932 and whose name changed to Varney Speed Lines in 1934. VAL flew the first privately contracted airmail flight in the US on 6 April 1926.

In 1927, William Boeing founded Boeing Air Transport to operate airmail routes under contract with the United States Post Office Department. Two years later, in 1929, Boeing merged his company with Pratt & Whitney to form the United Aircraft and Transport Corporation (UATC) which then set about buying, in the space of just twenty-eight months, Pacific Air Transport, Stout Air Services, VAL, and National Air Transport, as well as numerous equipment manufacturers. On 28 March 1931, UATC formed United Air Lines, Inc. as a holding company for its airline subsidiaries.

Coming back to the sale of the Pan Am TriStars, in terms of aircraft, United got eleven Boeing 747s, the six remaining Lockheed L-1011 Tristar 500s and a single DC-10-30. The Tristars had been oddballs in Pan Am's fleet pretty much as soon as they arrived. They were an even odder addition to United, who had never before operated a Lockheed product and was the launch customer for the rival DC-10. United sold them on as fast as possible though they werre all painted up into the Saul Bass 'tulip' colours. In 1989 they all went to Delta, which had a massive Tristar fleet of its own.

AirLanka

AirLanka was established as the flag carrier of Sri Lanka once the Sri Lankan government shut down the bankrupt Air Ceylon. Air Lanka's initial fleet consisted of two Boeing 707s, leased from Singapore Airlines. One Boeing 737 was leased from Maersk

Now with United, Pan Am's N501PA taxies past the camera. After a brief spell with United, it went to Delta as N759DA. *()*

AirLanka's 4R-ULC *City of Anuradhapura* at the hold at London Gatwick. *(Richard Vandervord)*

Air and maintained by Air Tara. On 24 April 1980, the lease ended; Air Lanka received a replacement Boeing 737 leased from Royal Brunei. On 1 November 1980, Air Lanka commenced wide-body operations with a leased L1011-1 from Air Canada.

On 15 April 1982, Air Lanka received its own L-1011 purchased from All Nippon Airways. With the introduction of the TriStars, the Boeing 707s were phased out and sold. Then another L-1011 was leased from Air Canada whilst the third L-1011 was purchased from All Nippon. On 1 May 1982, HAECO took over the maintenance of the two Air Lanka-owned TriStars, while Air Canada maintained two leased machines.

On 28 March 1980, Air Lanka signed a purchase agreement for two brand new L1011-500s. The first, 4R-ULA, was accepted on 26 August 1982 at Palmdale and was flown to Amsterdam as UL flight 566P. On 28 August, 4R-ULA *City Of Colombo* left for its inaugural flight from Amsterdam to Colombo as UL566, reaching it's destination on 29 August. This was followed by second -500, 4R-ULB, *City Of Jayawardanapura*.

By the mid-1980s, the TriStar was the mainstay of the Air Lanka fleet with four in service and a further one due to be added. Sri Lanka was dependant upon tourism for its survival, and the destruction on the ground of a TriStar by a terrorist bomb, was a major setback.

Air Lanka Flight UL512 - operated by 4R-ULD - was a flight from London Gatwick Airport via Zurich and Dubai to Bandaranaike International Airport, Colombo and Velana International Airport, Malé in the Maldives. On 3 May 1986, the Tristar operating the flight was on the ground in Colombo, about to fly on to Malé, when an explosion ripped the aircraft in two, destroying it. Flight 512 carried mainly French, West German, British and Japanese tourists; twenty-one people were killed on the aircraft and forty-one were injured.

The boarding of the flight had been delayed due to the aircraft being damaged during cargo and baggage loading. During boarding, a bomb, hidden in the aircraft's 'Fly Away Kit' - a container of L-1011 spare parts and consumables - exploded. The bomb had been timed to detonate mid-flight; the delay likely saved many lives.

The Sri Lankan government concluded that the bomb was planted by the Liberation Tigers of Tamil Eelam (LTTE) to sabotage peace talks between the

BWIA Internationals L-1011-500 9Y-TGN is seen at Heathrow. The airline was somewhat unusual in the their TriStars carried the registration at the top of the fin. *(Richard Vandervord)*

Above: 9Y-THA *Sunset Antigua* sweeps in to land. This L-1011 passed to Star Air as 9L-LED and was damaged at Charles de Gaulle airport Paris in 2005 when an engine caught fire during take-off. The aircraft was stored, and eventually broken up in April 2017.

Below: BWIA West Indies L-1011-500 9Y-TGN by now in the steelpan livery with '60th Anniversary' markings on the front fuselage. *(both Richard Vandervord)*

LTTE and the Sri Lankan government. They reported that a search of the aircraft the next day uncovered a parcel containing uniforms with the insignia of the Black Tigers, the suicide wing of LTTE.

In August 1991 the decision was made to replace the fleet of seven TriStars with five Airbus A340-300s starting in 1994.

BWIA British West Indian Airways

British West Indies Airways - known locally as 'Bee-Wee' - was one of the oldest airlines in the Caribbean. It was founded by a New Zealander Lowell Yerex, who also founded TACA. His private interest in the airline was sold to the Trinidad government in 1947. Initially, the airline operated a Lockheed L-18 Lodestar, but when Vickers Viscounts were delivered in 1955, the airline could expand its regional service considerably. In 1947 British South American Airways took over BWIA. When BSAA merged with BOAC two years later, BSAA became a subsidiary of BOAC but continued to operate as BWIA. The first transatlantic service was operated in 1960 with a leased Britannia from BOAC to London via Barbados and New York. The airline was nationalized in 1964. In 1966 Boeing 720 entered service with the airline replacing the Britannia. Boeing 727s were used since 1964 on a regional network. In 1980, BWIA merged with the then government-owned Trinidad and Tobago Air Service, providing BWIA with assets that enabled it to become a full-service airline, offering charter, scheduled and cargo services in domestic, Caribbean and intercontinental markets. That same year the airline gained permission from its government to order a pair of TriStar 500s, but no contract was signed. Two options were included, the total value being estimated at $85 million, and the first of an eventual fleet of four TriStar 500s were delivered in

Alia applied a number of different colour schemes to their L-1011s. Here JY-AGB is seen landing at Athens. *(Richard Vandervord)*

January 1980. The two options were confirmed that September for delivery in late 1981 and the middle of 1982.

By 1994, the airline had become partially privatised. A substantial reorganisation of its route network left London and Frankfurt the only European destinations. The airline ordered Boeing 757 and 767 aircraft, then cancelled the order in favour of Airbus A321 and Airbus A340 jets; in turn, this order was dropped after only two A321s were delivered. On 22 February 1995, the government of Trinidad and Tobago completed the privatisation of BWIA by turning over majority control of the common stock and management of the airline to a private group of US and Caribbean investors.

In the early 2000s, BWIA changed its livery to a new Caribbean green and blue colour scheme with its famous steelpan trademark, the national musical instrument of its home base. The TriStars survived with Bee Wee until 2004.

Alia/Royal Jordanian Airline

Alia (the Royal Jordanian Airline) started operations with two Handley Page Dart Heralds and a Douglas DC-7 aircraft, serving Kuwait City, Beirut and Cairo from Amman. In 1964, another DC-7 was added and service began to Jeddah. In 1965, Alia initiated service to Rome, its first destination in Europe. An Israeli air raid threatened the airline's progress during the 1967 Six-Day War when the DC-7 aircraft were destroyed. They were replaced by two Fokker F27 Friendship airliners.

A different Alia colour scheme - nicknamed 'strawbeyy and cream' - is seen here on JY-AGC, also at Ellinikon Airport, Athens. *(Richard Vandervord)*

JY-AGC in full Royal Jordanian colours about to lift off from Heathrow. I always thought this was a truly classy colour scheme. *(Richard Vandervord)*

The airline was established on 9 December 1963 and started operations on 15 December 1963 after a royal decree by the late King Hussein. It was named Alia (or Aalya) after King Hussein's eldest child, Princess Alia bint Al Hussein of Jordan (born on 13 February 1956). It is a common misconception that the airline was named after the King's third wife, Queen Alia whom King Hussein did not marry until 1972. The airline was founded with capital from private shareholders but the Jordanian government later took over the company.

In 1968, the airline joined the jet age when it introduced the Sud Aviation Caravelle, and expanded the route network to Nicosia, Benghazi, Dhahran and Doha. 1969 saw the addition of service to Munich, Istanbul and Tehran.

In 1970, Alia phased out the F27s and ordered Boeing 707 aircraft. Frankfurt and Abu Dhabi were added to the network. The 707s were delivered in 1971. In that year, service was initiated to Madrid, Copenhagen and Karachi. During the rest of the decade, Boeing 720s, Boeing 727s, and Boeing 747s were added to the fleet. A catering department was established, and duty-free shops were opened at Amman airport. Services were added to destinations including Bahrain, Dubai, Muscat, Rabat, Geneva, Amsterdam, Baghdad, Bangkok, Vienna, Damascus, New York City, Houston, and Ras al-Khaimah. In 1979, Alia became a founding member of the Arab Airlines Technical Consortium (AATC).

At the end of 1979, Alia ordered five TriStar 500s worth an estimated £142 million. Four more were to be added later, with a fifth machine for the Royal Jordanian Flight. They were put into service on European and trans-Atlantic routes.

In the 1980s, Tunis and Tripoli joined the route

Although apparently in Royal Jordanian colours JY-HKJ belonged to the Jordanian Royal Flight. *(Richard Vandervord)*

Air Portugal's CS-TEF is seen landing at spotters paradise that used to be Heathrow. *(Richard Vandervord)*

map, and Alia's IBM computer centre was inaugurated. Five Lockheed L-1011 Tristars, along with a number of Airbus A310s and Airbus A320s, joined the fleet. In 1986, Alia changed its name to Royal Jordanian when Princess Alia was nearing her divorce. Services were added to Belgrade, Chicago, Los Angeles, Miami, Bucharest, Singapore, Riyadh, Kuala Lumpur – in cooperation with MAS, Sana'a, Moscow, Montreal, Delhi, Calcutta and Ankara. This decade also saw the introduction of the Gabriel Automated Ticket System – (GATS).

The 1990s saw further expansion. Royal Jordanian and nine other Arab air carriers signed up for the Galileo CRS. The IMCS maintenance and engineering system was added, a new Amman city air terminal was opened at the 7th Circle of the Jordanian capital, and services to Rafah started, since then halted. The cities of Toronto, Colombo, Jakarta, Berlin, Mumbai, Milan and Tel Aviv were added to the network. In November 1997, Royal Jordanian became a code-sharing partner with TWA and moved operations into the TWA Flight Center at the John F Kennedy International Airport in New York.

TAP Air Portugal

The flag carrier of Portugal founded by the Portuguese civil aviation authority in 1944. First flight was operated on 19 September 1946 from Lisbon to Madrid using a Douglas DC-3. Between 1953 and 1975, TAP was in private hands. The first jet aircraft was a Caravelle delivered in July 1962. The first wide-body airliner, a 747-200, was delivered in December 1971. Lockheed TriStars formed TAPs long haul fleet between 1983 and 1994. During the 1990s, TAP underwent massive renewal. The first long-range Airbus A340 joined the fleet in December 1994. TAP is invited to join Star Alliance, the world's premier Airline Alliance and became a member in March 2005. TAP Portugal was wholly owned by TAP Group, which also wholly owned Portugalia, a twenty per cent stake in Air Macau through SEAP. The airline served European capitals and industrial centres with Porto and Lisbon. Prague, Budapest and Zagreb are served in Central Europe. TAP serves many cities in Brazil, Caracas as well as Newark in the USA and Casablanca, Sao Tome, Luanda, Maputo, Bissau, Sal and Dakar in Africa. In June 2015 government sold its sixty-one per cent stake in the carrier to the Atlantic Gateway consortium, which is controlled by the founder of JetBlue/Azul David Neeleman and Portuguese bus company owner Humberto Pedrosa. The airline is listed as having operated seven TriStars.

Chapter Eleven

The RAF and Marshall Aerospace

Marshall Aerospace and Defence Group is an aircraft maintenance, modification and design company located at Cambridge Airport, which it also owns and operates.

Formerly known as Marshall's of Cambridge, it was originally founded by David Gregory Marshall in 1909. Initially operating chauffeur services, the company soon branched out into vehicle repair and dealership activities. During the 1930s, Marshall's became increasingly engaged in aviation; by the end of the Second World War, the company had trained over 20,000 aircrew for service within the Royal Air Force. It was also engaged in repair and modification of military aircraft during the conflict; it has been claimed that Marshall's performed work on over 5,000 aircraft.

During the postwar era, the Marshall companies have been involved in aerospace and specialist vehicle engineering; Marshall Aerospace forming a major part of the Marshall Group. The company performs all aspects of design, manufacture, maintenance, modification, conversion and logistic support of military, commercial and business aircraft. Traditionally focused on military customers, Marshall has increasingly orientated itself towards the civilian sector in recent decades. It employs over 4,400 people and is based on an 800-acre site with 1,200,000 square feet of covered hangar space.

Cambridge Airport has had a long association with Lockheed through its work on the support of the Hercules military freighter, but this association expanded with work on the TriStars, although there was no formal agreement between the companies.

The Falklands campaign created the need within the Royal Air Force for additional tanker/transport capacity. Before this campaign, the Victor tankers of 55 and 57 Squadrons had been expected to serve well into the 1990s to be replaced by the VC10 tankers followed by a new as yet specified design. However, the Falklands campaign underlined the importance

A typical set of underfloor fuel tanks ready for installation in the RAF TriStar tankers. *(Marshall of Cambridge (Engineering) Ltd)*

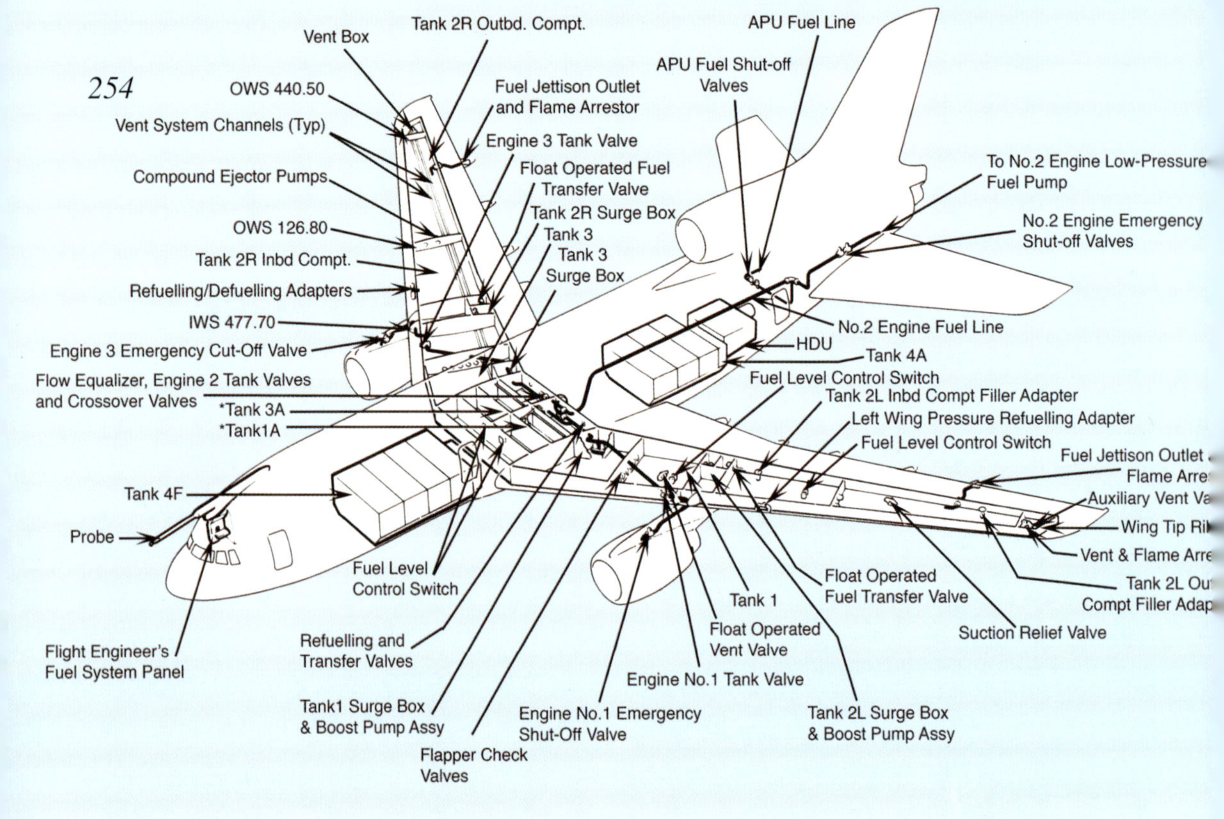

The fuel system as designed for the RAF TriStar tanker.

of long-range air-to-air refuelling, but it also prematurely used up the fatigue life on the Victor K2 tankers. Therefore, a replacement was required urgently, not only as an aerial tanker but also as a long-range transport to support the Falklands' military garrison.

In the second half of 1982, several commercial jet transports on the market made a conversion task the most cost-effective solution when the requirement was being established. The choice was between the six TriStar 500s with British Airways or the ex-Laker DC-10s. Marshall made the competing proposals in association with Lockheed for the TriStar conversion, and McDonnell Douglas with British Aerospace and possibly British Caledonian.

Following a detailed evaluation, the TriStar emerged as the final choice. Despite the availability of the KC-10A tanker derivative of the DC-10, there was little advantage in the conversion of a civil airliner. The decision to purchase the six BA TriStar 500s was announced on 14 December 1982 and the conversion contract was awarded to Marshall in February 1983. Marshall then became the UK design authority for the tanker/freighter conversion of the

Gear Up! RAF TriStar ZD948 seen climbing out of London Heathrow in something of a hybrid colour scheme. The aircraft is wearing its military serial, but also the 'last two' of G-BFCA, its previous civilian identity on the nosewheel doors and fin tip. *(Richard Vandervord)*

RAF TriStar ZD950 leads two Tornado 'chicks' out over the Moray Firth in Scotland. *(MoD via Jim Hughes).*

Lockheed TriStar for the RAF and rapidly constructed a new hangar, capable of accommodating five TriStars in work at any one time. During 1984, three more TriStar 500s were acquired from Pan Am, to a generally similar standard to the BA aircraft. The acquisition of the TriStar gave the RAF a tanker/transport capability that it had not previously.

The conversion and introduction into service of the TriStars was in several phases, two of the three ex-Pan Am TriStars entering service purely as passenger transports, leaving the third aircraft stored at Cambridge. Meanwhile, the BA aircraft were converted in three phases. The first four emerged initially as K1 - the K standing for kerosene - tanker/passenger aircraft, the first conversion making a successful two hour maiden flight from Cambridge at 08:30 hours on 9 July 1985. Four days later the aircraft took part in the flying display at the International Air Tattoo at RAF Fairford. The second conversion was the first to enter service with 216 Squadron at Brize Norton.

The aircraft had two Flight Refuelling Ltd Mk 17T hose drum units (HDU) mounted side-by-side in the rear cargo compartment in a pressure box, allowing air-to-air refuelling operations to take place while maintaining normal cabin pressure.

Each unit could independently ensure that no single failure would cause an air-to-air refuelling

RAF TriStar ZD950 seen at Marshall Aerospace not long after conversion. *(John Hamlin)*

The installation of the main deck freight door on the TriStar included a large reinforced area to maintain structural integrity of the fuselage.

The TriStar fuselage was very carefully destressed and very accurately supported before the installation of the large freight door cut-out.

RAF TriStar ZD948 seen at Brize Norton on 10 July 2004. *(John Hamlin)*

mission to be aborted, thus offering in-flight redundancy for critical missions. Additional fuel tanks were located in the below floor cargo compartments, a four-section tank in the forward compartment, and a three-section tank in the mid compartment. Each tank section consisted of an outer shell capable of withstanding cabin pressure and a rubber bag tank attached to the outer shell's inner walls. The bag tanks were interconnected, allowing fuel to flow from one to the other. Both groups of tanks incorporated a collector box at the rear in which were mounted four fuel flow booster pumps; the tanks also incorporated vent pipes that were connected into the wing tanks vent system.

All pipes within the pressurised area of the aircraft were of the double-walled type. The conversion provided for an increase in fuel capacity of up to a maximum of 100,000 pounds, with the transfer of fuel from either HDU at a rate compatible with the receiver aircraft, up to 4,000 pounds per minute at a pressure of fifty pounds per square inch at the probe/drogue coupling.

Refuelling operations were carried out over a speed range of 180-320 knots at altitudes up to 35,000 feet. Numerous other modifications were carried out to suit the TriStar's military role. Many aircraft systems had to be extended to cater to the extra demands of the tanker conversion. The flight engineers' console was extended to include the air refuelling, HDU controls and fuel management panels. The station also housed the controls and monitor screen for the closed-circuit television (CCTV) system, which was installed to provide a visual aid to monitor the in-flight refuelling operations. The camera was mounted on the centreline of the lower fuselage in a fairing forward of the drogue housing tunnels. The TriStars could also receive fuel at 4,000 pounds per minute, due to the installation of a probe attached to the upper surface of the forward fuselage above the cockpit roof. It was slightly offset to starboard to allow easier visual reference by the captain and was set with a negative incidence of seven degrees to compensate for the normal nose up incidence of the TriStar in flight.

Following the initial flight, development trials

The RAF TriStar fleet went through a period of toned down markings - here ZD949 is seen with a tiny fin-flash, emblem and roundel and a pastel shade of cheat line. *(Ian Frimston)*

ZA254, the prototype Panavia Tornado F2 formates with a Brize TriStar. *(Ian Frimston)*

continued with flights at varying weights and altitudes. For the trials, the TriStar was operated out of Cambridge Airport or RAF Brize Norton. The first dry coupling was made on a flight out of Brize Norton on 16 July 1985 with a probed Canberra aircraft from the Aeroplane Armament Experimental Establishment (A&AEE) Boscombe Down. With further evaluation and handling trials continuing, wet ground fuel flows to establish flow rates were conducted on a Hercules and Phantom at Cambridge and Boscombe Down, with a successful airborne dry coupling with an A&AEE Phantom on 9 October. The first Hercules coupling took place on 15 October. The TriStar operated out of Brize Norton and made a rendezvous with a Lyneham-based Hercules over the West Country. A successful dry coupling took place, followed by a wet contact with fuel transfer accomplished on the same flight. The TriStar was delivered to the A&AEE Boscombe Down on 28 October and subsequent aircraft were scheduled to leave Cambridge at three to four monthly intervals, having completed their initial flights in the hands of the company test pilots.

Since the original introduction into service, some changes were made to the operation of TriStars with the RAF, and three different configurations were used in the fleet of nine aircraft. Of the six ex-BA TriStar 500s, two were configured as tanker/passenger transport aircraft with the designation K.Mk1s, without the main deck cargo doors and 196 seats. The other four ex-BA aircraft were converted to the full tanker/transport standard as KC.Mk1s with the cargo door on the main deck. The interior was mounted on pallets, whether cargo, seats or a combination of both. When seats were loaded, galleys were also fitted on pallets. As the underfloor holds were full with the extra fuel tanks, the passengers' baggage was loaded on the main deck on pallets.

The first two aircraft were delivered to an interim standard, while number three and four were to full K1 standard. The fifth and sixth aircraft were to the revised K1 tanker/freighter standard incorporating a forward upper deck freight door, a cargo handling system with reinforcement where required. The first two aircraft were the next K1 conversions, followed by the remaining pair of aircraft. The three ex-Pan Am aircraft differed in detail, which made it impossible to modify them to the identical standard of the ex-BA aircraft.

They were designated K2 as tanker-passenger transports. There were plans for all nine aircraft to have Flight Refuelling Mk 32 refuelling pods under each wing, making them capable of simultaneously refuelling a pair of combat aircraft. The Mk 32A was a variant of the Mk 32 fitted to the VC10, but redesigned to take a seventy-four hose in trail and had a digital electronic logic system to control and monitor all the various mechanical and electro-hydraulic functions within the pod. However, this was cancelled, and the RAF decided to allocate the money to converting more VC.10s.

The modification of the ex-BA TriStars to tanker configuration involved the installation, with local reinforcing where required, of extra fuel tanks in the main underfloor forward C1 and rear C2 cargo compartments and twin HDUs in the aft end C3

An air-to-ground shot of the TriStar apron at Brize Norton.

A VC-10 co-pilots view of refuelling from a TriStar from Brize Norton. *(Ian Frimston)*

Is it Pinky or Perky? One of the two 'pink TriStars', ZD951 lands back at Brize Norton while wearing Operation Granby markings during the first Gulf War. *(MoD via Peter Davies).*

cargo compartment. The C3 entry, which allowed access to the HDUs without removal of the rear fuel tanks, was not present on the ex-Pan Am TriStars, reducing the available underfloor tankage accordingly.

In 1984, the RAF purchased three L-1011-500s from Pan Am, but owing to the detail differences, these could not be converted to the same KC1 configuration. Allocated RAF serials of ZE704 to ZE706, they received minor modifications at Marshall's but remained as standard airliners capable of carrying 250 passengers and were designated as the C Mk.2.

The fuel tanks themselves were very much like double size heavy duty underfloor containers, and were installed through the existing cargo doors and plumbed together. The forward C1 freight compartment held four fuel tanks with a pump/collector box, while the rear C2 compartment holds three tanks and a pump/collector box, increasing the TriStar fuel capacity by up to a maximum of 100,000 pounds.

By the end of 1987, three of the K1 aircraft were in service with the RAF, while ZD950 was in use with Marshall on a flight development programme to clear hose drum modifications and the new avionics fit. During the first six months of 1988, this development aircraft was operated on clearance trials at Boscombe Down, allowing air-to-air refuelling capability to be proved with all anticipated receiver aircraft. Meanwhile in the Marshall hangar, the first two conversions were being made to the full cargo configuration on ZD948 and ZD952.

The C4 cargo door installation consisted of an upper deck upward-opening freight door measuring 140 inches by 102 inches on the forward cabin's port

Another view of ZD948 at London Heathrow with yet another version of the hybrid colour scheme. *(Richard Vandervord)*

RAF TriStar ZE706 climbs away into the murk. *(Ian Frimston)*

side. To achieve such a large cutout in the fuselage, the entire aircraft had to be carefully supported and jacked to remove all stresses and loads from the structure otherwise significant distortion would have occurred. The actual installation involved cut out and reinforcing around the aperture of double the area of the door to cope with the structural loads. The cabin floor was reinforced to allow the carriage of 16,000-pound pallets, and power rollers and winches were installed to move heavy loads. The tanker/freighter variants were capable of carrying up to 100,000 pounds of freight or could be rapidly role changed to a 200-troop carrier or troop/freight mixed configuration, depending upon the type of pallets fitted in the fuselage. The first conversion with the C4 cargo door, ZD948 was subjected to a structural test programme in the new TriStar hangar, simulating a 2.5g turning load with the aircraft pressurised to represent the worst flight condition. During this structural test, the aircraft was fully instrumented to measure the relevant loads.

All nine RAF TriStars were operated by 216 Squadron, based at RAF Brize Norton, the home of all the RAF's heavy transports.

The 1991 Gulf War was waged by coalition forces from 35 nations led by the United States against Iraq in response to Iraq's invasion and annexation of Kuwait from oil pricing and production disputes. Operation Granby, commonly abbreviated Op Granby, was the code name given to the British military operations. Fifty-three thousand four hundred sixty-two members of the British Armed Forces were deployed during the conflict.

Within nine days of the invasion of Kuwait on 2 August 1990, twelve Panavia Tornado F3 interceptors from 5 (AC) Squadron and 29 (F) Squadron from RAF Coningsby had arrived in Saudi Arabia, alongside aircraft of the USAF.

RAF TriStar ZE704 is seen in the company of an RAF C-130 Hercules on a very snowy apron of RAF Mount Pleasant, Falkland Isles The airfield opened on 12 May 1985. *()*

RAF TriStars went through a number of different colour schemes, the final one being a medium grey, that could look gold in a certain light. Here ZD948 is seen over Afganistan in October 2008 with a pair of F-18C Hornets from USS *Abraham Lincoln*. *(USN)*

Later, Jaguar GR1 aircraft from RAF Coltishall, and Tornado GR1s, redeployed from service in RAF Germany to the theatre. Buccaneers from RAF Lossiemouth were also deployed to laser designate ground targets for the Tornado and Jaguar. This action had the effect of maintaining the confidence of friendly nations and limiting the potential for further Iraqi expansion. When an economic embargo was placed on Iraq, these aircraft also helped maintain it. The force of Tornado F3s was expanded to eighteen, drawn from the three British bases, then housing F3s - RAF Leuchars, RAF Leeming, and RAF Coningsby. They were based at the Royal Saudi Air Force airbase at Dhahran, where they flew patrols inside the range of Iraqi ground radar systems. Before the launch of the operation to liberate Kuwait, they flew over 2000 sorties. Victor tankers, based at Jubail Naval Base, provided AAR support to all the coalition aircraft. Hercules, VC10, and TriStar aircraft supplied both the Royal Air Force and other military endeavours; Nimrod MR.2P aircraft assisted naval operations. At bases in Tabuk, Dhahran, and Muharraq, the RAF deployed Rapier missiles as part of surface-to-air defences. In total, around 6,000 RAF

A grey TriStar on a grey day! ZD948 in low-visibility markings seen in more normal light. *()*

Gods view of tanking from an RAF TriStar. *(Ian Frimston)*

personnel were deployed to the Gulf.

The RAF TriStars played a major support role. On 6 January 1991, a single TriStar K1 with two crews was deployed to King Khalid International Airport, near Riyadh in Saudi Arabia as a tanker. Two TriStar K1s - ZD949 and ZD951 - during the deployment were painted in a pinkish desert camouflage earning them the nicknames of 'Pinky' and 'Perky'. The K.1s flew over ninety air-to-air refuelling missions totalling over 430 hours, the other TriStars in the fleet providing flight refuelling support for aircraft deploying to the Gulf, as well as transporting troops and equipment. None of the RAF TriStars retained the flight refuelling probe above the flight deck, as not only did the aircraft carry more than enough fuel internally for all normal operations, but it was discovered that modern large fan engines did not perform well with rapid changes of power when trying to approach a drogue. The large momentum of the aircraft is also difficult to control in close formation.

The four KC.Mk1s were used regularly on flight refuelling sorties from Brize Norton, the main training area being just off the east coast of Britain from The Wash to the north of Scotland. One of the operational changes from when the TriStars were first introduced is that the aircraft

ZD951 gets airborne in the Middle East in 2008. *()*

requiring fuel would now approach from the starboard side and wait their turn, formating on the port side when completed, if part of a formation group, or just departing if operating singly. Although most of the trade was the fast jets, VC-10s were about the largest aircraft to take on fuel.

After the outbreak of the Bosnian War in April 1992, the United Nations passed Resolution 781 on 9 October, banning military flights over Bosnia and Herzegovina. UN Resolution 816 was passed on 31 March 1993 that prohibited all non-authorised flights. On 12 April, NATO began Operation Deny Flight to enforce Resolution 816, under which two TriStars of 216 Squadron were deployed to Italy to provide AAR for fighters carrying out this policing of airspace. After the situation escalated in the 1999 Kosovo War, three TriStars were deployed once more to Italy under Operation Engadine in order to support NATO aircraft. Over the course of this Operation, five TriStars operated in the theatre, reportedly delivering 13.5 million pounds of fuel to 1,580 aircraft across 230 missions.

TriStars joined Vickers VC10s in the air-to-air refuelling role for Operation Veritas (Afghanistan), during which they provided aerial-refuelling for US Navy aircraft. In 2003, the RAF deployed TriStars to Bahrain as part of Operation Telic.

216 Squadron's disbandment ceremony on 21 March 2014. *(MoD via Kim Bolton Collection)*

Bruntingthorpe, Leicestershire, United Kingdom - 14 July 2018. The resting place of five stored ex-RAF TriStars.

This page shows three views of ZD948, sitting in the scorching sunshine without any engine or intake covers.

Behind the L-1011 is an ex-Olympic Airways Boeing 747, a de Havilland Comet, a Blackburn Buckaneer, Handley Page Victor and Avro Shackleton. (all author)

Above: framed under the tail of ZD948 is N405CS of ME Aviation Services, the former British Airways G-BFCC and RAF ZD950. Just visible is the tiny 216 Squadron emblem on the fin. Note also the Royal' and 'Force' has been painted out on the titling, leaving just 'Air'.

Below: With no intake covers or plugs and wearing the 30 Years commemorative emblem and very large 216 Squadron badge is ZD951. *(both author)*

By March 2021 the TriStars stored at Bruntingthorpe were starting to grow green coats - who knows how much longer they will remain in existance?

In October 2006, Marshall Aerospace was awarded a £22 million contract to modernise the TriStar under the project name of 'Minimum Military Requirements' (MMR). In early 2007, TriStar K1 ZD949 arrived at Cambridge Airport to undergo numerous upgrades, including a glass cockpit. However, due to the Strategic Defence and Security Review of 2010 these upgrades were halted and ZD949 was left at Cambridge Airport to be used for spare parts.

RAF TriStars supported the British airstrikes on Libya on 19-20 March 2011 as part of the coalition operations to enforce UN Resolution 1973.

In August 2013, a TriStar from 216 Squadron was detached in order to provide AAR support as part of 1312 Flight at RAF Mount Pleasant due to the forthcoming retirement of the Vickers VC10. The TriStar was replaced in this role in February 2014 by an Airbus Voyager KC3.

A disbandment parade started the official drawdown proceedings on 21st March 2014 with attendance from the Chief of Air Staff, Air Chief Marshal Sir Andrew Pulford. The parade, which took place within the 'AirTanker Hub' hangar at RAF Brize Norton, Oxfordshire, marked the end of 216 Squadron after ninety-six years of service, thirty of which whilst operating the TriStar.

The final sortie of an RAF TriStar was carried on 24 March by ZD948 and ZD950 which refuelled four Eurofighter Typhoons and a single Panavia Tornado GR4, ZD950 returned to base while ZD948 conducted flypasts over Cambridge and Derby before returning to RAF Brize Norton for the last time.

With many delays occurring in the delivery of the TriStar's replacement, the A330 Voyager, the life of the TriStar fleet, was later extended to March 2014. Retirement of the RAF L-1011 began in February 2014 with the first aircraft being delivered to Air Salvage International (ASI) at Cotswold Airport, where eventually it was parted for scrap. 12 March 2014 saw the next aircraft retirement with ZE705 delivered to GJD Services at Bruntingthorpe Aerodrome and ZD953 a week later, once again these airframes were be scrapped.

Following their service withdrawal, six TriStars made their last flights to Bruntingthorpe Aerodrome in Leicestershire while the remaining three were scrapped. ZD949 was the first to be scrapped on 27 May 2014 at Cambridge Airport, having last flown in November 2010 after the abandonment of the MMR upgrades. ZE706 followed this in June, which was also at Cambridge Airport as a spares airframe, ZD952 was scrapped at Cotswold Airport on 9 September 2014, having arrived there in February.

In 2017, Tempus Applied Solutions, an aerospace company based in the United States, procured the six remaining ex-RAF TriStars for further use. Four of the purchased airframes were AAR conversions, with the other two being pure freight versions. The company's intention was to restore three of the AAR tankers to service in that role, providing additional probe and drogue aerial refuelling capacity to the US Navy and NATO nations that utilise that particular method. The remaining three airframes were to be used as sources of spares.

Chapter Twelve

Accidents and Incidents

The L-1011 was involved in several aviation occurrences, including ten hull-losses, with 540 fatalities. Of the four pioneering widebody aircraft (Boeing 747, McDonnell Douglas DC-10, L-1011, and Airbus A300/A310 family), the Lockheed L-1011 had comparatively few accidents and a better safety record than its competitors.

Eastern Flight 401

Eastern Air Lines Flight 401 was a scheduled flight from John F Kennedy International Airport in Queens, New York, to Miami International Airport in Miami, Florida. On the day of the crash, Flight 401 was operated using TriStar N310EA, which had been delivered to the airline on 18 August 1972. The aircraft was fleet number 310, and the tenth TriStar delivered to the carrier.

The flight was under the command of fifty-five-year-old Captain Robert Albin 'Bob' Loft, a veteran pilot ranked fiftieth in seniority at Eastern. Captain Loft had been with the airline for thirty-two years and had accumulated a total of 29,700 flight hours throughout his flying career. He had logged 280 hours in the L-1011. His flight crew included thirty-nine-year-old First Officer Albert John 'Bert' Stockstill who had 5,800 hours of flying experience - with 306 of them in the L-1011, and fifty-one-year-old Flight Engineer Donald Louis 'Don' Repo, who had 15,700 hours of flying experience, with fifty-three of them in the L-1011.

A company employee - technical officer Angelo Donadeo - was returning to Miami from an assignment in New York - accompanied the flight crew for the journey, but was officially off-duty, and travelling as a 'non-revenue passenger'.

Flight 401 departed JFK Airport at 21:20 EST, with 163 passengers and 13 crew members on board. The flight was routine until 23:32 when the aircraft began its approach into Miami International Airport. First Officer Stockstill noticed that the landing gear indicator, a green light identifying that the nose gear was properly locked in the 'down' position, had not illuminated after lowering the gear. This was later discovered to be due to a burned-out light bulb. The landing gear could have been manually lowered, nonetheless. The pilots cycled the landing gear but still failed to get the confirmation light.

Loft, who was working the radio during this leg of the flight, told the tower that they would

Eastern's N309EA, the TriStar just one ahead of the ill-fated N310EA on the production line at Palmdale. This Whisperliner is seen at Isla Verde International Airport at San Juan, Puerto Rico. *(Richard Vandervord)*

discontinue their airport approach and requested to enter a holding pattern. The approach controller cleared the flight to climb to 2,000 feet, and then hold west over the Everglades.

The cockpit crew removed the light assembly, and Second Officer Repo was dispatched to the avionics bay beneath the flight deck to confirm via a small porthole if the landing gear was indeed down. Fifty seconds after reaching their assigned altitude, Captain Loft instructed First Officer Stockstill to put the L-1011 on autopilot. For the next eighty seconds, the airliner maintained level flight. Then, it dropped 100 feet, and then again flew level for two more minutes, after which it began a descent so gradual the crew could not perceive it. The airliner lost only 250 feet in the next seventy seconds, but this was enough to trigger the altitude warning C-chord chime located under the engineer's workstation. Repo, the flight engineer, had already gone below, and no indication was heard of the pilots' voices recorded on the CVR that they heard the chime. In another fifty seconds, the airliner was at half its assigned altitude.

As Stockstill started another turn, onto 180°, he noticed the discrepancy. The aircraft impacted into the Everglades at 23.42.12. The location was west-northwest of Miami, 18.7 miles from the end of runway 9L. The Eastern airliner was travelling at 227 miles per hour when it hit the ground.

With the aircraft in mid-turn, the port outer wing structure struck the ground first, followed by the No. 1 engine and the port main undercarriage, making three trails through the sawgrass, each five feet wide and over one hundred feet long. When the main part of the fuselage hit the ground, it continued to move through the grass and water. The aircraft's disintegration that followed scattered wreckage over an area 1,600 feet long and 330 feet wide in a southwesterly direction.

Only small fragments of metal marked the wingtip's first contact, followed forty-nine feet further on by three one hundred and fifteen feet long swaths cut through the mud and sawgrass by the aircraft's extended undercarriage before two of the legs were sheared off. Then came scattered parts from the No. 1 (port) engine, and fragments from the port wing itself and the port tailplane. About 490 feet from the wingtip's initial contact with the ground, the massive fuselage had begun to break up, scattering components from the underfloor galley, the cargo compartments, and the cabin interior. At 820 feet along the wreckage trail, the starboard wing's outer section tore off, gouging a fifty-nine-foot-long crater in the soft ground as it did so. From this point the fuselage's breakup became extensive, scattering metal fragments, cabin fittings, and passenger seats.

The three major sections of the fuselage - the most intact being the tail assembly - lay in the mud towards the end of the wreckage trail. The fact that the tail assembly - rear fuselage, No. 2 tail-mounted engine, and remains of the empennage - finally came to rest substantially further forward than other major sections, was probably the result of the No. 2 engine continuing to deliver thrust during the actual breakup of the aircraft. No complete cross-section of the passenger cabin remained, and both the port wing and tailplane were demolished to fragments. Incongruously, not far from the roofless fuselage centre section with the inner portion of the starboard wing still attached, lay a large, undamaged and fully inflated rubber dinghy, one of a number carried on the TriStar in the event of an emergency water landing. The breakup of the fuselage had freed it from its stowage and activated its inflation mechanism.

In all, seventy-five survived the crash - sixty-seven of the one hundred and sixty-three passengers and eight of the ten flight attendants. Despite their injuries, the surviving flight attendants were credited with helping other survivors and several quick-thinking actions such as warning survivors of the danger of striking matches due to jet fuel in the swamp water. Reports state that they sang Christmas carols to keep up hope and draw the rescue teams' attention, as flashlights were not part of the standard equipment on commercial airliners at the time. Of the cockpit crew, only flight engineer Repo survived the initial crash, along with technical officer Donadeo, who was down in the nose electronics bay with Repo at the moment of impact. Stockstill was killed on impact, while Captain Loft died in the flight deck's wreckage before he could be transported to a hospital. Repo was evacuated to a hospital but later succumbed to his injuries. Donadeo, the lone survivor of the four flight-deck occupants, recovered from his injuries. Frank Borman, a former NASA astronaut and Eastern's senior vice president of operations, was awoken at home by a phone call explaining a possible crash. He immediately drove to Eastern's Miami offices and decided to charter a helicopter to the crash site as the swampy terrain made rescue difficult and Eastern had not heard any news of progress in rescue efforts. There he was able to land in a swampy patch of grass and coordinate rescue efforts. He accompanied three survivors on the helicopter to the hospital including a flight attendant and passenger who lost her baby in the crash.

Most of the dead were passengers in the airliner's midsection. The swamp absorbed much of the energy of the crash, lessening the impact on the aircraft. The Everglades' mud may have blocked wounds sustained by survivors, preventing them from bleeding to death. However, it also complicated the survivors' recovery, as organisms in the swamp caused infections, with gas gangrene potential. Eight passengers became infected . All the survivors were injured; sixty received severe injuries, and seventeen suffered minor injuries that did not require hospitalisation. The most common were fractures of ribs, spines, pelvises, and lower extremities. Fourteen survivors had various degrees of burns.

Robert 'Bud' Marquis, an airboat pilot, was out frog gigging with Ray Dickinsin when they witnessed the crash. They rushed to rescue survivors. Marquis received burns to his face, arms, and legs - a result of spilt jet fuel from the airliner but continued shuttling people in and out of the crash site that night and the next day. He received the Humanitarian Award from the National Air Disaster Alliance/Foundation and the 'Alumitech – Airboat Hero Award' from the American Airboat Search and Rescue Association for his efforts.

The National Transportation Safety Board (NTSB) investigation discovered that the autopilot had been inadvertently switched from altitude hold to control wheel steering (CWS) mode in pitch. To explain, in this mode, once the pilot released the pressure on the yoke - also called 'control column' or 'wheel' - the autopilot maintains the pitch attitude selected by the pilot until he moves the yoke again. Investigators believed that the autopilot switched modes when the captain accidentally leaned against the yoke while turning to speak to the flight engineer, who was sitting behind and to the right of him. The slight forward pressure on the stick would have caused the aircraft to enter a slow descent, maintained by the CWS system.

An investigation into the aircraft's autopilot showed that the force required to switch to CWS mode was different between the A and B channels. Thus, the switching to CWS in channel A possibly did not occur in channel B, thus depriving the first officer of any indication the mode had changed Again, to explain, channel A provided the captain's instruments with data, while channel B provided the first officer's.

After descending 250 feet from the selected altitude of 2,000 feet, a C-chord sounded from the rear speaker. This altitude alert, designed to warn the pilots of an inadvertent deviation from the selected altitude, went unnoticed by the crew. Investigators believe this was due to the crew being distracted by the nose gear light, and because the flight engineer was not in his seat when it sounded, so would not have been able to hear it.

The final NTSB report cited the cause of the crash as pilot error, specifically: 'the failure of the flight crew to monitor the flight instruments during the final four minutes of flight and to detect an unexpected descent soon enough to prevent impact with the ground. Preoccupation with a malfunction of the nose landing gear position indicating system (the burnt-out landing gear indicator light) distracted the crew's attention from the instruments and allowed the descent to go unnoticed.'

In response to the accident, many airlines started crew resource management training for their pilots. The training was designed to make problem-solving much more efficient in a flight deck, thus causing less distraction for the crew. Flashlights became standard equipment near jumpseats, and all jumpseats were outfitted with shoulder harnesses.

Over the years, rumours began to circulate that Eastern Air Lines employees made sightings of the dead crew members, particularly Captain Robert Loft and second officer Don Repo, sitting on board other Eastern L-1011 flights.

These rumours speculated that reclaimed parts of the crashed aircraft were salvaged after the investigation and refitted into other L-1011s. Gossip regarding the sighting of Don Repo and Bob Loft's spirits spread throughout Eastern Air Lines to the point where Eastern's management warned employees that they could face dismissal if caught spreading ghost stories.

While Eastern Air Lines publicly denied their airliners were haunted, the media reported that they had removed all the salvaged parts from their L-1011 fleet. Over time, the reporting of ghost sightings stopped. The story of the crash and its aftermath was documented in John G Fuller's 1976 book *The Ghost of Flight 401*. A TV movie *The Ghost of Flight 401*, was aired in February 1978. Based on Fuller's book, it focused on the ghost sightings surrounding the aftermath.

Eastern Air Lines CEO and former Apollo astronaut Frank Borman called the ghost stories surrounding the crash' garbage.' Eastern considered suing for libel, based on assertions of a cover-up by Eastern executives. Still, Borman opted not to, feeling a lawsuit would merely provide more publicity for the book. Loft's widow and children did sue Fuller, for infringement of Loft's right of publicity, for an invasion of privacy, and intentional infliction of emotional distress, but the lawsuit was dismissed and the dismissal upheld by the Florida Fourth District Court of Appeal.

According to Robert J. Serling's 1980 book From the Captain to the Colonel: An Informal History of Eastern Airlines (Dial Press, 1980) the claim that wreckage from Flight 401 was installed and later removed from other Eastern aircraft was false, and no Eastern employees had ever claimed to have seen or believed in the alleged ghost sightings. Sceptic Brian Dunning claimed that the origin for the ghost sightings was a joke made by an un-named Eastern Air Lines captain after an emergency landing in which he quipped that he 'thought Don Repo's ghost was on the plane.' I tend to concur.

Delta Air Lines Flight 1080

This was a scheduled flight notable for the incident on 12 April 1977 during the San Diego to Los Angeles leg of the flight. Heading the flight was Captain Jack McMahan, the other flight crew members being First Officer William 'Will' Radford and Second Officer Steve Heidt.

At departure, the gross weight of N707DA was 300,000 pounds with 42,000 pounds of fuel, forty-one passengers and a crew of eleven.

During taxi out, Radford performed a flight control check of the stabiliser, ailerons and spoilers while Captain McMahan made the rudder check. The proper control response was verified by the SPI (surface position indicator) and no abnormal control 'feel' was experienced.

The flight departed San Diego at 23:53 Pacific standard time, an over-water departure to the west on Runway 27. The clearance was a Scorpion Six departure to Los Angeles at an assigned altitude of 10,000 feet.

Immediately after liftoff, an abrupt nose-high excursion in pitch was experienced that was controllable although Captain McMahan did hit the full-forward limit of the control column during this abrupt pitch up.

A climb attitude of fifteen degrees pitch was re-established with airspeed increasing, the gear was retracted and landing lights extinguished. The aircraft appeared to return to a normal takeoff flight profile.

At an altitude of around 400 feet and an airspeed of around 170 knots, the pitch started to become excessive, exceeding 18°. Captain McMahan was exerting a push force on the control column and trimming electrically using thumbwheel trim when the thumbwheel movement stopped. The pitch controls were sluggish, and he immediately attempted to utilise the mechanical trim wheel which served as a back-up system and overrode the electric trim. There was no response. McMahan discovered that the trim was already zeroed out with full nose-down stabiliser trim as indicated on the stabiliser trim indices and zero stabiliser indicated on the SPI instrument. He reset the electric trim switches, but the thumbwheel trim remained immovable.

At this time the two pilots went on instruments at 800 feet above mean sea level and Captain McMahan started a right turn on course. He remarked to First Officer Radford that he was having trim problems and asked Second Officer Heidt to check the hydraulic system. Captain McMahan was not overly concerned at this time as the L-1011 had a fine primary flight control system consisting of a flying stabiliser, four independent hydraulic systems, a well designed light legend to alert the pilot of a malfunction and plenty of redundancy in the system. He was confident that one of several possible procedures would correct our pitch problem.

Captain McMahan unlatched and reset all switches associated with trim - pitch trim, mach trim and pitch trim monitor - with no effect. First Officer Radford conducted an area test of the switch lights to verify light integrity as there were no lights illuminated on the various panels. Second Officer Heidt double-checked hydraulics and checked for any opened circuit breakers. By 3,000 feet, all emergency procedures for trim, pitch axis jam, flight control path jam and hydraulic malfunction were exhausted with no effect on controllability.

San Diego Departure Control was informed that the crew were experiencing a pitch problem and was asked to stay with the airliner. Later the crew received a handoff to Coast Approach.

The first officer and the Captain were both on the controls at this time and exerting full forward force on the control column. The aircraft continued to pitch up, and airspeed continued to decrease.

They were also experiencing a roll problem. In attempting to maintain a right bank, the two pilots hit the stops a couple of times in roll control.

Captain McMahan abruptly reduced thrust on all three engines and recognised a modest change in control feel. He then advanced No. 2 throttle full-forward, but almost simultaneously, he had to increase thrust on engines 1 and 3 to prevent any further loss of airspeed. He observed pitch correcting back through twenty degrees to somewhere around eighteen degrees and the airspeed slowly increased above 140 knots. 'I had to further increase thrust on the No. 1 engine to compensate for a left roll tendency. I felt certain that we were about to recover from a most desperate situation.'

As soon as possible, about 150 knots, the flaps were retracted from ten to four degrees, and the airspeed started to increase at a better rate. Performance data called for 198 knots before going to the clean configuration.

Radio contact with Coast Approach was established, and informed that they were experiencing control problems. They acknowledged immediately with an offer of assistance, and the airliner cleared direct to Seal Beach VOR to maintain 10,000 feet.

Simultaneously, as reaching on top of the clouds, the airspeed increased sufficiently to allow the remaining four degree of flaps to be retracted. With an indicated airspeed of around 190 knots, still climbing sharply with no control over pitch, it became evident that the aircraft would climb right on through their assigned altitude of 10,000 feet. Coast Approach was advised, and they responded with a block altitude of 10,000 feet to 12,000 feet. Climbing through 11,500 feet with no improvement in the ability to control pitch, it was clear that the crew could not maintain 12,000 feet either. They informed the Coast Approach, and they very cooperatively replied. 'We have you on radar, and all altitudes are clear. We will stay with you.'

Approaching an altitude of 14,000 feet, they had no alternative except to retard the thrust on Engines 1 and 3. The aircraft slowly responded with a slight pitch change, and so the crew attempted to descend back to 10,000 feet. They were unable to stop the descent rate at 10,000 feet, but with constant power adjustment, they could regain control at 9.500 feet. They were soon back up to 10,400 feet, then below 10,000 feet again and finally fairly well stabilised there.

The pitch attitude to maintain level flight was twelve to forteen degrees with thrust equivalent to climb power due to the induced drag. The airspeed stabilised at 195 to 197 knots. The throttles were severely staggered to maintain control over pitch and a roll tendency. No. 2 throttle was well in advance of No. 1 and No. 1 in advance of No. 3 throttle. The airspeed had to be controlled below 200 knots, or the aircraft would again start climbing. 'I was quite concerned about the extreme nose-high attitude of twelve to forteen degrees pitch and the amount of thrust required to maintain level flight. It appeared that we were working within a narrow airspeed envelope - too fast and control over pitch and altitude war impossible, too slow and a stall would occur.'

The flight attendants were briefed on the situation at this time. The flight deck told them that there was a control problem, but that it was now

N751DA of Delta about to depart London Gatwick. It was a colour sceheme that always looked good. *(Richard Vandervord)*

pretty well under control and they should not be overly concerned about the unusually high deck angle. To improve the centre of gravity, we asked them to move all the passengers forward and, as a precaution, to position them as near the emergency exits as possible. The flight deck crew assured them they would keep them fully informed of progress and course of action.

Now the decision had to be made where to go from here. The partially disabled airliner was halfway between San Diego and Los Angeles and had to be landed - but where?

Low ceilings, poor visibility and a heavy overcast virtually eliminated Los Angeles, Long Beach and El Toro airports. Going back to San Diego was out of the question. The decision was made to proceed to Los Angeles, even though the weather was marginal with 700 feet and four miles visibility. Most importantly, the airliner was stabilised in smooth air, and over water, with plenty of altitude to work with in the event of further difficulties. Los Angeles offered the best chance for a long, straight-in, stabilised approach to Runway 6R. Plus, it was an approach that the pilots were were familiar with.

The flight attendants were briefed on the landing plans and instructed to prepare for emergency evacuation. The flight crew told them to prepare for the worst and hope for the best. In a low-key manner, an announcement was made to the passengers that, in accordance with company procedures, precautionary measures were being taken to ensure their safety and that they would be landing in Los Angeles in a few minutes.

Having decided upon the 'where', it was now a question of 'how?' They had very little pitch control, a roll problem, and none of the emergency or abnormal procedures were effective. There was a confounding number of unanswered questions.

Captain McMahan decided that he would try one step at a time, using incremental flaps, verifying pitch control with each increment and attempting to establish a configuration of 22° flaps and an airspeed of 165 knots for the approach and landing. At 4° flaps the aircraft pitched down slightly and he was able to recover about one-half inch of control column movement from the full-forward limit. At 10° flaps the additional pitch-down gave me another half-inch of control response. The aircraft was stabilised at 180 knots, 10° flaps, 12° pitch, and one inch of control movement was available. Even though they were still severely limited, this felt like a major victory.

They tried the autopilot to determine if it had some trim authority that could be used. The aircraft pitched up, and so the autopilot was disengaged.

While maintaining 180 knots air, speed and the 10° flap configuration, the pilots could manoeuvre the aircraft reasonably well and follow radar vectors to position for a 6R instrument approach.

The pilots continued to 5,000 feet and intercepted 6R runway instrument localiser and glideslope fifteen miles from the runway threshold. The approach was made with 10° flaps, and 100 knots indicated airspeed with a sink rate of 800 feet to 900 feet per minute. The pitch attitude 12° nose up, making the possibility of a tail strike at touchdown feasible.

The approach checklist was completed then, at 2,500 feet, when the landing gear was extended, the aircraft again pitched up. The pilots shoved the control column full forward, but the airliner continued to climb while the airspeed deteriorated, and they were going above the glideslope.

They were so close and yet so far. Once more Captain McMahan increased thrust on No. 2 engine, reduced thrust an engines 1 and 3. The aircraft responded slowly, and he was able to manoeuvre back down to reestablish glide slope tracking. Eighteen degrees of flaps were selected, and the airspeed stabilised at 170 knots.

Upon reaching 700 feet, they broke out of the overcast and visual contact with the runway was established. The aircraft was aligned with the runway and had a sink rate of 800 to 900 feet per minute, which was perfect for the selected touchdown reference point. It was just fly the aircraft to touchdown, which was made at approximately 165 to 170 knots IAS in the first one thousand feet of Runway 68.

After fifty-five minutes of airborne time, they were on the ground. There were no tail strikes, no blown tyres. The pilots exited the runway at taxiway No. 47 and taxied to the ramp.

An equipment substitution was provided, and the crew and passengers continued Flight 1080 without further incident.

Post landing investigation found that the pressurisation and depressurisation of the L-1011 during flight cycles had caused water to be pushed inside a bearing, heavily corroding it and causing it to become jammed during a routine control surfaces check before takeoff.

Lockheed redesigned the elevator systems to be redundant upon failure of the bearings, added a seal to the bearing and a deflector to reduce the amount of water contacting the part. Lockheed also modified the pilot's manual to improve the

Pitch Axis Control Assist Procedures. The FAA further made it mandatory for pilots to be informed of these changes.

For his skill in landing the crippled airliner, the Captain, Jack McMahan was awarded the FAA's Distinguished Service Award. The airliner was repaired and continued to fly for Delta until 1985.

Saudia Flights SV163 and 162.

Saudia Flight SV163 was a scheduled Saudia passenger flight that caught fire after takeoff from Riyadh International Airport en route to Jeddah, Saudi Arabia on 19 August 1980. All 287 passengers and 14 crew onboard the Lockheed L-1011-200 HZ-AHK died from smoke inhalation after the aircraft made a successful emergency landing at Riyadh.

The captain of the flight was 38-year-old Mohammed Ali Khowyter, a Saudi who Saudia hired in 1965. Khowyter's records described him as a slow learner and in need of more proper training. Khowyter had 7,674 flying hours, including 388 hours in the TriStar. The first officer was 26-year-old Sami Abdullah M Hasanain, who joined the airline in 1977 and had previously worked as a trainee. He received his type rating on the TriStar eleven days before the accident. At one point during his training, however, Hasanain was removed from flying school due to his poor performance. Hasanain had 1,615 flying hours, including 125 hours in the TriStar. The flight engineer was 42-year-old Bradley Curtis, an American who was hired by the airline in 1974. He had needed to pay for his own training as an L-1011 flight engineer to keep his job. Curtis had 650 flying hours, including 157 hours in the TriStar.

Flight SV163 departed Qu'aid-e-Azam International Airport in Karachi, Pakistan at 18:32 local time bound for Jeddah International Airport in Jeddah, Saudi Arabia, with a scheduled intermediate stop at Riyadh Airport. The flight arrived in Riyadh at 19:06 Saudi time. There was a two-hour layover for refuelling. During the layover, several of the passengers disembarked. After refuelling, the flight took off at 21:08 bound for Jeddah.

Almost seven minutes into the flight, the crew received warnings of smoke from the cargo compartment. The crew spent the next four minutes trying to confirm the warnings, after which Flight Engineer Curtis went back into the cabin to confirm the presence of smoke. Captain Khowyter decided to return to the airport, and First Officer Hasanain radioed their intentions at 21:20. At 21:25, the number two engine's thrust lever became jammed as the fire burned through the operating cable. Then, at 21:29, the engine was shut down during the final approach.

At 21:35, Khowyter declared an emergency and landed back at Riyadh. After touchdown at 21:36, the airliner continued to a taxiway at the end of the runway where it exited the runway, stopping two minutes and forty seconds after touchdown at 21:39. The airport fire rescue equipment was stationed back on the runway landing section, with emergency personnel expecting an emergency stop and evacuation. This meant they had to rush after the aircraft, which had used the entire length of a 13,000 feet runway to slow and then exit onto the taxiway. The airliner stopped facing in the opposite direction from landing.

Once the aircraft had stopped, the crew

The burnt out remains of HZ-AHK, after the engines had been salvaged. *(Phil McCrackin Collection)*

reported that they were shutting down the engines and about to evacuate. On arrival at the aircraft soon after, however, the rescue personnel found that the two wing-mounted engines were still running, preventing them from opening the doors. These were finally shut down at 21:42, three minutes and fifteen seconds after the aircraft came to a stop, at which point communication with the crew was lost. No external fire was visible at this time, but flames were observed through the windows at the rear of the aircraft. Twenty-three minutes after engine shutdown, at 22:05, the R2 door was opened by ground personnel. Three minutes later, the aircraft burst into flames and was consumed by fire.

Why Captain Khowyter failed to evacuate the aircraft promptly is not known. Saudi reports stated that the crew could not get the plug-type doors to open in time. It is assumed that most passengers and flight attendants were incapacitated during the landing roll, or they did not attempt to open a door on a moving aircraft. It is known that the aircraft remained pressurised during the landing roll as the cabin pressurisation system was on standby, and the aircraft was found with both pressurisation hatches almost completely closed. The pressurisation hatches should have opened completely on touchdown to depressurise the aircraft. The crew were found still in their seats, and all the victims were found in the forward half of the fuselage. Autopsies were conducted on some of the non-Saudi nationals, including the American flight engineer. All of them perished from smoke inhalation and not burns, which indicated that they had died long before the R2 door was opened.

A 196-page report of the incident was submitted by E Dreifrus, Director of Civil Aviation, Presidency of Civil Aviation Saudi Arabia to H.E. Sheikh NasserAl-Assaf 16 January 1982.

The investigation revealed the fire had started in the aft C3 cargo compartment, but the source of the fire could not be determined. The fire was intense enough to burn through the cabin floor, causing passengers seated in that area of the cabin to move forward before the landing. Saudi officials found two butane stoves in the burned-out remains of the airliner, and a used fire extinguisher near one of them. One early theory was that the fire began in the passenger cabin when a passenger used his own butane stove to heat water for tea. Still, the investigation found no evidence.

After the event, the airline revised its training and emergency procedures. Lockheed also removed the insulation from above the rear cargo area and added glass laminate structural reinforcement. The National Transportation Safety Board recommended that aircraft use halomethane extinguishers instead of traditional hand-held fire extinguishers.

Saudia Flight SV162 experienced an explosive decompression of the cabin while climbing through 29,000 feet over international waters near Qatar's State on 22 December 1980. The aircraft, HZ-AHJ, had departed Dhahran, Saudi Arabia, and was en-route to Karachi, Pakistan. An emergency descent was initiated, and a successful landing was made at Doha International Airport in Qatar. Two children passengers were killed when they were ejected from the aircraft through a hole in the cabin floor which had resulted from the forces of explosive decompression.

Post landing investigations resulted in this summary in the official report 'Probable Cause: "The Presidency of Civil Aviation determines that the probable cause of this accident was an in-flight, fatigue failure of a main landing gear inboard wheel flange resulting in the rupture of the aircraft's pressure hull and explosive decompression. The failure of the flange was the result of the failure of the B.F. Goodrich Company and the Lockheed Aircraft Company to properly assess the safety hazard associated with the type of wheels installed on aircraft HZ-AHJ. Contributing to the accident was the lapse of effective quality control procedures by the B.F. Goodrich Company and the failure of the Federal Aviation Administration to provide adequate surveillance of the manufacturer".'

Eastern Air Lines Flight 935

On 22 September 1981, N309EA, operating as Eastern Airlines Flight 935 departed on an international scheduled passenger flight from Boston, Massachusetts, to San Juan, Puerto Rico, with an en-route stop at Newark, New Jersey. According to fifty-eight-year-old Captain Adam C Kagel, the Boston to Newark flight was normal. Flight 935 taxied from the Eastern Airlines ramp, received an IFR air traffic control clearance and was directed to runway 22L at Newark International Airport for takeoff.

The airliner departed Newark at 1125, using a reduced thrust takeoff power setting. The takeoff and initial climb were normal. According to forty-year-old First Officer Richard B. Donica, as the aircraft was climbing through 800 feet, they noted that the yellow warning light for the No. 2 engine fan airborne vibration monitor (AVM) had illuminated momentarily, indicating an abnormal level of vibration, then went out and did not come back on. Using the broad band vibrator filter selector, the Second Officer John L. Barrett, Jr., aged forty-nine, determined that while the No. 2 engine N1 and N3 rotor readings were normal, the N2 rotor reading was high and off the scale. The flight crew stated that when power was reduced at 1,000 feet in accordance with the normal procedures, all AVM readings were normal. Shortly thereafter, the No.2 engine oil filter pressure warning light, which measures pressure differential across the filter, illuminated indicating that the filter could be blocked and that the filter might be operating in the bypass mode. The flight crew then slowly retarded the No. 2 engine throttle to near idle.

Oil pressure was steady at 50 psi, and the oil quantity was fifteen quarts. Both readings were within normal limits. The captain directed the second officer to check the abnormal procedures section J in the Flight Manual for corrective action to be taken when the oil pressure filter warning light illuminated.

All engine parameters, including AVM readings, were normal when the aircraft was levelled at 2,000 feet in accordance with departure instructions. Under Flight Manual procedures, the flight crew slowly reestablished climb power while monitoring all engine instruments. According to the flight crew, as the aircraft climbed through 10,000 feet, they heard and felt a loud explosion accompanied by heavy aircraft buffeting. They stated that there was no warning and that immediately after the explosion, numerous warning and caution lights illuminated.

The second officer called out that the No. 2 engine had failed and that hydraulic systems A, B, and D had been lost simultaneously. There were no concurrent pressurization problems. No. 2 engine was shut down immediately, and the crew performed the engine shutdown and multiple hydraulic-system-failure checklists. Since the No. 2 engine fire warning systems would not test properly, the flight crew discharged the fire bottle as a precautionary measure.

The flight crew requested air traffic control clearance for an immediate descent and landing at John F Kennedy International Airport, Jamaica, New York. The request was granted, and the flight crew was given headings to jettison fuel ai 10.000 feet to reduce aircraft gross weight from 393,000 lbs. to 345,000 lbs. Airspeed was reduced from 320 to about 270 knots IAS to reduce buffeting. The captain and first officer noted that their rudder pedals were jammed in a neutral position.

The flightcrew made an approach to JFK Airport using elevators, ailerons, and differential power for aircraft control. The aircraft was landed on runway 22L at 1212. Crash, Fire and Rescue units were standing by, and after the aircraft stopped on the runway, they inspected the exterior of the aircraft for damage and leaks and determined that there was no immediate danger. The captain taxied the aircraft to a parking gate, and the passengers and flight crew deplaned normally. No one was injured.

Inspection of the aircraft revealed that the No. 2 engine fan shaft had failed and that the fan assembly had moved forward about twelve feet in the No. 2 engine inlet S-duct before breaking through both sides of the duct.

An inspection of the aircraft showed a section of the No. 2 engine low-pressure compressor fan module, including the disc, the blades, and an attached twenty-six-inch-section of the fan shaft was missing from the engine. A coincidental thirty-inch-section cf the fan module fail-safe shaft was also missing. As the fan module separated, it cut a spiral path through the S-duct and struck the left side of the fuselage about nine feet forward of the engine's front flange. The module then cut through the aircraft fuselage, leaving a clear cruciform-type impact mark at the upper right-hand side of the S-duct.

The fan module created a forty by twenty-inch hole on the left side of the aft upper fuselage S-duct and a seventy-five by eighty-six-inch hole on the right side of the duct as it passed through. The rear pressure bulkhead was punctured in ten places with dents and scratches over a forty-eight-inch square area. The aft centre lavatory was damaged slightly. A six-inch piece of a one-inch-diameter steel rod, used to support the S-duct, was found on the floor of the toilet. The rear pressure bulkhead below the cabin floor level was not damaged. The S-duct was damaged internally from next to the fan blades forward about sixteen feet.

Holes in the S-duct coincided with the holes in the fuselage. Holes were punctured in the top surface of the horizontal stabiliser centre box beam. There was a hole in the forward spar web, but no holes in the rear spar. The left stabiliser contained eighteen holes in the top surface and two holes in the lower surface. The damage pattern was from top to bottom. The right stabiliser was not damaged.

Eastern Air Lines Flight 855

On 5 May 1983 TriStar, N334EA, operating as Eastern Air Lines Flight 855 en route from Miami International Airport to Nassau International Airport, experienced the loss of all three engines near Miami, Florida. The flight crew succeeded in restarting one engine in time to land the aircraft at Miami International Airport safely.

N334EA had flown into Miami a day earlier where it underwent overnight maintenance, which included a check of the magnetic chip detectors inside the jet engines. This involved removing the master chip detector from each engine and replacing it with a new one. Each chip detector had two O-rings, which served as oil seals. The replacement chip detectors were not fitted with O-rings, a fact which escaped the mechanic who fitted them. After the chip detectors were fitted, each engine was motored for ten seconds to check for oil leaks. None were found. The aircraft was signed off as serviceable and returned to service.

Eastern Air Lines Flight 855 took off from Miami International Airport at 08:56 carrying 162 passengers and ten crew. On the flight deck was Captain Richard Boddy (58), Captain Steve Thompson (48) and Flight Engineer Dudley Barnes (44). On this flight, Captain Thompson served as a supervisory check crew member.

At 09:15, while descending through 15,000 feet, the low oil pressure indicator on the TriStar's number 2 engine illuminated. The flight engineer noted that the No.2 engine's oil pressure fluctuated between fifteen and twenty-five pounds per square inch, although the minimum pressure required for normal engine operation was thirty pounds per square inch. The captain ordered the flight engineer to shut down the engine.

By this time, the plane was about fifty miles from Nassau. The crew elected to return to Miami to land. Flight 855 received a clearance back to Miami, as well as instructions to begin a climb to FL20.

En route back to Miami, low oil pressure lights for engines No.1 and No.3 illuminated, and the oil quantity gauges for all three engines read zero. At 09:23, Flight 855 informed Miami air traffic control of the engine gauge readings but stated, 'We believe it to be faulty indications since the chance of all three engines having zero oil pressure and zero quantity is almost nil.' At 09:28, at an altitude of 16,000 feet, the No.3 engine failed. Five minutes later, the No.1 engine flamed out while the crew attempted to restart the No.2 engine. Cabin lights went off, and flight deck instruments stopped working. The aircraft descended without power from about 13,000 feet to about 4,000 feet, at a rate of descent of approximately 1,600 feet per minute. The crew successfully restarted the No.2 engine on the third attempt and executed a one-engine landing at Miami at 09:46. After the landing, the No.2 engine's power was insufficient for the aircraft to taxi; a tug had to be used to tow it to the airport terminal, where the occupants disembarked normally. None of the 172 passengers and crew aboard was injured in the incident.

The National Transportation Safety Board Aircraft Accident Report AAR-84-04: Eastern Airlines, Inc, Lockheed L-1011, N334EA determined that the probable cause of the incident was as follows: 'The omission of all the O-ring seals on the master chip detector assemblies leading to the loss of lubrication and damage to the airplane's three engines as a result of the failure of mechanics to follow the established and proper procedures for the installation of master chip detectors in the engine lubrication system, the repeated failure of supervisory personnel to require mechanics to comply strictly with the prescribed installation procedures, and the failure of Eastern Air Lines management to assess adequately the significance of similar previous occurrences and to act effectively to institute corrective action. Contributing to the cause of the incident was the failure of Federal Aviation Administration maintenance inspectors to assess the significance of the incidents involving master chip detectors and to take effective surveillance and enforcement measures to prevent the recurrence of the incidents.'

It was subsequently established that the engines needed to be run for at least 30 seconds with no O-rings fitted before an oil leak would become apparent.

Barnes, Boddy and Thompson were each presented with an Award for Outstanding Airmanship by the Airline Pilots Association.

British Airtours KT101

On 27 May 1985, British Airtours TriStar Flight KT 101, operated by G-BBAI, from Palma Airport, Mallorca, Spain, overran the runway on landing at Leeds Bradford Airport, West Yorkshire, after a rain shower. Twelve of the 412 people on board suffered minor injuries when exiting down steep rear ramps. The aircraft was severely damaged.

The nose landing gear strut folded backwards during the overrun, leading to severe damage to

KT101, operated by G-BBAI after it overshot the runway at Leeds Bradford.

the underside of the forward fuselage. The undersides of both wing-mounted engines were flattened, and both wing engines suffered ingestion damage. The aircraft's main wheels also dug deep troughs in the area, damaging the buried airfield lighting cables. The accident report concluded that the overrun was caused by the inability of the aircraft to achieve the appropriate level of braking effectiveness due to restricted thrust reverse options and recommended that both the scheduled wet runway performance of the TriStar and the condition of the surface of runway 14 at Leeds Bradford Airport should be re-examined.

Delta Flight 191

Delta Air Lines Flight 191 was a regularly scheduled Delta Air Lines domestic service from Fort Lauderdale, Florida to Los Angeles with an intermediate stop at Dallas/Fort Worth International Airport. On 2 August 1985, the TriStar N726DA operating as Flight 191 encountered a microburst while on approach to land at DFW. The aircraft impacted ground over one mile short of the runway, struck a car near the airport, collided with two water tanks and disintegrated. The crash killed 137 people and injured twenty-six others. The National Transportation Safety Board determined that the crash resulted from the flight crew's decision to fly through a thunderstorm, the lack of procedures or training to avoid or escape microbursts, and the lack of hazard information on wind shear.

Jordanian inflight fire.

A Jordanian Airline L-1011 experienced an in-flight fire while at 24,000 feet approaching Singapore Airport. The flight crew experienced electrical faults, and an overheat warning in the cheek area adjacent to the C+3 cargo compartment. Shortly after that, a fire warning occurred for the number two engine. Smoke began pouring into the aft cabin, and flames were seen entering the cabin through a floor grill on the aft left side. A flight attendant reported firing a Halon extinguisher at the fire, and they disappeared. At about 14,000 feet, the aircraft experienced a sudden depressurisation. The smoke subsided in the cabin, and the aircraft landed with no more problems.

Investigation revealed that a fire began with an arc from a power feeder cable to a titanium bleed air duct. The titanium ignited and fed by the 400 °F bleed air, which exited the ruptured duct continued to burn. A three-foot length of the duct was consumed in the incident. The hot air and molten titanium then ignited some epoxy/fibreglass ductwork in the area. The gases produced by the overheated resins caused the fire to spread around the aft pressure bulkhead and into the overhead. Fire impingement on the aft pressure bulkhead melted and shorted wiring, causing the number two engine fire warning and then causing a rupture of the bulkhead and depressurisation of the cabin. Since most of the burning was on the surfaces of materials and gases produced, the

The final resting place of N726DA after the crash at Dallas Fort Worth.

sudden rush of air due to the hole in the bulkhead blew the fire out. With this flight for the main fuel line running just under the cabin floor, Luck was almost penetrated by fire just forward of the aft pressure bulkhead. All 118 passengers and crew survived. The aircraft was later repaired and placed back into service.

- On June 28, 1991, LTU International L-1011 registration D-AERI, suffered an interior fire during maintenance in a hangar at Düsseldorf Airport. Four engineers escaped injury, but the aircraft was declared a total loss.
- On July 30, 1992, TWA Flight 843, an L-1011, had its takeoff aborted by the captain after liftoff from JFK, in response to a false stall warning. The aircraft landed too hard, breaking a wing spar and starting a fire. All 292 passengers and crew evacuated safely, with only ten minor injuries. The airliner was destroyed by fire.
- On August 23, 1995, Delta Air Lines Flight 157, an L-1011 Tristar 1, suffered a rapid decompression after the pressure bulkhead failed. The flight crew initiated an emergency descent to 14,000 feet, and the plane landed safely at Los Angeles International Airport with no deaths or injuries to the 226 passengers or ten crew. However, the aircraft was substantially damaged and later written off.

Chapter Thirteen

TwiLight of the TriStar

The TriStar was an effective and economic airliner, but it became more maintenance-intensive and parts for the once very advanced systems were becoming harder to obtain.

However, Lockheed teamed with Delta, the largest remaining operator, to provide comprehensive support for the remaining aircraft in service. This combined the knowledge of the manufacturer with the unrivalled experience of an operator of the aircraft from first delivery in 1973, its fleet growing eventually to fifty aircraft of all versions used both domestically and on international flights.

As well as charter operations, the TriStar found a useful niche with cargo operators, Marshall of Cambridge having established a good reputation for reconfigurations based on the knowledge gained with the tanker conversions for the RAF.

In March 1991, Saudia was having discussions with the Lockheed Commercial Aircraft Centre about the conversion of their TriStar fleet to cargo aircraft, while Pemco was also hoping to proceed on a major conversion programme for an unnamed customer, which was delayed due to uncertainty caused by the Gulf situation.

Wide-bodied aircraft had proved difficult to convert to economic freighters because the cross-section beam strength with the large cut-out of the cargo door was difficult to achieve without incurring unacceptable weight penalties. The floor strengthening and loading systems also increased the weight.

In July 1992, Lockheed Aircraft Services (LAS) announced the launch of the Lockheed 2000 freighter conversion, to be fitted with a 170 inch by 114-inch upward-opening cargo door on the port side of the forward cabin. The aircraft was expected to carry a payload of 122,000 pounds over distances of around 2,500 nautical miles. The major conversion work was to be done at the Lockheed Aeromod Center in Tucson, with Lockheed Aeronautical Systems of Marietta providing technical support to provide optional increases in take-off weight, landing weight, zero fuel weight, range and payload up to 154,000 pounds. LAS had contemplated working with Marshall Aerospace. Still, they rejected it, as the earlier military conversion was claimed not to be cost-effective for commercial applications, although Marshall had worked closely with Lockheed for the vital design data. Avtec of Basle was appointed as a marketing partner. The Marshall design had proposed a maximum payload of between 113,000 and 144,500 pounds loaded through a 102-inch by 138-inch cargo door.

Marshall Aerospace was not discouraged and confirmed in August 1992 that it was still offering cargo conversions of the TriStar. However, the door size had been increased to 114 inches by 154 inches. In an agreement with Lockheed Aeronautical Systems (LASC), which had approved the original RAF conversions by Marshall, LASC would publish a service bulletin covering the work. Despite some encouraging interest for the conversion of up to fifteen aircraft by LAS, no orders were placed, and the Lockheed-based TriStar freighter programme never started.

Civil freighter conversions

Lockheed seriously investigated a cargo conversion of the L1011, but it was Marshall Aerospace that really tackled the job. Their confidence and expertise followed on from their success with the tanker conversions for the RAF. Marshall selected the L-1011-200 as the model for the conversion, increasing the gross weight from 466,000 to 474,000 pounds.

The cargo capacity consisted of up to twenty-three 89 inch by 126-inch pallets on the main deck, with sixteen LD-3 containers up to a weight of 36,116 pounds in the forward underfloor hold and a further eight containers in the rear underfloor hold carrying

The capacious interior of a L-1011 once the passenger interior was stripped and a cargo roller-mat system was installed.

up to a weight of 18,100 pounds. Marshall had the manufacturing capability to complete up to three cargo conversions at a time, with any additional capacity being passed to Lockheed Martin in Greenville, which were capable of converting two other aircraft.

In addition to its work on TriStars for the RAF, Marshall also received a contract from British Airways to complete the Sunset III conversions on the long fuselage TriStars. This work on the longer-range L-1011-50s and L-1011-200s involved ten aircraft. Basically, it consisted of moving the below main deck floor galleys to the upper deck to increase the capacity of the C1 cargo bay and to reconfigure and refurbish the passenger cabins. This work was completed to a Lockheed service bulletin and did not involve Marshall in any design work, the first aircraft completed was G-BHBR.

Although the TriStar was still a very advanced aircraft in its systems, newer aircraft were becoming available, replacing the fleets in service with the initial operators. This put on the market a number of modern, highly economical wide-bodied jets with an adequate fatigue life to keep them commercially viable for many years.

Marshall Aerospace was in close communications with airliner manufacturers, which might well take TriStars in part exchange for their new products, to work in conjunction with Marshall to offer a cost-effective freighter conversion capability to the existing airframes. Conversion to freighter or freighter/passenger (combi) could be made to any existing airframes by fitting the C4 upper deck cargo door on the port side using the experience gained with the RAF aircraft's conversion. The freighter conversion programme was fully supported by Lockheed. The main deck could be reinforced depending upon the operator's requirements, and the total maximum load in the main cabin was twenty-three 88 inch by 125 inch pallets.

In addition, sixteen LD-3 containers up to a weight of 36,000 pounds could be carried in the forward cargo hold, and eight more up to 18,000 pounds in the rear cargo hold. A typical single class combi layout could have seating for up to 202 passengers, a cargo load on the main deck of 58,400 pounds in eight cargo pallets and below floor cargo capacity of up to 63,750 pounds.

The Marshall civil cargo conversion of TriStars was launched by an order for three conversions from American International Airways (AIA) in July 1994, with options on a further five. A batch of ex-British Airways TriStar 200s was allocated to this programme, and by the end of 1996, twelve aircraft had either been converted and had entered service or were in the conversion programme. In early 1995

International Air Leases (IAL) placed an order for three conversions of ex-Gulf Air TriStar 200s for operation by Miami-based Arrow Air, and International Lease and Finance Corporation ordered a further conversation of an ex-LTU L-1011-200 for Millon Air, also based at Miami.

The first civil freighter made its maiden flight from Cambridge on 11 August 1995 and was handed over to Conrad 'Connie' Kalitta, President of AIA, on 16 August as N102CK. Although the initial conversion had taken some fourteen months, Marshall planned to reduce the work period to between three and four months, depending upon the customer specification and additional work required to bring the aircraft up to date on modifications and service bulletins. The first aircraft entered service during mid-September operating services on behalf of Millon Air to South American destinations.

Compared with the modifications for the RAF, the major change in the conversion programme was to support the airframe neutrally and build the cargo door surround directly into the airframe before introducing the British Aerospace Aerostructures Manchester-built cargo door. In the case of the military conversions, the door surround had been jig built separately and then installed into the structure. Marshall Aerospace successfully overcame the difficulties of producing an economic wide-bodied cargo conversion capable of carrying significant loads over medium and long ranges.

Stargazer

In 1993, Marshall Aerospace took on yet another major conversion programme. The work formed part of the NASA Space Programme, namely modifying a former Air Canada L-1011 into a satellite launch platform for the Orbital Sciences Corporation. Previously a NASA B-52 had fulfilled the function, but it was now in need of replacement.

Orbital Sciences Corporation was an American company specialising in designing, manufacturing, and launching small- and medium-class space and rocket systems for commercial, military, and other government customers. In 2014 Orbital merged with Alliant Techsystems to create a new company called Orbital ATK, Inc., which in turn was purchased by Northrop Grumman in 2018. Today, the former Orbital Sciences Corporation's remnants are a subsidiary of Northrop Grumman known as Northrop Grumman Space Systems.

Orbital was founded and incorporated in 1982 by three friends who had met earlier while at Harvard Business School - David W Thompson, Bruce W Ferguson and Scott L Webster. Initial capitalisation for Orbital was provided by Fred C Alcorn, a Texas oilman and Sam Dunnam, a Texas businessman in September 1982. In 1985, Orbital procured its first contract for providing up to four transfer orbital stage (TOS) vehicles to NASA. In 1987, the Orbcomm constellation seeds were planted when Orbital began investigating a system using low Earth orbit satellites

Main picture: N140SC with Pegasus attached.

Inset: Modifications to the TriStar included the support and attachment structure underneath thefuselage, a release mechanism, aerodynamic fairings to accommodate the Pegasus satellite, Various systems, umbilicals, and equipment for testing and launching it. *(Marshall Aerospace)*

Above: Pegasus in flight!

Right: The Pegasus, which was fifty-two feet long and weighs 40,000 pounds, had a twenty-two foot wingspan, fitted under the fuselage, with an anhedral tailplane.

The fin was recessed into the unpressurised hydraulic service centre via specially designed doors. The underside of the aircraft was monitored by video cameras. *(Marshall Aerospace)*

to collect data from remote locations. In 1988, Orbital acquired Space Data Corporation in Arizona - one of the world's leading suppliers of suborbital rockets- thereby broadening its rocket business and manufacturing capabilities. This was followed by opening a new facility in Chandler, Arizona in 1989 to house the company's expanding rocket business.

In 1990, the company successfully carried out eight space missions, highlighted by the Pegasus rocket's initial launch, supposedly the world's first privately developed space launch vehicle. This claim was contested as Pegasus received significant funding from NASA and DARPA. Shortly following the successful Pegasus launch, Orbital conducted an IPO in 1990 and began trading on the NASDAQ stock exchange. In 1993, Orbital established its headquarters in Dulles, Virginia, and then successfully conducted the Taurus rocket's inaugural launch.

The former Air Canada TriStar 1-15 was delivered to Cambridge in June 1992 for the modification programme to commence and due for flight test in the first quarter of 1993. Modifications to the TriStar included the support and attachment structure underneath the fuselage, a release mechanism, aerodynamic fairings to accommodate the Pegasus satellite, payload air conditioning system, a nitrogen purge system, umbilicals, launch panel operator station, and equipment for testing and launching the satellite. The Pegasus, which was fifty-two feet long and weighed 40,000 pounds, had a twenty-two-foot wing which fitted under the TriStar's fuselage, with an anhedral tailplane. The fin was recessed into the unpressurised hydraulic service centre. Christened *Stargazer,* the modified TriStar N140CS, successfully completed its maiden flight from Cambridge on 12 July 1993. The satellite was launched at an altitude of 38,000 feet and could carry both the Hybrid Pegasus and the larger Pegasus XL. The RB211 engines were modified to give ten per cent higher power at the moment of release to counter the substantial rearward movement of the centre of gravity.

The first Pegasus launch to use Stargazer was conducted on 27 June 1994 as the maiden flight of the Pegasus-XL. Previous launches used the NASA-operated Boeing NB-52B *Balls 8*, which was also used for four subsequent launches, as the original Pegasus could not be launched from *Stargazer* due to clearance issues. A modified version, the Pegasus-

H, was introduced to rectify this.

In 1999, the Stargazer returned to Cambridge for modification to carry the joint NASA/ Orbital Sciences X-34. This would have served as a test bed for new technologies requiring a high-speed, high-altitude flight environment. However, when NASA cancelled the project in March 2001, the aircraft was placed in storage in the Mojave Desert, Arizona. The programme was later re-activated with the Pegasus, and Stargazer air-launched a Pegasus XL over the Pacific on 28 June 2003.

Stargazer was also used for captive tests and transportation of the X-34 hypersonic research aircraft; however, drop tests used *Balls 8*. Orbital Sciences also offered the aircraft for research flights. It is capable of carrying a 51,000-pound payload to an altitude of 42,000 feet.

Pegasus launches using *Stargazer* were usually conducted from Vandenberg Air Force Base. Launches have also been conducted from the Cape Canaveral Air Force Station, the NASA Kennedy Space Center, the NASA Wallops Flight Facility and from launch sites outside the US: Kwajalein Atoll in the Marshall Islands and Gando Airport in Spain.

In 2015, *Stargazer* was re-painted to reflect Orbital Sciences' merger with Alliant Techsystems and then, on 15 December 2016, successfully launched CYGNSS on behalf of NASA on its second attempt. The first attempt on 12 December was cancelled due to the hydraulic system's issues responsible for separating the Pegasus rocket from the launch aircraft.

Stargazer launched the Ionospheric Connection Explorer on 11 October 2019, an operation that was originally scheduled for June 2017 but was postponed when an anomalous piece of vehicle data was observed during a ferry flight. The data was related to the rudder position of the Pegasus XL rocket and was observed during a routine in-flight vehicle health check. The launch was delayed multiple times throughout 2017 and 2018 and 2019, finally occurring 11 October 2019. As of April 2021, Stargazer is the only L-1011 aircraft flying.

Flying Hospital

A further conversion, this time not by Marshall Aerospace, was that of an ex-PSA TriStar into a flying hospital. First announced in July 1995, the conversion was undertaken by Lockheed Martin Aircraft Services for Operation Blessing International Relief and Development. In the $14.5 million contract, the TriStar was the largest self-contained hospital aircraft ever built.

On the main deck, there was seating for sixty-seven medical participants, in business-class size seats that was used for in-flight travel as well as a classroom on the ground. A closed-circuit television system made it possible to present training and educational seminars to in-country health care professionals. A large video screen enabled a group of individuals to observe an operation and hear the surgeon's voice as he or she explained the procedure.

There were Eye, Ear, Nose, and Throat (EENT)/Dental Suites. Two fully-equipped operating stations permitted the performance of EENT and dental surgeries. Multi-drawer compartments were used to stow medical equipment and supplies during flight.

There were examination areas used for special examinations and minor surgical procedures and a Nurse's work station for administrative duties and system monitoring.

There was a Preoperative and Postoperative

P4-MED, The Flying Hospital at Tucon, Az.

Recovery Area capable of handling up to twelve patients awaiting surgery or recovering from surgery in the Surgical Suite, where there were three surgical tables and associated equipment.

The lower deck, which was reached by the special door provided for PSA for a lower cabin entry, is fitted with a pharmacy and a check-in/check-out reception, while the galley and crew rest area doubled as a consulting room. The aircraft was designed to operate independently on station in Third World countries for a week at a time and was fitted with auxiliary ground power generators and a water purification system, the overall conversion was completed by June 1996.

The TriStar carried its own oxygen generation system, nitrous oxide system, medical air system, medical Vacuum system and Water Purification System, along with its own ability to provide electrical power for the medical systems by a Ground Auxiliary Power Unit and by a diesel generator that was carried in the lower (cargo) bay. These units were removed from the aircraft and set up on location.

When the Flying Hospital visited the Farnborough Air Show in September 1998, seven medical missions had already been completed to a number of countries, including El Salvador, the Ukraine, Brazil and Bolivia, with missions planned to India and Nicaragua before the end of the year. In addition to helping to cure sick people in these countries, the medical team helped train local medics to carry on the work of the Flying Hospital after it had departed.

VIP Aircraft

Several L-1011s were modified by Lockheed Aircraft Services to VIP aircraft with a variety of deluxe interior features. American Trans Air operated several all first-class L-1011s on round-the-world tours, with only 100 seats total in this configuration. Another organisation to use the VIP TriStar was the Las Vegas Sands Corporation, an American casino and resort company based in Paradise, Nevada. Its resorts feature accommodations, gambling and entertainment, convention and exhibition facilities, restaurants and clubs, as well as an art and science museum in Singapore.

The corporation used its fleet of TriStars to ferry not only executives around its worldwide resorts, but also offered complimentary free transportation to high rolling gamblers to and from its numerous casinos.

It has several resorts in the United States and Asia.

The internal layout of a typical VIP TriStar 500

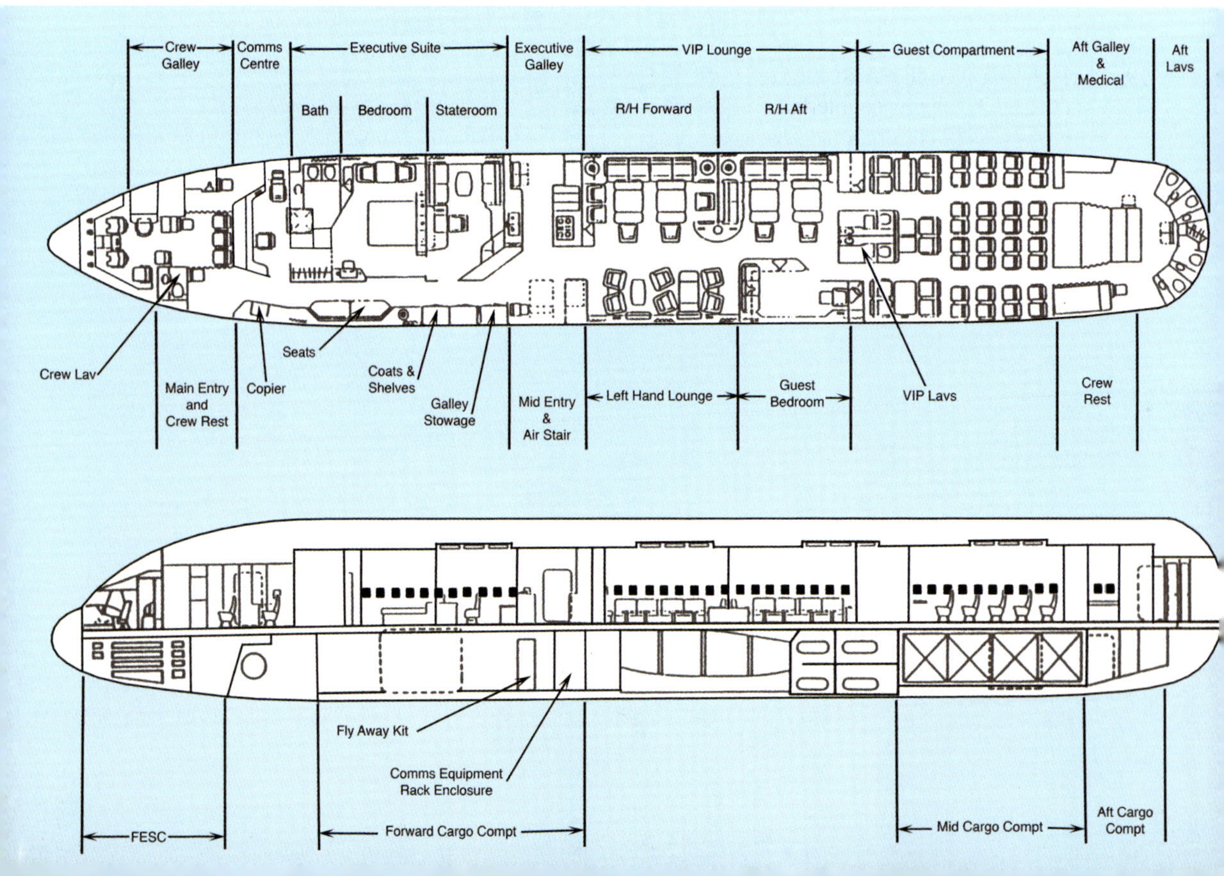

Among the properties it developed in the United States are two resorts on the Las Vegas Strip: The Venetian and The Palazzo, since sold.

In Asia, the Marina Bay Sands located in Singapore was added to the company's portfolio in 2010. Through its majority-owned subsidiary Sands China, the company owns several properties in Macau, including the Sands Macao, The Londoner Macao, The Venetian Macao, The Plaza Macao, and The Parisian Macao. It is the largest casino company worldwide.

The new applications of the L-1011 accomplished through modification added a whole new dimension to the continued use of the TriStar.

A gradual run-down.

By the end of 1990, a total of 237 TriStars were still in active service, with Delta and TWA in the USA, Caledonian Airways and LTU with five and ten respectively used for charter flights in Europe, Saudia with a fleet of seventeen TriStar 200s and All Nippon Airways with eleven TriStars used from Tokyo.

However, by the end of 1991 the worldwide fleet of active TriStars had grown to 244, out of the original 250 built, as it still provided a very cost-effective means of air transport. One year later, the fleet had begun the decline in numbers to 191 TriStars in airline service, with growing numbers arriving for desert storage. TWA had also filed for bankruptcy and submitted a recovery plan in early 1993, which involved the TriStar fleet declining to five aircraft by 1997, being counterbalanced by more modern and economical aircraft. Slowly, L-1011s trickled down to charter and third level operators as the major carriers disposed of their fleets, often via ACMI - Aircraft Crew Maintenance and Insurance - Leasing Companies. Most, but not all of these known airlines, some large, some single aircraft operators, are listed below in alphabetical order. It is worth noting that I say 'operated by', not owned by - I learned many years ago that unless you actually saw the suitcases of cash exchange hands, it is challenging to prove ownership!

Aer Lingus - Ireland

The national airline of Ireland commenced operations using de Havilland DH.84 Dragon, serving Dublin and Bristol. Aerlinte Eireann was formed in 1947 to operate transatlantic service, but operations did not start until April 1958. The two airlines eventually merged to form today's Aer Lingus. In May 1959, Aer Lingus entered the jet age when it put BAC 1-11 into service. The first Boeing 737 was leased in May 1965. In April, Aer Lingus received its first own Boeing 737-200. Aer Lingus used Boeing 747 for its transatlantic service to New York and Boston from the late '70s through the early 90's. With the acquisition of Airbus A330's, the airline aggressively expanded its North American network, as the type is more economical in less dense markets than a 747. They added Chicago, Los Angeles and Baltimore (later transferred to Washington Dulles) to its North American network. The airline has extensive network linking points in Ireland with UK and continental Europe using Airbus A320s and A319s. It was listed as having operated four TriStars.

Aer Turas Teoranta - Ireland

Aer Turas started operations in 1962 as an air taxi service from Ireland to the UK with a single de Havilland Dragon Rapide. They soon began to focus on freight rather than passenger operations and were quite successful for many years. In the 1980s Aer Lingus acquired a majority shareholding in Aer Turas. The airline is listed as operating three TriStars. However a decade later, soaring insurance costs,

G-BBAF was leased to Aer Lingus as *Cilian* for a time. *(Richard Vandervord)*

N10112 in AeroPeru markings climbs out from Miami. *(Richard Vandervord)*

increased competition and the turbulence following September 11th terrorist attacks in the USA all contributed to an overall operating loss and ultimately resulted in the company going into receivership.

Aero Continente - Peru
Aero Continente was a full-service passenger and cargo airline and began operations in July 1993. It has become Peru's largest airline after the demise of AeroPeru in 1999. The airline started as a domestic carrier, but international flights to neighbouring countries and Miami were inaugurated soon after. In 1999 Aero Continente established its subsidiary in Chile. Chile Government shut down aero Continente Chile in 2002 because of suspected drug trafficking. In June 2004, US authorities banned the airline from entering the USA and the airline and prohibited USA companies and citizens from dealing with the company because of alleged drug trafficking. This effectively grounded the airline since its equipment and insurer were dependent on American ownership. The airline attempted to restart as Nuevo Continente owned by its employees, but this effort also failed. The airline is listed as having operated one TriStar.

Aerolift Sierra Leone - Sierra Leone
Listed as operating one TriStar.

AeroPeru - Peru
The airline was established by the Peruvian government to replace Aerolineas Peruanas SAPSA and military controlled SATCO as the national airline. The airline was privatised July 1981. In 1990 Aeromexico purchased a forty-seven per cent stake in Aeroperu. Aeroperu had financial difficulties throughout its life and in 1996 suffered two major losses of aircraft due to negligence. The airline ceased operations in March 1999. The airline is listed as having operated three TriStars.

Air Afrique - West Africa
It was a Pan-African airline that was mainly owned by many West African countries for most of its history. It was established as the official transnational carrier for francophone West and Central Africa because many of these countries did not have the

SE-DSD of Air Ops under short-term lease to Air Afrique at London Heathrow. *(Richard Vandervord)*

capability to create and maintain a national airline. The headquarters in Abidjan, Ivory Coast.

Air Afrique began a steady decline in the 1980s, yet many years later the company was still considered the most reputable carrier in West Africa and even one of the top five airlines of Africa. Poor management, corruption, and the downturn in the aviation industry after the 11 September 2001 attacks led the airline to a crisis that ended with its liquidation in early 2002. It is listed as having briefly operated one TriStar.

Air Algérie

The origins of this airline can be traced to Compagnie Generale de Transports Aeriens CGT, which provided scheduled passenger service in Algeria and between Algeria and France. The airline did not start to operate as Air Algerie until 1953 when the above-mentioned company took over Compagnie Air Transport. At this time, Douglas DC-3s and DC-4s formed the backbone of its fleet; both types were retired in 1971. In 1962 Algeria became an independent country and a year later new Algeria government took a controlling interest in Air Algerie. The 1970s were most turbulent for the airline. First, the fleet was modernized with the purchase of 737's and 727's, and the Algerian government took over the airline in 1972. In 1974 the Government purchased the remaining shares still owned by Air France, and Air Algerie became effectively nationalized. The airline's first wide-body was Airbus A300, which they leased in 1974. In 1984, Air Algiers spun off its domestic service and formed a separate domestic division called Inter Air Services.

TF-ABG of Atlanta Iceland seen at London Heathrow. *(Richard Vandervord)*

TF-ABM in what is left of Air Atlanta colours is parted out at Pinal Airpark, Arizona. *(Richard Vandervord)*

Air Canada's C-FTNA on lease to Air France. *(Kim Bolton Collection)*

In 2004 Air Algerie retired its last Boeing 727, which together with 737 accounted for the majority of business since their introduction in 1971 and 1972, respectively. In 2005 first Airbus A330 entered service. It is listed as having operated eight TriStars.

Air Atlanta- Iceland

One of the largest ACMI lease provider with over 1000 employees and fleet of thirty aircraft. Thua company was founded by Captain Arngrimur Johannsson and his wife. Air Atlanta provides both passenger and cargo leases and specialized in wide-body aircraft. A large portion of its business are Hadj leases to airlines serving the Muslim world, but the company also provided its own passenger and cargo charters since 1992. In 2004 Air Atlanta purchased the majority shares of UK charter airline Excel Airways. In 2005 Air Atlanta acquired another Icelandic airline Islandsflug through its holding company Avion Group. A year later, Avion Group acquired French charter operator Star Airlines. The airline is listed as having operated eleven TriStars.

Air Charter Express - Ghana

Meridian Airways is a Ghanaian registered cargo airline based in Ostend-Brugge Airport, Belgium. They started operations as Air Charter Express in 2007 with a Douglas DC-8-63/AF. They were operating two DC-8s on cargo charter flights from Ostend Airport to the Middle East. The airline also operated charter flights for the British Ministry of Defence from RAF Lyneham. Two new DC-8-63F's arrived at Ostend Airport with Meridian Air colours. In 2009, Air Charter Express was renamed Meridian Airways. It is listed as operating one TriStar.

Air France - France

Air France operated one TriStar - C-FTNA - on lease from Air Canada from 1989 until 1991.

Air India - India

First called Tata Air Line, after one of its founders, Air India made its maiden flight in October 1932 to Karachi from Madras with de Havilland Moth. In July 1946, the airline adopted its current title Air

V2-LEK in Air India markings at London Heathrow. *(Richard Vandervord)*

India. In 1948 airline flew its first international flight to London by way of Cairo and Geneva with a Lockheed Constellation. Air India was nationalised in 1953 - in 1960 first Boeing 707 joined the fleet and put Air India into the jet age. Boeing 747's came in 1971. Air India traditionally concentrated on international traffic, passenger as well as cargo. The airline leased Ilyushin IL-76s and DC-8s as cargo machines and operated a scheduled cargo network. Air India has an extensive network connecting India with Gulf states to cater to India's migrant workers. Its network includes major cities in Europe, North America, Australia, East Africa and the Far East. In January 1986, Air India received its first Airbus A310. In 2005 Air India established its low-cost carrier subsidiary name Air India Express which operates from thirty-three destinations in India to the Gulf States and Singapore. It is utilised primarily by migrant workers. In 2007 first Boeing 777s arrived, beginning long haul fleet renewal. The airline is listed as having operated two TriStars.

Air Luxor

The airline began its operations as an executive jet charter owned by Mirpuri family. This operation was transformed into a charter airline in 1997. The executive jet operations became the core of Netjets European expansion. Air Luxor started scheduled airline operations in 2001. The airline offered long-haul flights to Africa and Brazil and also operated feeder service from Paris Orly to its hub in Lisbon. Air Luxor is listed as having operated three TriStars. The airline faced financial difficulties and its air operation certificate was withdrawn in October 2006 along with some of its fleet being impounded. The airline was sold to Canadian Investment Company Longstock Financial Group and was rebranded to HiFly Airlines. Plans to operate under HiFly brand were already in place before the Mirpuri family sold the bankrupt airline.

Air Margarita - Venezuela

Air Margarita operated between Santiago Mariño Caribbean International Airport, Venezuela and Miami International Airport, Florida with a Tristar leased from Caledonian and a DC.9 that never entered service. The airline is listed as having operated two TriStars.

Air Mauritius - Mauritius

The national airline of Mauritius commenced inter-island operations almost five years after its foundation using Piper Navajos aircraft. In its first five years Air Mauritius was a handling agent only. The airline's first independent international flight was operated in 1977 with leased Boeing 707 from British Airways. Later, in November 1984, the airline leased a Boeing 747SP from South African Airways and flew it on its inauguration flight to London. In December 2006, Air Mauritius received its first Airbus A340-300. In April 1988, Air Mauritius received two Boeing 767 to replace 747SPs. It is listed as using one TriStar.

Air Ops - Sweden

The charter airline started operations after Air Sweden's collapse in 1993. The company was registered in Honduras but operated from Sweden and later acquired a Swedish AOC. Operations commenced using one Lockheed L-1011 Tristar. Air Ops specialized in ad hoc leases to other carriers, including United Nations humanitarian and military flights. The company shut down in May 1995. After that, a new company was formed around its assets called Air Ops International, which lasted only for a few months. The airline is listed as having operated nine Tristars.

Air Rum - Sierra Leone

Little is known of this operator, apart from the fact that it is listed as having operated five TriStars.

SE-DSB in full Air Ops markings at London Heathrow. *(Richard Vandervord)*

Ground engineers work on air transat's C-GTSZ between services.

Air Scandic - UK
Air Scandic was an airline from Jersey, Channel Islands, operating charter flights for various UK tour operators, most of which operated out of Manchester Airport. It is listed as having operated one TriStar.

Air Transat - Canada
Air transat is based in Montreal, Quebec became that country's third-largest airline, operating scheduled and charter flights, serving sixty destinations in twenty-five countries. Air transat is owned and operated by Transat AT Inc. an international, vertically integrated tour operator with nearly twenty business units in right countries. The company is headquartered in Montreal, Quebec, Canada.

Transat was founded in the early 1980s by Jean-Marc Eustache, Lina De Cesare and Philippe Sureau as 'Traffic Voyages'. The company was a wholesaler specializing in travel from Québec to France.

In 1987, the company changed its name to Transat and was listed on the stock exchange through an initial public offering that generated $8.25 million. The company used the proceeds to establish its own airline, Air transat, founded by François Legault with other business partners such as Jean-Marc Eustache, Philippe Sureau, Lina de Cesare, Yvon Lecavalier, and Pierre Ménard.

Air transat made its inaugural flight on 14 November 1987, travelling from Montreal to Acapulco. Six years later, Air transat assumed defunct Nationair's maintenance base and aircraft.

The airline then embarked on a series of acquisitions to solidify its position as an outgoing tour operator in Canada and France and develop new destination markets. In 1988, Transat expanded its retail distribution presence with the acquisition of an interest in the franchisor Consultour.

The company had broken into the French market very early on with Vacances Transat (France), the largest tour operator offering travel to Canada, and soon expanded within France, the UK and the rest of Europe. It acquired French tour operator Look Voyages in 1996, Greek tour operator Tourgreece in 2001, British tour operator Canadian Affair in 2006, and French tour operator

9L-LOC of Air Universal in front of a threatening sky at London Heathrow. *(Richard Vandervord)*

CS-TEB of euroAtlantic airways comes into London Heathrow. *(Richard Vandervord)*

Amplitude Internationale which specialized in travel to Tunisia.

Legault left the company in 1997 with no forewarning after a dispute with business partners, who only found out after the fact.

Air Universal - Sierra Leone
This airline from Sierra Leone is listed as having operated two TriStars.

Air Zarco - EuroAtlantic Airways
euro Atlantic airways was founded by Tomaz Metello the majority stakeholder, and the remaining shares are owned by Grupo Pestana and CEO. Euro Atlantic was founded as Air Zarco and specialised in ad hoc ACMI and dry leases and charters. In May 2000 airline changed its name to Euro Atlantic Airways. It is listed as operating one TriStar.

Aircraft Machinery Works (AMW) - Chad
Believed to have been used as arms running outfit. CEO: Duane Egli. Listed as having operated one TriStar.

Airline History Museum - USA
Preserves one TriStar.

Algerian Government
Listed as having operated one TriStar.

American Trans Air - ATA Airlines - USA
Founded as Ambassadair in 1973. First Flight as American Trans Air 1981. Operated scheduled charters" for tour operators, as well as ad hoc and military charters. In 1999 ATA purchased Chicago Express and turned it to its feeder airline at Midway. A year later, an order for thirty-nine Boeing 737-800s was announced, and ATA entered the low-cost scheduled market using Boeing 737NG and 757s. Its network grew rapidly from coast to coast. ATA entered bankruptcy 26 October 2004 and reduced fleet and scheduled operation considerably. The company exited bankruptcy with financing from Matlin Patterson. ATA became a private airline owned by ATA Holdings. In 2004 ATA and Southwest Airlines agreed to codeshare their flights,

American Trans Air wore a number of different schemes in their time. This one on N190T... *(Richard Vandervord)*

...and this on N164T when their changed their name to ATA! *(Richard Vandervord)*

and ATA became Southwest Airlines Travel charter and leisure provider. Its scheduled flights were cut, and the airline focused on its Military and leisure charters flights. Hawaii and the Caribbean became its major markets. The airline sold most of its slots at Midway to Southwest and withdrew from the Indianapolis market. It also sold its Ambassadair Travel Club. In 2007 ATA Holdings changed its name to Global Aero Logistics and acquired World Air Holdings (World Airways, North American Airlines). The planned deal of acquiring DC-10s from Northwest for its military contract fell apart as the decision was made to transfer those to World Airways instead. Further cuts in scheduled service were made in 2008, and loss of military business, as well as rising fuel prices, caused the airline to file bankruptcy again and cease operations in April 2008. The airline is listed as having operated twenty-seven TriStars.

Antrak Air - Ghana

Scheduled passenger services. CEO: Asoma Banda Listed as operating one TriStar.

APA International Air - Dominican Republic

APA International Air was an airline based in Santo Domingo, Dominican Republic, that was operational between 1980 and 2001. The airline is listed as having operated two Tristars.

Arrow Air - USA

Arrow Air was formed in 1980 as a subsidiary of International Air Leases, which was owned by George Batchelor. It received CAB authority in March 1980 to provide charter services. Cargo charters began in March 1981, with scheduled cargo services beginning in August. By the end of August, the company entered the passenger charter

OB-1545 of APA, based on a previous Faucett scheme. *(Richard Vandervord)*

N306GB undergoes conversion into a civilian freighter at Marshall Aerospace, Cambridge for Arrow Air. *(Marshall Aerospace)*

business. Scheduled passenger flights began in July 1982. The airline did operate a passenger DC-8 in sub-service for LOT for a year beginning August 1987. Passenger charters resumed in 1993. A former employee turned whistleblower caused another investigation in 1995, which resulted in the airline's grounding in March. Cargo operations resumed in June. Arrow was sold to Fine Corp. (parent of Fine Air) in April 1999, but both airlines were operated separately. In September 2000, Fine Corp. filed for bankruptcy; in 2001, the two airlines were merged under the Arrow Air certificate, and began trading as Fine Air Services. In May 2002, the airline was sold to an investor group which brought it out of bankruptcy and reverted to the Arrow Air name. The company re-entered bankruptcy on 28 January 2004, and was sold to a new investor group in June, once again exiting bankruptcy. In January 2005, it began using the trade name Arrow Cargo. In 2008 it entered into an alliance with MatlinPatterson Global Opportunities, a private equity investment firm, which owned Global Aviation Holdings (which owned World Airways and North American Airlines) and had controlled VarigLog. Due to heavy losses, the airline ceased operations on 30 June 2010 and filed for bankruptcy. It was listed as having operated three TriStars.

Aviation Development Company - Nigeria

Although the parent company Aviation Development company was set up already in 1984, the airline

Visiting London Heathrow is SE-DTC of Blue Scandanavia. *(Richard Vandervord)*

operations did not commence until January 1990. ADC operated scheduled domestic service with regional flights to neighbouring Freetown, Accra and Banjul. ADC was the first Nigerian airline to trade publicly when its issues were floated on Nigeria's Stock Exchange in 1994. On 29 October 2006, one of its 737s crashed after takeoff near Abuja. Nigerian authorities ordered the suspension of its operations following the accident. Its AOC license was withdrawn in May 2007 after ADC failed mandatory re-capitalization order by Nigeria's civil aviation administration. Listed as having operated one TriStar

AWA African West Air - Senegal
Listed as operating one TriStar.

Bismillah Airlines - Bangladesh
Listed as having operated one TriStar.

Blue Scandanavia
A charter passenger airline formed in 1985 as a charter subsidiary of Transwede Airways. In 1996 airline was acquired by tour agency Fritidsresor and renamed Blue Scandinavia. In 1998 Britannia Airways acquired a majority stake in the enterprise and its name changed yet again - this time Britannia Nordic. After Fritidsresor tour operator was acquired by Thomson tours of UK in 2005, the airline was operating as Thomson but was renamed Tuifly Nordic in May 2006. TUIfly specialises in IT charters from Scandinavia to resorts in the Mediterranean, Canary Islands, Caribbean and Southeast Asia, mainly on behalf of Fritidsresor. The airline is listed as having operated one TriStar.

Boeing Capital Corporation - USA
Wholly owned subsidiary of Boeing Company. BCC provides financing and leasing services primarily to support Boeing's other businesses. The company has offices in Hong Kong, Los Angeles and Moscow and its headquarters are in Renton, Washington. Known to have operated two TriStars.

Bourtuqalieh Air - Jordan
This airline is listed as operating a Tristar.

Caribbean Winds Airways - Antigua and Barbuda
This airline is listed as operating one TriStar.

Chile Inter Airlines - Chile
The airline is listed as operating two TriStars.

Classic Airways - UK.
ACMI operator using British World Airlines AOC certificate. Listed as having operated two TriStars.

CSDS Aircraft Sales & Leasing - USA
The company focus is on buying, selling, leasing aircraft, helicopters and material to global clients. Has offices in USA, Singapore and Paraguay. Listed as operating six TriStars.

Damascene Airways - Syria
This airline is listed as having operated one TriStar.

Dragonair
Hong Kong Dragon Airline Ltd. is a scheduled passenger airline based in Hong Kong and operating domestic and international flights throughout the region. Dragonair was founded by Kuang-Piu Chao. Since 2006 Dragonair is owned by Swire Group Ltd., the parent company in Cathay Pacific. Dragonair commenced operations in July 1985 on a scheduled route from Hong Kong to Kota Kinabalu in Malaysia using Boeing

All is not as it seems - N765BE in the colours of the ficticious airline Northeast, for the movie *Die Hard 2* starrring Bruce Willis. The aircraft was being opeerated by Hawaiian Airlines at the time. *(Matt Black Collection)*

V2-LEO of Caribbean Winds Airways wearing a basic scheme. *(Richard Vandervord)*

737-200 aircraft. In 1990 Swire Group purchased a controlling interest in Dragonair. The long-time foes Cathay Pacific and Dragonair have become sister companies. Economic development in mainland China fuelled Dragonair's growth. The airline operated Lockheed Tristars transferred from Cathay Pacific on its trunk China mainland routes.

Beginning May 1993, Dragonair underwent massive fleet renewal when its first Airbus A320 arrived, followed by wide-body Airbus A330s in July 1995. In 2000 Dragonair ventured into all Cargo business. Dragonair planned long-haul expansion of its passenger service to the USA and Australia. This alarmed Cathay Pacific, and in September 2006, Dragonair became a subsidiary of Cathay Pacific. This resulted in its Cargo operations being transferred to Cathay Pacific and all long-haul plans had to be cancelled.

The airline was a member of IATA and an affiliate member of OneWorld airline alliance. The airline's bulk of business is on routes to secondary cities in mainland China and Taiwan. Dhaka, Bangalore, Kathmandu, Hanoi, Phuket, Kota Kinabalu, Pusan and Manila are served on its international network. The airline was listed as operating three TriStars.

Ducor World Airlines - Equatorial Guinea

Cargo charter airline replacing Liberia World Airways. Believed two have been used as arms running outfit. CEO: Duane Egli. Listed as having operated five TriStars.

Ecuatoriana

Ecuatoriana was the national airline of Ecuador. The airline was formed by private domestic and foreign (American) interest in 1957 as Compagnia Ecuatoriana de Aviacion. The airline commenced operations using Curtiss C-46s, DC-4s and DC-6s. Major restructuring commenced in July 1974 when it adopted a new corporate identity and changed its name to simple Ecuatoriana. The airline was nationalised at this time. The Ecuador Air Force was providing technical and managerial assistance. Airline traditional routes were from both of its hubs in Ecuador, Quito and Guayaquil to Panama City, Lima, Miami, New York, Caracas, Bogota and Santiago. In the 1970s, Ecuatoriana used Boeing 707s and 720s on its international routes, and some were painted in distinct abstract "psychedelic" colour schemes to compete with Braniff's colourful jets. In 1983 airline obtained its first wide-body aircraft, Douglas DC-10-30s, from Swissair. Ecuatoriana

C-FTNC on lease to Egyptair by Air Transat. *()*

opened routes to Madrid and Canada. The airline was mismanaged, had built a reputation of an unreliable airline, and by 1993 had to stop operations. Brazil's VASP bought fifty per cent interest in airline and restarted its operations in 1996 using Boeing 727s and a DC-10 from its fleet. In 2000 VASP sold its stake to Lan Chile. Ecuatoriana leased Boeing 767s from Lan Chile. In 2004 airline ownership changed hands again, and Bolivia's LAB became the owner together with the Ecuadorian government. LAB was at the point of collapse at this time as well and could not help Ecuatoriana survive. All operations were suspended in 2005, and the company was liquidated. The airline is listed as having operated one TriStar.

Egyptair - Egypt
The national airline was founded in 1932 as Misrair Airwork. The first flight was conducted in 1933 on domestic service from Cairo to Mersa Matruh (Alexandria) using de Havilland DH.83 Dragon aircraft. Misrair changed its name in August 1960 to United Arab Airlines when it merged with Syrian Airways. This union lasted only a year. The present title was adopted in October 1971. In 1960 Egyptair became the first African or Middle Eastern airline to fly jet - de Havilland Comet IV. Egyptair's network stretches from Tokyo, Osaka, Seoul, Bangkok, Almaty, Beijing, to New York, Montreal and Johannesburg in the South. Accra, Kano and Lagos are served in West Africa. In Europe, Egyptair serves Berlin, Frankfurt, Dusseldorf, Paris, London, Budapest, Moscow, Amsterdam, Geneva, Madrid, Milan, Rome, Vienna, Istanbul, Larnaca and Athens. The airline is listed as having operated two TriStars.

Evergreen International Airlines. - USA
Evergreen International can trace its history back to 1926, when Johnson Flying Service began operations from Missoula, Montana, as a flying school. Following World War Two it operated C-47s in smoke-jumping services and later moved into the aerial firefighting business. It entered the passenger and cargo charter business in the 1950s, flying Ford TriMotors, a DC-2, DC-3s and C-46s. Its name was changed to Johnson Air, then Johnson International Airlines. In 1975 it was sold to Del Smith and was merged with Intermountain Aviation, a former CIA front company based at the old Marana Army Air Field. The new name of the merged company became Evergreen International Aviation. The airline began passenger and cargo charters and briefly operated scheduled passenger service in the late 1970s. In 1981 EIA begun scheduled freight service for UPS and continued to do so until UPS established its own airline in 1988. It also developed a Boeing 747 airborne tanker for fire fighting. Today, EIA operates ACMI freight services as well as contract cargo flight for the US military. It is a subsidiary of Evergreen International Aviation, which operates Evergreen Helicopters and also owns a museum at the

Faucett - Peru OB-1504 in the early colour scheme. *()*

company's headquarters in McMinnville, Oregon. The company is listed as having operated one TriStar.

Fars Air Qeshm
Qeshm Air was an Iranian airline; it had its headquarters in Tehran, Iran and operates scheduled domestic and international passenger services as well as charter flights. The airline was founded in 1993 as Faraz Qeshm Airline. It established its services by leasing airplanes from other airlines. The company's first routes were from Tehran to Qeshm, and from Tehran to Dubai. By the year 2000, Qeshm Air had seven aircraft in its fleet.

Faucett
The airline was established by an American, Elmer J Faucett and a group of Peruvian businessmen. Operations started on 15 September 1928, making Faucett one of the oldest airlines in the world. In its beginning airline served the domestic market with Stinson Detroiters. After World War Two, Douglas products DC-3, DC-4 and DC-6 were used. In April 1968 its first jet, a Boeing 727 secondhand from Braniff, was delivered. In 1971 a BAC 1-11 was acquired. The airline focused on the domestic market and also provided charter cargo and passenger service abroad. Panama and Miami were served frequently using Douglas DC-8s in cargo configuration. In 1982 Aeronaves del Peru took a controlling interest in the airline. Faucett declared bankruptcy in November 1999 and liquidated thereafter. The airline is listed as having operated four TriStars.

Fine Air - USA
Fine Air was founded by Frank and Barry Fine, who owned the aircraft leasing and maintenance firm Agro Air Associates. It received its operating certificate in November 1992, and began to operate cargo services from Miami to the Caribbean and Central and South America. The airline went public in August 1997, but a plane crash three days later sent shares tumbling, forcing the company to void the stock sale and repay investors. As a result of the accident, the airline suspended operations on 4 September while the FAA reviewed its operations which it resumed in late October. Fine Air entertained the idea of acquiring Southern Air Transport in July 1998, but the two sides could not agree on terms. In April 1999, Fine's parent acquired Arrow Air from International Air Leases. On 26 September 2000, the parent and both subsidiaries filed for bankruptcy due to high fuel costs and heavy debt load associated with the Arrow acquisition. The airline merged into Arrow Air in February 2001,

Left: Almarwa of Fars Air Qeshm with SPA on the nose-wheel door.

Below: OB-1504 of Faucett in the later, dramatic red and white colour scheme. *Richard Vandervord)*

however, the merged airline traded as Fine Air Services. Listed and operating four TriStars.

Five Star Airlines

Five Star was an airline of The Interface Group which operated GWV Travel, a major tour operator. It purchased two L-1011s from TWA and planned to operate these airliners during the winter charter season, then lease them back to TWA during the summer. During the winter 1984-85 season, the airliners were leased to IASCO, which operated them for Five Star. In May 1985, it received CAB authority to operate domestic and overseas charters. The airline operated for four winter seasons and suspended operations for the season on May 15, 1989. It elected not to continue operations but leased its airliners to American Trans Air during the winter season for operation as Five Star.

Garuda Indonesian Airlines

In 1938 KLM formed the Indonesian airline KNILM. In December 1949 Dutch government and Indonesia government formed Indonesia's national airline Garuda with the assets of KNILM which ceased to exist. Like many other airlines, Garuda started operations with war surplus Douglas DC-3s. Garuda also used Catalinas, and in September 1950 first Convair CV-240 joined the fleet. In July 1954 Indonesian government took full ownership of the airline. The first turboprop, a Lockheed Electra, was delivered in January 1961. Garuda was also one of a handful of airlines to order Convair CV-990 jets, of which the first example arrived in September 1963. The same year Garuda acquired domestic operator Merpati Nusantara, but preserved the brand. In 1965 Garuda inaugurated first European destination, Amsterdam. Indonesia's historical ties to the Netherlands made Garuda a loyal Fokker customer. First Fokker F-27 joined the fleet in 1969 and was used on a domestic network. Same year Douglas DC-9s began to arrive. In August 1971 first Fokker F-28. The type became the backbone of Garuda's domestic operations for the next twenty years, and Garuda was the largest Fokker operator in Asia.The first wide-body aircraft was a leased Douglas DC-10 that joined the fleet in 1973 and replaced the DC-8s on Garuda's long-haul routes. Throughout 1980s Garuda flew a mixture of DC-10s, Airbus A300s and Boeing 747s to Australia, Europe with technical stops in the Persian Gulf, Saudi Arabia, Japan, Korea, China and the Philippines. The regional network includes destinations in Malaysia, Singapore, Thailand and Vietnam. In 2002 Garuda was put on a list of airlines banned from operating in the European Union, effectively ending Garuda's traditional routes to Frankfurt, Paris and Amsterdam. In 2009 Garuda approved to fly in Europe and starts again in 2010 Europe flight to Amsterdam via Dubai(In 2012 changed to Abu Dhabi with A330-200.. This airline is listed as having operated two TriStars.

Globe Jet Airlines

This ACMI Leasing company based in Lebanon is listed as having operated four TriStars.

Goliaf Air - Sao Tome & Principe

Listed as operating one TriStar.

Hawaiian Airlines - USA

Hawaiian Airlines can trace its history to Inter-Island Airways, founded in 1929 to provide mail and passenger service throughout the Hawaii Islands. The airline commenced operations in November same year between Honolulu and Maui using Sikorsky S.38 flying boat, this marked first commercial flight between Hawaii islands. The current name was adopted in 1941. The same year Douglas DC-3s joined the fleet. Airline's first jet was a Douglas DC-9 introduced in 1966. Hawaiian traditionally focused on intrastate routes, but in 1984 airline introduced long-haul flights starting to Micronesia. The airline received its first wide-body aircraft, a Lockheed Tristar, in March 1985 and introduced flights to West Coast. In 2003 Hawaiian filed for bankruptcy

N763BE of Hawaiian Air, with Suntrips of California promotion on the vertical fin. *(Richard Vandervord)*

protection. The airline retired its fleet of Douglas DC-10s, which replaced Tristars in early 1990s with leased and brand new Boeing 767s. It was able to restructure its labour obligations and emerged from bankruptcy in June 2005. Hawaiian serves west coast gateways as well as Manila, Sydney, Papette and Pago Pago in American Samoa. The bulk of its business is still intrastate island traffic. The airline is listed as having operated eight TriStars.

Holiday Airlines - Turkey

Holiday Airlines began operations in the summer of 1994 using Airbus A320 aircraft serving mostly the German tourist market. At the end of 1994, Holiday Airlines had to cease operations when two of the A320s were repossessed temporarily, but services were restarted in 1995 using two leased Airbus A300B4. Holiday Airlines was in such need of an aircraft to meet the demand that they used the Boeing 727-200, the Tupolev Tu-154 and the Yakovlev Yak-42. By September 1996, Holiday Airlines was refused rights to fly to its key market Germany. By November 1996 the company ran out of cash and had to cease all operations. The airline is listed as having operated one TriStar.

IASCO

IASCO began operations in 1959, providing flight crews to foreign operators, flight training at Napa (CA) airport, aircraft leasing, and air-taxi cargo services. It operated a fleet of Citations, Falcons, and Cessna Titans for Emery Express and Learjets on a Los Angeles to Columbus route for Purolator Courier. In April 1980, it was authorised to replace the Lears with a 737. In October 1983, it received CAB authority to operate scheduled passenger and cargo authority. IASCO operated several 727s for Emery and Burlington, neither of which had its own FAA operating certificates. It also operated a pair of TriStars for Five Star Airlines. In April 1985 began trading as Spirit of America and a year later it acquired CAM Air International, but the airlines continued to operate separately. It lost both Emery and Burlington contracts in 1989 and ceased operations on 16 June.

Iberia - Spain

The airline was founded by Horacio Echeberrieta and Deutsche Luft Hansa, which held a stake in the new airline until September 1944, when Iberia was nationalised. The first route from Madrid to Barcelona was operated in December 1927 using ex DLH Rohrbach Roland. Year later, Barcelona to Berlin flights were inaugurated with stops in Marseille, Geneva, Zurich, Stuttgart and Erfurt. However, this company was integrated into Lineas Aereas Subvencionadas SA (CLASSA) - a state-owned company, in 1928. Iberia was formed again in June 1940 from its predecessors LAPE (Lineas Aereas Postales Espanolas, which itself was founded in 1935) and started operations like many others with Douglas DC-3s, which were augmented after the war with DC-4s. The airline, from its beginning, concentrated on serving the Spanish speaking world, namely west Saharan Africa and the South and Central Americas. Buenos Aires and Montevideo were served from 1946 and North America from 1954. In the 1950s, Convair CV-440s were used on European network and Douglas DC-4s on Iberia flights to the Americas and Africa. In July 1961, the first jet joined the fleet, a Douglas DC-8, which was put on the Madrid - New York route on 2 July 1961. A year later, the Sud Caravelle arrived and was used on Iberia's European network. The first wide-body aircraft, a Boeing 747, arrived in 1970. Iberia introduced Boeing 727s and Douglas DC-9s on its domestic and European network and Douglas DC-10s and Boeing 747s were used for long-haul work

SE-DPV of Air Ops in the colours of the short-lived Impala Air, taken around 1994. *(Richard Vandervord)*

throughout the 1970s and 1980s. In the 1990s fleet modernisation took place when DC-9s and Boeing 727s were replaced with MD-87s, Airbus A320s and A319s. The long haul fleet was replaced with Airbus A340s. In 2001 airline was privatised. Since 1999 it was a member of Oneworld airline alliance. Iberia also provides maintenance for other airlines. The airline is listed as having operated two TriStars.

Impala Air - Burundi
This airline is listed as having operated one TriStar.

International Air Leases Inc.
An aircraft and aircraft engine leasing company, listed as having operated eight TriStars.

International Air Services / Air Express Liberia - Liberia
Listed as having operated two TriStars.

Istanbul Airlines
This airline is listed as having operated two TriStars.

Jordan Aviation
Jordan Aviation is the airline arm of JATE Group which owns Suday Travel agency, Red Sea hotel in Aqaba, Al Shoruk Construction Company, Philadelphia Transportation (a Bus company in Jordan), Alexandria Airlines of Egypt and Bremenfly airline of Bremen, Germany. Jordan Aviation provides charter flights for tour operators, ACMI leases to other carriers and pilot training through its sister company Arabia Professional Skills Development Company or APSD. Jordan Aviation is owned by its CEO Mohamed Al-Khashman. The airline is listed as having operated one TriStar.

Kallat El Saker Air - Libya
This airline is listed as having operated one TriStar.

Kampuchea Airlines
Listed as operating eight TriStars.

Kitty Hawk International - American International Airways - Connie Kalitta Services
Founded by drag racer Conrad Kalitta to haul parts for the automotive industry. Originally began as a contract freight operation as Connie Kalitta Services, a one-man operation utilising Cessna 310s. In 1991 CKS acquired the certificate of defunct American International Airways and changed its name to American International Airways. The new AOC gave it passenger-carrying authority. It was sold to the Kitty Hawk Group in September 1997. Renamed Kitty Hawk International, Boeing 747s, L-1011s and DC-8s remained on this certificate, while 727s and DC-9s were transferred to Kitty Hawk Air Cargo. Kitty Hawk International went bankrupt in 2000, and Kitty Hawk International was closed. Some assets were sold to start-up Kalitta Air because Conrad Kalitta wanted to resurrect the airline he had built up over the decades.

Kuwait Airways
The flag carrier and national airline of Kuwait was established by Kuwait ruler and a group of Kuwaiti businessmen in 1953 as Kuwait National Airways. Operations commenced in April 1954 between Basra and Cairo using Douglas DC-3s. The airline received its first turboprop aircraft in September 1958 when a Vickers Viscount was delivered. It changed its name to Kuwait Airways the same year, and BOAC took over management. In March 1962 the first jet service using a De Havilland Comet 4C was inaugurated on route Kuwait - London. Private interest was bought out in 1964, and the state of Kuwait became the sole owner. In 1968 first Boeing 707 joined the fleet. The first wide-body, a Boeing 747, joined the fleet in July 1978. This jet enabled Kuwait Airways to introduce long-haul routes as far as New York and Manila. In 1983 first Airbus A310 and Airbus A300 arrived, followed three years later by Boeing 767. The airline suffered a great setback in 1991 as a result of the Iraqi Invasion. Most of its fleet was destroyed, and all operations were suspended. After the war, Kuwait

N103CK of Kallita/American International Airways. *()*

Airways rebuilt its former network, and new aircraft were ordered, namely Airbus A320s, A340s and Boeing 777s. Listed as operating one TriStar.

LAM Linhas Aereas Mocambique

LAM is the national airline of Mozambique and was established in November 1980 as a replacement of DETA Mozambique, which was founded in 1936. The state enterprise was transformed to a public company in 1998, but the government of Mozambique retained ninety-one per cent of shares, with the remaining nine per cent going to the employees. The airline operates a domestic network and serves international destinations Luanda, Dar-Es-Salam, Nairobi and Johannesburg. LAM has code-shared agreement with TAP on flights to Lisbon. LAM is a member of IATA. The airline is listed as having operated one TriStar.

Liberia World Airlines - Liberia.

Arms running outfit headquartered in Gibraltar and using a Liberian AOC. Renamed Ducor World Airlines 8/01. CEO: Duane Egli. Listed as operating one TriStar.

Lignes Aériennes Congolaises - Democratic Republic of the Congo

Listed as having operated one TriStar

LUZAir

Luzair - Transportes Aéreos, S.A. is an airline based in Lisbon, Portugal, specializing in wet lease and ad-hoc charter operations. It was founded in 1997. The airline is listed as having operated two TriStars. In 2000, Luzair developed into an airline consulting and brokerage business. Worldwide ACMI charter.

Mahan Air

The first private airline (Mol-Al-Movahedin Credit Union) in Iran commenced operations in May 1993 with a fleet of Tupolev Tu-154s on domestic routes. The airline received its first wide-body aircraft, an Airbus A300, in 1999 and expanded internationally with flights to Dubai. The airline also specializes in air charters. In 2008 Mahan experienced rapid expansion with flights to Istanbul, Dusseldorf, Delhi, Bangkok and Denpasar. This airline is listed as having operated one TriStar.

Millon Air - USA

Owned by Ebsco Corp, Cargo. Listed as operating one TriStar.

NEBA North East Bolivian Airways - Bolivia

Listed as having operated one TriStar

Northeast Airlines - Swaziland

Listed as operating one TriStar.

Nordic East Airways - Sweden

A passenger charter airline operating charter flights throughout Europe, Middle East and North Africa under its own brand, inclusive tour operators as well as for other airlines, namely LTU and Deutsche BA. Airline was founded by Gunar Ohlsson in 1991. Airline started operations using Douglas MD-80's leased from SAS. In 1995 airline acquired its first wid-body aircraft, an L-1011-1 Tristar. The airline is listed as operating three TriStars.

Nordic European Airlines - Norway

Nordic European Airlines began its life in 1991 as Nordic East Airways using Douglas DC-9-21 aircraft on charters to the Mediterranean region. In 1992 the airline received two MD-80s. Because they needed an aircraft with a longer range than the MD-80s, the airline acquired Boeing 737-300 aircraft and the DC-9s and MD-80s were returned to the leasing companies while additionally a 737-400 was acquired. In 1995 Nordic East acquired two Lockheed L-1011s from Cathay Pacific, and with those, and a third aircraft added later, the charter work was expanded. The business comprised sub-charter duties for other carriers like the German LTU. The airline changed its name to Nordic European Airlines - NEA at the end of 1996, but by the next year, the airline was in financial difficulties and operations

SE-DTC of Nordic East. It was formerly VR-HOH of Cathay Pacific. *(Richard Vandervord)*

SE-DVI of Novair comes in for another landing. The airliner was formerly JY-AGJ of Alia Rya Jordanian Airlines. *()*

were suspended in March 1998, with the international business of the airline in receivership. The airline is listed as operating two TriStars.

Novair - Nova Airlines AB - Sweden
All inclusive tour charter operator wholly owned by Kuoni Travel Ltd. Listed as operating four TriStars.

Omega Air Ltd - Netherlands Antilles
Listed as having operated one TriStar

Orient Thai Airlines
The airline can trace its beginnings to Cambodia International Airlines, founded by current chairman Udom Tantiprasongchai. It started scheduled passenger flights in the mid-1990s. CIA was ordered to leave Cambodia, and the company moved to Thailand and operated briefly as Orient Express Air. The airline since changed its name to Orient Thai Airlines and started to operate charter flights in Southeast Asia, including South Korea and Japan. The majority of its charter operations serve the leisure travel market to and from Thailand's resorts. It also provides Hadj flights on behalf of other carriers, including Air India and Saudia. The airline is listed as having operated nine L-1011s. Thai Orient also provides logistic support to UN. Orient Thai and its low-cost domestic subsidiary One-Two-Go has earned a bad reputation from its customers and numerous complaints and warnings, including suspension of AOC from civil aviation authorities in Thailand, Japan, South Korea and Hong Kong. Poor customer service, inadequate pilot training and safety procedures are often cited. The airline operates a scheduled route between Hong Kong and Bangkok. The airline also ventured into the all-cargo charter business.

Peach Air - UK
All-inclusive tour charter airline owned by Carlson Leisure Group, which also owned Caledonian Airways. Peach Air commenced operations for the tour operator Goldcrest in spring 1997. Carlson Leisure Group was acquired by Thomas Cook Group and as a result Peach Air was integrated into Caledonian Airways. The airline is listed as operating three TriStars.

Phoenix Aviation - Kyrgyzstan
This airline is listed as having operated one TriStar.

TF-ABE of Air Atlanta Icelandic, but in the colours of Peach Air.
(Matt Black Collection)

PLUNA - Primeras Líneas Uruguayas de Navegación Aérea

The national airline of Uruguay wholly owned by the government of Uruguay. The company was founded in 1935 by local businessmen led by Alberto and Jorge Marquez Vaeza and British investors. Operations commenced on 20 November 1936 on Montevideo - Artigas using De Havilland Dragon secured with the help of British ambassador to Uruguay at the time, Sir Millington-Drake. After the war, Douglas DC-3s were purchased and PLUNAs network included destinations in Argentina, Brazil, Paraguay and Bolivia. PLUNA was nationalized in 1951. In June 1958, the first turboprop joined the fleet - Vickers Viscount. After PLUNA obtained its first Boeing 707 in 1985, intercontinental expansion was possible, and New York and Miami were added to the network, followed by Madrid. In 1994 VARIG purchased a forty-nine per cent stake in PLUNA, which at this time faced considerable financial difficulty. After VARIG's own bankruptcy in 2005, the Uruguay government purchased VARIG's share and became ninety-eight per cent owner of PLUNA again. PLUNA is listed as operating one TriStar.

Rich International Airways

A charter airline founded as an all-cargo operator in 1969. Since 1982, the airline also operated passenger charters. Rich International operated worldwide with the bulk of its capacity on trans Atlantic charters. By 1984 airline ran into financial problems. FAA revoked its AOC due to maintenance irregularities, and the company entered chapter 13 bankruptcy protection. Entrepreneur George E. Batchelor purchased the airline and turned it around, enabling the company to exit Chapter 13 by 1991. The company held US Military Air Command contract and operated wide-body L-1011 Tristar's that were made available after Eastern's bankruptcy. Again in 1996 FAA cited maintenance violations and revoked its license. FAA might have had overreacted as the violations were minor. Operations ceased on 1 September 1996. The company was liquidated by next summer. The airline is listed as having operated fifteen TriStars.

Rollins Air

Scheduled passenger and executive air charter service throughout Caribbean. Company was founded by Capt. Claudius Rollins. Company also provides full ground handling service at La Ceiba International airport. In the summer of 2010, Rollins Air operated charter flights to the World Cup in South Africa from Central America using a Lockheed Tristar.

Royal Aviation - Canada

Michel Leblanc founded the airline in 1991. Royal was acquired by Canada 3000 in 2001 in an all-stock deal. While the takeover/merger was touted in glowing terms in press releases, analysts quietly shared the opinion that Royal had few options and little time left based on the terms of the transaction. Michel Leblanc received Canada 3000 shares worth $84 million and became a Canada 3000 vice-chairman. Almost all of Royal Airlines aircraft was re-painted into the Canada 3000 livery. However, in the months after the merger with Royal Aviation, several of the former Royal Aviation aircraft had a mixed livery, with the Canada 3000 logo and Royal Aviation tail design to recognise the merger between the two airlines. Canada 3000 also purchased Royal Cargo, renaming it Canada 3000 cargo. Canada 3000 cargo was later sold off and became Cargojet Airways. Only a few months after the merger closed, Leblanc was fired from Canada 3000 in June 2001 in a bitter feud, as Canada 3000 filed a lawsuit against him for allegations of fraud and misrepresentation. However, the allegations were

Most certainly a hybrid colour scheme! SE-DPP of Air Ops with Hawaiian Airlines stripes and Sudan Airways titles on the forward fuselage. *(Richard Vandervord)*

Star Air's 9L-LDN on finals. *(Richard Vandervord)*

never proven in court, and Lelanc subsequently sold off all his shares of Canada 3000 before they stopped trading. In November 2001, the entire Canada 3000 company suddenly ceased operations with no warning for travellers or employees. The company filed for bankruptcy, citing a downturn in air travel during the weeks following the 11 September 2001 terrorist attacks in the United States. The airline is listed as operating three TriStars.

RAK Airlines
Airline founded by decree of the crown prince of Ras Al Khaimah was to start operations in late 2006. It planned to operate eight aircraft on scheduled passenger and cargo flights to Lebanon, India, Pakistan, Sri Lanka, Egypt and Iran. It was listed as operating one TriStar.

Royal Jordanian Air Force
Listed as having operated one TriStar.

Sky Eyes Airlines - Thailand
Listed as operating one TriStar.

Skygate - Netherlands
This airline is listed as having operated a TriStar.

Skygate International - Kyrgyzstan
Listed as having operated two TriStars.

SriLankan - Sri Lanka
The national airline and flag carrier of Sri Lanka can trace its history to Air Lanka, which was founded in 1979. The government of Sri Lanka was the sole owner of the airline until 1998 when the company was partially privatised. Emirates Airlines of Dubai purchased a forty per cent stake in the airline and gained management control of the airline. New brand Srilankan was introduced, and airline operations were streamlined. The airline is listed as having operated one TriStar.

Star Airlines
Worldwide IT charter operator. Airline was formed in 1995 as Société de Transport Aérien Régional by Cedric Pastrour and owned by Transat A.T. a Canada's tour operator which owns Air Transat. The airline was acquired in November 2006 by XL

Angola Airlines CS-TEC on a stand at London Heathrow. *(Richard Vandervord)*

Leisure Group of UK and transformed into its France subsidiary XL Airways France. In 2008 XL Leisure Group collapsed, but XL Airways France and XL Airways Germany were purchased by investment bank Straumur-Burdaras and continued operations. The airline is listed as having operated on TriStar.

Star Air - Gibraltar

Charter and ACMI Lease airline registered in Gibraltar with headquarters in Amman, and a base airport at Queen Alia International, Amman. It is lisated as having operated four TriStars.

Sudan Airways - Sudan

Government founded airline and flag carrier of Sudan. Operations commenced in July 1947 with DeHavilland DH.104 Doves, provided by Airwork Ltd of UK. In 1952 the airline put in service DC-3s and two years later operated its first International flight from Khartoum to Cairo. The first turboprop was a Vickers Viscount which entered service in January 1962. Sudan Airways was the first African airline to introduce the F-27 turboprop in January 1962. The first jet, a de Havilland Comet, was delivered in November 1962. The airline modernized again in 1974 when a Boeing 707 was delivered. Sudan Airways was banned from flying into the EU so its entire European network had to be abandoned. The airline is listed as having operated three TriStars.

TAAG Angola Airlines - TAAG Linhas Aereas de Angola

The flag carrier of Angola was formed as DTA and begun operations using De Havilland Dragon Rapides. In July 1940 the airline started its scheduled service. Domestic routes Luanda - Pointe Nore, Lobito - Mossamedes, Lobito - Nova Lisboa were established. In 1946 the first Douglas DC-3s joined the fleet and were in use until 1975. In 1951 DTA joined IATA. The first turboprop aircraft, a Fokker F-27 Friendship, joined the fleet in 1962. The airline adopted the current title TAAG in 1973 after Angola gained independence. In November 1975 it received its first jet, a Boeing 737. In 1977 TAAG leased its first Boeing 707 from British Caledonian. The same year TAAG also acquired Soviet-built Yakovlev Yak-40s and Antonov An-26s. In 1991 TAAG established its charter and air-taxi subsidiary Angola Air Charter. On 11 November 2006, Angolas Independence anniversary, TAAG received three new Boeing 737-700s and two new Boeing 777s. TAAG serves a dense domestic network. Its International service includes Rio de Janeiro, Lisbon, Windhoek, Johannesburg, Kinshasa, Dubai, starting in 2009, Bangui, Addis Ababa, Douala. However, in June 2007 EU banned TAAG from flying in Europe because of its poor safety standards. TAAG contracted SAA on its Lisbon route since. In May 2009 TAAG passed IATA standard. The airline is listed as operating one TriStar.

TACV Cabo Verde Airlines

The national airline of the island nation of Cabo Verde founded and owned by the government of Cabo Verde. The airline was formed in December 1958 but had to suspend operations in 1967. TAP of Portugal provided technical assistance to restart operations. TACV served Cabo Verde archipelago with links to Ilha do Sul, Boa Vista, Sao Vicente, Sao Nicolay Foco and Maio from its base at Praia. In 2004 TACV started its long-haul flights using leased Lockheed TriStar and later Boeing 757. Boston, Amsterdam, Fortaleza, Paris (CDG), Las Palmas and Lisbon are served. The airline also code-shares with Air Senegal on flights to Dakar and Gambia International Airways to Banjul.

Tara Air Line - Ireland

Listed as having operated one TriStar.

Tajikstan International TriStar 500 CS-TEB awaits another load of passengers. *(Richard Vandervord*

Tajikistan International Airlines - Tajikistan
Listed as having operated on TriStar.

Thai Sky Airlines
A passenger and cargo charter airline catering to the leisure industry in Thailand. The airline was privately held by Thai and Hong Kong investors. Operations commenced in May 2005 using three Lockheed Tristar aircraft on Bangkok - Hong Kong and Bangkok - Kuala Lumpur routes. The airline had to stop operations in August 2006 because of financial difficulties resulting in a lack of spare parts for its fleet of Tristars.

Time Air Sweden
Charter airline specialising in leisure flights to the Mediterranean on behalf of tour operators. The airline is listed as having operated two TriStars.

Tradewinds Airlines
FAR Part 121 Cargo and passenger charter airline based in Greensboro, North Carolina. The company was founded in 1968 as Blue Bell, later Wrangler Aviation Inc. and commenced operations in 1969 using Lockheed L-1049H Super Constellation freighter. In its early years, the company operated CL-44 and Lockheed Constellations. In 1991 Tradewinds introduced Lockheed L-1011 freighters, its first wide-body jet, operating a total of nine machines. In 1997 passengers charters commenced, mainly troop transport for Air Mobility Command. In 1999 Tradewinds introduced Airbus A300B4 freighters, followed in 2004 by its first Boeing 747F. The airline filed for bankruptcy on 25 August 2008 and was acquired by Sky Lease I, owner of Centurion Air Cargo, in December.

Trans Mediterranean Airlines
First all Cargo airline in the Middle East was formed in 1953. Operations commenced using Avro Yorks on ad-hoc cargo transports from the airline's base at Beirut International Airport. Scheduled operations started in 1959. At that time, TMA introduced Douglas DC-4s. The first jet was put in service in 1966 when TMA leased a Boeing 707 from World Airways of USA. In 1971 TMA became the first Cargo Airline to have a round the world service when its Boeing 707s completed the circle by adding New York-Anchorage-Tokyo leg. In 1976 TMA became the first airline in the Middle East to use Boeing 747 aircraft. From 1985 to 1986, due to civil war, TMA had to stop operations.

TMA was a member of IATA and holds ISO 9002 quality certification. It operated a scheduled and charter network stretching from New York to Tokyo, including Europe, Middle East and Southeast Asia. TMA also provides full overhaul service for Boeing 707 type, except the engines. In 2010 operations were restarted as TMA Cargo. The airline is listed as having operated one TriStar.

Tunis Air
The national airline of Tunis was formed as a joint-venture between Tunis Government and Air France. Airline's first aircraft was Douglas DC-3. In 1954 Douglas DC-4 joined the fleet, and scheduled flights commenced to Paris. Airline's first jet, Sud Caravelle, was delivered in August 1961. In 1971, fleet modernisation began when the airline took delivery of Boeing 727 and 737 jets. Tunis Air also ordered Airbus A300 for its high-density routes to France, first being delivered in November 1982. In October 1990, Tunisair received its first Airbus A320. The airline is listed as having operated one TriStar.

Wilmington Trust Company
Wilmington Trust was founded on July 8, 1903, as a banking, trust, and safe deposit company by DuPont president T. Coleman du Pont. In 2010, it became a subsidiary of M&T Bank. The company provides trust services to aircraft owners and lessors. The company is listed as operating two TriStars.

Thai Sky Airlines HS-AXA was formerly with Delta. *(Phil McCrackin Collection)*

Worldways Canada's C-GIFE. *(Richard Vandervord)*

Worldways Canada - Canada.
Worldways Canada was founded in 1973 by R T Moore and commenced operations in 1974. In 1983, Worldways purchased four Douglas DC-8s from CPAir. The airline operated worldwide charters. The company ceased operations in November 1990 because of financial difficulties and went into liquidation in 1991. The airline is listed as having operated six TriStars.

Yes Linhas Aéreas Charter - Portugal
Charter airline founded as a subsidiary of Portugal's flag carrier TAP with fifty-one per cent stake and Viagens Abreu, the largest tour company in Portugal with forty-nine per cent stake. Yes operated charters primarily to Brazil and the Caribbean. Because the airline was not profitable TAP, which later increased its holding toseventy-five per cent decided to shut down the operation at the end of 2003.

Zaire Airlines Hewa Bora Airways
Zaïre Airlines was born in 1994 from the merger between Shabair and Zaïre Express. In April 1997, when the country changed its name to the Democratic Republic of Congo, the use of the term 'Zaïre' became prohibited. Thence the company changed its name to Congo Airlines. Later on in 2001, the airline was rebranded Hewa Bora Airways. Chairman and CEO: Stavros Papaioannou. The entire Hewa Bora Airways fleet was blacklisted in European airspace. The Lockheed TriStar 500 and the Boeing 767-200ER were the last airliners accepted in Europe before new noise regulations and storage of the 767 definitively banned the airline. Hewa Bora Airways was the last airline that was allowed to operate from the Democratic Republic of Congo into Europe. AOL withdrew by DRC Govt 16 July 2011 due to a poor safety record. The airline is listed as operating one TriStar.

Yes Linhas Aéreas Charter CS-TMR. *(Richard Vandervord)*

Dubbed the Whisperliner due to its quiet takeoffs and a noticeable lack of noise in its passenger cabin, the production of L-1011 continued until 1983. The L-1011 fleet had a remarkable in-service rate that reached 98.1 percent reliability.

The financial troubles proved too much to overcome. A total of 250 TriStar airliners were produced by Lockheed, and the L-1011 marked the company's final commercial passenger airliners. But the company exited on a high note, having created, in one pilot's words, 'the most intelligent airliner ever to fly.'

Bibliography

Company Publications

The Lockheed Star: Vol 37, No.4. March 5 1970.
The Lockheed Star: Vol 37, No.5. March 12 1970.
The Lockheed Star: Vol 37, No.6. March 19 1970.
The Lockheed Star: Vol 37, No.8. April 16 1970
The Lockheed Star: Vol 37, No.9. May 7 1970.
The Lockheed Star: Vol 37, No.10. May 21 1970.
The Lockheed Star: Vol 37, No.11. June 4 1970.
The Lockheed Star: Vol 37, No.12. June 18 1970.
The Lockheed Star: Vol 37, No.16. July 30 1970
The Lockheed Star: Vol 37, No.17. August 13 1970.
The Lockheed Star: Vol 37, No.18. August 27 1970.
The Lockheed Star: Vol 37, No.19. September 10 1970.
The Lockheed Star: Vol 37, No.21. October 8 1970.
The Lockheed Star: Vol 37, No.22. October 22 1970.
The Lockheed Star: Vol 37, No.23. November 5 1970.
The Lockheed Star: Vol 37, No.24. November 19 1970
The Lockheed Star: Vol 37, No.25. December 3 1970.
The Lockheed Star: Vol 38, No.1. January 1971.
The Lockheed Star: Vol 38, No.2. January 21 1971.
The Lockheed Star: Vol 38, No.3. February 4 1971
The Lockheed Star: Vol 38, No.4. February 18 1971.
The Lockheed Star: Vol 38, No.5. March 4 1971
The Lockheed Star: Vol 38, No.6. March 18 1971.
The Lockheed Star: Vol 38, No.7. April 1 1971.
The Lockheed Star: Vol 38, No. 8. April 15 1971.
The Lockheed Star: Vol 38, No.9.April 29 1971.
The Lockheed Star: Vol 38, No.10. May 13 1971.
The Lockheed Star: Vol 38, No.11. May 20 1971.
The Lockheed Star: Vol 38, No.11. May 27 1971.
The Lockheed Star: Vol 38, No.12. June 10 1971.
The Lockheed Star: Vol 38, No.13. June 24 1971.
The Lockheed Star: Vol 38, No.14. July 8 1971.
The Lockheed Star: Vol 38, No.15. July 22 1971.
The Lockheed Star: Vol 38, No.16. August 5 1971.
The Lockheed Star: Vol 38, No.17. August 19 1971
The Lockheed Star: Vol 38, No.18. September 2 1971.
The Lockheed Star: Vol 38, No.19 September 16 1971
Lockheed L-1011 Engineering Description Series - Vol 1: Summary.
L-1011 Engineering Description Series Vol 2: Performance and Flying Qualities.
L-1011 Engineering Description Series Vol 3: Flight Station.
L-1011 Engineering Description Series Vol 4: Interiors, Galley and Cargo.
L-1011 Engineering Description Series Vol 5: Airframe.
L-1011 Engineering Description Series Vol 6: Propulsion.
L-1011 Engineering Description Series Vol 7: Electrical.
L-1011 Engineering Description Series Vol 8: Hydraulics and Flight Controls.
L-1011 Engineering Description Series Vol 9: Avionics.
L-1011 Engineering Description Series Vol 10: Pneumatics, Air Conditioning, APU.
L-1011 Engineering Description Series Vol 11: Safety.
L-1011 Engineering Description Series Vol 12: Aircraft Noise.
L-1011 Engineering Description Series Vol 13: Airport Compatability and Ground Operations.
L-1011 Engineering Description Series Vol 14: Maintainability and Reliability.
Lockheed Horizons - Issue 8. Lockheed California January 1970.
Meet The Professionals - TriStar. The Most Intelligent Jet Transport In The World. Lockheed California Company, May 1973

Books and Periodicals

L-1011 TriStar and the Lockheed Story, Douglas J Ingells: Aero Publishers Inc. 1973
Airlines & Airliners No. 11 L-1011 TriStar: Airline Publication & Sales, London 1974
Airliner Tech Series Volume 8 Lockheed L-1011 TriStar, Jim Upton: Speciality Press 2001.
Modern Civil Aircraft: 8 Lockheed TriStar, Phillip Birtles; Ian Allan Ltd 1999.
Colours in the Sky: the history of Autair and Court Line Aviation: Graham M Simons, Pen & Sword 2018
Aircraft Illustrated Monthly magazine 1968-1990 Ian Allan Ltd
Air Pictorial Monthly magazine 1968-1990
Aviation News Bi-monthly magazine, 1971-1986 Alan W Hall.
Air Enthusiast Vol 4 No. 7 - July 1973
Air International Vol 18 No.4 - April 1980

Airline Material, Inflight Magazines, Adverts etc.

Air Canada
British Airtours
British Airways
Caledonian
Cathay Pacific
Court Line Aviation.
Delta Air Lines
Eastern Air Lines.
LTU
Pan American Airlines
Trans World Airlines
United Air Lines

Index

The interior of Thai Sky Airlines' HS-AXE. Even allowing for the small size of the economy seating and the wide-angle lens, the interior of the TriStar was spacious. *(Temil Soket Collection)*

The interior of a British Airways TriStar. The pictures on the bulkhead could flip over and become a screen to show movies from the overhead projector, just out of shot. *(Bob Lehat Collection)*

Down the back!
The circle of toilets built in front of the rear pressure dome of the TriStar.
(Robin Banks Collection)

Delta's economy class L-1011 interior - note the 'airfones' in the seatbacks. The airline offered the US's first public air-to-ground telephone system with Airfone. The first iteration of Airfone service only permitted air-to-ground calls and frequently dropped link-ups. *(Rick O'Shea Collection)*

The first class area of Air Universal's L-1011. The rectangular 'box' in the ceiling, is the overhead projector used for showing inflight movies. *(Trimore Simango Collection)*

S

T

U

V

W

X

Y

Z

And finally - not the best of images, and to be honest, I have never worked out if these ladies are public relations models or the 'real thing'! Court Line Aviation and Pacific Southwest flight attendants (above) epitomised everything fun, sexy and exciting about TriStar travel in the 1970s - sadly, both in both terms of hostesses and aircraft, the likes of these wont be seen again! *(PSA Collection)*